Roy Hattersley is a writer and politician. He has been a Labour Member of Parliament for twenty-nine years and was Deputy Leader of the Labour Party.

He is the author of eleven books. He writes for the *Mail on Sunday* and is a weekly columnist for the *Guardian*. He has been voted Columnist of the Year.

Roy Hattersley

BETWEEN OURSELVES

PAN BOOKS

LONDON, SYDNEY AND AUCKLAND

First published 1994 by Pan Books
a division of Pan Macmillan Publishers Ltd
Cavaye Place London SW10 9PG
and Basingstoke

Associated companies throughout the world

ISBN 0330 32574 4

1 3 5 7 9 8 6 4 2

A CIP catalogue record for this book is available from the
British Library

Phototypeset by Intype, London
Printed and bound in Great Britain by
Cox & Wyman Ltd, Reading

The author and publishers gratefully acknowledge permission to quote from
The Complete Dorothy Parker (Penguin Books).

CONTENTS

Sounds and Furies

Up For Adoption

Contents

Literature Has Got Me Into This Mess . . .

Living at this Hour

Brief Lives

Contents

Purely Fiction

Where the Heart Is

Contents

Strictly Personal

Heroes and Hero Worship

Out and About

Contents

Between Ourselves

It all began in the Year of Victories. The Allies had defeated Germany and Japan. Labour had won the General Election. And I had passed the eleven-plus.

Because of the coincidence of those glorious achievements, the pattern of my life was set during 1945. I sat on the terraces at Bramall Lane to watch my first game of county cricket and stood on the terraces at Hillsborough to see my first professional football match. The leaflets which I pushed through Shalesmoor letterboxes that year were the beginnings of a lifetime of leaflet distribution. Most important of all, on my second day at the Sheffield City Grammar School, I queued up outside the 'stock room' behind Room L13 and was given a battered parcel of books which included *More Essays by Modern Masters*.

It was nothing like the most important book in the pile. That distinction belonged either to the Warwick *A Midsummer Night's Dream* or North and Hilliard's Latin Primer. However, it was *More Essays . . .* which changed my life. It was more than twenty years before their influence had its full effect. But, from the moment I read Hilaire Belloc, G. K. Chesterton, Robert Lynd, J. B. Priestley and E. V. Lucas, I felt that 'I want to write like that.' It was J. B. Priestley with whom I identified most closely. He wrote about town halls, brass bands, millstone grit and 'the windy roof of the world' that travellers had to 'share with the curlews'. They were part of my life as they were part of his.

Nobody told me that the essays were really only recycled newspaper articles. These days I gladly accept T. S. Eliot's judgment that journalists are in no way inferior to other sorts of writers and are separated from them only by temperament – the ability to work well under pressure and the need to earn small sums of money at short notice. But in 1945, I would have been profoundly disappointed to think that what I had read between hard, if dog-eared,

1

covers had first been published in the *News Chronicle*, the *Morning Post* and the *Illustrated London News*. The usual cliché concerns the indignity of Lynd and Lucas being wrapped round fish and chips. I would have been horrified by the thought of Belloc and Chesterton being torn into neat squares and hung from nails on the back of lavatory doors.

At first, I only attempted to write the inconsequential essay in my mind as I sat with my parents in the circle of the Sheffield City Hall and waited with mixed feelings for the local philharmonic society to begin its concert performance of Edward German's *Merrie England*. I wanted to write about our evening out. But I did not want to write about the words and music. What interested me were the men who moved the grand piano from one side of the stage to the other, the women who could compress their coughing into pauses in the performance and the young couples who had come to impress each other with their musical knowledge. When I wondered for a moment if such details of everyday life were worth recording, I recalled that they were at least as interesting as *On Running After My Hat*, *On Moving House* and *What I Found In My Pocket*.

It was not until I was in the sixth form that I offered anything for publication and then only after a combination of persuasion, coercion and flattery. My account of a school trip to North Yorkshire contained what I intended to be a satirical comparison between the blisters that affected the half dozen geographers who climbed Ingleton, Whernside and Pen-y-Ghent, and the frostbite which eventually doomed Captain Scott's last expedition to the South Pole. The master in charge – unable to distinguish between attempted irony and youthful insensitivity – requested, but did not require, the removal of the contentious passage. I argued and won. Arguing with editors – without reproducing my early success – has now become a feature of my life. Irony remains a cause of constant embarrassment. When I wrote that I thought of myself as Chatterton, 'the marvellous boy' who killed himself at the age of eighteen in despair that the world would ever recognise his genius, correspondents marvelled at my conceit.

When I was the age at which Chatterton died, the idea of writing for a living never entered my head. In my declining years

I shall romantically pretend that, having heard the call to serve the Labour Party, I had no time even to consider any other career. It will not be the whole truth. Although I was part of the brave new postwar world in which horizons were said to be limitless, I never believed that journalism was a career which was open to the likes of me. I am not sure who I thought worked for the *Sheffield Telegraph* and the *Star*. Perhaps I believed them all to be potential Neville Carduses on their way to distinction at the *Manchester Guardian*. But like Oxford and Cambridge, a motorbike and a trial with Yorkshire, journalism seemed out of my reach.

Writing crept up on me. It began with unreadable slabs of two thousand words, written for the leader page of the *Sheffield Telegraph* and occasionally reprinted by Harry Evans at the *Northern Echo* for an additional fee of two pounds ten. Then, out of the pale blue, came Iain Macleod's barely believable offer of regular space in the *Spectator*. At least some of the reasons why Macleod thought that I might be employable are explained later as part of the introduction to my pantheon of heroes. At the time it seemed like an episode from an unconvincing political novel. Sometimes, it still does. Almost as important as the offer of work was the effect that the work had upon me. I became addicted to writing. Now, without at least a thousand words a day, the withdrawal symptoms are unbearable.

When Keith Waterhouse told me that Arnold Bennett considered hanging a sign outside his house, 'Articles Written While You Wait', it seemed to me the model of the good life. The consequence of my obsession is almost half a million words a year and a total lack of discrimination about the commissions which I accept. At a *Punch* lunch in 1984, Frederick Forsyth heard me agree to write an article for a drink anthology – 800 words on lemonade for £50. As we left, he took me aside for what he regarded as essential advice. 'That's very risky. If you do it regularly, you will get a reputation, for being a £50 man.'

There was also unexpected criticism from some commentators who thought that I should devote all my time to the Labour Party instead of offering the world my opinion on the poetry of Elizabeth Barrett Browning, the state of county cricket and Augustus Welby Pugin. I was consoled by the total absence of any complaints from the Labour Party and the character of the journalists who urged me to spurn delights and live laborious days. Edward Pearce demanded that I write less. John Cole hoped that I would write more. At the 1982 Labour Party conference, Sir Thomas McCaffery (Chief of Staff to Jim Callaghan) approached me as I returned from a much needed tea-break. 'The last speaker', he said, 'claims that you write more words in a year than Charles Dickens.' McCaffery seemed alarmed. I was delighted. I thought of putting up a notice outside my house, 'Articles Written While You Wait'.

Instead I wrote an article about Elizabethan England. 'The glory of the age was that a man could be both a poet and a pirate without either being asked why he wasted his time writing sonnets when he might have been sacking Cadiz, or told that he should have been at home composing a masque instead of searching for Montezuma's gold.'

Because of my pathological inability to reject any offer of work, I was able to make my selection for this anthology from an eclectic selection of magazines and newspapers. As well as work done for the newspapers for which I wrote (and write) regularly, I have chosen from articles written for *The Times*, the *Sheffield Telegraph*, the *New Statesman*, the *Financial Times*, the *Independent*, the *Daily Mail*, the *Sunday Express*, the *Daily Telegraph*, the *Mail on Sunday*, the *Sunday Correspondent*, the *Glasgow Herald*, the *Radio Times*, the *Literary Review*, the *Times Literary Supplement*, the *Evening Standard* and the *Wall Street Journal*. Columns written for the *Mirror* and *People* during general election campaigns were too concerned with the issues of the week to retain their interest. Leader page features written for the *News of the World* in the early seventies are equally dated. I turned down two invitations to write for the *Sun*. One of them was genuine. The other was as near to an adult joke as anything that I have known that paper produce.

At the end of the press conference that launched Labour's 1992 campaign somebody asked if the modern party was guided by any coherent philosophy. Neil Kinnock invited me to reply and I got carried away. After several minutes of ideological exegesis (and a good deal of coughing and shuffling from the assembled journalists) Neil laid a restraining hand on my arm. When I got back to my office, there was an invitation (allegedly) from Kelvin MacKenzie on my desk. Would I like to write 'Twenty Things You Didn't Know About T. H. Green'?

Most of the articles reprinted here were, naturally enough, originally published in those magazines and papers with which I had or have a stable relationship. I wrote fifteen *Spectator* articles in the year before I first joined the government and I was a *Punch* columnist for seven years. I wrote Endpiece for the *Listener* for almost four. Endpiece has now been at home in the *Guardian* since 1982. For many years, I wrote frequently if not regularly for the *Observer*. Donald Trelford (who was editor for most of that time) commissioned my first piece – 'My Most Memorable Christmas', when he worked for the *Sheffield Telegraph*.

All the articles in *Between Ourselves* have been reprinted in their original form, except for the correction of small factual errors which kind readers were quick to point out. The original titles – not always to my liking – have usually been left undisturbed.

However, my work for *Punch* and the *Observer* is, at least in terms of column inches, under-represented. I wrote about the press for *Punch*, and articles about newspapers do not travel well. Most of my work for the *Observer* was meant to be a contribution to the national political debate. *Between Ourselves* is meant to be an escape from that sort of thing.

After I resigned the deputy leadership of the Labour Party, I chose to write for the *Sunday Times*, because the offer I was made included twelve political articles each year. When I sat on the Labour front bench I wrote about day-to-day politics (as distinct from political ideas) with an undisguised lack of enthusiasm. Politics was the subject about which I made speeches. I wrote about the great little things of life – always remembering, as E. M. Forster explained, '*The Seven Pillars of Wisdom* is about the war in the desert in the way that *Moby Dick* is about catching a whale' – and tried (through what I wrote about sand and fish) to reveal some sort of truth to myself if to nobody else. But I thought that, when I stopped making speeches, I would also want to abandon writing about literature and life in general and begin writing about politics in particular. I was wrong.

These days, aside from the urge to write fiction, I want to

examine and describe other people's writing. 'Literary criticism', wrote T. S. Eliot, 'is a distinctive activity of the civilized mind.' That may not be quite the right description of seven hundred words written for the *Sunday Express*. But a man's reach must always exceed his grasp, or what's the *TLS* for?

That civilised activity has taken hold of me in an entirely uncivilised way. I was always puzzled by the political correspondents' vicarious interest in politics. Why, I wondered, since they are so clearly interested in the subject do they not become politicians themselves, instead of sitting smug and secure in the gallery, telling bolder spirits how they should behave? The same criticism cannot be made of literary critics. To write about writers, they must ply the trade themselves.

Much of what follows is lit. crit. of a sort. The whole section on novels and novelists, the dozen book reviews and the essays on Shakespeare, Dryden, Ibsen, Yeats, Henry James, Dorothy Parker and Robert Browning are all writing about writers. And the authors, on whose ideas and judgments I depend, are welcome intruders into what I have written about my constituency, my origins, my humiliations and my pleasures.

The chance to write regularly for thirty years is a bonus which I have enjoyed thanks to the indulgence of editors. The first was David Hopkinson of the *Sheffield Telegraph*, then Iain MacLeod offered me space in the *Spectator*. Alan Coren at the *Listener* and *Punch* used to ask me to mark the jokes in the margin of my copy so that he could be reassured that I was producing humorous articles. David McKie (then assistant editor of the *Guardian*) persuaded me to move Endpiece from the *Listener* to what I hope is its natural home. Peter Preston continues to tolerate my idiosyncratic opinions.

Thank God for the *Guardian* and for the privilege of writing Endpiece for twelve years without ever missing a column through illness, holiday or sloth. The time has come to confess the cause of my fidelity. Back in 1982, when the column had barely begun, the rabbi of a progressive synagogue in North London regularly wrote to me with fulsome expressions of admiration for my work. One letter explained that he sometimes tried his amateur hand at writing light essays and, by chance, he had crudely drafted thirteen hundred words on the subject which (much to his subsequent surprise) I had chosen as my topic for the week. Would I cast my expert eye over his humble effort?

His Endpiece was better than mine. For a full decade I have lived in fear that if I were to miss one week, he would advance into my space and that, having established his frontiers, he would occupy my territory for ever.

My greatest gratitude is due to Tony Howard. As editor of the *New Statesman* he allowed me to write on frivolous subjects. At the *Listener* he commissioned my first regular column. As deputy at the *Observer* he bought my longest, and most ideological, articles. Now he regularly persuades me not to snatch at every job in journalism that is dangled in front of me. As obituaries editor of *The Times*, he has one major service yet to perform.

Sounds and Furies

It would have been much better, at least as far as television is concerned, if I had been born either twenty years earlier or twenty years later. I refer, of course, to the benefits which I would have enjoyed as a viewer. For although there was a time when I gnawed at a sound bite almost every day, I have spent many more hours watching television than I have wasted minutes performing in front of the camera. And that explains the problem. I was in my very late teens when the light of John Logie Baird first shone upon me. Had I been rising forty I might have possessed the wisdom to treat the intrusive newcomer with caution. If I had been born into a world which was already glorified by *Animal, Vegetable and Mineral*, *What's My Line?* and *Dixon of Dock Green*, I would have grown up with a small screen in the corner of my living room and learned to take it for granted.

Unfortunately television and I met when I was at an impressionable age. It was, at least on my side, infatuation at first sight and I demonstrate the consequent debasement of my critical faculties by describing my condition as 'still hooked'. My admiration of *Coronation Street* is so great that two of the paeans of praise which I have sung about it appear elsewhere in this anthology, properly jostling for space with celebrations of plays by Ibsen and Shakespeare. The confusion in viewers' minds between the facts of their life and the fiction of Granadaland ('The Sunny Side of the Street') did, however, seem a proper topic for inclusion here amongst articles which concern the vicissitudes of appearing on political programmes, the inside story of *Question Time* and the hideous tedium of making television films.

My panegyric to *Spitting Image* ('Spit Roasted') was an expression of genuine affection – though whether that was the result of the aforementioned infatuation, the absence of any critical faculty, or my status in the programme as eponymous hero, 'all round good sport' and 'amiable old duffer', I must leave others to judge. Since 1986, when the piece appeared in the *Sunday Express*, I have qualified my enthusiasm for the programme with an admission. If I were Kenneth Baker – portrayed as a slug, sliming my way through life – I might feel differently.

When – after the second election defeat – I gave up the deputy leadership of the Labour Party I wrote two valedictory articles. One concerned the inconvenience of moving rooms. The other ('Liberation With a Dash of Dignity') celebrated my emancipation from the duty to provide ten-second homilies for news bulletins. Although Gerald Kaufman telephoned to complain that I had not specifically renounced 'the walking shot' (which 'establishes' performers and also makes them look ridiculous), I felt absolved from more than the sound bite. I am no longer obliged to appear in television broadcasts which, because of their composition and format, do not attract me.

I did spend some happy moments with a microphone clipped to my tie and blinding lights in my eyes. The *Panorama* programme which ended with a fish choking to death on the studio floor ('Fish Out of Water') was not typical of my almost thirty years before the television mast. But the description of seven days in Blackpool ('In the Nick of Time') really was what always happened during the last week in every September for almost ten years.

My relationship with most television interviewers survived the strain of nearly twenty years of highly political party broadcasts. So my comments on John Nott's famous walkout from *Nationwide* ('Nott Answering') were never intended as retaliation for a lifetime of ravagings by Sir Robin Day – notably on *Question Time*. Sir Robin Day is to that series as Arthur Askey was to 'The Bee'. The comedian (Mr Askey that is) used to say, 'This is the song which made me famous. Or is it the song which I made famous? Anyway, one of us is pretty good.'

Sir Robin will, I hope, be gratified by the re-publication of 'Tropical Tangle of Grammar and Gramophone' in which I compared his interviewing technique (favourably) with the style employed on *Desert Island Discs* by Sue Lawley.

Miss Lawley took exception to my critique of her style. But then, Mr Plomley's sleepy lagoon has caused me nothing but trouble. Somewhere in the literary sections of this book there lies buried a quotation from W. H. Auden.

> *When I try to imagine a*
> *faultless love*
> *Or the life to come, what I*
> *hear is the murmur*
> *Of underground streams,*
> *what I see is a limestone landscape.*

I wanted a recording of Auden reading the last verse of 'In Praise of Limestone' on my desert island as a tribute to the country in which I was born and bred. There was panic in Broadcasting House. Somebody had read the whole poem, including the opening stanza about 'the flirtatious male who lounges against a rock'. Michael Parkinson, being a fellow south Yorkshireman, was deputed to speak to me in private.

Mr Parkinson, though miles away, was the cause of the only real row I had on *Question Time*. Before the programme began, Sir Robin expressed polite surprise that Henry Kissinger's only interview in Britain could be conducted by a figure best known as a chat-show host. During the broadcast, Sir Robin caused me considerable annoyance by demanding a 'straight answer' on the subject of abortion. Was I in favour, yes or no? In vain did I suggest that the topic was too complex for so simplistic a response. So I expressed my pleasure that Parky was the man chosen to interview Dr Kissinger. For some reason, Sir Robin felt unable to join in the congratulations.

In its original format, *Question Time* was not so much a discussion programme as a star vehicle for Sir Robin and I was one of the full supporting cast. It became much more worthy and much more dull. It is also a classic example of privatisation's invariable consequences. The company which won the contract was able to make the best bid, because it cut the workers' (that is to say panellists') wages. As Westminster Refuse Department, so *Question Time*.

During one of the interviews with which he launched his anthology of broadcasts, Sir Robin confessed that once he treated me with less than courtesy. *The Times* – translating me from 'veteran panellist' to 'veteran victim' – asked me, in the wake of Sir Robin's shocking confession, to compare new interviewers with old ('Enlighteners or Entertainers'). A week later – having appeared for the second time on *Clive Anderson Talks Back* – I was able to tell *Guardian* readers why the undoubtedly smart people who host television chat shows appear even smarter than they really are. What a less august newspaper might have called 'sensational revelations' about 'how showbiz smarties give their viewers the run around' did not even cause a gentle flutter in television's dovecotes. Perhaps the headline ('Picking Yourself Up from the Cutting Room Floor') lacked the essential drama of a 'film and tell' exposé.

When I next met Mr Anderson face to face at the pre-Cup Final broadcast, I took the opportunity of making a number of comments about him being unable – since we were what the BBC is pleased to call live – to cut out my best jokes. I am assured that millions of soccer fans had no idea what I was talking about. More humiliating still, Arsenal won the cup. As I said in my *Listener* article about *Question Time* ('Getting On'), that's showbusiness.

'Getting On' was the sort of smart title that I hate. But I am constantly reminded that titles are none of my business. At least I managed to change the 'come on' for my Esther Rantzen interview from 'Teeth of Gold' to something marginally better. My dissatisfaction with titles is chronic and only exceeded (as a cause of potential brain damage) by the annoyance that I feel when space, which might be filled with my words, is occupied with somebody else's pictures. Both grievances are long standing. Almost forty years ago a piece which I wrote about the Edinburgh Festival for the *Sheffield Telegraph* was cut to accommodate a picture of Marlene Dietrich and my suggested title – 'Morningside Becomes Electra', chosen as a subtle reference to the season of Eugene O'Neill films which had been organised by the city's cinemas – was rejected in favour of 'A Week at the Edinburgh Festival'. The guilty man went on to be editor of the *Observer*. There is no justice in journalism.

Yet I still regard writing a thousand words as superior in every way to making television programmes. If you wonder why, read 'Give and Take on the Not-so-small Screen'.

Spit Roasted

Most days of the week somebody – in a bus, on a train or just passing in the street – asks me what I think about *Spitting Image*. The same thing always happens when I visit a school in my constituency. At first the carefully assembled pupils make meticulously prepared enquiries about overseas aid and teachers' pay. Then one of them takes a deep breath and chortles the question which has the whole class laughing. 'Do you enjoy *Spitting Image*?'

My reaction is always a disappointment. For I am supposed to explode with rage at the mention of the programme's name, denounce Messrs Law and Fluck as dangerous subversives and promise to put Central Television out of business when the Labour government is elected. But I cannot produce the eagerly awaited outburst. I *do* enjoy *Spitting Image*. It is one of the television shows that I hurry home to watch. I switch on the repeats, too. It makes me laugh.

At least, it makes me laugh most of the time. But before I separate the nuggets of pure gold from the dross that washes around them, I ought to confess that I have two reasons for being biased in favour of the programme. The first is the explanation that I give to earnest television researchers. I am the eponymous hero of *Spitting Image* – the only image that actually spits. The second cause of my undoubted prejudice can be more simply explained. *Spitting Image* treats me gently – at least by its own especially offensive standards.

As portrayed in *Spitting Image*, President Reagan is a geriatric mental defective with painted cheeks and dyed hair. David Steel is a glove puppet. Norman Tebbit is a Hammer Film mutation produced by crossing a Hell's Angel with a werewolf. Margaret Thatcher is represented in a way which cannot be adequately described in a family newspaper. But I am no more than a bungling old duffer, the sort of uncle who comes round at Christmas to set up the electric train set and fuses all the lights. I doubt if I would enjoy the programme half so much if I were Princess Michael of Kent.

Nor would I watch the programme with such regularity if it concentrated its ridicule on minor members of the Royal Family, film stars and television personalities. Lampoons are funniest and most effective when they attack hard targets. Of course the occasional pot shot at a sitting duck can be amusing. The Duchess of York (spraying on freckles through a colander), David Coleman (so confused that he thinks that every sporting event from the Grand National to the Boat Race is a football match) and Paul Daniels (starring in a remarkable resemblance to the BBC's sheep-dog programme, *One Man and His Wig*) were all hilarious items. But they do not compare with the moments of vicious political satire. For the lampoon, from the early pictorial satirists right down to *Spitting Image*, is at its biting best when drawing blood for some political purpose. The wound is only justified when the teeth sink in for what the satirists, at least, ultimately believe to be a 'good cause'.

Of course that makes some of the *Spitting Image* jokes what is conventionally described as sick. A pregnant Irish chambermaid was persuaded by her Arab boyfriend to fly to America with a suitcase in which he has packed a time-bomb. In the same week, Margaret Thatcher is said to have offended the US President for the first time in their six years of political infatuation. So *Spitting Image* has Ronald Reagan kissing the Prime Minister goodbye at the airport with the words 'just take the suitcase on the plane, Margaret'.

That sketch was rough – not so much on the President and the Prime Minister (who are big enough to look after themselves) as on the imprisoned housemaid and her bewildered family. But it was rough with a purpose. *Spitting Image* was trying to make a point about American intolerance of allies who step out of line. The sketches about South Africa are even rougher. And I have friends who argue that apartheid is no laughing matter under any circumstances. But the 'recordings' of President Botha's speeches with spoof captions translating them into English put the doctrine of white supremacy into proper perspective. 'Good evening, every-one' his message to the nation began. 'Good evening, white people' read the sub-titles. The idea that one race is intrinsically superior to another is, of course, absurd. Ridiculing apartheid will help to speed its destruction.

But then, I believe that there is no subject that we cannot laugh about. The sin is not choosing the wrong subject but doing the job badly. *Spitting Image* provides examples which justify that theory. Samantha Fox is a ludicrous figure who fully deserves the Fluck and Law treatment. But interviewing the most famous parts of her anatomy is simply not funny. Talking nipples have a limited charm, not because we should not make jokes about breasts, but because we should only make good jokes about breasts.

Ideally we should make only good jokes about politicians. But too often all that we get is the dreary old one-liners about parliamentary windbags and the Westminster gasworks. *Spitting Image* tries to do better. There was one assault on Prime Minister's Question Time which ought to have struck a chord with everybody who has watched or taken part in that artificial event – increasingly built around an opening request for the Prime Minister to list her day's engagements.

The object of this complicated exercise is to catch the PM on the hop by going on to ask a question she has not anticipated – something like, 'But will she, during her busy day, introduce policies which reduce the level of unemployment?' But, while some shots hit target, the whole process grows increasingly arcane. The complications were brilliantly ridiculed one Sunday night by the latex and papier-mâché puppets. My supplementary question (for which I was warmly congratulated by Neil Kinnock) was, 'Why do I have to ask the Prime Minister for a list of her engagements before I can ask her a supplementary question?' I took the consequent rebuff with good grace. For it was one of those nights when I was not dressed up in the blue and white scarf and knitted woollen hat of the Sheffield Wednesday supporter.

There will, I know, be those who say that politicians who enjoy *Spitting Image* defend the programme because they are flattered by inclusion in the cast list. Not true. Most of us have grown out of the idea that any publicity is good publicity. I could easily live without the newspaper cartoons which portray me as having six chins, a huge wart and extreme opinions. But then, they are rarely funny. *Spitting Image* usually is. And to those who make us laugh, much is forgiven.

Sunday Express Magazine, 28 September 1986

Enlighteners or Entertainers

During the last of the many interviews with which he publicised his anthology of television conversations, Robin Day admitted that he had once been rude during a broadcast. I was the victim of whom he spoke, and I remember the incident vividly. But, until I heard Sir Robin's confession, I had never imagined that I was owed an apology for being told to 'chuck it'.

That is a mild rebuke by today's standards, and was also entirely justified. It was the beginning of the general election campaign, and I had decided, before the interview began, to have a row on the programme. I was opposed to Labour's defence policy and it seemed to me that the best way to avoid being pursued on the subject for four long weeks was to use my first confrontation with the media as a declaration of war on journalists. Having admitted my disagreement with the party, I denounced Sir Robin for mentioning it, and accused him of a wilful determination to damage the opposition. The tactic worked. Later interviewers treated defence and foreign policy with gratifying circumspection.

I was delighted to read Sir Robin's account of his self-defined brutality. For some time, I have been worried about my treatment at the hands of Jeremy Paxman – who has always interviewed me with formal courtesy. Since he does not enjoy a gentle reputation, I had begun to fear that he thought of me as an old duffer who might expire in his studio chair if he were pressed too hard. Sir Robin's reminiscence reassured me that I had once been treated in the spirit – if not quite in the manner – with which Mr Paxman treated Ann Taylor on 5 April.

Admittedly, Mrs Taylor – Labour's education spokesman – had clearly gone to the studio with a precise idea in her mind of what she was going to say, whatever the question. That is how politicians are taught to behave. It is the interviewer's task to prise the studio 'guest' (a strange word in these circumstances) away from the prepared text. If the job is done brutally, the programme's purpose is lost in a confusion of embarrassment and sympathy – assuming, that is, that the broadcast's purpose is concerned with parties and

16

policy rather than a demonstration of the interviewer's bravura technique.

In the case of Paxman v. Taylor, the question which the Labour shadow side-stepped was not even asked by the man whom the BBC pays to probe. It was put by James Pawsey, a Conservative MP who preferred to cross-examine his Labour opponent rather than deal with the point that Mr Paxman put to him. Having three times avoided saying whether or not she supported the teachers' test boycott, Mrs Taylor was rewarded by a request (from Mr Paxman, no less) to allow him 'to get a word in edgeways'. The result was viewers who sympathised with Mrs Taylor rather than the issues involved. *Newsnight*'s duty is to make people think about issues, not good manners.

The Paxman–Taylor contest raised the whole issue of what television interviewers are for – enlightenment or entertainment. If they aim to enlighten, the interviewer is no more than the means by which the interviewee's ideas, intentions, and character are exposed. If the object is entertainment, the interviewer becomes a star with an existence which is quite independent of the men and women who are cross-examined. The 'interviewer as star' is the death of serious political broadcasting. For it diverts attention from the real issues. But it is not the only cause of aggressive questioning which obscures rather than reveals the truth.

What are we to think of one Iain MacWhirter who – on *Westminster Live* a couple of weeks ago – interviewed Denis Healey on the subject of Bosnia? Lord Healey was – wrongly in my view – opposed to the threat of military intervention. His opposition caused Mr MacWhirter to ask whether that meant he did not care about ethnic cleansing.

It was all depressingly reminiscent of local radio reporters during the sixties – usually young ladies dressed like Fidel Castro who thought that they had a duty to 'take on' the visiting politicians. 'But surely, Mr Hattersley, you agree that Labour would bankrupt the country?' They, in their turn, provided happy memories of old cowboy films in which the greenhorn comes into the saloon and challenges the old gun-fighter. Of course, the gun-fighter always won. On *Westminster Live*, Lord Healey duly drilled his assailant between the eyes.

Win or lose, why do they do it? After his now notorious joust with John Hume last month, the usually excellent John Humphrys was protected from criticism by the sort of friends we could all well do without. He was, they said, tired. His passion for work, they explained, sometimes left him exhausted and exhaustion often impairs judgment.

I have now listened to that *Today* interview a dozen times, and I do not attribute the constant interruptions either to fatigue or any other sort of involuntary error. 'Nothing has changed' in Northern Ireland, Mr Humphrys said. '. . . face the reality . . . That's the reality.' The problem was that the interviewer had a point of view of his own.

He actually told Mr Hume, 'You had a very fair crack of the whip,' as if the item were a debate between them rather than a radio journalist obtaining information from a politician. The problem of over-aggressive (and therefore uninformative) interviews sometimes has the most basic of causes – the 'presenter' believes that he is a political animal in his own right rather than the representative of the informed and inquisitive listener and viewer.

My objection to the 'star system' in current affairs interviews, like my reservations about the presenter allowing his own views to play a part, has nothing to do with politicians' hubris.

Politicians do try to use broadcasts as vehicles for their own propaganda. They do answer the question which they would have liked to be asked rather than the one which was put to them. The interviewer has a duty to drag them back into line. But harassment and interruption are not the best ways of securing that desired end.

What politicians most fear is the brief question followed by incredulous silence. Mr Julian Haviland, formerly of ITN, used regularly to confound me by asking, 'Why?' or 'How?' As I wrestled to construct an answer, I longed for Robin Day's subsidiary clauses which, as they urged me to be frank, and impressed me with the importance of the question, gave me time to think. I do not urge politeness for politeness's sake.

The courteous (and spuriously humble) interviewer is most likely to expose the truth, and that, not self-projection, is the interviewer's job.

The Times, 3 May 1993

Fool's Gold

The critics were wrong. *Hearts of Gold* is not all dross. Indeed, in one particular, it glories in a distinction which few other programmes can boast. It employs a designer of genius. The titles, which precede the Esther Rantzen Awards for Previously Unsung Heroism, encapsulate the spirit and content of the programme with indisputable brilliance. The humorous cameos illustrate the 'kindness and courage' to which the programme is dedicated. A dragon is slain by St George, played by Richard Baker. Grace Darling, who pulls for shore and saves shipwrecked sailors, is Jan Leeming. Queen Elizabeth I, for whose convenience Sir Walter Raleigh ruined his cloak, turns into Sue Lawley. *Hearts of Gold* is bravery and compassion as seen on television, virtue sold like soap powder after celebrity endorsement.

It claims to be an unabashed celebration of natural goodness. And, in a way, it undoubtedly is. But it is also an amalgamation of every top-of-ratings trick that ever pushed a programme up the charts. Occasionally, it turns into *This Is Your Life* – surprising its startled guests by contrived confrontations with the beneficiaries of their previous goodness. It is all done to the applause of a studio audience who clap to cue.

Thus soldiers who contrived – with undoubted courage – the escape of a concentration-camp victim were first told of Esther's sorrow that the woman, who owed her life to them, could not be in the studio. Then, on she came, the woman who (when a girl) they had hosed down, deloused and hidden in a hayloft. Esther apologised for 'fibbing' and the temporary aura of popular sanctity was intensified by her blouse which appeared to be made from a stained-glass window.

In *Hearts of Gold*, the sacred and the profane are measured out in equal doses. Showbusiness and social work walk hand-in-hand into Britain's living rooms. That is the importance of the programme. It is an unashamed partnership of the jokes which made Esther Rantzen a television star with the overt concern which has elevated her into the champion of the deprived, the abused and the neglected. Doctors, who raised money for a scanner by playing in a jazz band, were introduced by a patient on whom they had successfully operated. The scanner, he explained, helped them to locate his three tumours so precisely that the 'mess' was reduced. Esther pulled a face which made the audience laugh. The whole thing is an extraordinary combination of the incompatible. If the Pre-Raphaelites had painted it, the title on the frame would have been *The Apotheosis of Rantzenism*.

It is a description to which I do not think Ms Rantzen would take great exception. She might jib at its pretentiousness, however. For she insists that she is the type of person who, when recognised in the street, is greeted with 'Hello, Esther' not 'Look, it's Esther Rantzen'. Indeed, she seems genuinely to believe that she is not a star – though whether it was wholly becoming for her to raise the subject of her non-stardom is a question which I have pondered since we met. The idea of false modesty troubles me less than the absence of theatrical judgment. Star she certainly is, even to the point of looking twice as big on screen as she is in real life. Indeed the problem with the Rantzen programmes is that they are made as star vehicles. *That's Life!* could not survive without her. *Hearts of Gold* is Rantzen from start to finish.

The explanation for the uninhibited diet of schmaltz comes in two parts. Esther likes people to be happy. So she provides programmes for those viewers who write to say, 'I know when I come home from a horrible day, there have been babies born, people married and miracles of surgery. I want to hear about them.' On the other hand, the importance of catharsis must not be underrated. 'Every time we tell a story of pain, we get letters from people who say, "I thought I was the only person".' To reinforce the final point she produced a whole file full of agonised letters from women who in childhood had been sexually abused. It was impossible not to be moved even by the properly anonymous transcripts.

Ms Rantzen's mission is to 'influence public opinion' – particularly in its attitude towards little children. It is her conviction that Britain is a 'nation of child-haters' who think that anybody under ten years of age should be neither seen nor heard. It was her strong views on that subject which got her into so much trouble about the Duchess of York's decision to leave her infant daughter in

Britain when she accompanied the Duke in Australia. 'Some demon in my brain said, "The Duke and Duchess of York were probably advised that the baby would puke." ' She now insists that she never meant to criticise the Duchess and said so at the time. And she is anxious to explain that the local reporter who filed the story was himself astonished by the storm which it provoked. Implausible as it all sounds, Ms Rantzen is a difficult lady to disbelieve.

That is, in part, because the casual acquaintance does business with her through a sheet of magic glass which neither distorts nor obscures but filters out anything that might be damaging or disobliging. Ms Rantzen remembered that, after we had appeared together on *Any Questions?*, I told her that she was nicer than her programmes had led me to believe – a view which I still hold. But she had forgotten that, before a previous programme, I had been forced to interpose myself between her and an irate George Brown who objected to public breast-feeding. Once her memory had been jogged, she spoke eloquently of being natural and open about such things.

We had already dealt with transplants – Ben Hardwick, the baby who had been featured on her programme and had, as a result, won a temporary lease of life. Ben's eventual death 'dealt transplant surgery a shattering blow'. In life and death, Ben pointed the same moral. People, given the chance, will help their fellow men, women and children. Television provides the chance. It also provides imaginative and innovative broadcasters with an opportunity to reach out and tap the well of kindness. Only the hidebound and stuffy will object to a little innocent fun being used as the loss leader which attracts the customers into the 'love thy neighbour' supermarket.

Reticence is not a virtue which Esther Rantzen values highly, though she confesses (or claims) to have hated dressing up as a charlady in order to advertise the first broadcast of *Hearts of Gold*. But, as a woman of genuine compassion, she ought at least to consider the problems which the absence of reticence creates – even for the causes she holds dear. It is impossible simultaneously to be the spirit of St Margaret and the ghost of Marie Lloyd. Money may be donated towards the cost of a new scanner; women may be encouraged to talk about the trauma of their childhood; children may be protected from abuse, but in the end even kindness is cheapened. Compassion becomes a music-hall turn, brought on stage between the conjuror and comedy vocalist. I do not suggest for a moment that Esther Rantzen wants such a result. But it is the result produced by the programmes which bear her exclusive label. What intrigues me is why a woman of such obvious intelligence does not realise it.

Listener, 17 November 1988

Fish Out of Water

I see that *Newsnight* promises to 'use all the speed and diversity of television techniques of the eighties' to bring to our screens 'the more exciting and perceptive coverage that viewers are demanding'. No one can be certain towards which previous programme that implied criticism is directed. But I suspect that one of the techniques of the sixties which is now regarded as a sure way of producing less exciting and perceptive viewing was the constant cheap employment of Members of Parliament as lump labourers.

We were, in fact, treated exactly like stevedores before the docks were decasualised. *Tonight* would leave simultaneous messages at the House of Commons for Shirley Williams, Brian Walden, Ivor Richard and me. The first one to return the call would be signed on to discuss the day's events in front of an audience of four or five million people. The deal was usually done at about five o'clock, leaving the lucky winner with a full twenty minutes to discover half a dozen facts about the Licensing and Gaming Bill, the repeal of the Rent Act, or the latest offensive in Vietnam.

For me, the delight of being numbered among the many who were called always turned into terror when I became the one who was chosen. I took it for granted that my contemporaries and competitors were armed with information about the issue of the moment long before they received the fateful call. As I was carried off to Lime Grove by radio cab, a single-column cutting from the *Guardian* in my hand, I always cursed Shirley Williams, Brian Walden and Ivor Richard for the dilatory way they returned telephone calls, and, thus, became the instruments of my humiliation.

I rarely felt better after the ordeal had ended. Television broadcasts begin in a thousand different ways – with audience or without, outside or in, surrounded by diagrams or lost in a sea of pale blue canvas. But the end is always the same. Before you can unclip the microphone, a person runs in to offer sincere congratulations on participating in one of the best programmes the BBC (or Thames, or London Weekend, or Granada, or Anglia) has ever put out.

We received exactly that accolade when the stage collapsed in the converted Birmingham cinema that used to be the home of ATV. The paeans of praise were just as loud on the day when I wore a check suit that so distorted the picture that I was forced to borrow a blazer from a cameraman. Later in the week a kind friend asked me if I 'had played the part of Rupert Bear'. But the director thought it had all been 'terrif'. I was just as much a success on the night that the trout died at my feet on the studio floor.

If not my finest performance, the trout incident was undoubtedly my finest television hour – the moment of courage that I would like remembered if the British Broadcasting Corporation lasts for a thousand years. It took place at the height of the Cod War, and *Panorama* was considering how the nation would survive if our supply was suddenly cut off. One ingenious alternative to stealing the fish that had suddenly acquired Icelandic nationality was 'trout farming'. To provide visual relief from the sight of six solemn faces, talking soberly about a sad subject, a huge tank had been brought into the studio. Inside it were what appeared to be a couple of dappled whales.

These cultivated trout did not realise that the broadcast was live. They thrashed the water so fiercely that the tank overturned. The water that engulfed me from knee to toe was soon forgotten. Wedged between my shoes and the plastic desk which separated me from the camera were two dying monsters, and neither of them was prepared to go quietly.

Until that day I had never believed the legend about silent creatures crying out at the moment of death. If Pavlova told the same stories about trout that she insisted were true of swans, she was right. They barked like hyenas with laryngitis. Just as one got its thrashing tail firmly wedged inside my left trouser leg Mr David Dimbleby turned to me for an opinion.

At first I thought of simulating a coughing fit in the hope that I could mime for the noise coming from under my desk. In the end, fearful that my thespian talents were not capable of sustaining this drama of life or death, I denounced the intransigence of the Icelandic government *very loudly*. 'Bit emphatic, I thought,' my private secretary said when I got back to the Foreign Office. 'Notice anything else?' I asked him. 'No,' he said. 'Apart from that, pretty uneventful.'

I will never know whether the camera turned to me at that moment because of malign fate or simple malice. I do, however, recall that at another time I was caught off guard at the express instruction of the director. It was on one of those *Election Specials* that used to follow each by-election during the dying days of the Labour government. Mr Austin Mitchell was contesting and – rather to everybody's surprise – winning Grimsby. As Mr Robin Day read out the result, I naturally assumed that all attention would be focused on him.

A group of sympathetic technicians at the back of the studio caught my eye, and I raised my hand to them in the sort of salute Charlie George used to give the North Bank crowd after he scored a goal for Arsenal. I also silently expressed an opinion about the Conservative Party similar to the judgment Mr George used to make about referees after his goals were disallowed. This incident was transmitted into lounge and living room all over the country. Astonishingly enough, the reaction of lip-readers crouching in front of their flickering screens was ecstatic. 'Let yourself go more often,' one lady wrote. 'That way it doesn't look as if somebody is working you from the back.'

Usually somebody *is* trying to work me from the back. I never set out for the BBC or ITN without advice echoing after me as I argue with the driver about whether or not he is supposed to be bringing me back as well as taking me there. 'Sit up straight. Look at the person you are talking to. Keep your hands away from your face. Try not to wriggle. For heaven's sake do not pick . . .'

Not that I am, in principle, opposed to artifice. My problem is being able to carry it through. On my way to be confronted by Mr Robin Day I always resolve to counterfeit uncontrollable anger. If there is anything that viewers like more than Mr Day shouting at people, it is people shouting at Mr Day. Once I did actually lose my temper. The response was extraordinary. Nobody shared my (momentary) judgment of Mr Day's talents. But, while they disagreed with what I said, they would have died for the chance to hear me say it again.

In 1978, at the height of World Cup fever, I played 'keepsy-upsy' on the streets of Hamilton with George Robertson, the Labour candidate in that famous by-election. Our display of ball control, transmitted to every Scottish home, would certainly have increased his majority had I not inadvertently allowed my judgment of Scotland's prospects in Argentina to be recorded at the same time. But even that incident had a happy ending.

The television crew, tired of filming my cultivated feet, decided to do my job for me and strode towards the Co-op in search of a typical housewife. They accosted exactly the sort of lady I tried to keep off television programmes about the cost of living – not very young, not very rich, not very happy. 'Tell me,' they said, zooming in on her grim, Calvinistic face, 'is the government doing enough about inflation?' She paused for a moment. And gave her considered reply. 'Taking into account the pressure of world commodity prices, I think selective intervention is the best option at their disposal, and it has certainly stabilised prices.' I dribbled off down the High Street.

Listener, 31 January 1980

Nott Answering

I am by nature a partisan person. So if someone had prophesied that John Nott might one day unfasten the microphone which was tearing a hole in his tie and stalk out of the *Nationwide* studio like an offended giraffe, I would have prayed for the prediction to come true. For the viewing public does not approve of that sort of thing. They expect politicians to take it on the chin, punch it out toe-to-toe or live out some other anatomical metaphor that keeps their posteriors firmly in the studio seat. Walking off displays either apprehension about what is to follow or distaste for what has gone before. Cowardice in the face of Robin Day is a capital offence. So is condescension – at least as far as Sir Robin is concerned.

Now my dream of petty party advantage has come true. And I am still glad that Mr Nott made a minor spectacle of himself. But my reasons are rather different from those which I would have anticipated. Of course, none of the Conservative conference delegates who told him that he 'did exactly the right thing' really meant it. By behaving like an angry stick insect the Secretary of State for Defence diminished himself and further lowered the level of popular esteem in which politicians are held. But he also struck a blow for sensible television interviews. I, at least, am prepared to sacrifice a small piece of Mr Nott's reputation to promote that cause.

There is, I know, great concern amongst the younger end of the BBC production staff about the way in which some of their current affairs programmes turn out. The political interview cannot sensibly be used as a star vehicle. It may well be that last week's little public *frisson* will liberate the critics who, for years, have only mumbled under their breath, and allow them to insist that politics on television should concentrate on the ideas and performance of the parties, not the character and personality of the interviewer.

Of course, I lay myself immediately open to the charge that I reflect nothing more than the opinion of the professional politician's trade union – an institution which would like to include in the BBC Charter a clause guaranteeing a soft ride for every politician who ever looks into a camera. In fact, quite the reverse is true. Sensible members of my profession do not mind being roughly handled. Being human, they may grow annoyed at being chivvied and chased from one half-sentence to the next. But they do not fear the constant interruption. There are all sorts of cheap popularity to be gained from both the soft answer that demonstrates composure and the quick retort that displays confidence.

Any politician who wrestled Robin Day to the studio floor would shoot up the popularity charts. And I myself was inundated with wholly unironic compliments on my compassion when (a fortnight ago on *Panorama*) I laid my hand on his be-knighted arm and urged him not to get upset. It is all good clean fun. The gladiatorial interview is the current affairs equivalent of all-in wrestling. There is a lot of action and nobody gets hurt. But nobody gets enlightened either. Jackie Pallo versus Big Daddy is simply cheap entertainment. Robin Day versus John Nott should be something more.

It should, ideally, be an opportunity for a politician's policies to be discussed and the weaknesses of both his plans and his personality to be exposed. And that – believe me – is best done by allowing the subject of the interview to finish the occasional sentence. It is, of course, harder work for the interviewer who has to prepare himself by mastering (say) the intricacies of the various nuclear options rather than by simply picking up gossip about a minister's popularity or a party's divisions.

David Dimbleby does it. So does Gus Macdonald of Granada, John Tusa of *Newsnight* and, above all, Alastair Burnet of ITN. To elevate the sporting metaphor from wrestling to cricket: being interviewed by any of them is like batting against a remorseless fast bowler who always aims for the stumps. Bumper after bumper flying over the batsman's head neither intimidates the participant nor entertains the audience.

The kind of interview which politicians fear most is the kind that used to be conducted by Michael Charlton and Julian Haviland. Both of them were meticulously courteous. Neither of them ever raised his voice. But both persisted in calmly asking difficult questions. In my ministerial days, when I was to be cross-examined by such formidable opponents, I always asked colleagues to prepare me for the ordeal by helping to anticipate the most lethal sallies.

The suggestions which made me break out in a cold sweat and anticipate counterfeiting throat infection were the apparently soft options – the genuine request for information followed by a silence that had to be filled by my ignorance, the offer to allow me to clear up the impression of inconsistency, puzzled concern that one of my answers was factually wrong. I used to pray that they would cover my fumblings and mumblings with hectoring interruptions.

But I do not mean to discuss the techniques of television interviewing simply in terms of a politician's preferences. Television influences our attitudes towards serious matters no less than it develops our taste for Pot Noodles or Cup-a-Soup. So the worst sort of television interview has been a major force in the trivialisation of politics. For it has created the false and fatuous impression that the great questions of the day can be answered 'yes' or 'no' and that anyone who says that the world is too complicated to be governed in monosyllables is prevaricating. I know that last week in *Nationwide* John Nott did nothing for his own reputation. But I cannot help thinking that the wrong man left the studio.

Punch, 13 October 1982

Getting On

The people who run the programmes would rather resign than admit it, but *Question Time* and *Any Questions?* have far more in common than the superficial similarities of an audience which asks and a panel of four participants which answers. Indeed, in one important particular, they are identical. Both are planned and produced in the clear belief that they are something more than mere broadcasts.

From time to time, both programmes have produced footnotes to history. I sat knee to knee with Margaret Thatcher when, back in 1974, she told the *Any Questions?* audience that Britain was 'not yet ready for a woman prime minister'. And Francis Pym and I were side by side on *Question Time* when he announced his opposition to any one party 'winning too large a majority' in the forthcoming general election. The result of Mr Pym's indiscretion was his removal from the Cabinet by the woman prime minister who, less than ten years earlier, did not believe that her time had come. But unlike other current affairs programmes, *Question Time* and *Any Questions?* have never condescended to exploit participants' indiscretions. *Weekend World* and *This Week, Next Week* issue press statements concerning astonishingly frank revelations. *Question Time* and *Any Questions?* are above that sort of thing.

Indeed, talking to Barbara Maxwell (the editor of *Question Time*) and Carol Stone (producer of *Any Questions?*), I wanted to plagiarise S. J. Perelman. When James Thurber asked him to comment on the *New Yorker*'s social purpose, moral perspective and aesthetic obligation, he answered, 'Jesus, Jim, it's just another ten cent magazine.' Thurber wrestled Perelman to the ground. And I have little doubt that the equally formidable Mesdames Maxwell and Stone would have reacted to similar heresy with equal violence.

It even took courage to ask what happens when nobody 'spontaneously' offers to ask the burning question of the moment. The answers were incredulous. By definition, the topics which the audiences volunteer *are* the burning questions of the moment. For both programmes are able to assemble a near perfect (though unscientific) cross-section of national opinion. To insinuate an idea or to prompt a participant would be to 'suggest that the people who appear do not represent what the country is thinking'. That is why *Question Time* did not discuss the City – its salaries and its scandals, its contribution to the economy and its standard of values – until months after the Big Bang. 'With the general public, that is the *thinking* general public, it wasn't an issue until much later.'

Neither programme began in a way which suggested the development of such infallibility. *Any Questions?* was born in Bristol, during October 1948, as a regional diversion and for years after it was networked on the old Home Service. It retained its West Country flavour with Ralph Wightman and A. G. Street offering fireside wisdom almost every other week, and the producer taking home for his dogs the meat that was left over from the pre-broadcast supper. Now Carol Stone has a backlog of almost 4,000 outstanding invitations. She makes her choice by resolutely refusing to go to the same place twice and attempting to cover most of Britain during her forty-five-week season.

The origins of *Question Time* are even humbler. A similar programme was attempted back in the early seventies – with no better purpose than filling in the gap left by *Panorama*'s summer holiday. Six 'senior politicians' were assembled in a Birmingham hotel and Mr (as he then was) Robin Day announced to the waiting world that on such a night as this important people gave important answers to important questions. Unfortunately, the producers had not taken the precaution of vetting the contributions before the live broadcast was transmitted. So Peter Walker, Brian Walden, Sir Reginald Eyre and I were asked our opinion on the increased rate which was being levied by the Thame and Wray Water Board. I am assured by viewers that our answers were universally inadequate.

Then, in 1979, Bill Cotton junior (then Controller of BBC1) made a long-term five-nights-a-week booking of the Greenwood Theatre in East London. His intention was to use it for the chat show which Michael Parkinson was due to host from Monday to Friday. But John Gorst – head of television current affairs – objected to so much time being diverted from grave issues, and the board of governors agreed that, on Thursday evenings, the slot (and the theatre) could be used for something unequivocally serious. Robin Day – his great days with *Panorama* and Mr Macmillan in Moscow behind him – was more than available. He was hanging about with a contract but no adequate way of serving out his time. Indeed, the devil was finding work for Mr Day's idle brain. He complained about the quality of the programmes on which he did not appear and attempted to impose his will on those ones which employed him. *Question Time* solved all the problems. Now it is a national institution.

Its imitators multiplied. Television South had *Questions* with David Jacobs in the chair. Radio Telefis Eireann broadcasts *Questions and Answers* under the guidance of Olivia O'Leary. In Scotland, Margo MacDonald presided over *Scottish Questions*. And on Channel Four there was a sports discussion, in exactly the same format, with Donald Trelford (the editor of the *Observer*, no less) playing the role of Sir Robin Day. Naturally enough, politicians long to take part. And messages are received from chairmen of great companies asking if they can be found a place on the panel. They are invited to lunch at the BBC – where Barbara Maxwell (who bridles at the word 'audition') decided if they would be successful participants. Often they would not.

The real object of the fortnightly lunches is to find new talent. It is an enterprise about which Sir Robin Day was openly sceptical. *Question Time* is not, he insists, '*Opportunity Knocks* for aspiring junior ministers' and works best when the participants are 'generalists' with 'established ability to argue a case'. And he believes that the audience (both at home and in the Greenwood Theatre) enjoys the programme most when the argument is conducted between four well-known controversialists. He suspects his editor of attempting 'positive discrimination' in favour of women. Barbara Maxwell pleads guilty to trying to exploit 'the still largely untapped reservoir' of female talent. They also disagree about an aside made by Sir Robin during a recent programme. She says that he complained about the 'women shouting instructions in his ear'. He insists that he spoke in the singular not the plural.

To justify the view that *Question Time* works best when the rival cases are argued by men and women with 'appropriate and established reputations', Sir Robin cites the case of Baroness Warnock – Mistress of Girton, chairman of numerous government inquiries and 'clearly a person of conspicuous talent'. During her appearance on the programme, she was asked to give the first answer to the first question and politely declined. The chairman insisted that she accept his invitation, but feared that his insistence changed his whole relationship with panel and audience. He would prefer – or says that he would prefer – to do no more than hold the ring, see fair play, act as umpire, clarify a point here and expand a detail there. He seeks to interfere only when the inadequacies of the panel force an aggressive role upon him. As he explained his desperate desire not to intrude between the viewers and the real stars of his show, I realised what an inadequate participant I must have been over the years. On each appearance I made the adversarial contest was ended with a fall, knock-out or submission.

My invitations to appear on the programme are, like the Order of the Garter, wholly unconnected with any damn nonsense about merit. For senior members of the major parties, a regular place at the Greenwood Theatre is guaranteed – guaranteed, that is, by the convention of the programme, for despite the suspicions that lurk in the minds of politicians who have not taken part, neither the panjandrums of Smith Square nor the moguls of Walworth Road (nor, for that matter, the satraps of wherever the various Liberals and Democrats now have their offices) are allowed to nominate the *dramatis personae*. Indeed, in the upper reaches of both parties there are dark suspicions that the BBC invites a proportion of its *Question Time* guests just to demonstrate its independence.

Sir Edward du Cann – when chairman of the 1922 Committee and my ever obliging pair – once asked me (in a tone which implied reproach at betrayal) how my Tory opponent on the programme had been chosen as the Conservative champion. I could only reply that, despite appearances to the contrary, it had not been arranged by me. Inadvertently it had been arranged by the government, for at the time they were reluctant for serving ministers to take part lest, horror of horrors, Environment answered a question on Health, and Defence offered an opinion on Transport. Now, ministers – or still lucid ex-ministers – virtually monopolise the Tory input.

With regret and reluctance, I find the BBC not guilty on all charges. To construct a list of the rebels of the far right is to ensure the question: 'Why do none of their troublemakers ever appear?' John Carlisle of Luton and Anthony Marlowe of Northampton are not kept off our screens because of the damage which their expressed opinions would do to the Tory Party. They are simply not the stuff of which serious discussion programmes are made. Labour rebels are more reasonable and more lucid and the most attractive of them get elected to the national executive. It is a cross which the People's Party will have to bear as long as *Question Time* lasts.

And that, I suspect, will be a very long time. Sir Robin Day speculates on other programmes about the joys of retirement, reminds his young admirers that he is almost sixty-five and refuses to commit himself beyond the end of his next one-year contract.

Modestly, he insists that there are many other television journalists who could do the job, though he refuses to mention anyone by name. Certainly both Sue Lawley and Donald McCormack of *Newsnight* have chaired the programme with distinction in Sir Robin's absence. But, when they did it, *Question Time* was different.

The influence of chairmen on such programmes is enormous. Once upon a time David Jacobs saw his role on *Any Questions?* as tossing the bone into the kennel and letting the dogs fight over it. And it worked very well. John Timpson, his successor, spent so long reading a contrived introduction for each participant that I always assumed that the audience switched off before the first question was asked. Now Jonathan Dimbleby persists in remembering that he is a real journalist and nips in from time to time with an interesting point of his own. Only Sir Robin dominates.

In my opinion it does not always make for sensible discussion – a view I have held since he brought the house down by demanding of me 'Do you agree with abortion or not? Yes or no?' – but it does make for compulsive viewing. And that is all that we should ask of the programme. The pretensions are all part of the public relations, the irascibility an essential ingredient in the star appeal. I make no complaint. I will never be forgiven for saying so, but that's show business.

Listener, 19 May 1988

In the Nick of Time

It all began with *Any Questions?* I arrived, as always, ten minutes before the programme began, and Carol Stone, the producer, did not even smile when I quoted Stephen Sondheim's line about the hero always coming in the nick of time. It was a bad sign. For ten years she has smiled at that quotation, once every six months. During the rehearsal, we were all asked to name our favourite television soap and I confidently nominated *Bread*. From then on, the curse of the Boswells was upon me. There followed eight days of unremitting work. Once upon a time, I used to think of appearing on radio or television as a sort of commando raid involving sudden and brief hand-to-hand fighting. After my week in Blackpool I regard a comparison with trench warfare as being more appropriate.

I had meant to travel via Liverpool. But my pilgrimage to the shrine of Joey, Grandad and Lilo Lill had to be postponed, for I was instructed to arrive in Blackpool no later than five o'clock. A line of television cameras awaited me on the steps of the Imperial Hotel. Behind them, Peter Mandelson, the Labour Party's director of publicity, was gesticulating emphatically. I read his coded message correctly. Speak to me before you speak to the world. Unfortunately, the television reporters did not afford Mr Mandelson proper precedence. I gazed, eyes glazed, into the cameras, only thinking of the awful message which awaited me. Had a loved one died, or, worse still, had Ron Todd turned against me? After twenty years of regular cross-examination, politicians develop the technique of talking about one thing and thinking about another. Yes, I did expect to be re-elected. No, I did not anticipate a second ballot. Yes, it would be a mandate for change. When it was all over I rushed up to Mandelson and asked him to give it to me straight. He spared me nothing. My jacket collar was turned up.

With Jeremy Paxman on *Breakfast Time* at 7.45 the following morning, not one of my hairs was out of place. I had already endured an interview with IRN – sensible enough questions via a transmission system which echoed my own answers back through the headphones. Interviews with Mr Paxman are a joy. For he asked one question throughout the entire interview – escalating the level of aggression and incredulity. Ten minutes later on radio's *Today* Brian Redhead exhibited his now-famous talent for genial assassination. It is not until the programme is over that the victim of Mr Redhead's unique technique realises that he has been mugged. As I left the makeshift studio Brian told me, 'I've been headhunted. Man telephoned me and asked if I was interested in being editor of *Punch*. Said "course not".' Glory alleluia. *Today* will remain the best current affairs programme on sound or in vision.

At lunchtime, I was interviewed leaning perilously on the brass railing which runs around the Winter Garden's balcony. Through the vertigo, I heard myself saying, 'Yes, I had expected to be re-elected. No, I had never anticipated a second ballot. Yes, it was a mandate for change.' Against my better judgment, I agreed to an eighteen-minute interview with Sir Robin Day on *Conference Day*. My better judgment turned out to be absolutely wrong.

At 6.15 Sir Robin began to talk to me about the subject of the morning's debate – the 'aims and values' of socialism. Philosophical discussions are rare events at party conferences and even rarer items in television programmes. But for over a quarter of an hour we examined the work of John Rawls and argued about how governments should behave 'when liberties collide'. As usual, Sir Robin and I tried to be smart at each other's expense. But unusually, neither of us took exception to the other's impertinence. I began to look forward, with unaccustomed pleasure, to Thursday evening's *Conference Question Time*.

I am told that I appeared later that night on *Newsnight* and I have a vague memory of a member of my staff congratulating me on 'getting Peter Snow off defence after the first question'. If in the future I remember the occasion at all, it will be because of the comments of my family and friends. They thought I looked 'tired' (not to be confused with 'tired and emotional') and wondered if I should have been quite so stern when Peter Snow attempted to ask a supplementary question on defence.

On Tuesday, I had no formal duties other than sitting within visible admiration range of the party leader and applauding enthusiastically during his big speech. My duty done, I strolled back to the hotel for an early cup of tea – only pausing to tell every television camera, on which I could focus, that the enthusiasm had been genuine. Before I got through the Imperial's door, I was handed an advance copy of a speech which Ron Todd was to make later that evening. From then on it was all bobbing and weaving. My only hope was to avoid converting a collision into a pile-up. 'Wait for it to go away,' we all agreed.

By Wednesday morning, we had decided that 'anyone who thinks it will go away doesn't understand politics'. Something had to be said – but not too much. *The World At One* offered an opportunity. My staff made them an offer. I would discuss the prospects of the party in general but not Ron Todd in particular. They refused and countered with a compromise – one Ron Todd question, a bridging supplementary and on to the wider issues. Unworthily, I wondered if the bargain would be honoured and was reproached with the news that the interviewer would be Jim Naughtie. The phrase echoed around the conference hall: 'Jim plays fair.' And so he does, but I forgot that he plays hard as well. At the end of the interview the windows of the recording booth were steamed up with my sweat. It took a recording for *The World Tonight* to bring my temperature back to normal.

Outside, BBC Television waited with a request of their own – three questions; one Ron Todd and two general. 'Promise,' I said, 'that if you only have time for one . . .' John Harrison was explicit. 'All or nothing,' adding that if it turned out to be nothing I'd better not complain about my time being wasted. It turned out to be nothing and I made no complaint. The best politicians can hope for is to be told the truth about what the programme-makers intend. Then we take it or leave it and accept the consequences.

On Thursday evening I meant to do no more than watch the extract from my interview with Peter Sissons which they put into the Channel 4 news bulletin. But when Mr Sissons announced that I had promised 'no betrayal', I decided that an interview which dealt with so novel a political concept ought to be seen in full. So I delayed my departure for the Norbreck Hydro and *Conference Question Time*. Barbara Maxwell, *Question Time*'s editor, did not even smile when I told her that the hero always comes in the nick of time. It was a bad sign. She has smiled at that quotation twice a year since 1979.

My fears were justified. Tony Benn began with a plea to keep personalities out of politics. As a result, he won my award for the Most Sanctimonious Performance of the Week, beating by a short head David Owen who, on *Any Questions?* six days earlier, had answered a question on the Gibraltar inquest with a statement of his gratitude to the SAS.

Inevitably, I turned nasty and lost the Labour Party several thousand votes from amongst the ranks of those gentle viewers who take politicians at their face value and believe that we should all be nice to each other. Annoyed by my indiscipline, I forgot that the BBC World Service was waiting outside the Norbreck ballroom. Two hours later they caught up with me. With embarrassment added to remorse, I recorded another interview on defence.

Later that same night I was told that the *Today* programme had made a special request for me to appear on their final conference broadcast – a flattering invitation only partly spoilt by the knowledge that they had told Neil Kinnock's office that if he was too busy 'they'd have to have Hattersley again'. I got to the studio just in time, as the eight o'clock news was ending, and told Brian Redhead that 'the hero always comes in the nick of time'. He smiled.

Listener, 20 May 1988

The Sunny Side of the Street

For *Coronation Street*'s most passionate supporters, the line between fact and fiction has always been difficult to draw. When William Roache visited Lichfield – to support the Tory candidate in the mid-Staffs by-election – a woman in the shopping centre shouted, 'Go home to Deirdre.' Mrs Roache was confidently awaiting her husband's return at their house in Cheshire. Deirdre was Mrs Barlow, deserted wife of the much-derided Ken.

It is not surprising that the sight of the actor results in instant recognition of the character he plays. For twenty-five years, William Roache has appeared each week in our living rooms as Ken Barlow – failed schoolmaster, failed journalist and failed husband. And *Coronation Street* prides itself on being true to real life. Its audiences identify rather than fantasise.

Of course it is more than a replica of the real world. It does what the 'realistic' English novel sets out to do – reflects rather than reproduces reality and, by dramatising the life of specific individuals, illustrates the habits and attitudes of a whole class or generation. When Newton and Ridley were threatening to turn the

Rover's Return into a 'fun pub', exactly the same desecration was destroying the public house in which I once drank after my constituency surgeries. As the inn sign went up over the front door – a teddy bear in goggles flying a biplane – we all wished there was a local Bet Gilroy to fight off the new barbarism.

It has become fashionable, in circles where fashion is important, to criticise *Coronation Street* as romanticising northern life and painting a wholly sentimental picture of the industrial working class. Channel 4 devoted a whole broadcast to a bombardment of Granada's flagship. Although Granada decided to return the fire, there is no doubt that *Coronation Street* has begun to accommodate some of the criticisms about its indomitable good nature. In the past six months we have had a cataclysmic marriage breakdown (preceded by months of furtive adultery), an unwanted pregnancy and bitter disagreement about the possible consequent abortion, an adoption savagely contested by an estranged grandmother, a young wife hideously unsympathetic about her husband's unemployment and a husband despairing at the mean-mindedness of his disagreeable wife. In short, *Coronation Street* has contracted a mild version of the *EastEnders* syndrome.

Once upon a time there was a murder in *Coronation Street*. But in *EastEnders*, homicide is a persistent storyline. For the past ten weeks a boxer, on the run from an unjust murder charge, has been a central figure of this principal plot. He was 'shopped' by a drug addict who had been reformed by imprisonment in his own house. Not surprisingly, after the dependency was cured, the moral degeneracy persisted. In the *EastEnders'* Queen Vic, there have been residents afflicted with Alzheimer's Disease, dipsomania, and at least the fear of Aids. 'Dirty Den', its first landlord, was liquidated by his gangster associates after fathering a schoolgirl's baby. How different from the home life of our own dear Alec and Bet in the Rover's Return.

I doubt if life in the East End of London is anything like as squalid or desperate as *EastEnders* makes it out to be. The programme is a caricature. *Coronation Street* is a caricature as well. But it chooses to emphasise the more genial side of life. It is essentially a happy programme in which the good are rewarded, the wicked punished (though not very severely) and most people live contentedly ever after. Hearing Mr Roache defend Ken Barlow to an audience at the Edinburgh Television Festival, I was struck by the plea that he made for tolerance. Ken, he said, had behaved badly but he had paid an awful price for his sins. In *Coronation Street* only the virtuous are allowed to enjoy themselves throughout the series.

It is the optimistic view of life which *Coronation Street* typifies that makes it such attractive television. It is important not to make too serious a claim about its virtues. It is, after all, entertainment – though entertainment of a superior quality with wonderfully naturalistic dialogue and an almost invariably high level of acting. The real question we have to ask ourselves is simple enough. Do we want a series that sends us to supper hopeful about the future of mankind, or one that spoils our digestion by convincing us there is something essentially squalid about human nature? *Coronation Street*'s strength is that it is on the side of hope.

It is important that *Coronation Street* resists the temptation to develop what its critics would, no doubt, describe as a harder cutting edge. Some of its best characters are essentially comic in an almost Dickensian sense of the word. Jack and Vera Duckworth, like Bet and Alec Gilroy, are an ill-matched husband and wife who thrive on their animosity in the manner of Beadle Bumble and Widow Corney. In consequence they make us laugh. In *EastEnders* you are more likely to find a modern version of Mr Murdstone tyrannising his weak wife and brutalising his stepson. It may be no more than a matter of taste, but I prefer to smile between half past seven and eight o'clock.

When, last year, I gave the *Coronation Street* Lecture at the Edinburgh Television Festival, I was asked to defend my contention that in some episodes the programme compared with serious literature. Foolishly I said that Alma Sedgwick, in her unswerving loyalty to her perfidious lover, reminded me of Anna Karenina. We knew that Vronski would behave badly, but part of Anna's attraction was the certainty that despite her protestations, she would stand by him. Alma, I said, had the same limpet attraction. Embarrassed by so pretentious a comparison, I said that I would run away with Alma Sedgwick as soon as she asked me to do so.

A fortnight later, a tabloid newspaper telephoned my office.

Alma, they said, was desperately worried about the Gulf war and was anxious to listen to the debate in the House of Commons. If I would obtain her a ticket, the newspaper would be pleased to take us both to lunch and publish a picture of our earnest political discussion. It was some moments before I had the presence of mind to say that Alma could neither come to lunch nor to the House of Commons. For Alma does not exist.

The importance of *Coronation Street* lies in the fact that no one would have made a similar telephone call hoping to obtain a photograph of a middle-aged politician having lunch with Anna Karenina.

Daily Telegraph, 5 November 1991

Tropical Tangle of Grammar and Gramophone

I missed my first chance to hear the programme for which the whole nation has waited since 1942. But, as the combination of person and programme promised to be the biggest festival of kitsch for fifty years, I made a point of listening to *Desert Island Discs* last Friday morning. I was not disappointed.

Honesty requires me to explain that, although I am an enthusiast for the programme, the programme has treated me like a liquidated member of the Supreme Soviet after one of Stalin's purges. I was not invited to the anniversary party at which – according to the publicity – all previous participants discussed alternative luxury objects and held literary discussions at which all talk of Shakespeare and the Bible was prohibited. The reason why I was ignored was more painful than the snub itself. I have been written out of the history books.

They actually asked me to be castaway last summer. And when I thanked them for the honour of inviting me a second time, they denied absolutely that I had been on the show before. I suspect that, down in the bowels of Broadcasting House, a wall is decorated with composite photographs of *Desert Island Disc* laureates – and that some of the faces have been obliterated. The non-persons are (or were) the dissidents of the revisionist Michael Parkinson regime.

It is only fair to say that as well as having a strange relationship with *Desert Island Discs*, I am not terribly close to John Major. My affection for him had not been increased by a problem which he had caused me on the day before I heard the choice of records which Conservative Central Office had made on his behalf. During Question Time in the House of Commons, I had to quote from one of the Prime Minister's previous answers. That is always a daunting task. Last Thursday my difficulty was grammatical. Ad-libbing about VAT in June, Mr Major refused to give a 'categoric assurance' that it would not be increased. He added for emphasis that no government could ever make such a promise: 'None have and none will.' Considering how to reproduce those five words spoilt my lunch at the American Embassy. Fearful that the error would be attributed to me, I considered following the habit of my fellow Sheffielder, Mrs Stainless Stephen, and speaking the punctuation.

Brevity is all at Question Time and I doubted if the Speaker would allow 'as the Prime Minister said. Ping. Ping. None have and none will. Pong. Pong.' I could have added '*sic*'. But it might have been misunderstood.

In short, I listened to last Friday's *Desert Island Discs* through a haze of complicated prejudice and what I write about it is probably conditioned by the bias. So I was probably wrong to suspect that when the Prime Minister twice spoke – with dismissive envy – of 'double firsts', a small effigy of Douglas Hurd was metaphorically rotating on the turntable. In consequence, it is better for me to concentrate on the questions rather than the answers.

Even dealing with what ought to have been the least conten-tious parts of the programme requires me to admit that I do not admire Sue Lawley's peek-a-boo interviewing technique. Whatever you may say about Sir Robin Day's mannerisms, his questions do sound like demands for information rather than invitations to be chased around the studio. But even Miss Lawley's style (which I am sure does not reflect her admirable character) is no excuse for treating a serious subject with such frivolity. And the Prime Minister is, whether *Private Eye* admits it or not, a serious subject.

On *Desert Island Discs*, Mr Major announced that no one need sleep rough in London. He went on to claim that the crisis of mortgage repossessions had largely been solved. Both assertions were left to hang unchallenged in the tropical air. Perhaps the producers thought that argument was inappropriate because the programme is not political. Clearly, Mr Major did not share that opinion. At first I was prepared to believe that he really liked the Elgar and I can easily imagine him listening to Diana Ross. Nor did it surprise me when he chose Don Bradman being bowled for a duck at the end of the last Test innings. But he did not mention that the England team gave three cheers before Bradman took guard and John Arlott subsequently said that you cannot bat with tears in your eyes. Funny, I thought. Funny. Perhaps such sentimentality is out of fashion. Then he ended the programme with 'The Best is Yet to Come' and I understood it all. The image makers had been at work.

Perhaps the programme could not avoid being hijacked. But even at the human interest level – the standards that we expect from château-bottled gossip like *In the Psychiatrist's Chair* – all the best opportunities were left buried in the sand or sunk amongst the coral reefs.

The Prime Minister said that the desert island fantasy was most appealing at quarter past three on Tuesday and Thursday afternoons. I can think of few other interviewers who, having been given that opening, would not have gone on to ask if he was really saying that he did not enjoy Prime Minister's Questions and what it was that he found so unattractive about the occasion. Perhaps he was merely counterfeiting humility. Or it may be that he hates wrestling with the grammar.

I am still worried about the way I quoted his answer last Friday: '... no government at any stage give [*sic*] categoric assurances.' There is nothing that you can do with that sentence except start again. Better a tropical moon, the sleepy lagoon and Sue Lawley.

Guardian, 3 February 1992

Liberation With a Dash of Appropriate Dignity

No more 'two shots'. My deputy leadership of the Labour Party is, like the old king's life, drawing peacefully to its close. There are still two weeks to go before I emerge from the Walworth Road chrysalis and begin to flap my way through politics like an elderly, overweight but joyously independent butterfly. But even last week – when the onerous obligations of office still weighed me down – I had a little flutter of freedom. 'Now we'll do the two shot,' the television interviewer said.

Majestically, I rose from my seat and left the studio. Fortunately, I had the presence of mind to remove the microphone which had been clipped to my tie. So I avoided the embarrassment of being dragged back to the chair, like a dog that runs after a rabbit without remembering that it is tethered to its kennel. As revolutionaries from Cavour to Kossuth will confirm in heaven, the act of liberation must be performed with appropriate dignity.

The true beauty of the occasion would have been lost if, in making my declaration of independence, I had knocked over the glass of brackish water or swept from the corner of the desk the rubber hair brush which is left, just out of sight, for the use of broadcasters who are sufficiently reckless to run it through their hair.

The 'two shot', I ought to explain to the uninitiated, is a device which was invented for the convenience of the television interviewer, the humiliation of the interviewee and the general suppression of truth. It requires the victim to be the instrument of his own destruction. In consequence, sadists love it. You will therefore understand that escaping from the typical television studio, without having performed this distasteful act, is something of an achievement. More sensitive readers may prefer to be spared the details of how a 'two shot' – not to mention a 'noddy' and a 'reverse' – is actually carried out. But for me, a description of those related processes is a catharsis in itself.

Even as I write, it seems incredible that men and women who, no doubt, love their mothers, feed their budgerigars, water their window boxes and pay their poll tax are prepared, once inside the BBC and ITN, to inflict such degradation on other human beings. A politician – wholly committed to the public good and only concerned with the wider dissemination of truth – agrees to be interviewed. He, or she, is asked a number of ignorant, contentious, biased and probably ungrammatical questions.

The replies are measured, balanced, accurate and constructed in flawless English. The interviewer then says, 'We'll just do the two shot,' or, 'The noddy will just take a couple of seconds.' The instruction is often preceded by a few words of cringing ingratiation such as, 'You must have done this a thousand times before,' or, 'You've probably been through this more often than me [*sic*] so I won't explain.'

Pictures are then taken of the interviewer pretending to ask questions, the politician pretending to listen and them both pretending to be immensely impressed with each other.

It is all either done in risible silence or with the person who is not facing the camera talking (but not being recorded) so that the perceptive viewer can see the muscles move in the back of his neck and believe a real interview is taking place.

If this television variant of a Noh play was only a waste of time, it might be tolerable. But it is all done in order to allow the tyrants of television to cut up, compress, misinterpret and generally defile the excellent interview which preceded the pantomime.

Many years ago in Brighton, I described a Labour prime minister as being received 'not ecstatically but sympathetically' and went on to support some parts of his speech and criticise others. Being in thrall to television – and anxious to be invited back – I then agreed to take part in 'reverses', or something of that sort. On the news bulletin that night, when asked how the party conference had reacted to the leader's address, I answered 'not ecstatically'. I then set out my criticisms of what he had said. Watching the programme, even I found it difficult to believe that I had said anything complimentary about the performance. Then I remembered that, in between each of my answers, there had been a brief glimpse of the interviewer nodding like a stuffed dog in the back window of a motor car.

Chained as I was to the rock of responsibility (a condition which encouraged me to construct ridiculously pretentious metaphors) I let the vultures of television pick at my liver for more than twenty years. But after 19 July – switching the image from Prometheus to Pinocchio – I have no strings to tie me down. So no more 'two shots'. And no more waiting 'whilst we find out if the recording is satisfactory' or breakfast broadcasts before half past seven, or facing into the wind so that my hair gets blown about but the interviewer's stays neat or facing into the sun so that I am the one who squints, or doing it again because 'it was a bit longer than we really need.'

In fact, after 19 July, no more television tyranny. That is if, after that date, I am ever again asked to give an interview.

Guardian, 29 June 1992

Picking Yourself Up from the Cutting Room Floor

The suit said it all. At least, had I worn it on the programme for which it was bought, it would have spoken with ready-made eloquence about both my state of mind and the role which I was cast to play on the late-night television chat show. It was, in itself, a perfectly good suit – blue worsted, single-breasted and designed to exude modest respectability. The moment that I saw it on the rack, labelled 'Middle-aged, portly', I knew that it might have been made for me. A couple of small alterations were necessary to ensure a perfect fit. But the salesman had no doubt that it could be cut down to size in time for me to wear it whilst I received exactly the same treatment from Mr Clive Anderson.

The suit was duly delivered to the studio in a large plastic bag which was gratifyingly decorated with my name and a bogus coat of arms. Honesty requires me to explain why I did not put it on at once. My old friend Anne Robinson – of radio, television and poster hoarding fame – was in the make-up room having her lily gilded, and I tiptoed in to say hello. She subsequently denied having seen me in the mirror, but I can think of no other reason why she should have begun to speak in a loud voice about the running order of the programme. The clear implication of what she said was that whoever preceded her occupied the position of 'full supporting cast'.

I decided to reprove her with a little gentle irony – not, in my experience, always an effective weapon against lady tabloid journalists, but the best form of retaliation I could think of at the time. I therefore spent the next ten minutes constructing a crude cardboard star which I would have hung on Ms Robinson's dressing-room door had I not been approached by a young lady who wished to wire me for sound. No sooner had I been plugged in than a second functionary – distinguishable from the first only by the colour of her leggings – said that I'd been lost, was late, and that the recording was about to begin. I must change my suit at once and proceed to the studio.

It was then that I discovered that the jacket sleeves, which should have been shortened by an inch, had been lengthened by the same amount. Admittedly, I have stubby fingers. But not since I was five have they been hidden beneath my cuffs. My first idea was to push the surplus worsted upwards. Do you recall the puff sleeves of the 1950s – tight up to the elbow and bulging around the biceps? They do not look good on a middle-aged portly politician. Through my panic, I recalled that there is no regulation of the Royal Television Society which requires chat show guests to appear with their extremities exposed. So I thought of sitting in front of my host, rude but not risible, with hands in pockets.

Then I realised that I had to approach Mr Anderson across a broad stage. To have advanced towards him with arms which apparently descended to knee level would have been an appropriate entrance for a monkey impersonator, but I was there to plug my new novel, and my counterfeit persona was intellectual rather than simian. I changed back into my old grey flannel.

I was preceded on the programme by a person known as Meat Loaf – a popular entertainer of some sort who aggressively made clear that his name was two words not one. But it was suit-induced tension rather than fear that I was on the wrong programme which made me lose my nerve. Instead of waiting for Mr Anderson's cross-examination, I began to interrogate him. Was it, I asked, true that Kenneth Baker had been offered £5,000 to appear on the show and still declined the invitation?

Before I had finished the question, I felt certain that I was doomed. The razor-sharp television personality was certain to reply with a revelation of the fee that I would receive. He would then make a comment about the relative values of his guests. To my astonishment, Mr Anderson gulped, paused and muttered something pompous about not discussing other people's earnings. Sadly, that passage was left out of the subsequent broadcast.

We went on to discuss football and Mr Anderson expressed doubts about whether or not I had paid real money for my Coca-Cola cup final ticket. The taboo on discussing finance being lifted, I reassured him that I had actually made out a cheque. That passage also failed to make it into the final programme. Reassured by a rather good joke about Chris Waddle – Anderson said that we were both dribblers (*Private Eye, circa* 1970) and I said that each of us was regarded as the best in England but neither of us got picked (Labour Party, *circa* 1983) – I bowed out. As I left the studio, Ms Robinson was taking command of the programme and, no doubt in a fit of remorse, trying to talk about my book. Mr Anderson was gasping again. You guessed it. Anne Robinson Talks Back was not transmitted.

Do not believe, compassionate reader, that my evening was wasted. My book was plugged. More important, I learned one of life's lessons. As a result, I took my suit back to the tailor with absolute confidence that, on the following day, it would be made into a perfect fit. I had learned from the Clive Anderson show that if you keep cutting and stitching together anything can be made to look smart.

Guardian, 10 May 1993

Give and Take
on the Not-So-Small Screen

Like Queen Victoria, John Cole is so 'secure in the affection of the people' that no 'jumped-up Birmingham radical politician' possesses the power to inflict even superficial damage on his reputation. So I can report, with a clear conscience, an unhappy episode in our long (and previously friendly) relationship. It concerns a cry for help which received a wholly inadequate response from inside that avuncular tweed coat.

Just after Christmas, the BBC invited me to make three television films and I telephoned Mr Cole for his advice on how I should pursue what was, for me, a novel activity. 'Have you,' he asked, 'signed the contract?' I told him that I had. 'Then,' he replied, 'I have no advice to offer you.'

It is possible to argue, in Mr Cole's defence, that his response was not encouraging. There was certainly no suggestion that weeks of joy stretched out ahead of me. But his comment did contain the fatalistic implication that, having taken the Director General's shilling, I should not complain about being left to die in No Man's Land – or the Television Centre as we film-makers call it.

The films being finished, I have no doubt about what Mr Cole, from the depth of his experience, should have told me. 'Flee the country. Feign serious illness. Employ Mr Carter-Ruck to find the clause in the agreement which allows withdrawal at the onset of chronic frustration and terminal boredom.' He said none of those things. In consequence I have, for weeks, been exposed to a group of people who really do think that a picture is worth a thousand words. Worse, they believe that nouns and verbs only exist to help with the display of images. My role was to act as the hooks and wire with which their works of art were hung on television's wall.

I might have forgiven them their distaste for the English language had they not all been so nice to me. Throughout my weeks of continual bad temper they remained courteous, kind, sympathetic, polite and understanding. It was intolerable. I recalled my years in the Boy Scouts when I was encouraged to smile and whistle under all difficulties, but I identified not with my indomitable patrol leader but with the difficulties which never got him down. We were vocationally incompatible. Television is team work. Writing is not. Now I understand why, when he went to Hollywood, Scott Fitzgerald got drunk every night.

There were, early on in my brief screen career, moments of unworthy pleasure. People really do say 'it's a take' and 'very quiet please in the studio, we're rolling'. I got 'cued'. Indeed, I found the instructions so confusing that I had a semaphore system that was all my own. It was called 'a special wave for Roy'. But when I speculated on the possible metaphysical connotation of that concept – Virginia Woolf, the Hellespont, Venus arising from one – I was urged to concentrate on the coloured tape which marked the spot on the studio floor from which I began my walk towards the camera.

If the licence fee goes up next year, blame it on the amount of coloured tape which, thanks to me, has been stuck on studio floors since last February. No longer do I scoff at President Ford's alleged inability to walk and talk at the same time. Were I even to contemplate contempt, a dozen reproaches would float into my mind. Roy, you were a little breathy towards the end. Roy, you fluffed on 'ideology'. Roy, you forgot to turn to camera one. Even when Roy remembered, it was still 'one more time' – just to make sure or because the lights were not quite right or to get another camera angle. At first my only consolation was the blonde make-up lady who mopped my brow during lulls in the action and put drops in my bloodshot eyes to make them how they would have been but for the previous day's filming. This, I thought, is at least like *Sunset Boulevard*. Then I remembered that I was Norma Desmond.

According to the critics, the first programme was a great success. No credit is due to my writing – short, repetitive sentences which, in the words of the director, 'worked best when they said what I was going to say, said it and then said it again'. My performance will be remembered, at least by me, for the way in which I clutched the front of my suit. Somebody had told me that a jacket which was a size too big would make me look thin. I looked fat, but the jacket looked a size too big. Unless I held the lapels together, as if I were trying to stem the flow of blood from a gaping wound, it became obvious that I was wearing a cream shirt.

I have not worn a cream shirt since primary school. But white glowed and, because of the clever tricks being performed by the director, blue did not register with the camera. When I wore a blue shirt, the screen showed a space where my chest should have been. Through the gap in my thorax, Sofia Airport was clearly visible. It was right at the beginning of filming. But I still said, with feeling, 'O that this too, too solid flesh would really melt.'

Last Friday, there was a party at Richmond to celebrate our achievement. I could not be there because of constituency duties. But I know what went on. When the band struck up the first tune, the director ran forward. 'Sorry, but you came in too early.' In the bar, orders for gins and tonics were rejected. 'I'm afraid you were rather breathy when you asked for ice.' The interval was delayed because the lights needed to be re-arranged. When the blonde make-up lady's fiancé tried to kiss her she told him to stop until she had powdered his nose. Despite all that, I am sorry to have missed the festivities. But then, there will be other parties. I cannot say the same about films.

Guardian, 31 May 1993

Up For Adoption

Never, at any time during my thirty years in the House of Commons, have I been able to think of myself as a Birmingham Member of Parliament. And, for the last quarter of a century, I have not even tried very hard. I am the Member of Parliament for Sparkbrook. It is the interests of that earth, that realm, that single constituency which concern me. When what is good for Sparkbrook is also good for the city by which it is surrounded, I can do a fair imitation of Joseph Chamberlain's ghost. But I still cannot identify with the Bull Ring, Aston Villa or the old jewellery quarter.

It is a character failing which I increasingly share with my constituents – more and more of whom patronise a jewellery quarter of their own. It is situated along each side of the Stratford Road at more or less the point where the Sparkbrook and Sparkhill wards meet, and is made up of genuine goldsmiths who hammer out necklaces and bracelets in the back of their shops, display them in windows that gleam in the grimy sunlight and sell them not as adornments but as investments which appreciate far more quickly than bank balances. Now, half of my constituents are – like me – immigrants. Perhaps that is why I feel that I am theirs, they are mine and that I would not want to be elected for any other seat on earth.

That was not always my attitude. When I was 'adopted' as Labour candidate – back in 1962 – I was very near to becoming a political orphan. In those more comradely days, ambitious young men did not try to ease sitting Members out of their safe seats and I had been adjudged unworthy to fill any of the Yorkshire vacancies. Then Sparkbrook found me, took me off the streets and gave me a political home. To begin with, my only emotion was gratitude. But gradually as we grew on each other I began to feel a stronger attachment. In 1982, when the Boundary Commission threatened to divide the constituency into three pieces and distribute them about Birmingham, I decided that if Sparkbrook went I would go with it.

When I was first elected, Sparkbrook's ethnic minority was the Irish. Fifteen years later, most of them had moved south – first to the council estates and then to the owner-occupied suburbs. Sikhs and Muslims (Pathans, Kashmiris and Bengalis) gradually took their place. The Sparkbrook Carnival – Middle England out of the Irish Free State with a touch of the Caribbean added for flavour – was one of the last surviving relics of the old constituency. Now it has gone – along with the public houses which have been boarded up or turned into community centres, and the chapels which have become gurdwaras and mosques. An Endpiece that I wrote for the *Listener* ('Carnival in Sparkbrook') described one of the last great summer celebrations in Farm Road Park. My description was inadequate. Some critics would say corrupt. Amongst the army of infants who marched under the slogan 'Children of the World Unite' was a group of fake Orientals who defied my description. They wore home-made pigtails, gloriously false drooping moustaches, and old lampshades tied on their heads to look like hats. Those who remembered the instruction walked with their arms folded. The oldest boys carried a dragon banner. 'Little Chinese' did not sound quite right and I was told that 'Little Chinamen' certainly had racist (and probably sexist) overtones. So I pretended that they did not exist. My only excuse is that established society had made the same mistake about the ethnic minorities for most of the previous decade.

During the decade which followed, Sparkbrook became increasingly Muslim. Islam was never, numerically at least, the dominant force that some commentators pretended. But it has left its permanent mark on the constituency and upon me. By the time that Salman Rushdie published *The Satanic Verses*, the Sparkbrook Muslims thought that I was theirs. And so, in many ways, I was. Nobody in Sparkbrook wanted to hang the author. But my refusal to support the call for the book to be banned caused great offence and, far worse, the feeling amongst the Khans, the Hussains and the Mirzas that they had been deserted by their only influential friend. Their reaction was mild compared with the response of enlightened opinion to my suggestion that the paperback should be postponed as a gesture of reconciliation.

In polite society my reputation sank even lower after I wrote, for the *Independent* ('They Must Be Like Us'), a reply to Fay Weldon's assault on Islam's attitude to women. Amongst the first to throw me a social lifeline was Ms Weldon herself. In a remarkably generous letter she confessed to 'voicing strong opinions on subjects about which I am no expert'. And she asked me to arrange for her to visit Sparkbrook. Throughout the day I tried not to behave as if the constituency belonged to me. Fay tells me that I failed.

I suppose that I became so committed to the Muslims at Sparkbrook because they were mine and in such obvious need of a friend. They suffer double deprivation – the penalties of poverty and the damage done by racialism. On the afternoon that Enoch Powell made his second celebrated attack on the black and Asian British – not 'rivers of blood' but 'active volcano' – I was opening an extension to Clifton Primary School. Inevitably, I wrote about it. One of the governors, a Mrs Bi whose husband I had helped to get into Britain, was voluble in her gratitude. I solemnly shook her son's hand as she announced that I was 'responsible for him'.

Deprivation is not quite colour blind, but it certainly does not ostracise my white constituents. When I wrote about Amanda and her daughter Sapphire ('Poverty Trapped Inside an Army Surplus Anorak') *Guardian* readers sent cheques and postal orders to help the desperate pair survive. John Humphrys (who insisted that his help was not acknowledged) wrote his column about my column and added his fee to the fighting fund. Amanda wrote me a note of thanks that ended with the assertion that 'Xmas has come already, only better'.

My story of adult poverty ('Lady with a Limp') attracted less public attention because the victim was old. My description of three of my constituents who – by even the most prejudicial standards – were a clear asset to society ('Forget Conformity . . .') resulted in fewer racist letters than I had expected. But Dr Sydney Alder of Brighton did send me a page of nonsense which might have been written for a sketch from *Beyond the Fringe*.

> As a fellow socialist, I resent your attitude to Mr Churchill's article in defence of the British way of life. Why should the muezzin's call to prayer drown out the church bells in a Christian country? I am no racist. I have had a Muslim and Hindu partner in my

practice and my closest friend at university was a Hindu. Is Islam a religion or a political faith, because political statements issue often from religious figures with much frequency? Can we Christians have the same tolerance in the countries whence our new Britishers came?

As I sit at home writing and thinking – as J. B. Priestley recommended – of the readers who will stare at my column during the following week, I try to forget about Dr Alder.

Sparkbrook, in one form or another, has featured in my regular columns about four times a year – rather less than 10 per cent of the total output, rather more than Sheffield Wednesday and the Yorkshire County Cricket together, but less than Shakespeare. When I write about schools ('When We Were Very Young and All Was Well') they are likely to be Sparkbrook schools. The polling day which I described – when for a moment the hope of victory flickered again – was a Sparkbrook polling day. On 9 April 1992, I felt finally at home. Sparkbrook and I needed and wanted each other.

Carnival in Sparkbrook

Summer really ends when the party conferences begin and the silly season tales of teeth lost on the Blackpool sands give way to stories of reputations won in the Winter Gardens. The party leaders may be photographed smiling their way around the big dipper. But they – and their supporters – have only been allowed in the hotels and boarding houses because the genuinely joyous holidaymakers have gone home to save for next year.

From the moment the first delegate arrives we can only count the days until the signs of spring inevitably appear again. A trumpet of a prophecy, O wind! If winter comes, can the Sparkbrook Carnival be far behind?

The Sparkbrook Carnival takes place each spring. It is certainly not the biggest and probably, by objective standards, not the best of the summer celebrations in my constituency. At Acocks Green the crowd is twice as large and is offered delights as diverse and diverting as a caged-bird show in the billiard room of the Sons of Rest pavilion and a tug-of-war competition in which local public houses heave away for the coveted 'Hattersley Shield'. They are more adventurous in Balsall Heath. There, real ale is on sale for all the afternoon and most of the evening, the streets are closed to traffic, and children ride donkeys so recently brought from the seaside that they still have sand between their toes. But, for me, the only true sign that another summer is really on its way is the Sparkbrook Carnival, for in Sparkbrook they have a contest for the best-decorated lorry and usually I am the judge.

The lorries – or 'floats', as we experts call them – draw up in line alongside the iron railings which once enabled Farm Road Park to be emptied and locked as soon as dusk, and its attendant moral dangers, descended. Most are decorated by (and with) the youth clubs, play-groups, Wolf Cub packs and infant schools of the area. Some are the permanent coach-built advertisements of the armed forces and nationalised industries. A few are so crude and casual that they are not really part of the competition, just the teeming, huddled masses of black and white Sparkbrook youth out for a joy-ride.

The professional displays, sent, for example, by the Midlands Electricity Board in a heroic bid to improve its sponsor's popularity, I mentally disqualify *at* once. In my mind, if not in the published rules, the real contest is between the groups of local children: nursery classes turned by their teachers into hosts of cardboard daffodils and fields of paper poppies; self-conscious 'Schools of Dance' pirouetting uncertainly on the back of coal lorries as they attempt to keep their tutus clean; whole crews of primary school pirates, every man blind in one eye and forced to wear a black patch; West Indian girls' football teams, augmented by guest appearances of men with balloons inside their shirts and bright red patches painted on their cheeks.

There is always a comic policeman who helps the real policemen to marshal the crowd for the presentation of the huge tissue-paper rosettes that the organisers have made in caricature of what they have seen at the *Horse of the Year Show* on television.

Occasionally the Air Training Corps band, the drums and fifes of the Boys' Brigade and the bugles of the Scouts all parade together, raising delicate issues of precedence that are always settled with honour and amity.

St Trinian's is regularly represented – a commentary upon the ease with which their uniforms can be obtained or the psychology of forty-year-old ladies. The elderly pupils always offer improper inducements to the judge and shake their hockey sticks in mock rage when they are rejected.

But the hazards of choosing the winner do not compare with the dangers of deciding who shall take part. The basic rule is simple enough. The competition is open to any decorated vehicle. No problem ever occurs about whether a vehicle is, or is not, decorated. For the organisers, quite rightly, regard twenty or thirty singing children as a decoration in itself. The real difficulty arises when decorators arrive without a lorry to carry them.

It is almost impossible to believe how improvident daleks, knights in armour and leprechauns can be. They will spend weeks building turreted castles and crocks of gold (complete with rainbow ends) only to discover on the morning of public manifestation that their creations are too big to fit the Co-op milk-float or that the promised lorry on which they were to be assembled is, after all, needed at the abattoir. Improvidence turns to anger and despair, then to the demand that, lorry or not, they take part anyway.

Of course we always capitulate – or at least allow them to take part in the competition. Parading along the busy main road that joins Birmingham to Warwick and Stratford is difficult. Thirty teenage crusaders carrying a plywood portcullis are inclined to overlook the sudden arrival of a double-decker bus. The risk of Humpty Dumpty falling off the back of his bread-van is bad enough. No sensible organiser will risk the paper centipede (with thirty-four legs but only one pair of eyes) being trapped between the brewery dray that carries the evangelical message of local Nonconformity and the steam engine that advertises the arrival of Leyland's latest model in the neighbourhood showrooms.

The same rule applies to bands. The purveyors of martial music, who can be relied upon to move forward at a regular and steady pace, are encouraged to march. Other musical ensembles –

Hard Rock, All Steel, Irish Accordion and, for all I know, Senior Citizens' Gypsy Violin – can only participate if mechanised, for it is assumed that they will make irregular progress, varying in both speed and direction and simultaneously holding up the procession and risking death from traffic moving in the other direction.

Imagine, therefore, my surprise when in 1977 I was told that nothing could begin before the arrival of a 'walking float' – an idea that seemed either to possess biblical connotations or to be a contradiction in terms. It was a unique, if not a special, year for the carnival. Much to the organisers' surprise the cameras of *Panorama* were present. They had come to Birmingham to film an interview about immigration. Without much difficulty their attention had been turned to a small example of the multiracial society in triumphant action – the Sparkbrook Carnival. The BBC, of course, believe that God made the world in six days simply so that it could be televised on the seventh. They were impatient. As the man responsible for their presence their impatience infected me.

It was then that I saw the 'walking float' appear over the stony, grassless mound of earth that is Farm Road Park. First came a line of children, sixty or eighty abreast. Behind, there was a second line and behind the second line a third and fourth. Three hundred children, of many races, most creeds and every colour, marching in something approaching unison is, in itself, a formidable sight. But these children bore a banner with a wonderful device and were dressed in celebration of their message.

There were little Frenchmen wearing their mothers' berets and carrying strings of Spanish and Israeli onions; Indians disguised as Red Indians; Jamaicans in their national costume of white flannels and cricket caps; Trinidadians in grass skirts with assegai and oval Zulu shields; Pathans dressed in the sort of clothes their grandfathers wore when they fought the British Army on the North-West Frontier; a disproportionately large contingent of cowboys representing North America; young Sikhs resolutely dressed as adult Sikhs, and two or three incipient Englishmen in paper bowler hats. Above them the banner proclaimed 'Children of the World Unite'.

It did not seem a moment for a rigid adherence to the rules.

We pinned the paper rosette on an infant Chinese waiter from the nearby takeaway and formed the children up into a column of four at the head of the procession. Most of the other competitors applauded. The ladies of St Trinian's wept a little. We marched off to the massed bands of the Scouts and Boys' Brigade. I think that the tune was called 'Imperial Glory'.

Listener, 11 October 1979

Afternoon at Home

My Christmas festivities always begin at Clifton Infants' School with a Friday afternoon party at which little Muslims and young Hindus join together with more conventional celebrators called O'Connell, McManus and Kelly to sing the songs of the Nativity. Father Christmas, his ascetic Indian features hidden beneath a conventional cottonwool beard, wears a scarlet coat that can compete in neither splendour nor brilliance with the saris worn by visiting mothers. Thanks to Clifton School, when I think of Advent I always remember the coming of strangers into Sparkbrook and how, in the end, they found room in our inns, our schools and – for the most part – our affections.

Christmas memories are, I admit, a strange beginning to a high summer essay. But I have an excuse. Last week I 'opened' the new Clifton School – a supernatural building in which architectural legerdemain has scaled everything down to the needs of four-foot/six-stone pupils without causing six-foot/fourteen-stone visitors to bang their heads on ceilings or become wedged in the apparently narrow doors. But the Clifton 'opening' defied laws of time as well as space. Children and teachers had been in happy occupation for nine months.

Although we did not know it at the time, our little ceremony took place on the day that Mr Enoch Powell spoke of the 'active volcano' of racial violence that he proclaimed was about to erupt in Britain. In the Clifton School playground, a hundred little lumps

of Mr Powell's potential lava glowed in anticipation of the afternoon ahead – the food and festivities that were to be enjoyed
after the red ribbon that fastened the handles of the new front
door had been untied.

The food disappeared almost before the last echoes of the
opening speeches died away. Sponge cake, on which cream had
been spread like mortar, fastening a top layer of strawberries to
the three-storey structure, was the first to go. Dhokla, a Gujarati
sweetmeat made of semolina, flour and ground rice, was the second
fastest down. Of course, we all drank tea, the cup that not only
cheers but binds together the two continents and is, I believe,
particularly enjoyed by Englishmen who resent alien intrusions and
revere our traditional customs – among which they number the
enjoyment of an Indian drink. Refreshed, we took our places in
the schoolyard and looked apprehensively at a sky that was greyer
than the tarmacadam.

We need not have worried. It rained, and it would be sentimental nonsense to pretend that we did not notice or that we did not
mind. But although the tiny drops of moisture glistened in my
neighbour's hair, I knew that nothing could dampen either Mrs
Bi's spirits or mine. We had seen the children in their classrooms,
possessed of a passion to perform that was far too strong for the
elements to exorcise. Mrs Bi is a parent governor of Clifton School.
Ten years ago I helped to get her husband into Britain. In rather
different ways we both felt responsible for one of the performers
whose enthusiasm defeated, if it did not deflect, the rain.

The performance began with the arrival of a clump of walking
trees; not so well disguised as Birnam Wood on its way to Dunsin-
ane, but an obvious clump of trees nevertheless. Each sapling wore
a pair of paper leaves sewn together to make a forage cap of which
Robin Hood would have been proud. Each seedling carried a stick
festooned with green paper streamers. When the action demanded
it, the sticks became branches that shook in the wind and the
streamers turned into foliage that fluttered in the breeze. The trees
were, in fact, the wood into which it is unwise to go on the day
the teddy bears have their picnic.

The teddy bears – Pakistani teddy bears, Brummie teddy bears
and Jamaican teddy bears, indistinguishable under their ochre

cardboard masks – danced and pranced in orderly, though unregimented, delight around the wicker hampers. The school gramophone played a jazz version of the song my own teddy bear was always brought downstairs to hear whenever it was broadcast, at a slower tempo, by Henry Hall on the old Marconi radio. Neither their energy nor their exuberance was exhausted by the time the lyrics required 'tired little teddy bears' to be taken off to bed. They were still pawing the air – and obscuring the view of seated parents – when the next act began. 'Teddy bears, sit down at once!' cried the headmistress with an authority and success that Mrs Whitehouse would have envied.

Following the teddy bears was not an easy task, but it was carried out with dignity – a comparatively rare quality in seven-year-olds – by half a dozen Asian girls dressed, I suspect, in their first adult saris. They swayed rhythmically and clapped in perfect unison to the slow music of the subcontinent, mimed the winnowing and grinding of corn, and then made way for folklore and fantasy of a more European sort. Even the severest critics of modern education could not complain that the curriculum at Clifton lacks breadth. There was a traditional fairy story in which Aniel, Smya and Hazifa played Hansel and Gretel and the witch. The human forest came back into verdant action. A classic prince rescued a classic princess. There was a dragon dance. A chorus of imitation tulip pickers wearing pointed paper Dutch hats sang about a mouse ('with clogs on') from old Amsterdam.

Of course, things went wrong, as things always will go wrong in infant schools. A huge eight-year-old called Mahmood, dressed in a pink leotard, looked so much like an Indian wrestler that from time to time the desire to act like one overcame him. A claret-coloured turban began to slip over one of its wearer's eyes, and a proud parent darted forward to set it straight. The mulberry bush around which the reception class danced had some trouble climbing into his bark-covered trunk. But the overall success was obvious, overwhelming and both audible and visible.

There was one moment – shortly after 'the dingle-dangle scarecrow in the flippy-floppy hat' – when one class struck up a tune that I have heard plagiarised at a hundred football matches: 'If you're happy and you know it, nod your head'. There was so much assent and affirmation on every side of the playground that I feared that a few small heads would be shaken off. Nothing was damaged. When the Hansel and Gretel song reached the moment for the wicked witch's laugh, the whole school joined in with a noise that broken necks would have made impossible.

By five o'clock it was all over and we were back inside the school, cleaning and clearing up. The sweet blue and pink popadoms had been taken for safe keeping into the staff room. Little girls collected, to carry home, the dolls which had been on display. The school pictures and paintings, hung from classroom walls, had become bedraggled from the brushing past of anxious parents and confident performers. A thin film of greasy city rain covered the golden circle and the wriggling yellow snake that had been painted into the playground. Walking down Ladypool Road, I bought a copy of the *Birmingham Mail* and read Mr Powell's volcanic metaphor.

The first thought of any decent reader at the end of such an afternoon could only be of the children – those of them who were old enough and wise enough to discover that the world is not always as welcoming as Clifton's friendly classrooms. But losing the optimism of innocence is the fate that we are heir to, and the urban poor have always suffered it earlier and more brutally than other people in other places. The second thought concerned the possibility that the eruption could happen.

I suppose it is possible that one day the children with whom I spent last Friday will burn down Clifton School. The rule that governs the writing of this column prevents much speculation about why that might happen or how it could be prevented. But were it to happen, through fear or failure, malice or mistake, one thing is certain. They would be burning down their own houses, their own schools, their own country. There is no question of their going home. They are home already.

Listener, 24 July 1980

Lady With a Limp

She looked no more than sixty. But in one of the loosely related clauses which made up her opening sentence she told me that she was eighty-one. As I tried to write down her story in something resembling logical order, I thought of the discrepancy between appearance and reality as the one favour that fate had granted her. For she was obviously poor and obviously crippled.

Cheap coats proclaim their cheapness with increasing vehemence as they grow old. Hers had once been an inappropriate baby blue. But it had faded into the watery grey of a foggy November sky. The padding had swollen into little bulges that stood out from the shoulders. And half of the seams were so stretched that the taut white cotton was visible between the pieces of cloth.

She walked with the aid of a stick – a huge piece of hawthorn which looked as if it had been made to help some giant farmer struggle over his upland acres. It lay incongruous and obtrusive on the plastic-topped round table that I use each Saturday morning as a desk. For I hold my constituency advice bureau in the back room of the Sparkbrook Labour Club. And the lady with the limp had come to see me with her problems.

Her rent, subsidised under the Council's housing benefit scheme, had gone up. But the subsidy had not gone up with it. On 6 October her arrears stood at £16. She had never been in debt in her life. There were a few pounds in her post office book, but if possible . . . The account of hidden treasure trailed out into stubborn silence. Clearly the contents of her savings account were not a welcome topic of conversation.

But it forced its way into the story of the second crisis. She had limped along to the local office of the Department of Health and Social Security to see if they would pay the cost of repairs to her surgical shoe. They would not. There was no scheme under which payment was possible. Was the problem her savings? For they could not be spent – under any circumstances.

The bank book had begun to fascinate me. I had read the stories of neighbourhood astonishment when the ragged recluse in the corner house died and was revealed to be a secret millionaire. Perhaps the signs of poverty deceived and my elderly constituent had thousands hidden away. 'How much?' I asked. It all spilled out in a stream of semi-consciousness. Three hundred pounds. For the burial. Not enough, but something. After all, there was no one else to preserve the decencies and maintain respectability.

A colleague, more generous and ingenious than I, took out his wallet and addressed our visitor in formal tones. 'There is', he lied, 'a fund which we administer here at the Labour Club and I think that I can speak for all the trustees in saying that the cost of surgical shoe repairs comes within our terms of reference.' The response was less than ecstatic. Assurances were demanded that the fund really existed and that the offer was not an act of personal charity.

There followed bogus threats of journeys upstairs to obtain and display account books and counterfeit requests for receipts – if they were available. The lady with the limp took a masculine purse out of her shopping bag, unfolded the extended leather lip which curled around its several pouches and tucked away the five-pound note amongst a collection of special-offer vouchers from the local supermarket. Embarrassed, I began to write down the details of her case in my notebook.

She had no children and she had been a widow for over twenty years. When her husband died she had got a job 'wire brushing' – one of the dirtiest jobs in the engineering industry. She had scrubbed away at swarf-covered castings for almost a decade. Then she had fallen down a flight of steps and life had begun to revolve round the weekly Giro from the Department of Health and Social Security.

Now I suspect that the lady with the limp – since ingenuity or desperation brought her to me – will soon find an improvement to her circumstances. The confusion between rent and subsidy will be resolved within days of the receipt of my letter. The DHSS will confirm that three hundred pounds is no impediment to the receipt of several 'discretionary payments' and their discretion will be guided by the note from the local MP. But she will still live in grinding poverty, surviving each week on approximately the cost of a first-class return ticket from London to Birmingham.

She was by no means the most desperate constituent to walk into my advice bureau this year. Indeed, this month I have met families who were facing greater crises. In the inner cities real poverty is becoming commonplace. The lady with the limp was typical of what happens when the old, the sick and the poor are paid just enough to survive. If the slightest extra thing goes wrong, survival becomes almost impossible.

In one sense her story speaks for itself. A nation which provides so little for its poor may possess the Elgin Marbles, a Nobel literature laureate and a national theatre with three auditoriums but it is still not civilised. It is not even honest. For it comforts itself that the poor are always with us and that there is no way in which old ladies with limps can be permanently insulated from the poverty which they almost take for granted.

But it does not have to be like that. Almost a hundred years ago, Matthew Arnold asserted as a self-evident fact that if we wished we could 'choose equality and flee greed. On one side inequality harms by pampering: on the other by vulgarising and depressing,' because we prefer to live in that sort of society. We owe the lady with a limp a lot more than the price of the repair to her shoes.

Guardian, 5 November 1983

They Must Be Like Us

The principle is clear enough. Salman Rushdie's rights as an author are absolute and ought to be inalienable. A free society does not ban books. Nor does it allow writers and publishers to be blackmailed and intimidated. The death threats are intolerable whether they are seriously meant or the rhetoric of hysteria. I have proclaimed those fundamental truths in mosques all over Britain – a considerably more daunting task than preaching the gospel of free speech at literary dinner parties. But it is preposterous to pretend that the first principle governing the publication of *The Satanic Verses* is the last word on the subject.

I accept my duty to defend to the death the right of others to express opinions with which I disagree. But I do not recall Voltaire requiring me to pretend I agree with ideas that I find offensive. *The Satanic Verses* is an intentional blasphemy. The choice of language allows no other interpretation. Mr Rushdie is entitled to abuse the religion in which he was reared and must be protected against those who want to intimidate him into silence. But the idea that we all have a duty to applaud his calculated assault is a novel interpretation of the liberal obligation.

That idea has its origins in two distinct errors – the first of them entirely honourable. While extremists burn effigies, supporters of the intended victim will make insupportable claims about his virtues. Their error can be defended as nothing worse than sentimentality. But such a defence is not open to those who, outraged by the Rushdie death threats, write as if all Muslims are implicated in the blackmail and condemn the multi-racial community in which Islam exists. The proposition that Muslims are welcome in Britain if, and only if, they stop behaving like Muslims is incompatible with the principles of a free society.

Indeed, that proposition can only be described as racist. I do not use the noun as a term of abuse, but as a technical description of an attitude which contains two related fallacies. The first is the contention that a racial group has common characteristics which are shared by all its members. The second is that those characteristics make that group not so much different as alien.

Yesterday, in its leader column, the *Independent* criticised the creation of Muslim schools and described them as a barrier to integration. The objective which the newspaper had in mind was not integration at all. It was assimilation. Two days ago, in the *Independent*, Fay Weldon proposed that all children should be required to attend schools where 'one flag is saluted and one God worshipped'. Such a system would produce neither assimilation nor integration but bitter resentment against a society which required boys and girls to affect support for a religion in which they did not believe. Neither Catholics nor Jews would accept such a proposition. Nor should they be required to do so. Freedom is or ought to be indivisible – a liberty enjoyed by one group must be available to another.

In her *Independent* interview Ms Weldon applauded the 'uniculturalist policy of the United States' which 'welded its new people from every race, every nation and every belief into one whole'. Such fusion never came about. The black and Hispanic Americans were not prepared to lose their identity in what white liberals called the melting pot. British Muslims would react in just the same way. They are proud of their religion, their history, their literature. If Muslims abandoned their Islamic characteristics, they would be sacrificing more than a theological principle. Their material welfare would be in jeopardy.

The demand that Muslims should be allowed to worship their own God is not, of course, the suggestion that they should have an immunity from the law. Ms Weldon's assertion that 'there is a general feeling that if you arrest people with dark skins there is a suggestion that you are a racist' is nonsense. The police arrested young Muslims after the Bradford demonstration and the Westminster march. On the assumption that breaches of the peace had been committed, they were clearly right to do so.

Every group within our society must obey the law. But support for that principle is not the same as insisting that 'they' must behave like 'us'. The doctrine of assimilation is arrogant and patronising. It causes hardship to the ethnic minorities. Our present laws demonstrate the unhappy truth.

In her pamphlet *Sacred Cows*, Ms Weldon describes the Muslim community of bar-room fantasy – 'women with arranged marriages, their children in care, their high divorce rates, wife beating and intimidation'. That description is a travesty of Muslim society in Britain. Unfortunately our immigration laws are based on similar nonsense.

Ms Weldon is right, there is a tragic problem associated with arranged marriages. But the anguish of unwilling brides is not the typical tragedy. For every woman coerced into marrying a man she has not met, there are a thousand who argue that unless they are married 'in the traditional way' they will not 'feel married at all'. Unfortunately, because the government cannot distinguish between an arranged and a bogus marriage, husbands are prevented from joining their wives in this country. The whole cruel process is legitimised and perpetuated by our refusal to accept that in a multiracial society Muslims must be allowed to live according to Muslim traditions.

Thanks to our similar backgrounds and cultural experience, Ms Weldon and I find the idea of arranged marriages unattractive. But in a liberal society the important question does not concern what we prefer. The important issue is whether we are prepared to allow others to make decisions according to their own judgments rather than ours.

I have no doubt that Ms Weldon – and the editor of the *Independent* – believe themselves to stand for freedom. More than a hundred years ago, Matthew Arnold described the dilemma that middle-class libertarians have to face but often seem reluctant to overcome.

> Every Englishman doing what he likes was convenient enough so long as there were only Barbarians or Philistines [his not altogether complimentary terms for the upper and middle classes] to do what they liked . . . It has become inconvenient and productive of anarchy now that the populace wants to do what it likes to do.

In a free society the Muslim community must be allowed to do 'what it likes to do' as long as the choice it makes is not damaging to the community as a whole. Muslims are people too. The sooner we accept that, the sooner there will be racial harmony in this country.

Independent, 21 July 1989

Right of Abode

Aftab Ali settled in Birmingham during the swinging sixties. In those distant days, immigration from the Indian subcontinent conformed to an almost invariable pattern. Men travelled to Britain alone and, having found a house and job and saved the price of two or three air fares, 'fetched' their families to join them. The verb properly implies that a male initiative was needed to begin the process. Aftab Ali attempted to 'fetch' his wife (Saleha Khatum) and son (Abdul Alim) sometime during the early seventies. The result of his efforts was set out in a letter sent to me on 3 August 1988 by Timothy Renton, the Home Office minister who was once described in the House of Commons as expressing the views of the National Front in the accents of Bertie Wooster.

> Mrs Khatum and Mr Alim have on two previous occasions been refused entry clearance for settlement in the United Kingdom as Mr Ali's wife and son because the entry clearance officer was not satisfied that they were related to him as claimed. Their subsequent appeals to the appellate authorities were dismissed in 1981 and 1986. A third such application was refused on 14 July.

Some readers may wonder why on earth a sixty-two-year-old man should have spent almost two decades attempting to gain admission to this country for a woman of fifty-three who was not his wife and a man who was not his son. But no such perplexing thoughts seem to have complicated the mental processes of the entry clearance officers, the appeal adjudicators or Mr Timothy Renton.

Even when the husband suffered a massive stroke and the wife applied to visit him in hospital, these fortunate fellows still never doubted their judgment that Aftab Ali and Saleha Khatum were 'not related as claimed'. An application for a visitor's visa was refused. Tim Eggar at the Foreign Office was reassuring. 'I can confirm that at the time of the current refusal, the High Commission were fully aware of Mr Ali's medical circumstances.' The renewed suggestion that the government might show a little compassion was greeted by the Foreign Office – again in the person of Tim Eggar – with a letter which might have been written for Beachcomber. The joke was on Aftab Ali.

> Under Section 4(1) of the Immigration Act and Paragraph 12 of the Immigration Rules (H.C.169) the power to give or refuse entry clearance is exercised by Entry Clearance Officer (ECO) and I have no discretion to ask the ECO to reverse his decision. Such discretion under the 1971 Act is vested in the Home Secretary.

The 'exchange of correspondence' was passed on to Mr Timothy Renton. You guessed it. He could find 'no basis on which (he) would be justified in overturning the entry clearance officer's decision'. On 13 April 1989 a basis was provided. Cellmark Diagnostics – a division of Imperial Chemical Industries – carried out DNA tests to determine whether or not 'Abdul Alim is the biological son of Mrs Saleha Khatum and Aftab Ali.' Their report included an explanatory note which described the techniques involved. The conclusion was plain enough. 'It is one million times more likely that Aftab Ali and Mrs Saleha Khatum are the parents of Abdul Alim than both being unrelated.'

Thus armed, both the Joint Council for the Welfare of Immigrants and Aftab Ali's Member of Parliament made renewed attempts to obtain permission for his undisputed wife and son to visit him in hospital. The MP's letter to the Home Office included confidential information. The doctors believed Aftab Ali was dying.

On 5 September 1989, Lord Brabazon of Tara replied on behalf of the government. His letter included an extract from Hansard. It set out the government's attitude to the new technique of DNA profiling, 'the most accurate method of determining parentage'. The Home Secretary made clear that the possession of proof that a prospective immigrant had been wrongly refused entry would not, in itself, ensure admission to this country. Lord Brabazon advised that Mrs Saleha Khatum and Mr Abdul Alim should '. . . contact the High Commission in Dhaka in order to lodge reapplications'. His Lordship could find 'no grounds for giving priority over other reapplicants'. The waiting time for interview would be 'about twenty-two months'.

Abdul Alim and Saleha Khatum made new application to the High Commission and, as a result of various pressures and continual lobbying, they were given a 'priority interview'.

On 11 October, Saleha Khatum was granted the 'right of abode' in the United Kingdom and she flew to Britain the same day. Her brother-in-law met her at the airport. Aftab Ali – her undoubted and now undisputed husband – had died twenty-four hours previously.

Two questions remain. The first concerns the fate of Abdul Alim, the second relates to the reasons for the government's wilfully callous behaviour. Abdul Alim is still in Bangladesh. The government admits that it wrongly refused him entry ten years ago. But he is now over eighteen and his age is more important than the Home Office's error. The fact that his mother needs him in Birmingham is not sufficient reason to persuade the minister that they ought to rectify their earlier mistake. The reason for the government's heartless incompetence is explained even more easily.

The immigration rules – at least as they apply to the Indian subcontinent – are not designed to distinguish between those men and women who are entitled to come to Britain and those who are not. They are meant to keep people out – by delay, by contrivance, by obstruction and by intentional incompetence. At least one item of government policy is working exactly as the Prime Minister intended.

Guardian, 4 November 1989

Poverty Trapped Inside an Army Surplus Anorak

Had Amanda been a daughter of the middle classes, I would have immediately diagnosed her hollow eyes and sunken cheeks as symptoms of a terminal disease. But I had already noticed her clothes. Do not believe that denim is the great leveller. The fake sheepskin collar on her threadbare bomber-jacket confirmed a case of chronic poverty.

When I asked her to sit down, she began to cry. I claim no talent for comforting unknown women. So I looked helplessly at the baby in the battered pushchair. To my relief it did not follow its mother's example. Instead, it stared back at me from the depths of a gigantic army surplus anorak. Desperate, I asked the infant's name. Sapphire, her mother told me, between the sobs.

The problem was rats – rats which infested the ninth-floor flat, bit the baby and defied the most determined efforts of the council's rodent officer. At least, that was the problem which she asked me to solve. She went on to describe life in the tower block which, if the council had any sense of history, would be called the Cave of Adullam. It is the home of the disadvantaged, the distressed and the dispossessed. Each night, after the pubs close, one of her neighbours tries to kick Amanda's door down.

She was of course 'on her own'. In Sparkbrook that sad description is usually no more than a euphemism for one-parent family. But Amanda was, apart from Sapphire, 'alone' in every sense of the word. Her mother's 'boyfriend' would not 'have her in the house'. And her father, although sympathetic, 'had his hands full' with her brother, who was handicapped. My reaction was hideously inappropriate. I marvelled at the irony of a woman called Amanda being so desperately in need of love.

The shame that I felt at allowing my mind to wander over such trivialities is the excuse which I offer for my crass attempt at consolation. Sapphire, I suggested, must provide a pleasure which dozens of prosperous childless families would envy. Not being enough of a philosopher to dispute the need to choose between poverty and infertility, Amanda agreed with simple sincerity. I was left to ask the questions which are the necessary prelude to squeezing a few extra pounds out of the Department of Social Security.

Sapphire's father 'did not want to know' after her twin brother died. The silent presence in the army surplus anorak was reported to be fit and well – an item of information which I received with mixed emotion. For the children of the very poor, there is a passing advantage to be gained from minor illness. It often entitles them to a few extra coppers. At that moment, I felt that nothing was quite so bad as being poor.

That is, I know, a simplistic and unromantic view of poverty. But it is one which is often supported by those who have a first-hand knowledge of the condition. And it is far more convincing than all the theories of benevolent selfishness which have been invented to calm prosperous consciences. Looking at Amanda, I tried to believe that if she pulled herself together she could become an MP, write for the *Guardian* in her spare time and thus qualify to live in Westminster and own an almost new motor car. But the idea seemed about as convincing as the notion that, because prosperity trickles down the income scale, inequality is the remedy to poverty. Whenever I consider these questions, I come to the same conclusion. It is because I am relatively rich that Amanda is absolutely poor. The remedy for her condition and my conscience is, in the phrase, to spread it about a bit.

It may be argued that for her it is too late. But those who make that claim are the same people who, twenty years ago, would have said that it was too late for Amanda's mother. And now they must answer the question, 'Too late for what?' It is not too late for a warm coat, for regular meals and for a house which is not infested by rats. And it is not too late to avoid Sapphire being run down by the cycle of deprivation. Before you tell me that 'throwing money at the problem is not enough', let me tell you that without money being thrown her way, Amanda and her daughter are doomed. And there is, prosperous reader, nowhere for it to come from except you and me.

I do not mean a few pounds handed over in a fit of sudden benevolence or even a carefully covenanted regular donation to a registered charity. That would be good for our souls and consciences. But it is not what Amanda and Sapphire need. They need to live in a society which is organised to catch them when they fall and pays the price because of its compassion. Looking at those two human beings – with their pathetically ludicrous names – I could not honestly argue that the self-interest of the well-to-do requires them to vote for an extra penny on their own income tax. The chairman of British Telecom will not have his wage increase threatened by a revolution which either of them leads. We ought to look after Sapphire and Amanda because looking after them is right.

I remain sufficiently optimistic – and, some will say, sentimental – to believe that there is a majority in this country that wants Sapphire to escape from inside the army surplus anorak. What stands in their way are the politicians who will not take a chance on the voters' decent instincts. 'To find the Grail,' said Sir Galahad, 'we have first to believe in it.' If we believe in a more equal society, a more equal society will come about. Anyone who met Amanda and Sapphire would want that to happen.

Guardian, 4 November 1991

Bright Hopes

When the sun began to shine, it became one of the happiest days of my life. It started badly, for the latest opinion polls – planted in my mind by the previous night's late news – took root whilst I slept and I woke up worrying about the figures and the forecasts. But then, unable to find the light switch on the hotel bedroom wall, I stumbled towards the window and drew the curtains.

It was one of those mornings that exiled poets pretend are typical of England in April. If there had been elm trees where I was going the lowest boughs of their brushwood sheafs would have been in tiny leaf. The sky was so blue and the air so clear that no decent romantic could possibly have felt despondent. And only romantics stand in ten consecutive general elections.

There were rational reasons for feeling encouraged by the shafts of light that shimmered on the council house scaffolding. I was brought up to believe that Labour supporters – with holes in their shoes and threadbare raincoats – are most likely to vote when the weather is dry. The warm streets of my constituency would, I felt confident, be packed with enthusiastic socialists making their heroic way to the polling station. As Sparkbrook goes so goes the nation. So I took it for granted that the swing which I anticipated in Birmingham 11 would be reproduced all over the country.

Brothers, we were on our way – perhaps even taking one or two sisters with us.

My reception was encouraging. On normal campaign days half a dozen casual callers obstruct the efforts of the party workers. But last Thursday morning, the old Tandoori restaurant was packed from empty refrigerated display cabinet to collapsed counter. Some of the visitors were there to offer their felicitations. Others had a boon to crave. It was all gloriously reminiscent of the court scene from *A Man For All Seasons* – except that I reacted to each supplicant with a hubris which would have prevented Thomas More's canonisation. Doris Tombs and Mary Tuite were serene amongst the debris. Baghat Singh was calming the throng. Stan Yapp ordered me from the premises.

Sir Stanley Yapp was, I ought to explain, half of one of the many unique features of the Sparkbrook campaign. Together with Sir Richard Knowles, he made up the only pair of knights to be in command of a Labour constituency. Dick, Stan told me, had been exiled to Acocks Green; there to convey the elderly and the infirm to the polling station. Being leader of the council, he had attracted a larger crowd than that which had assembled to greet the putative Home Secretary. Unless I followed him to a similarly distant part of my once and future kingdom, the real work of polling day would not get done.

I was by no means sure what the real work of polling day was. Long ago, when Sparkbrook was Irish and marginal, the final hours were divided between energising identified supporters and cutting the sandwiches for the booze-up which followed the declaration of result. Now that we are safe and Muslim, one of those activities is unnecessary and the other unacceptable. The time is supposed to be spent calming the candidate. Did Organiser Sir Stan know something that I did not? Was Agent Sir Dick really driving his car like a rank and file volunteer or had he gone to confirm the bad news from the polling station?

The only way to find out was to make the grand tour myself. It is usually an activity which I avoid. For I think of myself as a working candidate and making stately progress from Seven Stiles comprehensive to Ladypool junior – shaking hands with policemen and returning officers along the way – is a bit too lord-of-the-manor for my taste. But it was the best intelligence-gathering operation that I could mount. So, rosette on lapel and heart in mouth, I set out. The result was bliss.

I travelled the streets of Sparkbrook for almost eight hours on and off, and I travelled slowly. For victory greeted me on every corner. After thirty years on the political streets, I believed that I could distinguish opponents from supporters at fifty yards. But, last Thursday, women with Tory shopping bags and men with Conservative shoes came up to me and, in the golden sunlight, said that it was time for a change. I walked to the count in the footsteps of those feet in ancient times.

Then they told me about the exit polls. At first, I thought that they were too bad to be true. When the results came in, they became the best hope to cling to. After the Lord Mayor had declared me elected, I had time to decide why the bright hopes of the Sparkbrook afternoon had turned into the grim night of the election results. I came to a desperate conclusion. The men and women who had greeted me in the sun were either the dispossessed and disadvantaged, or those who live and work amongst them. They had voted in the hope of something better. The other half in Britain had voted in fear of something worse. My happiest day had been spent in a tragically divided country.

Guardian, 13 April 1992

When We Were Very Young and All Was Well

Whenever I see the inside of a primary school, I wonder why anyone should want to be anything other than a primary school teacher.

My experience of juniors and infants is, admittedly, limited to ninety-minute bursts on Friday afternoons. So my comprehension of life and work amongst the miniature wash basins and low-level coat pegs is probably incomplete. Egg boxes, play dough and poster paint may not seem wholly attractive on cold Monday mornings when all that life has to offer is the sights and sounds (and the smells) of growing up.

Huw Wheldon once told me that, although he was a brilliant father for two hours every Sunday afternoon, his wife was only capable of sustaining successful motherhood for seven days a week.

In a similar spirit of envious admiration, I pay my tribute to the women and men (it is mostly women) who devote their days to the emotional, intellectual and bodily needs of reception classes and rising fives. Theirs is, I believe, an immensely rewarding profession. It is also a hard job.

All that being said, there can be little doubt that – even in the most disadvantaged schools – the bliss of being very young seems always to transcend the problems of growing up in deprivation. The joy seems to dissolve as double figures approach. At ten, girls make an unsuccessful attempt to become women and, two years later, boys begin to believe that there is something manly in behaving like Paul Gascoigne. But between four and six, human beings of both sexes exude a surprised pleasure at being alive. The enthusiasm is infectious.

Last Friday, in what is popularly believed to be the more prosperous part of my constituency, I was surrounded by a group of parents and staff who were united in a collective demand for more nursery places to be made available to children in their care.

We sat and talked about the problems which face one-parent families on minimum income support and the difficulties of encouraging the reading habit in houses which are overcrowded, underheated and shared with several other families. Our discussion included the bitter allegation that officials from the Education Department – who, it was assumed, travelled everywhere by motor car – could not understand the impossibility of leaving a four-year-old at a pre-school play-group at half past eight and then, by a quarter to nine, delivering his sister to a primary school which was two miles' walk away.

Whilst all the hard talking was going on, the objects of concern and affection were playing on the floor inside our huddled circle. It would have been wholly inappropriate to have thought of Thomas Gray. For, though regardless of their doom, they had only their species in common with the young gentlemen of Eton College.

As we talked about their prospects of entering school with a reading and natural age which matched each other, they beat away with their plastic hammers, rang the tin bells on top of their plywood trains and pumped the handles of their humming tops. After half an hour of concentrated discussion, I was lost. Not very successfully, I bent down and attempted myself to start a top humming. I was, an amused mother told me, trying to operate it upside down.

The headmaster, and the depressingly young teacher in charge of the infants' department, were almost as concerned about the feelings of the parents as they were about the prospects of the pupils. They did not want me to make speeches about the number of children in the school who qualified for free dinners or the percentage who, receiving an inadequate supplement to their weekly benefit, send their sons and daughters to school with sandwiches.

The only political point which I dared make was the paradox of nursery school provision. Pre-school places are most likely to be found in abundance in the areas which need them least.

At the end of our meeting, I promised to do all that I could to promote the children's cause and warned that my efforts would fail. Normally, I end such homilies with the stern reminder that there is not enough money to go round. But last Friday I decided that the assembled mothers knew that already. It is a lesson which they had learned at the end of each week, as they live on credit and wait to cash their Giros. The tops hummed on and the tin bells on the plywood trains rattled and rang.

There is no moral to this story. I certainly do not suggest that the joys of childhood are any compensation for the problems which childhood neglect will cause. Nor do I draw the conclusion that parents' devotion and teachers' dedication can fill the gap left by a government that spends taxpayers' money on bribing schools to opt out rather than on meeting the basic needs of the most necessitous families. The penalties of government partiality are too obvious to need any emphasis. I simply describe what I saw last Friday.

I saw a dozen children who had barely, if at all, reached the age of reason and because they were unconscious of the wicked world around them lived for the pleasure of the moment. It was a glimpse of what life must have been like in the Garden of Eden before the Fall. The serpent whispered worries about the future and the canker in the apple was the fear of growing up. Innocence is living for the moment.

Whenever I see the inside of a primary school, I wonder why anyone should want to be anything other than a primary school pupil.

Guardian, 1 January 1993

Bringing Home the Truth About the Very Poor

Sometimes I fear that this column is becoming obsessed with education, and sometimes I fear that it is not. This week, I suffer from the second anxiety. For last Monday morning, I was once again reminded that what is most wrong with this country – and does more damage than our reverence for the past and our instinct for deference added together – is the wilful neglect of the nation's most wasted asset, the children of the poor.

I spent the half day on a housing estate on the edge of my constituency, visiting parents whose children will start school next September. The teachers, who guided me from door to dilapidated door, make the tour each year – ostensibly to explain the hard facts of life in a reception class. Failure to make an early application for free meals may mean that, on the first day of term, new pupils are required to pay or starve. Sweatshirts bearing the school badge – relatively expensive, but good value for the price – can be purchased on request. Applications to sit next to friends from nursery or play-group will be sympathetically considered. Providing such essential information is only part of their purpose. The teachers are also there to learn.

They did not expect to make any startling discoveries about the parents. The families we visited all had older children already in school and it was I, not the teachers, who felt and expressed surprise that some of the mothers had forgotten the free meal regulations and the headmaster's enthusiasm for rudimentary uniform. But the children were deep and almost uncharted waters. A few clues about their character and likely conduct had been provided by the behaviour of their brothers and sisters. But rising five is a mysterious business.

Twenty minutes' observation – talking to mum whilst watching the subject of the conversation out of the corner of one eye – hardly provides a complete picture of problems and potential. But it sketched in some of the outline and we were helped in filling in a few of the details by the contents of a plastic carrier bag which we carried down every muddy path.

The bag contained educational toys. Most obvious amongst them was an eighteen-inch male doll made of plastic and in sumo wrestler proportions. He came in anatomically incorrect pieces – neckless head that sank down on his shoulders like the top of a Henry Moore statue, expandable arms that could be pulled out until they hung down to his knees, hands that seemed to be wearing Mickey Mouse's big white gloves and feet which were designed for stability rather than elegance. He brought out in the children what might be called the Frankenstein impulse – the desire to build a creature in human form.

The impulse affected different children in different ways. One (who had met the monster at playgroup) put him together, stood him on the carpet and turned his attention to more novel toys. Another had some difficulty in distinguishing arms from legs but, with a little help from his friends, eventually converted his Toulouse-Lautrec into Arnold Schwarzenegger. A third had to be persuaded even to look inside the carrier bag, for he was watching *Good Morning* on television. Cambridge seemed a million miles away, but was it not a Mistress of Girton who said that, in education, 'social factors predominate'? Nobody could have spent that half day in Birmingham without feeling that her judgment, although controversial at the time, was really too obvious to be worth making.

Yet there are people who doubt it still – the people who claim that the theoretical chance for every child to obtain an assisted place in an independent school is somehow related to social justice. One of the inhibitions which prevents the total destruction of that preposterous argument is a proper reluctance to tell the whole truth about the very poor – or at least about the proportion of that unhappy breed who have been overwhelmed by their poverty.

If you go into a room which is only furnished with a rotting three-piece suite and a television set, the paper peeling from the walls and the cigarette ends in the fireplace tell you that the children of that household are unlikely to get a fair chance. When you meet their mother – barely thirty but in appearance twice as old, rotting teeth and three daughters all with different second names – you know that they are very close to being doomed. She is incapable of rescuing them from deprivation. Only children with iron wills, indomitable courage and alpha intelligence can make the escape on their own. Most of them simply take refuge in their television sets. Who can blame the mothers for doing the same?

God knows, I have no moral judgment to make about such families. The concept of the undeserving poor – a peculiarly English heresy – is one of the most repulsive notions known to man. My only point is that such parents are in desperate need of help and that help is increasingly denied them.

We no longer even provide a clothing allowance which enables their sons and daughters to hide in the anonymity of a uniform sweatshirt. These are the bottom 10 per cent, the people who (in real terms) have become poorer during the years when the merchant bankers and the currency speculators have grown so rich. It is a rotten society which so blatantly neglects those of its members who need help most.

I left Birmingham worrying – like every Member of Parliament – about the prospect of tax increases. But I was worrying about whether or not the next Labour government would increase them by enough.

Guardian, 21 June 1993

Forget Conformity, Let's Rejoice in Our Racial Diversity

It was the letter in *The Times* that gave the game away. Winston Churchill – punctuating each paragraph with moral indignation – insisted that his Bolton speech had only one intention. Its purpose was to hold back the horrors of racial conflict which would engulf this country if more venal politicians were allowed to react to the fear of immigration by 'sweeping the whole thing under the carpet'. But the passion for plain speaking did not encourage Mr Churchill to say quite what he meant. The letter's opening paragraph made clear that, although he shied away from the word, Mr Churchill's real concern was the proportion of the British population which is black.

The revealing sentence ends with the assertion that many of our inner-city schools 'are over 80 per cent immigrant'. That claim is, by any honest use of language, simple nonsense. There are schools in my constituency in which 90 per cent of the pupils are Sikh, Hindu or Muslim. Almost all of them were born in Britain and can only be described as immigrants by a perverse definition of that word that also encompasses Mr Churchill's illustrious grandfather. The young Khans, Patels and Singhs may well have a foreign parent – as Sir Winston did. But their nationality is neither in doubt nor the cause of the apprehensions which the Bolton speech articulated. Their real offence is their colour, their cultural heritage and their determination to embrace two communities – Asian and British, British and black.

The future for them, and for the communities in which they live, depends on society's ability to accept and respect their dual personalities. Children of Asian parents, who grow up in Britain's inner cities, are not going to abandon their family religions because of complaints that muezzins calling the faithful to prayer are drowning the sound of church bells. Their parents regard Britain as a godless society in which Islam provides spiritual guidance that other faiths no longer even offer.

Complaining about the visible signs of their faith encourages their feeling of moral superiority and, at the same time, increases the fear that they will never be regarded as anything other than unfriendly aliens.

Both feeling and fear drive them back into their ghettos; not simply areas of our cities where, because they are surrounded by other Muslims, they feel secure, but ghettos of the mind in which they feel isolated from the rest of the country. The penalty for encouraging their alienation is immense. The responsibility lies as much with politicians who make coded speeches as with music-hall comedians who make overtly racist jokes. But the ethnic minorities themselves must take some of the blame. Whatever their other virtues, their public relations are a disaster, the Muslims worst of all.

Shenaz Javed is twenty-six. She was born in Preston, educated at Hutton direct-grant school and the University of Hull where she graduated with an upper second. She is now a solicitor in private practice – and also, by Mr Churchill's definition, an immigrant.

Salah Mohammed was born in Kashmir. He came to Britain (which he calls 'the mother country') in 1960. At that time, he could neither read nor write. He is now a foreman in a Birmingham factory which makes metal frames for ladies' handbags. A certificate awarded for twenty-five years' service with the same company hangs in his front room alongside pictures of Medina and Mecca. His three youngest children, all 'Churchill Immigrants', are students in higher education.

Mohammed Ishtiaq, a partner in a cash-and-carry warehouse and retail supermarket, spent his boyhood in Bradford. As a child, he worked in the family shop for two hours before school and two hours after lessons ended. He now employs twenty men.

These are the sort of Muslims about whom neither newspapers nor politicians speak. They are the antithesis of the popular stereotypes. The 'Paki caricatures' are well established: the unemployed social security scrounger with two wives, six children and as many child benefit books; the 'fundamentalist' fanatic who burns *The Satanic Verses* and hopes to hang Salman Rushdie; the corner shop grocer who undercuts his competitors by opening for eighteen hours a day and using his family as cheap labour. All of them, in the fantasy world of racism, tyrannise their wives, slaughter sheep in the backyard and scheme in order to bring their distant relatives into Britain.

Ironically, one of the principal causes of the Muslims' false reputation is their adherence to some of the stern Victorian virtues which their critics claim are sadly lacking in Britain today. They are obsessively thrifty, tirelessly industrious and insatiably ambitious for their children. Their piety is genuine and their acceptance of its obligations is absolute.

Of course the Islamic community, like every other, is not entirely homogeneous in character and conduct. But there is near universal respect for the Koran and the Koran sets out a way of life and offers an answer to every moral dilemma. Most Muslims living in Britain are unbending in their determination to preserve their own standards of value and to protect their exclusively Islamic view of the world. They want to be liked, to fit in, to succeed. But they want to be Muslims far more.

The cleverest among them live two successful lives. Shenaz Javed wears a lawyer's subfusc during the day and changes into salwar and kameez in the evening. In the office she takes equality with male colleagues for granted. She met her husband at the Chester 'crammer' where she took her law examinations and then married in the traditional way, with the groom and his male guests eating in one room and the bride garlanded and on display in another. She accepts, without question, the obligation of reticence which is imposed on her sex – she has never worn a bathing costume or jeans. But she represents Muslim women in matrimonial disputes with their husbands.

She has no doubt that the 'failure rate' of arranged marriages – once thought negligible because failure was never admitted – is now rising fast, as the old traditions and new environment come into conflict with each other. But she defends the habit with a passion which comes very close to being convincing. 'Marrying in the *bradhry* [the extended family] makes us feel responsible for each other. We have a duty to look after our relations and our husband's relations.' There is a long pause. 'Have you ever seen a Muslim woman in an old people's home?' She smiles. For she knows that I have not.

It is the family obsession more than any other Islamic attribute which causes resentment among the rest of the population and brings Muslims into conflict with the government. The early immigrants (the real thing, not the euphemism) settled in parts of our cities where housing was cheap. The second wave chose to live in areas where the neighbours understood Urdu, the shops sold Halal meat and a Methodist chapel had been converted into a mosque. For some of the Muslim British those inducements still apply. But others (articulate, prosperous and self-confident) choose to remain in the family community and to extend it according to the obligations of Islamic law. That is why Muslim families are in constant dispute with the Home Office over two classes of immigrants: spouses determined to join their partner in this country and elderly parents whose children want to support them during their declining years.

Salah Mohammed describes the benefits of the family instinct. 'We all stick together – worst times, best times, illness, money troubles, everything – we all stick together.'

Married for thirty years, he says that his wife feels an obligation to look after her mother-in-law that is greater than that which he feels himself. He attributes the sense of duty to the teachings of the Koran, strictures which he follows with the determination of a nineteenth-century evangelical divine.

Coming to Britain was his second upheaval. As a boy he had crossed the border which partitioned Kashmir and settled with his family in Mirpur. He cannot remember if he was eleven or twelve when he began work, but he does recall, with genuine sadness, that there was no time for him to learn the Koran. Both his sons, raffishly dashing but still Muslim, have enjoyed the opportunity which he missed – kneeling in the mosque for two hours after every school day and memorising the Last Testament line by line. Questions about the possible effects on their formal education are dismissed. The obligations of faith must be observed.

Thirty years ago, labouring in a foundry, Salah Mohammed found the heavy work impossible during Ramadan, when he fasted from dawn to dusk. The management refused to find him a lighter job. So he left. He did more than survive. He succeeded. Neither of his sons have any doubt that they will do the same. It will be a victory for faith as much as for character.

Mohammed Ishtiaq, working cheek by jowl with his accountant in the office at the back of the cash-and-carry, is equally sure that his success is the result of the mores by which he lives. He has no wish to move out into what Churchill called a 'leafy suburb'. He regards his part of the inner city as 'his village' and is proud of the contribution which he makes to its prosperity. However, when he dies, he hopes that his body will be taken back to Pakistan. But, I said, surely this is home. 'Of course,' he replied. 'But I have more family in Rawalpindi. That is where I shall be remembered.'

I told him that in thirty or forty years' time, his children and grandchildren would remember him here in England. 'Only Allah,' he said, 'knows that.' Perhaps. But one thing is certain. In life, if not in death, the Muslim British are here to stay – stay in Britain and stay steadfastly Muslim in custom and attitude. They will not be assimilated into a secular British society or disappear under a veneer of bogus conformity. We can either celebrate their virtues, build on their strengths and accept their differences, or we can encourage a climate of suspicion, distaste and fear. Common sense, as well as compassion, demands that we rejoice in our new diversity.

Sunday Times, 6 June 1993

Literature Has Got Me
Into This Mess . . .

On 26 April 1982, I arrived at my office in the House of Commons at a few minutes before half past nine. On my desk lay an envelope which had been addressed in the unmistakable hand of Michael Foot. Printed below the name was the stern injunction: 'Private and Strictly Confidential. To be opened by Mr Hattersley personally'. As I unfolded the letter, I noticed the date. The discovery that the letter had been composed before breakfast and typed shortly afterwards increased the mystery and heightened the tension. I had been Shadow Home Secretary for almost three years and it was the first time that the leader of the party had written to me.

> Some offences may sometimes be overlooked, and on the point of timing I merely note that you made the choice to deliver the attack at a moment of international crisis on the cowardly assumption, I suppose, that it might not even be noticed. I add also that all previous offences, a long list extending over a long period, will now be taken into account. I expected to find your resignation to be awaiting me. Since I am not even offered an apology, how are we to proceed?

For a moment, I believed that I had committed some terrible act of treachery. At primary school, when a teacher asked an unknown miscreant to confess some trivial offence, I always felt an almost irresistible urge to put up my hand – even when I had been nowhere near the scene of the crime. And, in a notorious cabinet meeting, when Jim Callaghan announced his intention of rooting out the mole who had leaked the government's new Common Market policy to the *Financial Times*, I almost owned up – even though I was not the offender. I suppose that I have a talent for guilt. I read on nervously.

Dorothy Parker was not only a poet, a short story writer, a wit, the best exponent, if not the creator, of that American institution, the wisecrack. She also gave a display of casual courage surpassing that of any of her New York contemporaries.

In those days, Endpiece was published on Saturday and, forty-eight hours earlier, Michael had read 'Her Couplets Runneth Over', my opinion of Mrs Parker's work. He later told me that he had worked on his response for most of the weekend. Eventually, what 'started out as a genial rebuke turned into a legitimate tirade'. His defence of a lady – with whom I had not previously assumed he had much in common – included the confident assertion that 'she justly counted herself in the socialist camp'.

Several times, during the morning, Michael's secretary telephoned me to say that I was expected to send a reply. I could imagine him sitting in his office, slapping his thigh and announcing that as soon as he received my response he would construct a second literary broadside. I failed him. I had no doubt that I could sustain and substantiate my criticism. But I was so disoriented by the whole bizarre episode that I could not concentrate on the construction of my rebuttal of his charges.

At lunchtime, I telephoned the leader's office and left the message, 'You win.' His letter had ended with the confession that he was a regular Endpiece reader and the hope that in the years which lay ahead my time would not be 'directed exclusively to such work'. I have always feared that, after my failure to rise to the Dorothy Parker challenge, Michael Foot believed that I would make a better home secretary than a literary critic. In search of consolation, I began to work on the next Endpiece. 'Literature has got me into this mess', Philip Roth wrote, 'and literature had better get me out of it'.

The Dorothy Parker article was the result of a chance encounter with a blackboard at the BBC. I was there to make a film in the *With Great Pleasure* series and, stumbling about on the set, I knocked into what looked like a chalked family tree. The lines were all there – spreading out and down – but only three words complemented them. Where the names of the founding father might have been, someone had written 'One Perfect Rose'. I could not identify the quotation. Neither could any of my fellow film makers. Then, during the afternoon, somebody said that the previous programme in the series had been a tribute to Dorothy Parker.

> *A single flow'r he sent me, since we met.*
> *All tenderly his messenger he chose;*
> *Deep-hearted, pure, with scented dew still wet –*
> *One perfect rose.*

> *I knew the language of the floweret:*
> *'My fragile leaves' it said, 'his heart enclose'*
> *Love long has taken for his amulet*
> *One perfect rose.*

> *Why is it no one ever sent me yet*
> *One perfect limousine, do you suppose?*
> *Ah no, it's always just my luck to get*
> *One perfect rose.*

My *With Great Pleasure* programme was written without joy. For writing scripts is mostly pain. It was dedicated to Philip Larkin whom I had known slightly when I was at Hull and I wrote a friendly note telling him that he was my chosen subject. He did not reply to me but the postcard which he sent to the producer said that, although he declined the invitation to take part, he wished the programme well. The week before the broadcast he sent the same message to me. His note ended, 'I'm sorry to learn that Endpiece is leaving the *Listener*. I enjoy it but not enough to persuade me to read the *Guardian*.'

His dislike for the programme that I made about him was the subject of several posthumously published letters. I made them the theme of one Monday's column. My sadness that he did not approve of either me or my encomium was, to some extent, moderated by the hope (which also appeared in the collected correspondence) that he would not outlive Kingsley Amis, his closest friend. If Kingsley were the first to go, his old pal would have to give the address at the memorial service. And Philip could think of nothing good to say about him.

Despite the rebuff from the grave, I persist in my belief that

'Dockery and Son' is an almost perfect expression of regret and that 'The Arundel Tomb'

> *. . . The stone fidelity*
> *They hardly meant has come to be*
> *Their final blazon, and to prove*
> *Our almost instinct almost true*
> *What will survive of us is love*

is an exquisite illustration of how hideous ideas can be beautifully expressed. Leaving the disillusion to the end of what first appears to be a poem in praise of love makes the cynicism doubly painful. I wrote about Larkin ('French Letters and a Passion for Poetry') in the belief that sharing none of his values, yet admiring him more than any contemporary poet, proved something about art occasionally transcending politics.

I have to believe that in order to justify my admiration for authors whose views on life I find less acceptable than their contribution to literature. I would not have chosen to go on a Lake District walking holiday with either Yeats ('Quickly Turn Away') or T. E. Lawrence ('Who Cares?'). Nor do I imagine that Tennyson ('Pre-Raphaelite Avalon') would have been a natural Labour voter. T. S. Eliot we know to have been High Church and High Tory. But he could produce literary judgments that surpass anything else that was written this century. In the first Annual Yeats Lecture he spoke of the poet as a Pre-Raphaelite.

> 'The Shadowy Waters' seems to me one of the most perfect expressions of the vague enchantment of that school. Yet it strikes me – it may be an impertinence on my part – as the western seas as seen through the back window of a house in Kensington.

It is enough to make an ordinary mortal give up writing for ever – or at least start to rewrite what had previously been thought adequate.

Eliot was one of the poets and critics who made fleeting appearances, through passing references, in column after column. So – at another extreme of art and life – did J. B. Priestley, whose essays (together with the work of Robert Lynd, E. V. Lucas, G. K. Chesterton and Hilaire Belloc) were a central theme of a talk which I gave at the Keighley Literary Festival. For some reason *Vogue* published most of my lecture. The *Vogue* readership proved remarkably knowledgeable about the Old Testament. Dozens of them wrote to explain that I was in error when I suggested that Joshua blew down the walls of Jericho. Apparently he employed someone else to do the demolition work. The lecture ended with the assertion, omitted in the edited version ('I Essay'), that writing fifteen hundred words about nothing very much is the most enjoyable of all human activities. That, however, remains my view.

Pre-Raphaelite Avalon

First impressions are not always the best. But they are often the impressions that we choose to keep and cherish. That is certainly how it is between King Arthur and me. My mental picture of the Round Table and all its knights is the one which was indelibly engraved on my mind and memory during a single shining hour over thirty years ago, when I first read *The Lady of Shalott* and *Sir Galahad*.

Sir Galahad reminded me of nothing so much as the local Methodist preacher who lived at the end of our road, a worthy but dull man whom I could not imagine singing 'Tirra lirra' by the river and encouraging young ladies to fall out of turret windows. Sir Lancelot, on the other hand, I took to be a bit of a lad. That was nothing to do with him and Guenever being (as Malory tactfully puts it) 'mischieved both'; a state of affairs I would not then have understood. It was his 'brazen greves' that gave the game away. It was clear to me that, like plus-fours and two-tone shoes, they were the mark of a bounder.

I read the poems in a tattered Victorian anthology of the minor works of Tennyson (Alfred Lawn Tennyson, as William Empson insists we should properly call him), which included drawings by an artist who owed a debt to both Aubrey Beardsley and Dante Gabriel Rossetti. The pictures were unashamedly romantic, the illustrations for an idyll, framed in garlands of ferns and flowers. All the horses were chargers or palfreys and they stood, with one fetlock prancing and pointing, on medes as full of tresse flowers as a squire's cloak.

Every line-drawn knight looked straight towards the horizon, where the apparition of the Holy Grail shone in the sky in place of the sun. The Grail was a miracle of Victorian Gothic craftsmanship – part of the great anachronism which made up the nineteenth-century portrait of Camelot. 'As a picture of the Middle Ages,' F. L. Lucas wrote, 'the *Idylls of the King* are about as adequate as a fancy-dress ball or parish pageant.'

But when the Victorians wrote about Arthur or attempted to map the Vale of Avalon, they were not trying to unearth historical truth. They were feeding their favourite fantasy about a golden age of nobility and chivalry which, although destroyed by lust and treachery, might one day come again. It was a creative fantasy, for it produced St Pancras station, the theory of perfect competition and the Pre-Raphaelite movement.

So the Knights of the Victorian Round Table who appeared in my dog-eared anthology were not mediaeval warlords or tribal chieftains – groups of men not famous for their preoccupation with the necessity of preserving the virginity of damsels in distress. They wore armour of the fourteenth, not the fifth, century and looked as if they had leapt straight from the top of a crusader's tomb.

The Victorians were looking for 'chivalrye, trouthe and honour, freedom and courtesye' and they chose to find it in the decades that separated Chaucer and Malory. And since the whole story of hands in lakes, swords in stones and worms in buds is a myth, the Victorians were perfectly entitled to set it in whatever period they found most convenient.

The Arthurian legend has remained for me an idyll ever since that first afternoon when I discovered that Sir Galahad had the 'strength of ten because his heart was pure'. It has survived Mark Twain as well as Malory, Rodgers and Hart, Lerner and Lowe, and Monty Python. It even survived Mr Graham Greene's savagely despairing account of the end of innocence of Mr Parkis, a divorce detective with aspirations for his son:

'He's called Lance, is he?'

'After Sir Lancelot, sir. Of the Round Table.'

'I'm surprised. That was a rather unpleasant episode, surely.'

'He found the Holy Grail,' Mr Parkis said.

'That was Galahad. Lancelot was found in bed with Guenever.'

Mr Parkis said sadly, looking across at his boy as though he had betrayed him, 'I hadn't heard.'

I hope that the idyll will survive BBC1's Sunday-evening serial, programmes in which fact and fantasy lie uneasily together. The myths are reproduced – indeed, a new one is invented. Two episodes ago Merlin went into voluntary retirement, promising to return in some future age. In Malory's he 'assotted and doted on one of the ladies of the lake . . . was shut in a rock under a stone and there died'.

But, apart from a splendid classically wizard-like Merlin, the people look ridiculous. King Arthur himself clearly plays in midfield for a second division football club and does his hair in a light perm as a tribute to Kevin Keegan. With the single exception of Lancelot, the Knights of the Round Table look like extras from a lager advertisement. And Sir Lancelot is clearly from the same agency, if not the same promotion. I saw him the other week on American television climbing, white and spotless, out of a disinfected drain with cardboard bacteria and bacilli impaled on his sword.

The Arthurian legend cannot survive the idea that you might meet the King after the show having a pint in the Pendragon Arms. Fantasy often hovers on the edge of absurdity as, for instance, in Malory's account of how Joseph of Arimathea prepared the red-cross shield of invincibility for Galahad. 'Then Joseph bled sore at the nose, so that he might by no means be staunched. And there upon that shield he made a cross of his own blood.' Nosebleeds and idylls are incompatible.

Once the story is touched by cold philosophy it collapses. What sort of chivalry provides Arthur with a sword that gives him a magical edge over all his opponents and a scabbard that acts as a coagulant whenever he is wounded? In the real world that sounds suspiciously like a boxer with a horseshoe inside his glove who uses illegal substances to close the cuts beneath his eyes. But in an idyll nobody complains to the Board of Control – particularly if it is a patriotic idyll about rural England and the champion who fought to maintain the old country and the old values.

And that is, or ought to be, the strength of every version of King Arthur's story. Descriptions of sunny England, spring and the maypole on the village green, or harvest-time as described by T. H. White:

> It was July, and real July weather, such as they had in Old England ... The dogs moved about with their tongues hanging out, or lay panting in bits of shade, while the farm horses sweated through their coats and flicked their tails and tried to kick the horseflies off their bellies with their great hind hoofs ... The best mowers mowed away in a line where the grass was still uncut, their scythes roaring in the strong sunlight.

It is an England that never existed, and never could have existed, a place where even the weather was perfect.

It is a far cry from the Industrial Revolution and the dark satanic mills which were just beginning to spread across England when the *Idyll* was written, but in some people's minds the Backward Glance to the England of their imagination actually pointed a way to what England might become. If those Infant Feet ever did walk here in ancient times the boy Jesus came hand in hand with Joseph of Arimathea, the same Joseph who on his second visit brought and left the Holy Grail for which King Arthur and his Knights quested.

That is the beauty of the myth the Victorians created. As long as you keep it a myth you can use it exactly as you choose. It can become a general theory about progress or improvement, or the simple evocation of a personal romantic experience.

I choose the second. Having read *Sir Galahad* and *The Lady of Shalott*, I was allowed to open four small leather-bound volumes that my father had given my mother after their first meeting. They were *The Golden Treasury*, Wordsworth, Keats and Tennyson, and on the flyleaf of the volume that contained the *Idylls of the King* my father had written a reference to a single line: 'Oh Enid, bake sweet cakes to bring us cheer.' I suppose it was then I decided that as long as you take a Victorian view of these things the age of chivalry is not passed.

Listener, 28 October 1979

Her Couplets Runneth Over

A month ago this column contained a sentence which implied that I was less than infatuated with the work of Dorothy Parker. Indignant letters, written half in disbelief that such a meaning was intended, are still arriving in my office. When in the *Listener* I was explicit about my dislike of both her poetry and prose the correspondence was simply abusive. The different reactions may demonstrate the different character of the people who read the papers in which Endpiece has appeared. Or it may prove that the more direct the style the greater the certainty of understanding. The truth is, I regard Dorothy Parker's writing as rubbish.

I realise that in part I dislike her so-called wit and wisdom for deplorable reasons. I cannot enjoy anything written by a lady who has become the apotheosis of the little black dress. I can imagine few things less entertaining than Mrs Parker sitting in the gloomy, mahogany-lined Hotel Algonquin working hard at being effortlessly funny. Long cigarette holders, pendant earrings, and impatience for the conviviality of the cocktail hour seem to me incompatible with literary genius. George Eliot never drank a dry Martini in her life. The Brontës chose to face death not flirt with it. If living quietly at home was good enough for Jane Austen there was no excuse for Mrs Parker to parade herself around New York.

There is, I think, a small nugget of sensible criticism buried under the heap of prejudiced dross. Mrs Parker has always reminded me of one of those chromium-plated standard lamps that stood in the corners of so many American pre-war apartments. From a distance they seem to shine very brightly. But in reality they throw very little light on anything. And Mrs Parker *worked* at being limited. Superficiality was her special talent. She was not one of those admirable persons whose frivolity or cynicism camouflages a serious nature. She was frivolous and cynical deep down inside. And I fear that I cannot separate my judgment of the tales from my opinion of the teller.

Believe me, I do not usually take against writers for such preposterously personal – and therefore profoundly philistine –

reasons. The only author with whom I completely identify is Thomas Chatterton, the 'marvellous boy' who so despaired of his infant talents ever being recognised that he killed himself before his genius was fully understood. Much as I worship the literary ladies offered above as examples of excellence, they were the sort of people whom I would have insisted on worshipping from afar. Nor are the men who stand beside them in my private pantheon exactly the sort of people to whom I would naturally warm.

I cannot imagine hurrying through my hotel supper in order to enjoy Match of the Day with Thomas Hardy, or playing Rodgers and Hart records so that I could sing along with D. H. Lawrence. If Milton were living at this hour I would treat him in the way that I treat all apostates who abandon old faiths and take up temporarily fashionable heresies. Much as I admire Browning's robust Victorian optimism, I suspect him of taking brisk walks and cold baths. But usually such incompatibilities are unimportant.

Yet I just cannot believe that Dorothy Parker has anything of interest to say to me. And, in consequence, I find it impossible to retain in my memory anything she has written – as I discovered a couple of weeks ago when I was impatiently wasting time at the BBC. The room in which I waited had recently been used for some sort of rehearsal. Chalked on the gigantic blackboard which dominated one of its windowless walls were the words 'one perfect rose'.

I knew that I had met the sentence somewhere before and inevitably I was touched by its blatant sentimentality. Perfect roses are only one aesthetic step away from gilded lilies. But those three words possess the special cheap charm of romantic excess. They are like the better titles of the best popular songs – The Way We Were, It Never Entered My Mind. They cram enough meaning into a single phrase to be almost considered poetry.

At first I thought that the hazy recollection was just coincidence and that the writing on the wall had prosaic origins. Perhaps Carmen had preceded us in the rehearsal room and some fastidious Don José had written up his exacting requirements as a reminder to a stage manager whose fastidiousness he did not trust. I was just enjoying the idea of the singer who could not perform unless he was certain that no worm lurked in the bud when someone nudged me, pointed to the scribble, and pronounced the dreaded name.

Had it been an unknown line of Tennyson I would have rushed home and looked it up at once. But it took me several weeks to face the indignity of reaching down the *Penguin Dorothy Parker* and thus admitting that I was interested. Accepting that I actually enjoyed reading the poem was an even greater indignity. I survived the trauma by reminding myself that the verse possessed an essentially ephemeral charm. In any case it is in the thousand-word essay not the twelve-line poem that the English language has its finest flowering.

However, I have rarely suffered such a cultural shock. I can only compare it with the discovery that J. B. Priestley has moved to Warwickshire and that a poem by Noël Coward has been insinuated into a serious collection of modern verse. I am past the time when I am prepared to have my prejudices disturbed. Fortunately a brief glance at a couple of the anthology's other 603 pages convinced me that no reappraisal was necessary. 'Lady make a note of this/One of you is lying' is, for me, the couplet that does not cheer.

But a residual disquiet remains. If the blackboard had contained a forgotten passage from *Sons and Lovers* how would I have reacted? Would I have recognised it as part of a perfect page? Or if the chalk marks had made up an unknown line from *Paradise Lost* would I have known at once that it was from a work of genius? Perhaps Mrs Parker is really better than I think. But as so many of her poems remind us, when it is too late for love the sensible and sophisticated decision is to admit it and turn away without regret.

Guardian, 24 April 1982

Little Englander

Fifty years ago this autumn J. B. Priestley set off on his *English Journey*. He was just thirty-nine and with *The Good Companions* already on the bookshop shelves his reputation as a popular but serious novelist was already secure.

His inconsequential essays had begun to add distinction to the foot of several newspapers' pages. Soon he was to write the meticulously constructed plays with the intriguingly ingenious plots. But the *Epilogues* which followed the *Nine O'Clock News* and made him a welcome visitor in a million wartime homes were still a decade away.

Yet despite the success which he had already enjoyed and the fame which still lay ahead, the story that began on a motor coach driving to Southampton is incomparably the greatest achievement of his eighty-nine years.

It is a miracle of straightforward English. Armed with 'the minimum of clothes, a portable typewriter, the usual paraphernalia of pipes, notebooks, rubbers, paper fasteners, razor blades, pencils, Muirhead's *Blue Guide to England*, Stamp and Beavers' *Geographic and Economic Survey* and, for reading in bed, the tiny thin paper edition of the *Oxford Book of English Prose*', he began to write about England as no one had written about it since Cobbett. Indeed, he wrote about this tight little, right little sceptred isle with an unselfconscious simplicity that Cobbett could not match.

When Cobbett rode through Hampshire he wrote about the changing pattern of commercial life. 'Between Southampton and Western Grove we cross a bridge over the Itchen River.' The countryside was littered with grand houses and 'just at the back' of the grandest of them all was 'another paddock place' inhabited by 'a man who was a coachmaker in the East Indies and whose father or uncle kept a turnpike in Chelsea a few years ago. See the effects of industry and enterprise!' Cobbett found it easier to grieve at other men's misfortunes rather than to rejoice at their success.

Priestley's vignette of the social and commercial condition of southern England is so subtle that at first the reader does not realise that it is a commentary on how we lived then. There are no booming exclamation marks, didactic asides. The story is told by a 'thinnish fellow, somewhere in his forties' who had 'a sharp nose, a neat moustache, rimless eyeglasses and one of those enormous foreheads – roomy enough for an Einstein – that so often do not seem to mean anything'.

The thinnish stranger wanted to talk and made an excuse to move across the coach's gangway. 'He was the kind of man who comes into a few hundred pounds in his early twenties and begins to lose money steadily . . . there are a few thousand like him up and down the country, especially in growing towns and new suburbs. At the end of one venture they begin another passionate search for an opening.'

The twentieth-century reincarnation of Messrs Micawber and Polly began his commercial critique in Surrey with gloomy news about the profitability of tearooms. By the time that the travellers had reached Hampshire, emigration to South Africa was on the agenda. The prospects for raincoats and waterproof hats, cheap furs, the shoe trade and wireless maintenance were all thoroughly discussed on the journey south.

I am far too much in awe of J. B. Priestley to allow myself the cynical suspicion that the man with the domed forehead and a flair for bankruptcy never existed. I prefer to think that in this, as in other encounters, Mr Priestley was fortunate in attracting into his company characters of unusual interest and humorous habits. I suppose that he sifted through three months of conversation and wrote down just the home-made aphorisms that kept the journey bounding joyfully along.

I have a vision of the red and round-faced Mr Priestley attracting a moving army of casual acquaintances. Not for nothing was he called 'Jolly Jack' – most often by people who had never met him. He looked approachably avuncular. And what he wrote about England confirms his good temper as well as his excellent judgment.

Other travellers through England – especially those who have set out during the last decade – have found much that displeased their eye, offended their sensitive susceptibilities and infuriated their passions for innovation and improvements. J. B. Priestley found much in England of which he disapproved.

He 'thought about patriotism' and wished that he 'had been born early enough to be called a Little Englander . . . that *little* sounds the right note of affection. It is little England that I love . . . I dislike Big Englanders. I wish their patriotism began at home so they would say – as I believe most of them would if they only took the trouble to go and look – "Bad Show!" to Jarrow and Hebburn.'

I am not sure whether or not William Cobbett loved England or if the England of October 1826 through which he made his way to Southampton was less lovable than the England of autumn 1933. But I am sure that, without the sort of fondness that J. B. Priestley feels, it is impossible properly to describe what life is like in this slightly tarnished golden jewel set in an increasingly polluted silver sea. *English Journey* is a love story written in simple language. It is also a masterpiece.

Guardian, 17 September 1983

Who Cares?

Last Sunday was open day at Bovington Camp. I was not there. I suspect that with the new Challenger battle tank on view my absence was barely noticed. Indeed, as the Royal Armoured Corps had omitted to send me an invitation to 'Open Day 83' it may well be that no one expected me to be present. So I do not use this column like the Court and Social pages of *The Times* to explain – as if I were a dowager duchess oppressed by age and arthritis – why I have failed to discharge my social obligations.

I fear that there is more than a touch of the N. F. Simpsons in my concern about my whereabouts on the afternoon of Bovington's exposure to the tank-loving public. Mr Simpson (elderly and literate readers will recall) is the author of an anti-logic play called *One Way Pendulum*, in which an aggressive barrister cross-examines a harassed defendant with the classic question, 'When you might have absented yourself from anywhere in Britain why, on that particular afternoon, did you choose to absent yourself from Norwich?'

Before elderly, literate and didactic readers reach for their pens and paper to expose the inaccuracy of the quotation, let me confess more serious guilt. My interest in my failure to visit Bovington is almost as irrational as the N. F. Simpson question. For when I saw the *Times*' photograph of the new battle tank, I could not believe that anyone within travelling distance of the Armoured Corps depot would actually choose to go there.

For Bovington is on the southern tip of Wessex. Ten miles due east of Casterbridge. In the real world, I have spent many hours driving across the moorland which surrounds it and cursing the great wounds that tank tracks have cut into the good Dorset earth. At least, I think that it was in the real world. For I was looking for Clouds Hill.

To do Bovington Camp justice, Clouds Hill would not have called me if the tank training ground had never existed. For Private Shaw (alias 352087 Aircraftsman Ross, T. E. Lawrence and, worst of all, 'Lawrence of Arabia') would not have used the cottage as a retreat and refuge for himself and the other squaddies who bashed out their basic training on the Bovington square. Colonel Lawrence, not surprisingly, did not enjoy his basic training. During the war in the desert, slow march in review order had played very little part in either strategy or tactics. And he had been through it all before, during the desperate days when he had attempted to lose himself in the RAF.

Lawrence sold a gold dagger, given him in Mecca in 1918, to repair the roof and ceiling of Clouds Hill. And, during his agonised years in the army, whatever he wrote was produced simply to finance cottage repairs. That such a dispossessed and disenchanted man should feel so deep an attachment to the place is, in itself, a reason for visiting Clouds Hill. So is the vision of its distinguished visitors – Thomas and Mrs Hardy, George Bernard Shaw (who left a copy of *St Joan* inscribed 'To private Shaw from public Shaw') and E. M. Forster who described the scene for the *Listener* in 1938.

There was no alcohol at Clouds Hill. For Lawrence still maintained his Islamic enthusiasm for coffee and tea. And there was very little food. Lawrence was the masochistic sort of aesthete who just put aside all fleshy pleasures and then acquired an intellectual anorexia nervosa which permanently suppressed his appetite. For the convenience of his friends, he kept a large supply of tinned fish and baked beans. They were eaten at will. I would gladly have visited Clouds Hill just to see where Thomas Hardy wandered the living room, eating pilchards straight out of their oily can. But the real reason of my visit was to read the words which Lawrence himself carved over the cottage door.

I find almost all that I know of Colonel Lawrence intensely unattractive (not least the dislike of alcohol and the detachment from food) though in mitigation I remember the way in which he writes. And of those who write well, much is rightly forgiven. It is difficult to imagine a more elegant complaint against happiness than his description of a portly Arab. 'I begin to suspect him of constant cheerfulness. His eyes had a confirmed twinkle and though only thirty-five he was putting on flesh. It might be due to too much laughter.' However, the words which he carved on his lintel were not his own.

They were Greek. The biographers print them in the ancient script and E. M. Forster offers *ou phrontis* as a modern version. Everyone agrees that they translate as 'I don't care' – the culminating and climactic line from a story by Herodotus concerning a young man who, at the banquet to celebrate his betrothal to a princess, disgraced himself and therefore forfeited both bride and dowry. We have no way of knowing if the reckless response to his rejection was genuine. For the suitor was drunk and his riposte was instantaneous.

Lawrence carved 'I don't care' above the door at Clouds Hill when he was stone cold sober. And in spite of his many talents, he was not a sufficiently proficient mason for the work to be done in a few minutes. He must have stood for hours, precarious on a chair or uncertain on a ladder, chipping away at the lintel and conscientiously engraving his cottage and his life with the motto by which he wanted to be remembered.

That is not the action of a man who believed what he carved. Indeed, it is the behaviour of someone who cared very much indeed, but hoped that little acts of bravado would convince the world that he did not care at all. For all its naïveté, that combination of characteristics is profoundly endearing. It makes up – at least in part – for the love of motorcycles, the inclination to be photographed in flowing white robes, even the antipathy to food and drink. For it demonstrates a secret vulnerability. Is it possible that people who could have gone in search of that house and that inscription chose, instead, to look at tanks?

Guardian, 9 October 1983

From the Original Story

On the evening of my arrival in Harvard I tried to combat my loneliness by sitting, silent and solitary, at the back of the common room in Winthrop House and listening to the director of the Smithsonian Museum give a lecture on a subject I no longer recall. But I remember vividly the question which followed his formal address. All I knew of the Ivy League I had learned from Scott Fitzgerald, and his striped-blazered undergraduates had not prepared me for the combat-jacketed students who surrounded me that evening.

They were opposed to the Smithsonian *in principle*, for it sanctified the artefacts of capitalism. They took particular exception to the *Spirit of St Louis* which apparently hangs from one of the ceilings in Washington's most famous museum, pretending to commemorate Lindbergh's solo flight across the Atlantic. They explained that in reality it was there to glorify the St Louis Chamber of Commerce which sponsored the venture. Until that moment I had believed that the name on the nose of the aeroplane was a tribute to one of those French soldier-saints.

The whole experience came as such a shock that when, next night, I saw a young man wearing a straw boater I followed him, hoping that he would lead me to a whole effete coven of Amory Blaines.

He turned out to be a member of the Harvard Drama Club on his way to another of the university's public lectures. That night's celebrity was Jim 'McArthur Park' Webb, who spoke briefly on the romantic musical. He dealt with his subject with the same simple certainty that I had observed in Milton Friedman twenty years before when the monetarist gnome had explained that we could end Britain's housing shortage overnight by allowing rents to rise until effective demand was satisfied. A good musical, he said, was four memorable songs and three acts. Boy meets girl. Boy loses girl. Boy gets girl back.

The formula has intrigued me ever since. And at last, after a whole decade, I have hit upon an idea which – although not original – will pack in the coach parties. True to the classic tradition, my musical has a chorus or narrator. He starts the show with a melodic question:

> *Who's that tapping at the window?*
> *It happens every evening after dark.*
> *From chimney-pot to basement*
> *There is not a single casement*
> *That has not been smudged and smeared by fingermark.*
> *Who's that peeping round the curtain?*
> *It really is a practice I deplore.*
> *For it's desperately unnerving*
> *When a ghastly gaze unswerving*
> *Stares in a window on the second floor.*

The narrator soon finds out. And he begins to tell the tale of the ghost and her two lovers. The characters gradually develop. One is a hypochondriac whose feeble constitution contrasts sharply with the muscular savagery of the anti-hero. The valetudinarian explains his wry philosophy:

> *As long as you've got your health*
> *Every day is sunny, every joke is funny, every bush a vine;*
> *As long as you've got your health*
> *Every baby's bonny, every goose is swanny, every day is fine.*
> *As long as you've got your health . . .*
> *I wish that I had mine.*

At this point (we are by now into the second act) the plot takes the sudden turn that Mr Webb believes to be essential. A conversation is overheard and misunderstood. As a result the star-crossed lovers separate and go bitterly on their different ways. An old family servant, instead of comforting the distraught suitor, reproves him for listening to other people's conversations:

> *Serves you right for listening at keyholes,*
> *Serves you right for crouching outside doors.*
> *For whenever an eavesdropper*
> *Slips and comes a frightful cropper*
> *All decent people join in the applause.*

As a second-act finale that takes some beating. Perhaps Cardinal Newman's lyrics (set to music by Edward Elgar in a show that never got to Broadway) match it for moral certainty. But neither Hart nor Hammerstein (why do all the really great lyricists have names which begin with H?) could have produced a wittier quintrain. And how, I wonder, would they have made the second change of mood and contrived the happy ending which is essential to the show's success – and still have remained faithful to the original work on which this smasheroo is based? I simply relied on the basic text. Thus the curtain comes down to the author's own words:

> *So they all end up together*
> *On the hills amongst the heather*
> *And in the quiet earth they'll lie content.*
> *Round their moorside mausoleum*
> *We will sing a last Te Deum*
> *And the harebells chime a soft accompaniment.*

> *CHORUS: All together let us sing*
> *Death, oh death where is thy sting?*
> *Grave, thy victory will be pyrrhic—*
> *Hence this joyful final lyric.*

> *Now three headstones in a row*
> *Mark the place where, down below,*
> *They lie at rest and safe from harm.*
> *As the moths go fluttering by*
> *Across Yorkshire's benign sky*
> *Their flapping wings will syncopate our psalm:*

> *CHORUS: All together let us sing etc.*

Of course, for the show to run and run, it needs a good title. I thought of a single word followed by an exclamation mark in the manner of Lionel Bart. Impresarios making offers should, therefore, mark their envelopes in the top lefthand corner with what will become a legend of the English musical stage, Heathcliff!

Guardian, 22 November 1983

I Essay

For over 400 years, the reputation of the English essay has been prejudiced by its French origins. When, in 1571, Montaigne published his *Essais*, he was foolish enough to comment on the nature of his work. Writers should let their writing speak for itself. But Montaigne, being an amateur, could not resist a little do-it-yourself literary criticism. 'It is,' he said, 'myself I portray.' Ever since then, essays have been defined as writing of an essentially *personal* quality. Every notable essayist of the last two hundred years has written in an essentially personal style, and those who have chosen to comment on their own technique have all emphasised its personal quality. Max Beerbohm insisted that 'the essayist's aim is to bring himself home to his readers'. Thackeray confessed that he had 'taken leave to egotise'. E. V. Lucas – the best essayist of the twentieth century, writing about Charles Lamb, the greatest of all essayists – said that the *Essays of Elia* were essentially about Lamb himself. Of course the glimpses of character are not literally accurate and the descriptions of experience are not historically true. David Cecil explains about Max Beerbohm:

> Max the essayist is no more the same as Max the man than Elia the essayist is the same as Charles Lamb the man. In each case the writer projects on to the page a personality not identical with his own, though founded on it, a figure made up of elements selected from himself and then re-arranged and displayed for his aesthetic purpose.

The essay's second characteristic – equally important but too often ignored – is its absolute dependence on quality of writing rather than importance of subject. Essays are not part of what De Quincey called the literature of knowledge. We do not read them to obtain information. There are some mighty works wholly concerned with improvement and education which have chosen to call themselves essays. But Locke's *Essay on Human Understanding* and Mill's *Essay on Liberty* are not, in our sense, essays at all. The real essayist – and therefore by implication the real essay – was properly described by De Quincey. 'The mark of our attitude towards the essayist is that we are indifferent to his subject. It is not his subject which engages us.' We have only to list the inconsequential titles of the great English essays to realise that that must be true: Steele's *Recollections of Childhood*; Johnson's *A Journey in a Stage Coach*; Hazlitt's *On Going a Journey*; Lamb's *Dissertation on Roast Pig*; Leigh Hunt's *Getting Up on Cold Mornings*; Robert Lynd's *On Moving House*; J. B. Priestley's *First Snow*; and G. K. Chesterton's *A Piece of Chalk* . . .

> I remember one splendid morning all blue and silver in the summer holidays when I reluctantly tore myself away from the task of doing nothing in particular and put on a hat of some sort and picked up a walking stick and put six very bright coloured chalks into my pocket. I then went into the kitchen (which along with the rest of the house belonged to a very square and sensible old woman in a Sussex village) and asked the occupant of the kitchen if she had any brown paper. She had a great deal; in fact she had too much; and she mistook the purpose and rationale of the existence of brown paper. She seemed to have an idea that if a person wanted brown paper he must be wanting to tie up parcels.

It is not *only* the essayist who writes about the inconsequential in a way which forces the reader to maintain interest in an intrinsically uninteresting subject. Jane Austen's novels are concerned with the emotional trivia which dominate the lives of silly girls. Turn them into television serials and we begin to wonder why anyone regards *Pride and Prejudice* or *Sense and Sensibility* as two of the great novels of our language. Then we open them again to find out what all the fuss is about and discover that the genius is neither plot nor characterisation but language. *Brideshead Revisited* enshrines –

indeed proclaims – values which I find wholly repulsive. But it is so beautifully written that it remains a joy to read.

The mark of the good essayist is his ability to pick up unconsidered trifles and make them worth considering. Any cub journalist (by-line Jericho) can dominate the front-page lead with an eye-witness account of how Joshua blew down the city walls. It takes a writer to capture space on page five for an account of how an elderly fanatic puffed away on his trumpet and nothing happened.

The English essay is, of course, essentially a form of journalism. T. S. Eliot offered two definitions of that strange art – both, in my view, amusing but inadequate. The first – 'work of only passing interest intended to make an immediate strong impression and destined to eternal oblivion after that instant effect has been produced' – he rejected as slander. The second he accepted.

> There is a type of mind, and I have a very close sympathy with it, which can only turn to writing, or only produce its best writing, under the pressure of an immediate occasion; and it is this type of mind which I propose to treat as the journalist's. The underlying causes may differ; the cause may be an ardent preoccupation with affairs of the day, or it may be (as with myself) inertia or laziness requiring immediate stimulus, or a habit formed by early necessity of earning small sums quickly.

That definition does not encompass essays and essayists. The earning of *small* sums – that at least is typical. So, I think, is the need for some sort of stimulus – though in the case of the essayist his appetite is likely to be whetted by some inconsequential personal experience rather than by some cataclysmic international event. Indeed, a writer who produces an essay every week or month – an essential aspect of the essayist's existence – would be extremely unwise to rely on indigenous inspiration. But he would be even more foolish to believe that he could, in Mr Eliot's definition, 'produce his best writing under pressure'.

I know that William Hazlitt slept all morning, thought all afternoon and then spent the evening producing a continuous flow of faultless prose which needed neither correction nor alteration, and that J. B. Priestley wrote without pause. But most essayists have possessed a less spontaneous talent. Their genius has been for writing and then re-writing. They had much in common with the cabinet-makers. The smooth and gleaming finish is essential. But it is nothing without the rigid structure. However, it is journalism.

Over the last 200 years, virtually every essay which has appeared between hard covers has begun life as newsprint. Richard Steele had an exclusive byline, 'From My Own Apartment':

> I went home, considering the different conditions of a married life and that of a bachelor, and I must confess that it struck me with a secret concern to reflect that whenever I go off I shall leave no traces behind me. In this pensive mood I returned to my family; that is to say, to my maid, my dog and my cat who can only be the better or worse for what happens to me.

The third essential characteristic of the essay is the establishment of a relationship between the writer and reader. Perhaps in more realistic terms it is described as an *imagined* relationship between the writer and his *imagined* readership. To sweat away at producing a regular, personal, inconsequential, readable 1,500 or 1,000 words, the writer needs to feel that he is doing it for someone. E. M. Forster – an essayist by our definition, but an essayist whose personal experiences were almost always literary – told us that he wrote for himself and one or two friends whose judgment he respected. All writers write chiefly for themselves. Most need the confidence that comes from at least the fantasy of gratified readers.

J. B. Priestley offered a different but related reason why essays must keep the newspaper connection:

> When a man is writing regularly in one place for one set of readers (and nearly all the essayists were regular contributors to the Press, appearing in the same periodicals at regular intervals) he comes to feel that he is among friends and can afford to let himself go. The secret of writing a good essay is to let oneself go.

An essayist cannot let himself go if he is encumbered by an imaginary obligation to be profound or to demonstrate his erudition. The essayist's constant temptation is to show off by acking his writing with obscure references and arcane allusions. The extraneous insertion is the mark of the second-rate essay and only proves that the author possesses *The Oxford Book of Quotations*.

Nothing stands so immovably between reader and writer as the 'difficult essay' – the essay written in a complicated or contrived form with the intention of demonstrating the essayist's syntactical agility.

I am not suggesting that every idea or every reference in every essay should be understood and recognised by every reader. Essays, like poetry, can be enjoyed in different ways by different people. The essay that is only comprehended by, and enjoyable to, readers who have read the complete works of George Eliot is a bad essay. If Robert Lynd can catch and hold our interest by writing about *Being Measured for a Suit of Clothes* – even though we know neither him nor his tailor – he ought to be able to command our delighted attention for a novelist whose books were of a higher quality than anything produced by Savile Row. Of course, reading *The Mill on the Floss* would add a little extra pleasure – as, I am sure, would meeting the tailor to whom Lynd was recommended by E. V. Lucas . . .

> The nearest approach to Turtle or Tompkinson or Tarbutt that I saw among the names on the shops was Pigeon, so I opened the door and went in. 'I want to be measured for a suit,' I said. 'Thank you, sir,' he said, 'what colour?' I said dark grey, for I had been told to say dark grey. As he looked among the rolls of cloth he asked, 'Any recommendation?' 'Mr Hereward gave me your name,' I said. 'We always like,' he said, 'to know the name of anyone who sends us a new customer so that we may write and thank him.' I had a curious feeling of elation at that. Here was I who had been called disgracefully shabby, and had been talked to as if I were a scarecrow or an old rag-and-bone man, and yet a respectable tailor was about to write and thank a man of fashion for having introduced me to him. 'Either,' I thought, 'I cannot be so shabby-looking after all, or the tailor sees that beneath a shabby waistcoat there possibly beats a purse of gold.'

The 'difficult' essay – like the 'difficult' poem – may create problems of comprehension for a variety of different reasons. The assumption is that – since the essay is an ancient form of writing which is associated with magazines which are read in college common rooms – it must deal with subjects too obscure or esoteric to interest the ordinary man or woman. In fact, quite the opposite is the case. The essay deals with the commonplace and makes it amusing and interesting. For that reason it is essential that the essay is not the exclusive preserve of the high-quality magazine. There is great joy in a whole page of a prestigious weekly. But the essay ought to be taken back to the people – in the mass circulation newspapers. Of course, it is there already. Perhaps the best essayist writing today is Keith Waterhouse of the *Mirror* – though he may not thank me for so classifying him, for he is essentially iconoclastic about 'great literature' and 'great writing'. Mr Waterhouse no doubt calls himself a columnist not an essayist. The two conditions overlap. The essayist may occasionally be controversial. The columnist is committed to controversy. The essayist may sometimes turn into polemicist. The columnist must be polemical by nature. The problem with persistent polemics and constant controversy is the subsidiary effect that their constant employment has on those who practise them. Those effects are, I fear, a tendency to shrillness, stridency and an ungenerous disposition. The essay can never be shrill or strident – try to imagine a personal shrillness or an intimate stridency. Nor can the essayist – revealing his character in 1,500 words – hate his fellow men. He can be gently didactic. But he cannot thunder with aggressive passion. It is his tendency to shout which, in my opinion, places Hazlitt second to Lamb in the essayist's pantheon.

With Lamb, on the other hand, we sometimes wonder if he is just a little too complacent about this wicked world. When he contributes to the sweeps' annual charity he expresses particular pleasure at the smell of sassafras tea – an unguent which assuages the condition which developed in their palates. The fact that they are all dying from their occupational disease seems not to have been noticed.

However, that aside, a generosity of spirit is essential in the true essayist and I conclude with a comparison to illustrate my point. Thomas Macaulay – overbearing, pompous and self-opinionated – said of Mr and Mrs Thomas Carlyle, 'God was good to cause them to marry each other. Thus making two people unhappy instead of four.' Leigh Hunt – who also knew Mrs Carlyle to be a difficult lady – expressed his joy at her occasional diversion towards humanity. 'Say I'm weary, say I'm sad/Say that health and wealth have missed me/Say I'm growing old, but add,/Jenny kissed me.' Leigh Hunt was not always so charitable. But in this instance I have no doubt which attitude to life represents the true temperament of the true essayist.

Vogue, September 1985

Glory

I have acquired a new ambition which, for all its modesty, seems no more likely to be fulfilled than some of the bolder aspirations I once cherished. I want to see *Glory*. Even as I write the sentence, I realise that it sounds like a Harlem evangelist's hope of heaven. But it is only obliquely related to gospel singers and the close harmony of salvation which began on the plantations of the Confederacy.

The *Glory* I want to see is a film about the American Civil War and the black battalions which loosed terrible swift swords in the grand army of the Republic. The nature of my employment prevents frequent visits to the cinema. It does, however, provide numerous *longueurs* in which I can invent plots and dialogue of my own.

In the *Glory* of my imagination, all the characters are built around the publicity picture of a young black infantryman which promoted the film. It might be better described as a portrait. For it showed only his tense profile under the cap which I always associate with the bearded, tobacco-chewing generals of the North. I bought a cardboard and paper copy of such a hat in the gift shop at Gettysburg before I walked the field of battle and saw the granite memorials that run along the crests of ridges like giant stepping stones. The plot which I write in my mind is not original. It is based on Robert Lowell's 'For the Union Dead'.

That poem describes the excavations of Boston Common. 'Behind their cage, yellow dinosaur steam-shovels' grunt as they 'gouge their underworld garage' from the ground. 'A girdle of

112

Puritan-pumpkin coloured girders braces the tingling Statehouse.'
Among those who watch the work is 'Colonel Straw and his bell-
cheeked Negro infantry' on the Civil War memorial . . . 'Two
months after marching through Boston, half the regiment was
dead.'

There was a time when I climbed the steep slope of the
Common twice a week, for the subway from Harvard Square spills
out its passengers nearby and I could never resist wasting a few
moments of bright New England morning by walking towards the
gold-domed seat of Massachusetts' government. John Winthrop,
the first governor of that state, called politics a house which is
built on a hill. I always thought of that lofty metaphor as I sweated
my way past the stone tributes to the witches burned on that God-
fearing soil. I never noticed the monument which 'sticks like a
fishbone in the city's throat'. Because of Robert Lowell, I marvel
at my blindness. 'At the dedication, William James could almost
hear the bronze Negroes breathe.'

Robert Lowell found 'no statues for the last war' on Boston
Common. Though 'on Boyleston Street, a commercial photograph
shows Hiroshima boiling over a Mosler safe, the Rock of Ages,
that survived the blast'. And as the poet crouched by his television
set 'drained faces of Negro schoolchildren rise like balloons'. Those
children are the descendants of the black Americans who fought
for a government of the people.

It was not until I read 'For the Union Dead' that I thought
about the black regiments of the Union. I had seen black GIs
driving great lorries through the wartime English countryside. But
children whispered to each other, without knowing what it meant,
that they were 'not allowed to bear arms'.

I had just begun to learn about poetry, and I would not have
believed that a poem had ever been written about black infantry-
men. Indeed, having not yet matured into Isaac Rosenberg, I would
have been sceptical about a poet finding inspiration in an infantryman of any race. Inspiring poetry seemed to be a part of life which
was out of bounds to other ranks. I knew about Herbert Asquith's
'Volunteer'. But in Sheffield, *circa* 1944, 'toiling at ledgers in city
grey' was thought of as an upper-class occupation. The muse was
only to be found in the officers' mess.

By the end of the second world war all that changed. F. T. Prince talks airily of Florence and Michelangelo. But when he describes 'Soldiers Bathing', the men take time to 'forget the fear and shame of nakedness' – a wholly working-class syndrome. And Henry Reed's 'Lessons of War' are certainly not being taught by gentlemen. In 'Naming of Parts', the drill sergeant's syntax often falls apart – but that is not an exclusively plebeian characteristic. In the lesser known 'Unarmed Combat', the idea of chivalry is expressly rejected: 'And never be frightened, to tackle from behind – it may not be clean to do so, but this is global war.'

Those lines are an intentional caricature. But the conclusion is serious enough and it is separated by thirty years of doubt and disillusion from Rupert Brooke's war, where the soldiers fought 'with hand made sure, clear eye and sharpened power'.

Henry Reed's final lesson of war is that 'we must fight not in the hope of winning but rather of keeping something alive'. For Colonel Shaw, still 'lean as a compass needle' on his Boston monument, the battle was in defence of the Union alive. And as 'he leads his black soldiers to death', some of them, no doubt, thought about the promise of emancipation. Their descendants, being black, found it almost impossible to escape the draft to Vietnam.

I look forward to seeing the real *Glory* – the film, as you will recall, not state of grace. But I hope the title is in part ironic – that the heroism of the soldiers is contrasted with the ugliness of war.

Most of all, I hope it excoriates those who sit at home and glorify battle. 'Shaw's father wanted no monument except the ditch where his son's body was thrown and lost with his "niggers".' Nevertheless, the patriotic citizens of Boston built one. The descendants of the black soldiers moved from the plantations of the South to the ghettoes of the northern cities.

Guardian, 17 March 1990

Romantic Attachment

Seventy-five Good Fridays on, the temptation to read about it was irresistible. So I reached down *The Green Flag*. By accident Robert Kee's monumental history of Irish nationalism fell open at a page on which three lines by Yeats were inset:

> *Know that I would accounted be*
> *True brother of a company*
> *That sang to sweeten Ireland's wrong*

According to Kee, Yeats's claim to be the inspiration of Irish volunteers begins with *Caitlin ni Houlihan*, a play which he wrote with Lady Gregory for the Abbey Theatre. Not for the first time, literature proved more interesting than politics. So I read on.

Caitlin ni Houlihan is a character from comparatively recent Irish mythology. During the uprising of 1798 she was said to have called at a peasant's cottage and urged him to join the rebellion. She knocked on the door, old and bowed. But her work for independence done, she was transformed. The peasant's brother, who watched her turn away, saw 'only a young girl and she had the walk of a queen'.

So that is the answer. For years I have wondered why the self-loving memoirs of Maud Gonne McBride are called *A Servant Of The Queen*. I do not propose ever again to read her detailed account of the praise which was heaped upon her from the salons of Paris to the Transvaal veldt. But I forced myself to consult the introduction:

> Tired, but glowing, I looked out of the window of the train at the dark bog land where now only the tiny lakes glowed in the fading light. Then I saw a tall, beautiful woman with dark hair blown on the wind, and I knew it was Cathleen ni Houlihan . . .

We were back with Yeats. Kee tells us that his battle against clichés was complicated by the 'romantic attachment he had formed for Maud Gonne'. We all know how it ended. She married John McBride who 'took his place amongst the sixteen men of imperishable glory who were executed in 1916'. That was the grieving widow's account of his death. Yeats's threnody is less romantic:

> *This other man I had dreamed*
> *A drunken, vainglorious lout.*
> *He had done most bitter wrong*
> *To some who are near my heart*
> *Yet I number him in a song . . .*
> *He, too, has been changed in his turn.*

I can never read those lines without being shocked at Yeats's willingness to offer his raw nerves for public scrutiny. Poets cannot afford emotional reticence and the cry of pain is, I suppose, an artistic achievement of a sort, particularly if it embarrasses the emotionally fastidious. Refusal to hide his feelings is one of the qualities that makes Yeats so Irish an Irish poet; that and the way in which the glory so often turns to despair and the beauty leaves only sadness.

Connoisseurs of disappointment will find few better examples of hopes being dashed than 'The Second Coming'. Despite the doubts, the first enquiry is deceptively optimistic: 'Surely some revelation is at hand?' The last question only speculates about the nature of the tragic outcome: 'And what rough beast, its hour come round at last,/Slouches towards Bethlehem to be born?' We know, from 'Oedipus At Colonus', that the only escape is the ultimate despair:

> *Never to have lived is best, ancient writers say;*
> *Never to have drawn the breath of life, never to have*
> *   looked into the eye of day;*
> *The second best's a gay goodnight and quickly turn away.*

After that, even the 'Lake Isle of Innisfree' seems attractive, notwithstanding the size of the wattle-built cabin and the nine bean rows.

Despite his professed affection for the bee-loud glade, Yeats undoubtedly preferred 'The light of evening, Lissadell,/Great windows open to the south'. He certainly enjoyed the company of 'Two girls in silk kimonos, both/Beautiful'.

Of course, it all ended in tears: for him, for Eva Gore-Booth and Con Markiewicz, and for the whole world. 'A raving autumn, shears blossom from the summer wreath.'

It would be unreasonable to expect the Irish airman, foreseeing death, to be full of joy about what lay ahead, though more senti- mental poets have attempted to send men into battle with merry smiles playing about their gallant lips. But Yeats's pilot despairs about his past as well as about his future. 'The years to come seemed waste of breath,/A waste of breath the years behind.' Per- haps, like a good Yeats hero, he was bitter about a second Helen in a second Troy who had 'filled (his) days with misery', then 'taught ignorant men most violent ways'.

The special desperation of the poet's personal tragedy is the frustration that came from the love of his life preferring a man who was not so much unworthy of her affection as unworthy of Yeats's rivalry. Yeats believed himself too good to be passed over for McBride. It is not quite so ignoble a reaction to rejection as first it seems.

When he thought of himself pacing the mountains overhead, it was certainly Mount Helicon he had in mind. And his face was hidden among the thousand stars which illuminate the gods. But he loved Maude Gonne McBride for her moments of glad grace and her pilgrim soul, while others loved only her beauty. He believed her to be so superior that he thought her suited only to a man as superior as himself.

Other young women would have been swept off their feet. Miss Gonne turned him down. In his sorrow he wrote despairing, and therefore essentially Irish, poetry.

Guardian, 5 April 1991

French Letters and a Passion for Poetry

Until the publication of his letters, I had always imagined that I got on rather well with Philip Larkin. We were acquaintances rather than friends, and we met not by arrangement but as a result of our mutual membership of the French Club in St James. Both of us made a habit of inviting guests who arrived later than the appointed time. When we grew bored with old (and in my case incomprehensible) copies of *Paris Match* and *Le Canard Enchaîné* we would complain to each other about the weather and whatever else had annoyed us during the morning.

I remember only two of our conversations. One included Larkin's suspicion that the figure sitting at the bar was not really Elizabeth Frink, but a cardboard cut-out of the sculptor which the management had balanced on a high stool in order to give the club some much-needed class. The other was a mysterious warning never to go into the kitchens. Until that moment, going into the kitchens was an idea which had never entered my head; but from then on the idea obsessed me. After a couple of weeks, I worked up enough courage to put my head round the swing door. Nothing seemed to have changed – not even the grease on the gas-rings, or the dust on the window sills – since the Free French founded the place. I never visited the club again. Warning me about those kitchens was the second disservice that Philip Larkin did me.

The first was perpetrated in Hull University back in the mid fifties. He reported me to the Dean for persistent late return of library books. I was guilty as charged, although there were extenuating circumstances. At the time, I was living a complicated literary life – reading *Brideshead Revisited* hidden inside Stigler's *Theory of Price*. But Larkin was unmoved by my plea in mitigation. The sub-dean (to whom the library's complaint had been handed down) was, however, wholly on my side. 'Did you know', he asked in his brisk geographer's style, 'that he's a poet? Better to humour that sort of chap.'

Larkin's friends have written that as he travelled to Hull for his interview, he feared that the librarianship would be denied him because of a poem that he had published a few weeks earlier. The Hull job description emphasised the arduous nature of the work involved and implied that the committee was looking for dedication rather than flair. They seemed unlikely to be impressed by an applicant who had written, 'Why should I let the toad work squat on my life?' The myth makers now say that Larkin was successful because his inquisitor had not read the poem. I doubt if they knew that he was a poet.

In those long distant days, Philip Larkin's poetry had no charm for me. Either the poems or I have improved with age. I now think of 'Dockery and Son' as certainly the most sad and probably the most moving poem to be written since the war. When BBC Television asked me to make a programme about a poet of my choice, I tossed up and the penny came down heads for Larkin rather than tails for Yeats. The object of my admiration wrote me a letter which – as well as noting my interest in his work – contained one of his few recorded jokes. 'I am sorry to learn that Endpiece is leaving the *Listener*. I enjoy it, but not enough to persuade me to buy the *Guardian*.'

Now we learn from his letters that he hated my programme with a passion. The one which appeared in the *Observer* was bad enough. But worse is to come. Had it not been for the Asylum Bill, which the House of Commons debates this afternoon, I would, tonight, be making a speech at the opening of an exhibition of the Larkin correspondence in the University of Hull. Amongst the exhibits on view is a note written on 15 June 1982 to one Colin Gunner. The organisers offered to cover it over during my visit.

> I think that you got Hattersley's number all right. What an extraordinary programme. 'It's my pleasure' – should think he could be got under the Trades Description Act. Bloody little pleasure about it, sitting there glowering like some Soviet Public Prosecutor. I got quite tired, waving two fingers at the small screen.

Where, I asked myself, did I go wrong? The answer seems to lie in my admission that I admired Larkin's poetry despite feeling absolutely no sympathy for his view of life and politics. Thinking about it – chastened by the criticism of my eleventh favourite poet – it still seems to me that what I said amounted to one of the greatest compliments that an author can receive. I felt much the same about *Brideshead Revisited* hidden away inside Joan Robinson's *Imperfect Competition* back in 1954. To loathe a writer's values and philosophy, yet to be enchanted by what he writes, is to elevate writing to its proper level – an occupation that should transcend petty questions of ideology and prejudice.

That is, at least, what I wanted to say in my *With Great Pleasure* programme. Unfortunately, Larkin turned out to be more political than me.

After ten years, I could not be certain that the broadcast worked out as I had intended and, anxious to deserve (if not to receive) the poet's good opinion, I asked the BBC for a video recording. They offered me one for the standard fee. The offer was declined in the best Larkin tradition. I wanted to be reassured that I had done him no wrong. But I was not so anxious that I was prepared to spend £36 just to make absolutely certain.

Guardian, 2 November 1992

Good Behaviour

It is hard to believe that Henry James was ever young. We know that he was born in New York, educated in Paris and Geneva and that he survived a year at Harvard Law School. But the image that he has impressed upon history is essentially middle-aged. He looks down the years from Sargent's portrait urbane, cosmopolitan and cultivated. His appearance – face furrowed by thought, but unlined by uncertainty – did not change during the last twenty years of his life. Even before he shaved off the beard, which had begun to show tell-tale patches of grey, he had the figure and demeanour of a mature and distinguished sophisticate. He always looked as if he moved effortlessly from dinner party to dinner party without ever leaving a stain on his waistcoat.

Superficially, James's writing confirms the impression of a socialite's concern with manners rather than morals. His novel *Daisy Miller* – an early commercial success – describes the tragedy that engulfed a young American girl who defied European conventions. The book's popularity was, in part, based on prurient speculation about the nature of Daisy's relationship with the Italian friend who keeps the reckless rendezvous in the moonlit Coliseum. But the story concerns something far more important than the line that divides innocence from indiscretion. Daisy Miller is a casualty of the conflict between the old world and the new.

The collision between American vitality and European tradition was one of James's abiding preoccupations. The explanation of how the obsession was born – together with the description of how the novelist set out to become a great man by making himself a great writer – gets Fred Kaplan's biography off to a flying start. It never flags, but glides, like its subject, to a polished end. James remained fastidiously well-mannered to the last. When, on his death bed, he was shown the insignia of the recently bestowed Order of Merit, he asked the servants to turn down the lights and hide his embarrassment.

James's attitude towards Europe was ambivalent. Although he became English by adoption and eventually by naturalisation, lived and worked in France and felt a constant urge 'to cross the Alps', his literary career was built on his early faith in American superiority. He believed that 'to be an American is a great preparation for culture', and wrote that he 'never read a good English novel . . . without drawing a long breath of relief . . . that we are not part and parcel of that dark, dense British social fabric'.

He learned to live with English society – even though his visit to George Eliot ended with the request that he dispose of an unread copy of *The American*, which his hostess and heroine did not realise he had written. But the prejudice, suppressed in life, remained in literature. His last three great novels all deal with the conflict between the European and the American personality.

In 1870, he offered his brother a clear, if less than gallant, opinion of English women. 'I revolt from their dreary, deathly want of . . . intellectual grace . . . moral spontaneity.' Ten years later, in *Portrait of a Lady*, Isabel Archer possessed both those American virtues and displayed them to great advantage against the background of an English country house. *The American* is an account of how transatlantic magnanimity triumphed over European perfidy. The paradox is that, after years of happy exile, James became so European that his novels were only 'American' because – like English novelists before him – he chose to write about Americans. The Americans about whom he wrote often reflected his early views in what amount to biographical vignettes.

In *The Princess Casamassima*, the strangely named Hyacinth Robinson advocates social reform which amounts almost to revolution – although he mellows after exposure to European culture. In the year that the novel was written, James described the English upper classes as 'rotten and collapsible', like the French aristocracy before 1789. To these well-known examples of self-revelation, Kaplan adds insights into James's character which appear in his less famous, indeed virtually unknown, minor work.

The Diary of a Man of Fifty examines 'anxiety, sexuality, commitment and marriage' and ends with the fear that caution may be the enemy of happiness. The story was written when he was thirty-six – and had already felt a barely containable attraction to Paul Joukowsky, Turgenev's companion. During the last twenty years of his life 'he fell in love a number of times'. To one of the young men who attracted him, he wrote: 'My life is arranged – if arranged it can be called – on the lines of constantly missing you.'

Whatever the failures of James's private (as distinct from social) life, the idea that he had periods of professional disappointment seems barely credible. He enjoyed the multiple blessings of a private income, the determination not to live on his inheritance and an apparently infinite talent for writing. But the living was not always easy. Kaplan paints a complete picture: the portly author, dressed 'in brilliant crimson cape and splendid black velvet hat', dancing at a 'Renaisssance ball' in Florence, is only one of the figures in his landscapes.

As late as 1895, with twenty years of great novels behind him, James had one of his short stories turned down by the *Century* magazine, and was asked to withdraw another for reasons that he described as prudish. There followed *The Next Time*, the history of 'a poor man of letters, who squanders his life in trying for a vulgar success which his talent is too fine for him to achieve'. No doubt the hero was envious of lesser authors' achievements. James himself remarked on (but did not rejoice in) the popular acclaim accorded to *The Importance of Being Earnest* and concluded that, with two smash hits 'running at once, [Wilde] must be raking in the profits'. He could not say the same for himself. In October 1896, he wrote that Macmillan's 'annual account of what accrues to me for 1895–96, from the sale of the 16 books of mine (some of them three-vol. novels) in their hands ... is £7 0s 5d'. *The Spoils of Poynton*, *What Maisie Knew* and *The Ambassadors* were still to come, each of them the brilliant consequence of whatever demon drove James on.

One of the many strengths of Kaplan's biography is the way in which he identifies what made James run. First, he believed in his destiny to become a commercially successful as well as an intellectually respected author. He regarded the publication of *The Europeans* as 'the beginning of my appearance before the British public as a novelist – as *the* novelist – of the future, destined to extract from the British public . . . a colossal fortune'.

Second, he was impelled by his character, temperament and experience to write down what he felt and thought. Sometimes his emotions were reproduced in fictional characters. On other occasions, his opinions were set out in essays. But what he wrote was always endogenous without being egocentric. Henry James wrote about Henry James, adding the genius of his imagination to the strength of his feelings. It is a quality that T. S. Eliot described as his simultaneous 'mastery over [and] escape from ideas', the true mark of his 'superior intelligence'.

Nobody who reads Kaplan's biography will doubt the greatness of that intelligence, or the service that James performed to civilised society by applying his genius to literature.

Sunday Times, 22 November 1992

Living at this Hour

When I discovered that Leo Tolstoy believed that William Shakespeare was a confidence trick perpetrated on gullible children by a corrupt and philistine establishment, I felt nothing but relief. I liked Shakespeare – particularly the histories – but my Uncle George had for many years held a very similar view to Tolstoy's. He had described *Henry V*, which we had seen together at the local cinema, as rubbish. The endorsement of his barbarism by a great novelist helped to assuage the shame that I had felt on the way home, when (in the full hearing of the whole bus queue) he had expressed scepticism about the French Court talking to each other in English poetry.

No explanation of my shame should be necessary. I regarded not liking Shakespeare as a sin which was comparable with spitting in the street, going to the pub before Sunday dinner and being tattooed. I still rejected Uncle George's views. But Tolstoy gave them a much-needed respectability. At fourteen, respectability is very important.

Sentiment sometimes clouds my memory of the Yorkshire boyhood by which I was shaped. But although I undoubtedly remember with advantage the runs I scored in local cricket and the girls I ogled at the youth club, I think that I remain relatively objective about the relationship between the bard and myself. For I also recall the bad times.

The first tragedy was a comedy. Like most children, I was weaned on the poor imitations of Lamb's *Tales* until *A Midsummer Night's Dream*. 'The story of a silly girl,' said Mrs Goodwin, a temporary teacher who was holding the fort for a schoolmaster who was waiting to be demobilised. I agreed with her then and I agree with her now. Even when I discovered the tragedies, the course of true enjoyment did not run smooth. Accounts of my unhappy experience at *Lear* and *Hamlet* ('Word Count') follow.

But they did nothing to dampen my ardour. Indeed, as that article makes plain, they simply confirmed my view that Shakespeare should be produced without distractions.

That is not a judgment which I confine to Stratford and the Barbican. It is a rule which I apply to plays and playwrights in general. Whilst the critics raved about the 1992 production of *An Inspector Calls*, I complained ('An Avenging Angel in the Alhambra Spotlight') about the destruction of the rigorous framework within which the real play had been built. I saw *Crazy For You* in New York and loved the music so much that I regretted ('Blue Rhapsody on the Pure Joys of Gershwin') that we were only allowed to hear the snatches which fitted into the re-written plot.

There is a lyric by Lorenz Hart which includes the complaint:

> *A man called Cruper plays the drums like thunder,*
> *But the melody is six feet under*

The song is called 'Must You Bury the Tune?' The same question needs to be asked about plot and dialogue. The related polite enquiry, which applies particularly to fancy productions of Shakespeare, is 'what makes the director think he knows more about the play than the author knew himself?'

I am an unrepentant adherent to the classical school of Shakespeare production. The actors should dress in Elizabethan costume and the men – doublet and hose except when togas, breastplates or cross-garters are appropriate – should advance in turn to the front of the stage and speak their lines clearly. It is the words which count. There should not even be small distractions from the poetry. I have seen a Stafford Romeo who spoke of love from beneath a Dexion balcony, and I have watched, in the same theatre, Lear's Fool hanging from the scenery like a Della Robbia infant Christ in swaddling clothes. Directors who allow such diversions should be forced to jump off Beachy Head.

The obvious fact that it is impossible to improve on Shakespeare does not mean that his work must be left inviolate. By the simple expedient of quoting from both texts, it was easy to demonstrate ('My Salad Days When I Was Green in Judgment') that *Antony and Cleopatra* was an improvement upon Plutarch. But I have absolutely no objection to other dramatists following the same distinguished path and imprinting their individual marks on the original classics. I prefer Rodgers and Hart's *Boys from Syracuse* to the *Menaechmi* of Plautus – though not to the *Comedy of Errors*. Stephen Sondheim's *A Funny Thing Happened on the Way to the Forum* – although nothing like his best musical – does not nip at Shakespeare's ankles. It runs parallel to, though somewhat behind, the master work which shares the same parentage.

I first saw Sondheim's *A Little Night Music* with Sven Anderson, the Swedish Foreign Minister. His host – the Foreign Office – thought that since it was based on Bergman's *Dreams of a Summer Night* it was an especially appropriate climax to his London visit. As a good Lutheran, he was troubled by the seduction of the young seminarian. But at least he understood the plot – which was an improvement on his experience on the first night in Britain. Again with Scandinavian origins in mind, Government Hospitality arranged for him to see *Rosencrantz and Guildenstern Are Dead*.

I saw *A Little Night Music* twice more during the next month and again many years later when it was revived at Chichester. I wrote about it ('Every Day a Little Delight') not least because I wanted to boast about my not altogether dignified meeting with the author, whom I had admired since I saw and recommended ('And One For Mahler') his almost forgotten masterpiece *Company*.

Inclusion of two of the articles which follow requires some sort of explanation. I do not refer to the two pieces on *Coronation Street*. They appear here by obvious right. My gratitude for the pleasure which the series has given me ('Dark Side of the Street') was greeted with incredulous disagreement by smart young critics. Their disapproval in no way contributed to the mild recantation I wrote ('The Soap Won't Wash') four years later. It is not what it used to be. But then, neither am I. I reject all suggestions that the programme needs a rest, in case the idea gains general acceptance that nothing good can be sustained for more than thirty years.

The two pieces whose reproduction in this section needs some sort of justification, concern two very different characters – Prime Minister, John Major and Twin Pillar of the World, Mark Antony. Perhaps comments on John Major ought to appear in the section of this book which deals with novels. For he is Mr Pooter made flesh. But during 1992 he developed the bad habit of quoting (I am careful not to say 'quoting from', which implies knowledge or initiative on his part) Shakespeare. On one Tuesday, he quoted a meaningless line from *Love's Labour's Lost* for apparently no better reason than the satisfaction of reading out the title. That was bad enough. But then, one Thursday, he observed, 'I seem to believe that Hamlet said something like...' My response ('Pooterish Pratfall from Shakespearian Heights') was the product of intense irritation – mixed with a little guilt about my loyalty to England's only real miracle.

The feeling of guilt rightly followed a betrayal of *Spanish Tragedy* or *Changeling* quality. One day in 1991 I wrote ('So Simply Serpentine') that Dryden's *All For Love* was a better play than *Antony and Cleopatra*. I can only plead that, at the time, there were extenuating circumstances which explained (though they did not excuse) my aberration. When I read my apostasy in cold print, I expected a thunderbolt to strike me down. Now I foolishly offer myself as target for the gods' revenge a second time.

And One for Mahler

I can remember the exact moment at which I first felt a desperate urge to write a thousand words in praise of Stephen Sondheim. Halfway through the second act of *Company*, Elaine Stritch proposed a toast to all the rich middle-aged women who eat expensive lunches in New York restaurants:

> *Another long exhausting day; another thousand dollars,*
> *A matinée, a Pinter play, a little piece of Mahler's.*
> *I'll drink to that! And one for Mahler!*

For the next three or four years I was occupied on other business and wrote very little apart from the occasional 'pl.spk.' or 'not convinced' on the bottom of cabinet papers so highly classified that it would be a breach of the Official Secrets Act even to recall that they had titles like 'Prices Policy: The Next Steps' and 'Amending Monopolies Legislation'. Then, just as Mrs Thatcher provided me with both time and opportunity, I was deterred from my devotional duty by Mr Sondheim himself – or at least by what he said during a television conversation with André Previn.

Sondheim appeared to be an amiable person, wholly belying Oscar Hammerstein's judgment that his genius had enabled him to develop from infant prodigy into fully-grown monster. But his explanation of how he wrote his music totally overawed me. According to Mr Sondheim, in his songs syllables are actually matched to semiquavers, and consonants are carefully paired with crotchets.

The discovery that Mr Sondheim laminated his words and music – not just making sure that they both ended at the same time, but actually dovetailing the two sorts of sound – seemed to disqualify me from holding an opinion on the songs I had been humming for half a decade. No doubt the musically educated always knew that Rodgers and Hart, Mozart and da Ponte, Newman and Elgar put it together like that. I did not. And the revelation that Sondheim's music was the product of such a complicated technique produced the suspicion that the songs I sang were only superficially connected to the songs he wrote.

Musical ignoramus though I may be, I have long suspected that Mr Sondheim suffered from pretentious critics who admired his mastery of paradox and applauded his perception of the human relationship's essential ambivalence. Until I saw him talking about his work in a way which apparently made sense to Mr Previn, I had always hoped that, despite all the fancy talk, Mr Sondheim smiled his way through the reviews and got on with the serious business of writing lovely lyrics and tremendous tunes. After I heard him talking about his art as if it were a science I began to fear that I knew nothing about him.

His touch of cold philosophy did, of course, help me to understand why lyrics can so rarely stand on their own feet and metre. Until then, I had been half inclined to put it down to problems of translation and the prosaic inadequacy of the English language. Spoken rather than sung, the 'Hallelujah Chorus' is undeniably repetitious. Even with a cardinal as its librettist, the song that stopped the show in *The Dream of Gerontius* would not have achieved immortality without a good tune for errand-boys to whistle:

> O *wisest love! that flesh and blood*
> *Which did in Adam fail,*
> *Should strive afresh against their foe,*
> *Should strive and should prevail*

may be pious, but it is hardly poetry.

And after the Sondheim interview I began to think that Italians reading 'Se questo mio core mai cangia desio, Amore mi faccia vivendo penar!' in cold print would find it just as banal as 'if this heart of mine should ever change in its desire, may love make me suffer for as long as I live' sounds to every literate Englishman.

The sudden addition to my knowledge did nothing to diminish my admiration and affection for Mr Sondheim's work. I still tried (and still failed) to sing simultaneously both parts of 'Too Many Mornings', the Puccini parody from *Follies*. On long car journeys I persisted with my invariable (and usually unwelcome) recitals from *A Little Night Music*. Baths were never completed without an extract from *Roy Hattersley Sings the Stephen Sondheim Songbook*. But I held the songs at arm's length as if they were too technical and too complicated accomplishments for tone-deaf ignoramuses to belt out.

I felt again the frustration I experienced back in 1950 after I had seen *Crime Passionel* at the Sheffield Playhouse. During the performance I had relished every moment of what I took to be a Central European civil war thriller. At school the next day I discovered that I had failed the play, or the play had failed me. I had been so busy enjoying myself that I had missed every one of Jean-Paul Sartre's philosophical messages and overlooked every item of social commentary.

There are plenty of philosophical messages and social commentaries in Sondheim lyrics, many of them so obvious that they are not even overlooked by me. 'Good things get better; bad get worse. Wait! I think I meant that in reverse,' says the cautiously happy husband in bewildered certainty. New York – 'a city of strangers' – is irresistibly repellent, and repulsively attractive, to the people who come to stare or to stay because of, not despite, its crowded loneliness.

The message is only *try* to connect and never be surprised or daunted when you fail to make contact. The moral is 'don't be afraid'. Lucky people share their problems with others and overcome them through complicated relationships:

> *Maybe you can show me how to let go,*
> *Lower my guard, learn to be free.*
> *Anyone can whistle,*
> *Whistle for me.*

Less fortunate survivors battle on alone:

> *Some people can be content*
> *Playing bingo and paying rent.*
> *That's peachy for some people,*
> *For some, humdrum people, to be;*
> *But some people ain't me.*

But the important thing is keeping going:

> *Good times and bum times,*
> *I've seen them all and, my dear,*
> *I'm still here.*

Those three examples of Sondheim's work seem to me simply good, sharp, taut lyrics – the first unashamedly sentimental, the second unapologetically brash, the third intentionally allowing the sentimentality to show through the brash veneer. They are a long way from being real poetry – even though a remarkable amount of meaning is packed into very few words – but they stand comparison with the words Lorenz Hart wrote for Richard Rodgers' music. I can offer no higher praise.

Lorenz Hart wrote for a generation of Americans who feared emotional failure and longed for material success – emergent urban middle-class Americans. 'I'll buy everything I wear at Saks. I'll cheat madly on my income-tax' is not the ambition of a Vanderbilt or Rockefeller, already 'disgustingly rich'.

It is a carefully constructed, highly polished, slightly self-satirical lyric for the verse of a first-rate popular song. And I propose to go on enjoying the work of Rodgers and Hart in exactly those terms. I also propose to recover my Sondheim self-confidence. I am sure that the great man himself is prepared for me to enjoy his words and music at whatever level I choose.

T. S. Eliot, writing about 'difficult' poetry, warns the reader against suggesting 'to himself that the poem is going to prove difficult'. There is, he reminds us, 'such a thing as stage fright, but what such readers have is pit or gallery fright'. I shall conquer mine. After all, that is what Mr Sondheim struggles to teach us. While other people say 'don't – it isn't right; don't – it isn't nice', his advice is very different:

> *I insist on*
> *Miracles if you do them;*
> *Miracles – nothing to them.*
> *I say don't*
> *Don't be afraid.*

Listener, 3 January 1980

Crimean Punishment, or the Case of Troilism and Cressida

It was, in a way, a tribute to the author's timeless genius. I do not know why the RSC decided to set its Barbican production of *Troilus and Cressida* in the Crimean War. But true believers in the audience made the natural idolatrous assumption. What William Shakespeare had to say about pride, passion, fidelity and – above all – the futility of war, was just as appropriate to the folly of Victoria's campaign against Russia as it was to the futility of Agamemnon's siege of Troy. And the wisdom of 1602 had lessons to teach even in the world of 1986. I sat in the stalls for three and a half hours, determined to concentrate on the high argument for turning a great play into a multiple anachronism.

I say multiple anachronism because the production was neither pure Sebastopol nor unadulterated Inkerman. The problem was not the protagonists' distressing habit of talking about Ithaca as they answered the field telephones or referring to Athens as they lit pipes and smoked cigars, it was the unintentional meanderings through time-space which left disbelief not so much willingly suspended as hanged by the neck until it was dead.

Shakespeare addicts tried to believe that the opposing French/ Greek and Trojan/Russian armies had been heavily influenced by German instructors. For when Hector and Achilles faced each other in personal combat, they put on what may well have been patently Heidelberg goggles and ducked across bar-room tables like extras from the *Student Prince*.

Paris, in a monocle, was exactly the sort of rapacious Prussian officer to whom Biggles took proper exception, whilst Ajax in a sheepskin coat might well have been a pilot in the Royal Flying Corps. Worst of all, when great Achilles enters, 'his drowsy blood' roused by the wounds of Patroclus into 'arming, weeping, cursing, vowing vengeance', he is accoutred not in breastplate and helmet but in the blue denim version of nineteenth-century mess kit and a single leather mitten of the sort often worn by heavy-metal guitarists.

It is now necessary for me to reveal my secret fault. I have engraved upon my mind a clear boyhood picture of the real Achilles. He has a round shield, embossed in brass and silver with the signs and symbols of ancient Greece. His helmet has a great red plume along the crest, and the bits of him that can be seen between breastplate and arm protectors, leg guards and Attic kilt, are golden brown. The Achilles with whom I was brought up would no more have worn blue denim than he would have risked going to war in sling-back sandals.

About Pandarus, I have no clear-cut boyhood memory, except the strong conviction that all offers of sweets should be refused. My opinion of him was, however, much improved last week by the discovery that he could play the piano whilst battles raged around him. There is something deeply impressive about an elderly ponce who dresses up like Dirk Bogarde in *Death in Venice* and calmly tinkles away on the ivories whilst assorted Trojans and

Athenians (or was it Russians and Frenchmen?) cut and thrust at one another. Unfortunately he persisted in playing on even when they stopped fighting and started talking – even though, if you understand my meaning, they talked Shakespeare.

I do not want my Shakespeare to be interrupted by sub Scott Joplin played on a honky-tonk piano. I am equally opposed to intrusions by off-stage artillery and Venetian blinds that are blown out of their window frames. I find difficult alien vowel sounds just as distracting. When Thersites spoke his first line in a thick Geordie accent, I laughed fit to burst. But then I remembered that he was not a thick Geordie but a very bright (and according to the programme 'disaffected') Greek or (according to the Warwick Shakespeare an 'independent minded Grecian'.) I would like to think that when directors ask actors to make northern noises they are signalling that the character in question has penetrating intellect or scintillating wit. But that is not my experience. And when Thersites makes complicated speeches, I do not – give or take the odd apostrophe – want to think about the accent at all.

I want to listen to the lines without diversion. And that obliges the director to avoid surprises. Anyone who wants to be amazed should buy tickets for something modern in Shaftesbury Avenue – amazed, that is, by anything other than language and ideas. Theatre-goers with language and ideas in mind should be given Shakespeare pure, even though it could not be Shakespeare simple. The costumes, the scenery, the make-up and the props ought not to come between the audience and the poetry.

None of that is to suggest that I did anything except enjoy the Barbican *Troilus and Cressida*. I admired the decadent Deep South set which would have been just right for *Gone with the Wind* as General Sherman's army closed on Atlanta. I marvelled at the superb acting. But when Ulysses told Achilles that 'Time hath, my lord, a wallet at his back,/Wherein he puts alms for oblivion,/A great-siz'd monster of ingratitudes', I just wanted to listen to the poetry. The Prince of Ithaca's General Service Medal just made my mind wander.

Of course, Shakespeare transcended it all. But that only served to convince me that, if he had wanted to set *Troilus and Cressida* within the Crimea, to do so would have been wholly within his capabilities. I am, I know, going to receive dozens of erudite letters which will tell me that in the first performance Helen was played by a man and Ajax wore doublet and hose not a bearskin cloak. But that is not the point. I do not ask for authenticity. All I ask is Shakespeare uninterrupted by distracting sights or disturbing words. It is not an unreasonable request to make during a performance of *Troilus and Cressida*.

Guardian, 31 May 1986

'My Salad Days When I Was Green in Judgment'

I would be extremely distressed were it widely believed that I chose today's subject for no better reason than the forlorn hope that it might impress the box office staff at the National Theatre. Of course, if those admirable men and women did come to that conclusion and, in consequence, promoted me on the waiting list for tickets to see *Antony and Cleopatra*, I would not be unduly offended by their error. But I propose to tell the rest of you something approximating to the truth.

The moment that I heard of the play's production, I bought an Arden edition and a *Penguin Masterstudy* by Kenneth Muir. It would be pretentious (as well as exhausting) to carry the Complete Works, Bradley, and Dover-Wilson on the train that bears me so frequently between London and Birmingham. And the twenty swaying minutes were my best hope of preparing myself for the moment when I sank into my seat on the South Bank. Preparation was essential, for I hardly know the play at all. And I have learned with the years that, in the case of William Shakespeare, the better you understand the text, the more you enjoy the play.

Ideally I would have read the Arden text first – carefully noting in the margin that when the soldiers say 'the gods make this a happy day for Antony', they really mean to say a 'lucky' day, and marking the Messenger's description of Octavia both to remind myself that 'station' should be read 'manner of standing' and to record the comparison with *Hamlet*, act III, scene iv, line 58, where the same form is used. Unfortunately, I took the wrong book into the lavatory, and being temporarily immobilised, began my critical study by reading Professor Muir's scholarly analysis.

Today I write about what I read for the simple reason that reading Shakespeare or reading about Shakespeare produces in me an irresistible compulsion to spread the word. I can only compare my obsession with the first time that I saw an aeroplane etching its vapour trail across a clear blue sky.

I ran in from the garden and demanded that my mother come out of the kitchen and share the miracle with me. I did not hold the arrogant belief that I knew more about vapour trails than had been revealed to her, or that, like me, she had never before experienced the wonder of seeing one. It just seemed too good to keep to myself. Shakespeare is the same.

The compulsion to write about him always wrestles with – and just manages to defeat – the fear of doing so. Second-rate writers have only to think about the sonnets to be confronted with the proposition that their only decent course is to burn their paper and break their pens. I recall Mrs Potter (who used to teach me English) asking a fellow pupil the meaning of the Wordsworth poem which explains 'her life was turning, turning'. When he suggested that it was about a ballet dancer, Mrs Potter inquired – with majestic courtesy – if he was 'any good at woodwork'. Every time I think of Shakespeare, I mentally reach for my saw and chisel.

It may be conceited to despair because of unfavourable comparison with brilliance so dazzling that everything seems dull. If so, I can only give thanks that the *Penguin Masterstudy* helped to restore my humility and to cure me of the syndrome. The therapy was provided by an insistent question that reading the chapter on Shakespeare's sources planted in my brain. If Plutarch suffers so badly from the comparison, who am I to complain?

It was on Plutarch's *Life of Marcus Antonius* that Shakespeare built his play. To be exact, Shakespeare worked from Sir Thomas North's translation of Jacques Amyot's translation of the original.

But since the idea that these two distinguished gentlemen destroyed Plutarch's prose style undermines my thesis, I am not prepared to consider the possibility that the words which Professor Muir quotes are anything except a fair copy. Among them is an account of Antony's first meeting with Cleopatra. It was Plutarch who first used the device of describing her approach in the words of Enobarbus; the old soldier who likes telling a good tale, but regrets that one of his best stories concerns a liaison of which he heartily disapproves.

Plutarch must take credit for the barge, 'the poop whereof was of gold, the sails of purple and the oars of silver which kept stroke in rowing after the sound of the music of flutes, howboys, citerns, viols'. Cleopatra herself was 'laid under a pavilion of cloth of gold tissue, apparelled and attired like the goddess Venus commonly drawn in picture and, hard by her, on either hand of her, pretty fair boys apparelled as painters do set forth the god Cupid'. It is, I am sure you will agree, all pretty good stuff. But compare it with what happens when a genius rearranges the words:

> The barge she sat in, like a burnish'd throne,
> Burn'd on the water: the poop was beaten gold;
> Purple the sails . . . the oars were silver,
> Which to the tune of flutes kept stroke, and made
> The water which they beat to follow faster,
> As amorous of their strokes.

The boys became 'dimpled' rather than 'pretty' out of respect for the proper cadence of the English language, and they 'smile like Cupids' instead of looking like a painter's-eye view of little love gods. In one sense it is no more than inspired sub-editing. In another it is a change so total that it alters the nature, not simply the quality, of the narrative. It enables Enobarbus to warm to his hyperbolic work and his audience both to recognise the exaggeration and to be enchanted by the scene which he describes. By the end of the speech, the old soldier begins to believe in his own rhetoric. Not surprisingly, for he is speaking Shakespeare's words. No doubt he, too, would go to any lengths to get tickets for *Antony and Cleopatra*.

Guardian, 25 April 1987

Word Count

For Shakespeare enthusiasts it has been a long cold winter. Just a year ago, *Troilus and Cressida* at the Barbican theatre was set outside Sebastopol during the Crimean War. And we all know what the weather was like there and then. *A Winter's Tale*, on the same stage, took its title so literally that everybody wore white and snowballed each other in order to drive home the seasonal point. *Twelfth Night*, at the Riverside Studios, was played as if the whole action of the play took place between Christmas Day and Epiphany. It actually snowed on stage.

And very good snow it was too. It fell like the gentle dew from heaven and glittered as brightly as Francis Thompson's filigree petals. It was such a good imitation of the real frozen thing that it 'settled' (as we used to say in Yorkshire) and gave a light covering to the various bits of scenery which the actors were required to sit on, or (in the case of Sir Andrew Aguecheek) fall over. When they stood up, or (in the case of Sir Andrew Aguecheek) were lifted to their feet, the synthetic snow stuck damply to their persons in a most realistic way.

It would be quite smart to write that men were all asleep when the snow came flying. It would also be hopelessly wrong. For the spectacular *Twelfth Night* banished sleep – more effectively than even Cawdor could have hoped to do – from the most exhausted member of the audience. And the snow itself caught and held enrapt attention.

For a moment, I wanted to shout – like the *Chorus Line* method actress practising being a toboggan – 'I see the snow. I see the snow.' And there's the rub. I do not want to think about snow falling on to the stage whilst I am watching Shakespeare.

I do not want to think about anything very much except the words. Whatever the weather. *Twelfth Night* has a thin little plot that depends on a couple of incredible coincidences and the principal characters being either so blind or so stupid that they cannot distinguish between men and women.

And *A Winter's Tale* has really very little plot at all. It is the words that count. If artificial snow (no matter how ingenious its preparation and convincing its appearance) distracts from the lines, it should melt and resolve into a dew like Hamlet's too solid flesh.

On the subject of lines especially devised to accommodate Shakespeare's overweight actors, it is worth digressing a moment into *Antony and Cleopatra* at the National Theatre. References to the tubby general's tendency to run to fat actually appear in the text. But although Antony would be classified in a ready-to-wear tailor shop as 'middle-aged portly', at the National Theatre he steps boldly into the centre of the stage and speaks the lines like the hero that he is. Admittedly, at the beginning of the play he rolls about a bit both on the floor and on Cleopatra. But for most of the time, the earthquakes which follow the meeting between one of the great pillars of the world and the serpent of old Nile are chronicled without interruption.

What is more, all the participants are properly dressed. The Romans mix and match the sort of armour that the Legions wore with a compromise between Elizabethan court dress and boiler suits. That is what, over the years, we have come to expect Shakespeare's characters to wear. In Florence, Illyria, Athens, Verona, Elysium, Padua, Venice, the Forest of Arden and Birnam Wood, they're all supposed to look the same. There is a convention in Shakespearian clothes on which we were all brought up. We feel at home with it. It does not build a barrier between the audience and the words.

I admit that I have been particularly sensitive about Shakespearian distractions ever since, as a boy at school, I went to the Sheffield Repertory Theatre to see a special school certificate performance of *Hamlet*. After the Prince of Denmark had interrupted a soliloquy to warn the boys in the stalls that they either shut up or he would, it was impossible to worry about all occasions informing against him. Worse was to come.

When Donald Wolfit's *King Lear* came to Sheffield, I went to see it wearing a pair of brand new shoes. The pain they caused was sharper than a serpent's tooth. Ever since then mention of the play has produced excruciating agony of the instep. I do not say that it is impossible to enjoy Shakespeare with crushed feet, but it is very difficult.

It is almost as difficult to enjoy it with crushed illusions. I recall the famous *Midsummer Night's Dream* of the 1960s which bounded along with wonderful vitality until various kings and courtiers wandered on to the stage swinging pieces of plastic hosepipe.

Those devices were, at the time, immensely popular with children; some of whom preferred them to hula hoops. Their attraction was that when whirled like a lasso, they emitted a noise which faintly resembled a bar of electronic music. It was not, in my view, the stuff that dreams are made on.

I am, of course, open to the accusation that I am not so much in search of dreams as of memories. Like most people, I was introduced to Shakespeare at school, where all the actors stood like stones and lifeless things and the costumes were made from mercifully no longer needed blackout curtains. But I think that a small truth is buried under the nostalgia.

If you could doubt it, go to see *Antony and Cleopatra* (if you can get a ticket) and listen to Enobarbus describing the Queen of Egypt's progress down the Nile. The National Theatre could, in the modern way, have augmented the speech with projections of the barge she sat in flashed on the screen at the back of the stage. Instead they let the poetry speak for itself. The words were worth a thousand pictures. That is how Shakespeare ought to be. We ought to listen to him.

Guardian, 23 January 1988

The Real Enemy of the People

Years ago, before the patricians of the Tory Party were driven into political exile by Conservative property developers, I sat behind Alec Douglas Home in the stalls of the Savoy Theatre. Together, in a separate sort of way, we laughed uproariously at Ralph Richardson confusing masons of the stone-carving variety with Masons who roll up their trouser legs, perform ridiculous rituals and claim that it is all done for charity.

During the interval one of Sir Alec's aides approached me as if we were old friends and happened to mention that, if I wondered why the Foreign Secretary was spending such a frivolous evening, the answer was to be found on the front of my programme. I had seen that technique in action many times before – the casual manner intended to conceal the carefully laid plan. What is more, in common with the rest of the audience, I knew that the author of *The Chiltern Hundreds* was the great man's brother.

As far as I was concerned no apology was needed. If, one day, we have a written constitution in this country, it must include a clause which requires all ministers to take an active interest in reading and writing as well as arithmetic. I would make a weekly book and a monthly play a compulsory part of the Prime Minister's duties. A panel of Privy Councillors should be called together to prepare both a reading list and a theatre guide. In an ideal world, it would meet under my chairmanship. Were we to assemble before the end of the year, I would insist that Margaret Thatcher went to see *An Enemy of the People* at the Playhouse Theatre.

That play begins with a straightforward, if slightly simplistic, attack on the privatisation of water. A town is about to become a spa, and build its prosperity on healing the sick, when its mayor (and chairman of the development company) is told that the natural springs are polluted.

In order to cut investment cost, they have been tapped too close to the town and below a tannery which pumps out lethal effluent. The bad news is borne by the mayor's idealistic, but irresponsible, brother; doctor to the spa. An independent survey confirms that the water is polluted and the scene is set for public good to wrestle with private greed. It is just the thing to send me rejoicing to the bar at the end of act one.

As *An Enemy of the People* was written by Ibsen, what follows is rather more complicated than a conflict between good and evil staged in the manner of a pre-war western film. Indeed the brilliance of the play lies in its characters possessing a bewildering combination of virtues and vices – not unusual characteristics in our families and friends, but a rarer phenomenon on stage where black is too often pitch, and white almost always driven snow. Indeed, the only characters who are wholly and unequivocally wicked are the politician and the journalist. And who will quarrel with that as a mirror of real life?

When I heard the politician explain that he was lying to preserve the town's prosperity and the journalist describe why suppressing the truth was necessary to save his paper from bankruptcy, I remembered a line from Carl Sandberg: '. . . I have seen his face a thousand times before.'

By the time of the second interval, *An Enemy of the People* has changed from an examination of commercial morality into a study of something far more complex. Dr Stockman – determined to expose the scandal – inspires, infuriates and intimidates in turn. Mrs Stockman – simultaneously anxious to support her husband and protect her family – excites both sympathy and irritation. It is her duty as a wife loyally to mount the barricades. But it is her obligation as a mother to fear for her children's welfare. And it is her right as a thinking human being to be afraid of what results from enthusiasm that turns into irresponsibility.

The small businessmen try to stick to their principles without upsetting the established order. A sea captain keeps the faith. But he is from a different world. Sacked from one ship he can always sail off in another. When Dr Stockman is evicted from his ransacked house, the captain's quarters are easily put at his disposal. For the captain spends little time in the land of avarice, deceit and betrayal.

Having established the point that good is not always as virtuous as it seems and vice is not always unequivocally evil, the author was ready to question the principle which dominated radical society, reverence for majority rule. Strict reference to the context requires the concession that Ibsen's assault upon democracy was specifically targeted on decisions for which democracy is wholly inappropriate – the chemical composition of water, the shape of the earth and its relationship to the sun and the strategy of an advancing regiment. I may be struck by Thor's thunderbolt for saying such a thing, but Ibsen's military analogy is, therefore, false. The scout, out on reconnaissance, must know what the body of men following behind do not. In matters of science, the majority may (by definition) be ignorant. But that is not the argument against general democracy.

I find the cult of the superman, particularly the scientific superman, deeply alarming. But – to pursue the military metaphor – the notion that a few understand what the many may not is only Ibsen's approach march. The battle concerns whether or not a majority can reasonably claim that democracy requires it to suppress the views of its critics, opponents, and anyone who gives them succour and support. For telling the truth – the inconvenient and expensive truth – Dr Stockman is sacked and dispossessed. Because of his reckless disregard for vested interest, his sons are sent home from school, bullied and beaten, his daughter loses the job she loves and his wife is denied her inheritance.

The truth is prohibited by ballot and its exponents are vilified and persecuted by reasonable people acting with proper moderation.

An Enemy of the People is about an elective dictatorship – even though it was written a hundred years before the phrase was coined. That is why my Christmas wish is for Mrs Thatcher to sit in the royal circle of the Playhouse Theatre and watch the story unfold.

The programme tells us that George F. Kaufman advised any playwright with a message to send it by Western Union. For years, the Prime Minister has not been accepting telegrams from her political opponents.

Ibsen is one of the few arguments which we have left.

Guardian, 17 December 1988

Every Day a Little Delight

Stephen Sondheim is coming back to town. *A Little Night Music*, triumphant in Chichester, will soon be wowing the West End. At least, I think that it will. It certainly deserves rave reviews and adoring audiences. But Mr Sondheim proved with *Anyone Can Whistle* and the first version of *Follies* that it is possible for a play to be a total triumph and the audience a complete disaster. His problem is simply explained. He expects the paying customers to think – an unusual experience in the stalls during a typical Broadway musical. Worse, he occasionally suggests that boy meets girl can sometimes be the beginning of a story without a happy ending. That is not the ideal note on which to complete an expensive night out.

A Little Night Music has a happy ending of a sort, even though love's victory is accompanied by death and desertion on stage. But it has a paradox rather than a laugh a line and, when trousers fall down, it is irony not farce which releases the forces of gravity. You can enjoy a Sondheim musical in whatever way you choose. The plots are built around life's contradiction. But the music is so romantic that it fills the air with enough emotion to set off the automatic fire alarms. He is the composer for all seasons. Throughout this Labour Party conference week, I have hummed the finale to *Night Music*'s first act – 'every day a little death'.

It was sycophancy of that superior quality which made me pay court to Mr Sondheim while I was in New York a couple of years ago. I visited him at home in one of those massive stone houses which look as though they were written by Henry James. It boasted a garden with trees, above which the lights of Manhattan skyscrapers twinkled like stage stars. Impertinently I asked how anyone could afford to buy an oasis in the middle of the world's most expensive concrete desert. '*Gypsy*,' he told me. '*Gypsy* paid for it.' The house next door was bought for half the price, twenty years earlier. '*Woman of the Year* paid for that one,' Mr Sondheim said. His neighbour is called Katharine Hepburn.

Gauche though I knew my behaviour to be, I stumbled about the dark garden, staring in the direction of the curtained window in the hope of seeing a silhouette of that incomparable profile. I tripped over several roots, bumped into numerous stone urns and bruised myself on various items of garden furniture. It did not matter. My abandon was not the product of infatuation alone. That night, a few more humiliations were neither here nor there.

I had been greeted on my arrival chez Sondheim by a lady who welcomed me in what I took to be fluent Serbo-Croat. Despite my lack of competence in that language, I gathered from her gestures that I should sit on the sofa in the ground-floor drawing room and help myself from a large bottle of white wine. As I poured my first glass, someone in the room above me began to play the piano and

I wallowed in the theatrical cliché that was going on around me. I went on wallowing for the next hour – though the extent to which I wallowed gradually diminished as the minutes ticked away. After ninety minutes the wine and my patience were both exhausted.

Although my sycophancy had been stretched perilously close to breaking point, it did not quite go twang. Faced with the choice between insulting my hero and continuing to endure his apparent contempt, I did what any civilised man would have done. I planned an elaborate lie. Tearing a page from my diary, I began to draft a message concerning a desperate, and much regretted, need to honour an urgent engagement. My lies having been committed to paper, I was about to wedge the note into a crack in the banister when Stephen Sondheim appeared in dishevelled glory at the top of the stairs. 'No more auditions tonight,' he said. 'There's an Englishman coming to see me.'

The apologies were profuse and reinforced by a second bottle of wine which – despite its damp and dirty condition – Mr Sondheim placed on the polished top of an antique table. Wanting to save him from his folly without acknowledging his confusion, I unobtrusively moved the bottle on to one of the highly decorated mats which seemed to have been provided to protect the varnish. Unfortunately my host noticed the thoughtful action and firmly replaced the dripping bottle on the table. 'That,' he said, 'is not a coaster. It is a seventeenth century Florentine puzzle.' He began to dab it with his handkerchief.

It was then that we went out into the garden and walked under the synthetic stars which might have illuminated the dreams of a summer night. Mr Sondheim suggested a visit to an off-Broadway musical which satirised on-Broadway shows. At the beginning of the second act, a dishevelled figure – almost identical to the man who had confused me with a mendicant tenor – appeared in the spotlight and parodied *A Little Night Music*'s most famous song in a tribute to the Sondheim commercial failures:

> *I thought that they'd like what I write. Sorry my dear.*
> *Where are the crowds?*
> *There ought to be crowds.*

Anyone who encourages jokes at his own expense exhibits a self-effacing self-confidence which guarantees an honourable mention in this column. If the paragon also writes marvellous music and weaves it round interesting ideas he gets a positive commendation. Stephen Sondheim is coming to town! Undeterred by our previous meetings, I shall be there cheering. Do yourself a favour and buy a ticket for *A Little Night Music*.

Guardian, 7 October 1989

Tickling the Twilight Zone

This year at Stratford, Susan Fleetwood plays a dashingly mature Beatrice. I mean the description to be wholly complimentary. To be described as dashing is such obvious praise that my adverb does not need to be defended against the charge of lacking chivalry. On the other hand, maturity is often only regarded as a virtue in cheddar cheese, malt whisky and the opinions of elderly men which lack all daring and imagination. But in *Much Ado About Nothing*, Miss Fleetwood makes maturity a quality which puts callow girls to shame. Her performance is consistent with the text. For Lady Disdain has seen more of the world than either Juliet or Ophelia have experienced. What is more, it puts middle-aged men in the audience at their ease. We know Benedick is an idiot to reject her right into the final act. But we do not feel the embarrassment of identifying with Melvyn Bragg's bank manager in pursuit of his teenage fantasy.

It is almost twenty years since I saw Miss Fleetwood in *The Playboy of the Western World*. She was, I have no doubt, magnificent. But all I can remember about that production is a question about the play asked of me by the guest of the government whom I had, out of duty, escorted to the National Theatre. 'Tell me,' the Shah of Persia's sister demanded, 'do I understand the plot rightly? A man hopes to become a hero by pretending that he has beaten his father to death with a shovel. What a strange place Ireland is.' If Miss Fleetwood had looked then as she looks now, it would not have been Iran's 'dragon lady' nor her judgment on that most distressful country which I remembered best about the production.

The Comedy of Errors is also in this year's Stratford repertoire. Antipholus of Syracuse and Antipholus of Ephesus are both played, until almost the very end, by the same actor. He is also mature. In fact – since he is a man and can, therefore, be described without any concession to gallantry – I do not hesitate to say that he might just pass for forty-two in the dusk with the light behind him. Yet he is pursued by his sister-in-law with a panting passion which millions of lean youths must long to experience.

From all this I conclude that middle age is coming back into theatrical fashion. Andrew Lloyd Webber is lucky that he was saved by a company lawyer's lisp from setting up the Really Youthful Company. From now on he should adopt names like Past It, Twilight, Wrinkles and Aging Gracefully.

It is only recently that the cult of youth has so dominated our lives that actors and actresses have had to counterfeit an infant vitality which had long since died. Sarah Bernhardt did some of her best work whilst handicapped with the infirmity of a wooden leg. As Hamlet duels with Horatio, Gertrude describes him as 'fat and scant of breath' in order to justify the part being played by a less than sprightly actor. To hammer the point home, Hamlet himself prayed that his too, too solid flesh would melt. If the play had been written 350 years later, most directors would have insisted on cutting the line out and sending Edmund Kean to a health farm for a month to make sure he got into his tights.

Admittedly, the evidence obtained from two matinées at Stratford-upon-Avon is slim. (Note the pejorative use of the word.) But I based a theory upon it. Society is beginning to abandon its worship of the young and emaciated. Theatres which want to flaunt their connection with William Shakespeare will soon remove 'All the world's a stage' from the scroll above the presidium arch and replace it with 'Let me have men about me that are fat' or simply 'Infinite variety'. That, you will remember, is not the promise of the last word in vaudeville but a reminder that age had not withered Cleopatra.

Neither had it brought wisdom to her or to Mark Antony. But that is the glory of their story. Both of them are old enough to know better. Romeo and Juliet should have been taken into care under a local authority supervision order. Ophelia caused all the problems that are usually associated with an adolescent girl's secret infatuation with an older man. But Antony was one of the pillars on which the world stood and Cleopatra was Queen of Old Nile. Both of them, as Plutarch might have put it, had been around a bit. Yet they were still ready – indeed determined – to demonstrate that life begins rather later than forty.

I am beginning to believe that Shakespeare – despite having done much of his best work while he was still young enough to play in goal for England – was a 'youthist', that is to say, prejudiced against the young. Henry V turned from idiot to hero. Othello might well have become Chief of the Imperial Venetian General Staff had it not been for a girl young enough to be his daughter. Falstaff's one attractive moment is when he announces that he no longer hangs about waiting to hear the chimes at midnight.

Beatrice – certainly as played by Susan Fleetwood – makes a similar point in a slightly different way. Wisdom comes with the years and (although it brings with it a couple of grey hairs) the package is well worth having. There may have been juveniles in the audience who actually admired the schoolgirl wit, the counterfeit contempt and the synthetic anger of act one. But none of those characteristics marked Beatrice out as an ideal partner with whom to enter an old people's home. The sensible Beatrice of act five decides to settle down and live happily ever after. That is real wisdom and it only comes with age.

Guardian, 30 June 1990

Dark Side of the Street

Last Wednesday Alec took his wife Bet to his daughter's birthday party. Father and only child had been estranged for over twenty years and, during those two decades, a lot of water has flowed along the Ship Canal. The small-time theatrical impresario has become landlord of the Rover's Return and the woman whom he described as his 'little girl' has made the social ascent from Salford back street to detached suburbia. Alec was anxious to impress his newly acquired son-in-law and apprehensive about Bet behaving like the barmaid she used to be. Inevitably (in the patois of his childhood) he showed himself up and let himself down.

The birthday present was a particular error. It was accompanied by what we can only suspect was a birthday card of the cute variety, for the smaller of the two gift-wrapped boxes was not opened. The larger one contained a picture of the sort which is purchased, not in an exclusive gallery, but in the fancy goods department of a large department store. Alec's daughter expressed her ironic gratitude in crude sarcasm which was, fortunately, too subtle for her father to recognise.

I suspect that millions of *Coronation Street* viewers admired the picture and, like me, marvelled at its recipient's ingratitude. But I am less certain how they reacted to the humiliations which were heaped on Alec's bald head. His son-in-law mispronounced his name – calling him (thanks to the meticulous writing which characterises the programme) by the middle-class variant which ends with an x, not a c. His daughter was openly hostile. And Bet, who admittedly has had a lot to put up with recently, did not even try to hide her contempt. In the past I have never liked Alec. Last Wednesday, I was totally on his side.

That is, I suppose, because during the last half-dozen years I have not climbed the social ladder with the speed and determination which *Coronation Street* has displayed during its years of remorseless upward mobility. Mike Baldwin's sweat shop has been demolished to make way for flats and maisonettes, and the profits from the sale badly invested in Spanish property. Curly Watts has become a management trainee. Alf and Audrey Roberts are looking for a house in a more desirable neighbourhood. Derek Wilton is obsessed with status and his wife, Mavis, although not quite sure what all the fuss is about, is wholly behind her husband in his quest for managerial respect. Ken Barlow – as his haircut proves, still the Peter Pan of soap operas – is no longer the programme's sole representative of the middle classes. It is all a long way from Ena Sharples's hairnet.

That is not the only change to have come about in the Street during the last ten years. We had a murder of sorts in the 1970s when Emily Bishop's husband was mugged. And we have had plenty of passion over the years as Elsie Tanner enjoyed enough amours to fill several hotel bookshop paperbacks. But the programme remained essentially gentle and almost invariably optimistic. Alan Bradley could not have inhabited the same world as Albert Tatlock. Len Fairclough was a rogue, but not a villain. *Coronation Street* has become harder as well as more middle class.

There will be those who argue that the characteristics of a three-times-a-week television serial are not a matter of any consequence. They will be wrong. In the early days of the programme, Richard Hoggart compared it to sliced bread – pre-wrapped and containing a special ingredient which meant that although it was slow to turn stale it was never quite fresh. He advocated the consumption of wholesome, stone-ground, genuine wholemeal. Even if his judgment was right, it was harsh. But at least he conceded that *Coronation Street* is the staff of life. There are other programmes which are so unrelated to anything which goes on in our daily life that they could not be credibly compared with anything which might be found on a normal breakfast table. That is why the changes in its tone and content are important. *Coronation Street* may not influence the nation's conduct, but it is a reflection of the country's behaviour. Not for nothing did Alan Bradley hope to make his fortune by setting up a security business. During the years when we have begun to pay for everything with credit cards, we have also begun to double-lock our front doors and display burglar alarm bells alongside our bay windows. *Coronation Street* is a caricature, but it is a caricature of the way we live now.

Caricatures can be either benign or malevolent and *Coronation Street* still comes in the kindlier of the two categories. Brian Tilsley may have behaved like an absolute swine. But his mother still loves him. And Gail's conduct would certainly scandalise middle-aged drinkers in most public houses. Yet even as the characters have hardened and become more prosperous, most of them have retained their warmth, hope and charity. Percy Sugden is infuriatingly helpful. All the Street rallied round when Rita Fairclough had her nervous breakdown. Slip on a piece of tripe in Coronation

Street and there is a collection box on the bar of the Rover's Return before you get back from hospital with the X-ray results. How different from the home life of our own dear *EastEnders*.

Twenty years ago, four out of five episodes of *Coronation Street* ended in a way which made me feel more hopeful about the world than I did when the programme began. Miss Nugent left Mr Swindley at the altar, but Jack and Annie Walker struggled on together into the twilight. Now, the feel-good ratio is down to no more than 50 per cent. And being depressed by *Coronation Street* depresses me in general. For I fear that, just as it mirrors changes in the social composition of society, it may also provide a more or less accurate reflection of the change from optimism to cynicism, which is the second characteristic of the last two decades.

There are some nights when, at eight o'clock, I have only one consolation. Speaking with a patronising, surprised superiority of which Ken Barlow would be proud, I say: 'Bloody good, wasn't it?'

Guardian, 1 January 1991

So Simply Serpentine

I expect to be struck down by a thunderbolt as the punishment for saying it, but I have begun to suspect that Dryden's *All For Love* is a better play than Shakespeare's *Antony and Cleopatra*. Of course, it lacks the poetry. There is no Enobarbus to teach Thomas North and Plutarch how they should have described the pomp and circumstance of the lass unparalleled. But, paradoxically, that is one of its strengths. Dryden described two middle-aged people with a problem. That is not the easiest way of holding an audience's attention but, done well, such simple stories are particularly appealing to those of us who rejoice in an unheroic turn of mind.

There is only limited merit in making the commonplace interesting. On television every evening of the week, soap operas attempt the task, with varying degrees of success. Dryden performed a more difficult and more complex trick. He first demonstrated the obvious truth that neither Roman triumvirs nor descendants of Ptolemy can escape the agony of common emotions. Then he showed how destructive, noble, and irresistible those common emotions can be. Though gods they were, as men they died. Or is it the other way round? I can never remember. *All For Love* has done nothing to clear my mind.

Shakespeare's Antony describes his love in the language of a man who rules one-third of all the world. 'Let Rome in Tiber melt and the wide arch of the rang'd empire fall. Here is my space.' Dryden's Antony postpones his desertion to explain how hurt he would be if Cleopatra were to take up with anyone else. One Cleopatra has immortal longings; the other complains that her paramour is using his children as an excuse for not leaving his wife. And Dryden's doomed lovers make no theatrical gestures of self-sacrifice. They are admirably demanding, properly selfish.

Admittedly Dryden fails to reproduce the attendant unpleasantness with the skill that Shakespeare employs. The Elizabethan Cleopatra requires her friends to be unpleasant about Antony's wife, and Antony himself spits out one of the bitterest gobbets of abuse ever to spatter the English language: 'I found you as a morsel, cold upon dead Caesar's trencher.'

But the audience is still left with the feeling that the lovers are star-crossed more by their rank and responsibility than by their character failings. It is character failings which have a universal interest. Dryden succeeds by making all talk about honour and duty sound like an excuse for not taking the final risk and not making the total commitment.

That is not to suggest that Dryden's lovers lack nobility. It is Shakespeare's Antony who longs to be with Cleopatra when they are apart, and chafes to return to Rome when together: a bad attack of what Stephen Sondheim called 'The-tell-me-that-you-love-me-Oh-you-did-I'll-see-you-later blues'.

Estranged from Cleopatra, Dryden's Antony seems to console himself with the thought that it was while he was 'in her arms' that the world 'fell mouldering from my hands'. But he cannot wait for the disintegration to start all over again. Without her, the universe – whole or crumbling – is no more than 'a black desert at the approach of night'.

Indeed Antony needs Cleopatra so badly that Dryden's title makes sense only if the world is defined as no more than power, wealth and prestige. If the world they wanted was simply happiness, they could easily have won it; all that prevented them was an unfortunate breakdown in communications and an overdramatic reaction to what, on the evidence of past follies, would have been no more than another temporary hiatus in their relationship.

I never feel that at the end of *Antony and Cleopatra*. Perhaps I lose sympathy because of all that nonsense about the pulleys heaving the dying lovers 'aloft' (as the stage directions demand) to the top of a convenient tower. Or I may suffer from anti-rugby-club prejudice, which makes me doubt if anyone who does all that singing and drinking on Pompey's galley could be the possessor of finer feelings.

I always want to tell Shakespeare's Antony to pull himself together and get on with the important business of sharing the world with Lepidus and Octavius Caesar. Dryden's Antony stimulates different emotions. He needs somebody to put an arm round his shoulder and tell him the important thing is to be happy, that nothing else really matters.

It all provides more evidence for my conviction that an account of the consequences of commonplace emotions is the most interesting sort of writing. I make no claim about its importance in the canons of literature, but it does help the reader to understand the ways of the real world. Thomas Hardy wrote something about 'war's annals clouding into night' before the simple stories died. Antony and Cleopatra's story ought to be told 'no less in pity than in glory'. Shakespeare said it, but it was Dryden who accepted the advice.

Guardian, 17 August 1991

Pooterish Pratfall from Shakespearian Heights

The Prime Minister was at it again last week – quoting from Shakespeare in a way which makes intellectually fastidious Members of Parliament (Gerald Kaufman and me) cringe with hugely enjoyable, more or less genuine and meticulously choreographed embarrassment. In the secret depths of his being, Douglas Hurd no doubt cringes too. But collective responsibility requires him to be a covert cringer.

We are able to relieve our injured feelings with contemptuous looks and dismissive gestures. He must resist all temptation to moan and scream. One day, the suppressed disdain will explode and scatter particles of justified intellectual snobbery all over the government front bench.

John Major's relationship with William Shakespeare is complicated by a couple of problems for which the Swan of Avon is in no way to blame. The Prime Minister speaks the lines in a way which is only appropriate for one of Peter Quince's rude mechanicals. And he prefaces his quotations with Pooterisms which, although intended to make his erudition sound spontaneous, serve only to render the charade ridiculous.

'As I recall my Shakespeare ...' and 'If I remember Shakespeare aright...' were bad enough. But last Wednesday, he confessed, 'I seem to believe that Hamlet said something like...' He might as well have asked, do I sleep or dream?

Charitable persons may argue that he could not begin, 'My private secretary, having searched the dictionary of quotations...' But such a frank admission would be no more risible than the pretence of intimate acquaintance with the Folio of 1623. It is time that a supplementary questioner asked him to set out the context or declaim the next line. Fortunately, the Prime Minister did not take part in Friday's tenants' rights debate. Had he done so we would have probably been told to 'see what a rent the envious Casca made'.

More important than Mr Major's particular faults are the pitfalls which his show of learning illustrates – booby traps into which we all deserve to fall if we choose to spew out a word or two of undigested genius without knowing (or even attempting to find out) what the full passage meant. On Wednesday the House of Commons was offered a sentence which, since it was untimely ripped from its proper place on the page, had only one literary merit. It was an example of pure bathos. 'At least, I am sure it may be so in Denmark' is, on its own, not so much a dying fall as a dead duck.

That line – in itself virtually meaningless – is the coda to a speech of savage power:

> *O most pernicious woman!*
> *O villain, villain, smiling damned villain!*
> *My tables, meet it is I set it down,*
> *That one may smile and smile, and be a villain.*

With Margaret Thatcher in her present humour and the Tory Party in a mood of post-Maastricht revolt, quoting the whole speech might have been regarded as deliberate provocation. Perhaps discretion is the better part of literary valour.

But if the job had to be done so badly, it should not have been done at all. Quoting from *Hamlet* was so obvious an addition to a speech on Denmark that it could only have been justified by a stunningly apposite quotation which came out of the speaker's head, not from a reference book. Dictionaries should be used to check, not to find, the right words.

Finding an appropriate bit of Shakespeare is too easy an occupation to be interesting. For Shakespeare said something about everything. Everyone who speaks in the next Maastricht debate could quote Shakespeare on the Danes without any fear of tedious repetition. The word Denmark appears nineteen times in the collected works; fourteen in verse and five in prose. On three other occasions it is apostrophised – once to denote the absence of a verb and twice to signify possession.

Since Denmark had co-operated with Britain in holding Europe back, Euro-sceptics could tell the Foreign Secretary, 'Let thine eyes look like a friend' towards that country, Federalists could insist that 'something is rotten' in that state. And it is not only the direct references that are relevant to our present discontents. Between 'more honoured in the breach than the observance' and 'how all occasions do inform against me', the Prime Minister had all of *Hamlet* at his disposal.

Similar choices can be made on every day of the week. Last Tuesday we gave the Finance Bill its second reading – at the end of which, 'the commons had been pill'd with grievous taxes' (*Richard II*). Wednesday was Earth Summit day, when we all promised not to 'make sop of all this solid globe' (*Troilus and Cressida*). On Thursday we debated community care – a system which was introduced 'rather than suffer questions for your residence' (*All's Well That Ends Well*). Today we discuss fishing. 'Fish' accounts for 0.0053 per cent of Shakespeare's total output. All that this afternoon's speeches need to give them a spurious literary connection is a Concordance and the mind of a philistine. My advice to those who are tempted – and to the Prime Minister – comes (almost) from Cole Porter. Don't brush up your Shakespeare. Stop quoting him now.

Guardian, 8 June 1992

Blue Rhapsody on the Pure Joys of Gershwin

When *Crazy For You* moves from Broadway to Shaftesbury Avenue, I shall be there on opening night – standing on the pavement outside the theatre, mounting a one-man demonstration against its production in London. My complaint will not concern the right of English Equity members to obtain employment in their own country. Nor will it be a protest against white actors being cast in black parts. I shall be there – home-made banner in hand – in my capacity as self-appointed life president of the George and Ira Gershwin protection society.

Crazy For You is based loosely – perhaps pendulously would be a better word – on *Girl Crazy*, the 1930 Gershwin hit. Like all good inter-war musicals *Girl Crazy* was built around an absurd story. Danny Churchill, accused by his father of wasting his time on wine and women, is removed from Princeton and enrolled in an agricultural college in Custerville, Arizona – a one-horse town which has the same number of women as horses. The one woman is Molly Gray, cow-girl and postmistress. Boy meets girl. Boy loses girl. Boy and girl are united and live happily ever after. Fortunately they both can sing.

With a plot like that, the show has to be carried by the words and music. So when – during one of the afternoons when the Democratic Convention did not meet because the television was otherwise engaged – I went to see *Crazy For You*, I wept no glycerine tears over the pointless changes which had been made to Bolton and McGowan's book. I sat back and waited for the glorious noise. What I got was quantity rather than quality.

Snatches of song from *Girl Crazy* were interspersed with fragments of songs from other Gershwin shows. But nothing was developed in the way which the Gershwins intended. Before one melody was absorbed, another tune pushed it out of the way. And, since most of the verses were omitted completely, the funniest and most poignant lyrics were cut out of the show in favour of brief choruses. Only one song – 'Loving Her' – was given the full and extended treatment. And that was so transcendently successful that it was difficult to comprehend why the director chose to chop everything else up and spit it out in little pieces.

Even more difficult to understand was why the director thought he was a greater authority on the works of George and Ira Gershwin than the Gershwins were themselves. What made him think that he could produce a better Gershwin musical than the Gershwins produced? It was Ravel himself who asked George, 'Why do you want to become a second-rate Ravel when you can be the first-rate Gershwin?' The man who cobbled together *Crazy For You* thought that Gershwin was a second-rate him. It is a sort of impertinence that is practised far too often on stage these days.

Nobody in his right mind objects to new plays being made from old. *The Comedy of Errors* is not an affront to the *Menaechmi* of Plautus and the *Boys from Syracuse* is a credit to them both. That is because neither Shakespeare nor the Rodgers and Hart musical was made up of bits and pieces from the parent work. They were theatre in their own right. Lorenz Hart was good. But he did not believe that he could improve on 'Come I will fasten on this sleeve of thine/Thou art an elm, my husband, I the vine'. So he thought of something quite different to carry the plot over the same hurdle. 'I heard from a wise canary, trilling makes a fellow willing/So, little swallow, swallow now.' Hart did not produce a pastiche but a new variation on the old theme.

The problem of pastiche is that the pieces rarely hang together to form a coherent whole. In the original *Girl Crazy*, 'Bidin' My Time' goes on for several choruses with the singers gradually falling asleep. In *Crazy For You* it becomes a high-speed yawn. The fun that the verse pokes at songs of indomitable happiness is not so much lost as thrown away. Without 'Some Fellas Love to Tiptoe through the Tulips . . .' and the subsequent contempt for 'Singing in the Rain', 'Painting the Skies with Sunshine' and 'Swinging Down the Lane', 'Bidin' My Time' becomes just another song.

The excuse for all this carnage is buried in the phrase 'bringing up to date'. In the name of that dubious objective Bizet's toreador becomes a heavyweight boxer. *Hamlet* is played in modern dress, Hedda Gabler shoots herself at the beginning of the play and the story of her growing dementia becomes a flashback, Peter Pan grows up into a businessman and rock versions are created of everything from Gilbert and Sullivan to sung mass. It is all hideously reminiscent of Neil Simon's *Goodbye Girl* in which an off-Broadway production of *Richard III* makes the eponymous villain gay in order to attract the attention of newspapers.

If *Girl Crazy* as originally written is not good enough to attract present day audiences, it should be filed away in the museum of old musicals and something brand new ought to be written to fill the theatres of London and New York. On the other hand, if it is as good as I believe it to be, it deserves to be revived intact. When *Crazy For You* comes to London I shall parade outside the first night with a banner which reads 'Gershwin Is Good Enough'.

Guardian, 27 July 1992

An Avenging Angel in the Alhambra Spotlight

For anyone who lives in London – and goes too rarely to the West End theatre – Bradford is a long way to travel simply for the pleasures of seeing a play. But I wanted to enjoy *An Inspector Calls* in its proper setting. I read from the programme notes that 'because of the unavailability of a suitable theatre' the play was first produced in Moscow and then, more than a year later, opened in London. But its natural home is the Bradford Alhambra. That magnificently bizarre building has been so comprehensively restored that it no longer looks like one of J. B. Priestley's 'Lost Empires'. But the evening's performance was the climax to an expedition which I thought of as Bruddersford Revisited.

The town hall in *The Good Companions* is 'a noble building in the Italian Renaissance style which always looks as if it has no right to be there'. Bradford's Victorian-Gothic extravaganza would only be completely at home in Camelot. Inside, the impression of fantasy is heightened by the perfect replica of the whole confection which stands at the top of the grand staircase. But, a couple of paces down any of the corridors, the visitors expect to meet the councillors and aldermen of *When We Are Married* – equally opposed to argy-bargy, hanky-panky and anything that is lah-di-dah.

These days, architects design churches that look like offices. In nineteenth-century Bradford they built offices to look like cathedrals. The tower of the Wool Exchange is now inhabited by the essential services of the nervous nineties – guidance, counselling and advice. And the great hall – in which men once argued over Sydney Greasy Futures – was locked and dark. But beyond the pointed glass panels of the doors, I could see the arches which hold up what can only be called a nave. Through the dusk, there was the faint glimmer of stained glass. In Victorian Bradford they must have haggled over wool prices in reverential whispers.

A different set of venerable values is represented in the

159

Alhambra. The majestic auditorium is higher than it is wide and the muses gaze down from murals above the stage and over the boxes. They are half-naked girls – barely, if at all, above the age of consent. It seemed just the right setting for a play about the double standards of middle-class morality and the hypocrisy of conventional respectability.

An Inspector Calls begins as an apparently traditional – and tautly constructed – detective story. It turns into a morality play. The arguments about its merits all turn on a single point. Is its message – that we are all members, one of another – delivered with the subtlety that comes from surprise or driven home like a six-inch nail? The Alhambra production set out to end the dispute, once and for all, by hammering away so hard that it flattened some of the sharpest parts of the dialogue.

The eponymous Inspector Goole is an avenging angel who confronts the Briling family with descriptions of the way in which each one of them has contributed to the death of a poor and pregnant girl. Their punishment is remorse, mutual mistrust and the consequent breakdown of their comfortable little community. Only at the end, when a telephone message warns that a real inspector is on his way, should we realise that Goole is not a detective with ideas above his station and a degree in sociology. But at the Alhambra he was supernatural from start to finish – calling down celestial spotlights to illuminate his victims and summoning representatives of the toiling masses to support his set speeches. They stood silent, and no doubt embarrassed, that they were required to wear the clothes of the 1940s in a play which, according to the dialogue, takes place in 1912.

Priestley meant the play to take place in the claustrophobic Brilings' sitting room. At the Alhambra, their whole house stood like a gypsy caravan in the middle of the stage and, one by one, the family ducked out of its tiny front door and clambered down to the cobblestones in order to confront the inspector. The audience clapped when the curtain went up. In my experience, it is always a bad sign when the set gets a round of applause. Like the best sort of football referee, scenery ought to contribute to the success of the action without intruding upon it.

An old-fashioned telephone kiosk made a fine splash of colour at the corner of the stage. But the dialogue does not explain why a prosperous middle-class family chose to use it instead of dialling from home. The answer is that they live in a doll's house on stilts which has been tipped up to illustrate the collapse of their world – just in case the playwright had failed to make the point clear in his text. Priestley's work was also enhanced by the creation of what amounted to an extra character. Edna, the servant, became Everycrone. She is on stage throughout, and for much of the time gives a silent imitation of Munch's 'Scream'. She was entitled – as was the rest of the intrinsically splendid cast – to ask a simple question: 'Why are they doing this to me?'

Part of the answer is provided by the programme. The director wanted his audience to understand the play's purpose. But that does not explain or excuse the decision to make its message more crudely obvious than Priestley intended. A great play and fine actors were done a disservice because of the desire to be new and different. Had the director spent a day looking at the Bradford Town Hall, the Wool Exchange or even the auditorium of the Alhambra Theatre, he might have realised that some works of genius are better left as their creators intended.

Guardian, 7 December 1992

The Soap Won't Wash

I stopped believing in *Coronation Street* in January when Tracy – once a disturbed adolescent, but now a teenage vamp – assailed her mother with the accusation of long-concealed adultery. The confrontation was conducted in the clichés of outrage. 'How could you?' the distraught daughter asked. 'How could you do it?' Ever since she asked the agonised question, I have fantasised about the pure bliss of Deirdre Barlow, estranged wife of the eternally youthful Ken, giving an honest answer.

'You were too young to understand how desperate we were in those days. Ratings were falling. The BBC had launched a rival soap. I felt dirty and I felt humiliated. But we had to live. Don't you dare judge me. If I hadn't have gone to bed with Mike Baldwin, you'd be auditioning for Baby June in the revival of *Gypsy* for the Blackpool summer season.'

The sudden disillusion marked a deterioration in the programme rather than an improvement in me. I still long for Elsie Tanner. But Gresham's Law of Soaps has driven the good programmes downmarket in pursuit of the bad. Everybody in *Neighbours* speaks as if the last thing that happened to them was a complete surprise. *EastEnders* seems to believe that anything that is depressing must also be realistic.

The Street can still produce moments which make viewers sit on the edge of their sofas. When Terry confronted Des at Lisa Duckworth's funeral, I really thought that they would jump into the open grave and grapple with each other across the body of the woman they had loved and lost. The idea would not have been original. But it would have been easily enough done. Before Laertes could leap on to Ophelia's corpse he had to urge the Elsinore gravediggers to 'hold off the earth a while'. But the obliging verger at the Granada cemetery did not begin 'to pile dust upon the dead' until Granada's camera had zoomed in on the silver coffin plate and Des's single rose.

Naturally enough, Terry was furious that his wife's lover had turned up at the cemetery. But his threats lacked the elegant menace of Hamlet's 'Yet have I in me something dangerous.'

A comparison between Shakespeare and *Coronation Street* is not as absurd as it first appears. William Shakespeare was the popular dramatist of his age. The audiences who cheered Coriolanus, booed Shylock and shouted warnings to Thisbe about the lion, would have laughed at the suggestion that their favourite playwright would one day be regarded as only suitable for highbrows and examinations. The tragic truth is that Shakespeare and the army of writers who produce our daily lather of soaps have a quality in common which, paradoxically, makes their work chalk and cheese. The Globe produced plays which reflected the spirit of its age. Its audience wanted heroism heroically expressed and villains who represented mortal sin. Granada and the BBC make soaps which do the same. *Coronation Street* and *EastEnders* viewers expect suburban adultery, social security fraud and grievous bodily harm.

It is all very modern but, to me at least, it is no longer moving. *Romeo and Juliet* is not the best play in the world. But think of how the contemporary comparison reaches its unhappy climax. Samantha Mitchell and Ricky Butcher – forbidden by their families to marry – ran away together and created one of *EastEnders'* few tender moments. Grant and Phil, the bride's brothers grim, turned briefly human.

It all ended in tears, as everything does in and around the Queen Vic. But who cares? Juliet, killing herself rather than face life without Romeo, was undoubtedly foolish. Sam, leaving her bone-headed husband for the lights of the West End and the dubious pleasures available to a hostess on a cruise liner, is simply squalid. Heartstrings only twang to the music of grand passion – and to the more agonised sounds of personal crises which we might, one day, experience ourselves. *Coronation Street*'s caricatures were once a convincing commentary on the way we live now. Any resemblance to you and me is now purely coincidental.

Once upon a time, we all wept for the Ogdens even as we recoiled from the idea of living next door to them. We all knew Annie Walkers and admired, as well as resented, their indomitable pretensions. When the chapel closed and Ena Sharples lost her job as caretaker of the parish hall, I almost wrote her a note of sympathy. And when Mr Swindley (the draper mad with love) was left by Miss Nugent at the altar, I wept into my fish and chips. Now I only wonder why Jim Macdonald (a retired soldier with a Belfast accent) never mentions the troubles in Northern Ireland; when Martin Platt (a trainee nurse) will notice the health service cuts; and what prevents a Muslim family from moving into Coronation Street.

The programme must remain irrationally hopeful. Viewers who want to be depressed should watch *EastEnders*. But it is possible to write about the seamy side of life without depressing the audience into switching off, or making the audience prefer life to art. Charles Dickens did it in *Nicholas Nickleby* and *Oliver Twist*. The difference was that Dickens believed in the artist's duty to change the world. *Oliver Twist* was meant to demonstrate the iniquity of the 1834 Poor Law. In *Nicholas Nickleby*, he specifically set out to expose what amounted to childhood slavery in the Dotheboys Halls of northern England. There have been drugs in the Queen Vic and homeless youngsters in the square, but I doubt if *EastEnders* has ever provoked an angry letter to an MP. Has anyone ever set out on a crusade after watching *Coronation Street*? Both programmes need to believe in something. They could do worse than begin by convincing themselves that entertainment can inform as well as amuse.

Sunday Times, 7 March 1993

Brief Lives

It is more than a decade since I wrote *A Yorkshire Boyhood* but, because of that brief memoir, literary editors are still inclined to think of me as 'our childhood reminiscence correspondent'. I accept their offers of work with reluctance. For the competition is very fierce in the bookshelves labelled 'when we were very young', and I am not sufficiently generous of spirit to enjoy publicising rival work. I was, however, persuaded to review both Richard Hoggart's *A Local Habitation* ('All His Yesterdays') and Blake Morrison's *And When Did You Last See Your Father?* I fear that what I wrote about them did very little to reduce their sales. Reviewing Alistair Horne's *A Bundle From Britain* ('Digression Therapy') provided a pleasure which I did not anticipate when I opened the Jiffybag. It vindicates the view, developed late in life, that it is not necessary to enjoy reading a book in order to enjoy writing about it.

I had been writing for years before I began to understand the true joys of contributing to book pages. Foolishly, in adolescence I was influenced by a piece of typical Malcolm Muggeridge nonsense. I had heard that unmistakable voice in some radio programme asserting that reviews were the last refuge of failed journalists.

The second mistake, which denied me for almost two decades the peculiar pleasure of commenting on other people's work, was the belief that the reviewer should approach his task with a mind unclouded by bias or preconception. Since I possess well-established prejudices on virtually every subject, my self-denying ordinance restricted the possible scope of my commissions to a point where I was virtually unemployable. Now I realise that my original judgment – it was probably a prejudice – was diametrically wrong. A reviewer should advance on his target reinforced by strong views. Those views may change as he turns the pages. But if the *tabula rasa* ever exists, it is not the stone on which a book review should be engraved.

There is a problem about books which are written by friends and enemies. Initially I felt unable to review Barbara Castle's memoirs, for I was once her parliamentary secretary and I admire her greatly. But when I told Michael Foot – a closer friend to Barbara than I ever was – that I could not bring myself to complain about her tone of self-congratulation, he brushed my inhibition aside with the judgment that 'there is much to be said in Barbara's favour and she says it all herself'. I stole the joke for my review ('Star Ahead of Her Time'). When Michael used it in his speech at the party which launched *Fighting All the Way*, Barbara accused him of 'plagiarising Roy Hattersley's bad jokes'.

Roy Jenkins, an assiduous postcard writer, was totally relaxed about my review of his memoirs in the *Sunday Express* and my attempt to imitate his style in the *Guardian*.

> I thought the *Guardian* piece v. funny and your *S. Express* review in the circumstances generous. Thank you. You complain that I did nothing 'to calm the jangling nerves' of H. Wilson when he was obsessed with plots and plotters. But I cannot resist pointing out that you were always complained of as the foremost of the plotters and that you figured in about half my rows with Wilson. I remember frequently urging him to deal with this fact by putting you in the Govt and later promoting you – which I thought would at least calm your jangling nerves if not his!

That postcard began the restoration of a relationship which had begun to break down when Lord Jenkins resigned the deputy leadership of the Labour Party. My friendship with Tony Crosland grew stronger with the years. But I include my review of his wife's splendid biography for reasons of which Susan Crosland may not approve. It contains the pompous assertion that 'I believe it wrong to write down or remember one's private conversations and then publish them.' In retrospect, I regret the pomposity. But I have not changed my mind about a principle. The Crosland biography is the ideal peg on which to hang my point. For, in reference to that context, I cannot be accused of elevating self-protection into a moral precept. Unlike some recently written memoirs, I can read between my own inverted commas without wincing.

The review of J. K. Galbraith's anthology ('The Height of Impudence') was written with genuine trepidation. For, as I wrote, in a declaration of interest, I admire him to a point that 'a man who did not possess his self-assurance would find embarrassing'. My anxiety was increased during the week before my piece was published. Galbraith (presumably in London to publicise his book) was Neil Kinnock's guest at dinner. Knowing the professor's habits I arrived early, and when the host bustled in, I was being entertained with a long account of how President de Gaulle had asked for 'the Harvard definition of the philosophy of tall men'. Galbraith, true to tradition, had quoted Governor Winthrop who, during the early years of the Massachusetts Commonwealth, constantly constructed metaphors about looking up to houses built on hills. The President was, apparently, much impressed but added: 'And we have a duty to tyrannise small men.' At that moment, no doubt inadvertently, Professor J. K. Galbraith stretched out his arm. His fingers touched the top of Neil Kinnock's head.

I suppose that I was asked to review Keith Waterhouse's *Theory and Practice of Lunch* because, at the time, *Private Eye* was paying five pounds to anyone who sighted me eating out. My insistence that lunch was too often work and rarely pleasure, although true, was not what persuaded the magazine to withdraw their offer. The 'sighting letters' stopped after Michael Palin contributed to the lengthy correspondence.

Sir,

I write to protest at the hounding of Roy Hattersley (Grovel *Eye* 645). What on earth can be wrong with a man who chooses to spend his hard-earned spondoolics on good food and female company? I find the behaviour of such a great trencherman far less reprehensible than that of *Eye* readers Susan Sampford and Anne Johnson whose informing activities can win them scholarships to the KGB any day. What was Anne Johnson doing at the 'expensive' Linden Hall Hotel, Longhorseley, anyway? Cleaning out the chimneys? Testing the sound system for Red Wedge?

As for her observation that 'I smiled, but he did not smile back', one cannot help feeling why the hell should he? The last thing you want after a nice meal is to have to grin at some sanctimonious bint who's going to rat on you in a national magazine.

I'm no psychiatrist but I believe the reason for Roy's epicurean habits may lie in the fact that he was born and brought up in Sheffield. This is one of the most gastronomically deprived areas in the Western World, indeed the food was so bad that many of us didn't eat at all until well into our teens. South Yorkshire was to the gourmet as the Nullarbor Plain to the forest ranger. Is it surprising therefore that we want to get stuck into the magret de canard at every opportunity?

Let's hope that Roy is big enough to shrug this off.

Palin, a Sheffielder like me, told the dinner at which he became Travel Writer of the Year that the award was the greatest honour that he had received 'in the last twenty minutes'. During the interval in the celebrations, I had offered him a ticket for the Wednesday v. United FA Semi-Final. The joke was a great success with the literati there assembled. In the following week, Henry Root claimed in his *Independent* column that he had thought of it first and that Palin had stolen it without attribution. The veracity of Mr Root's story is undermined by one simple fact. Palin's anecdote was true.

There is a lot of Yorkshire in 'Brief Lives' – including the complaint that Mike Harding, comedian and president of the Ramblers Association, had disqualified himself from writing about the Dales by choosing to live in Lancashire. Mr Harding took my criticism ('The Largest County') literally and wrote to denounce my irrational chauvinism. My reply contained an eloquent paragraph on the dangers of irony, supported a proposal (first advanced by Ian Aitken of the *Guardian*) that printers should invent an 'ironic type' which made a writer's intention clear, and a fulsome apology for having caused even inadvertent offence. J. B. Priestley believed that a 'benign disposition' was an essential characteristic of the successful essayist and I extended that dictum to cover book reviews – at least most book reviews.

It was not difficult to feel well disposed towards Robert Skidelsky's biography of John Maynard Keynes ('Prophet of Hope'). At the party held to celebrate its publication, there was much learned discussion about a metaphorical question which it was thought that I had posed about the great economist. 'The subtitle, *The Economist as Saviour*, must raise in sceptical minds the . . . question, "but was he sceptical?" ' Admiration for me intellectually was misplaced. The question was a misprint. I had only meant to ask 'was he right?'

On reflection I am inclined to believe that my original enquiry was one which reviewers should never make. It is not for us to ask fundamental questions about great men. We judge the judgments and ought to be satisfied with the pleasure which that provides.

The Largest County

The right to exploit both accent and origin for personal gain is part of the Yorkshire birthright. Ever since George Hudson's broad vowel sounds convinced soft-headed southern investors that he was the sort of man who could be trusted with their money, the professional Yorkshireman has marketed his commodity with instinctive skill. Easy brand identification has always helped sales. All the consumers know that Michael Parkinson, Brian Clough, Denis Healey and Keith Waterhouse come from Yorkshire. But who can identify the counties which gave birth to their competitors and counterparts, David Frost, Howard Kendall, Geoffrey Howe and George Gale? But as every advertising agency will confirm, the real selling point is the quality of the product.

The county itself – from the North Yorkshire Moors across to the Dales and right down to the rolling acres of what was once the East Riding – looks as though it breeds honest dependability and loyal courage. Its picture postcards all encourage belief in what George Orwell angrily dismissed as 'the cult of the north'. Cult it may be, but it certainly sells in southern bookshops. Yorkshire – how it looks, what it stands for and the sort of people who are supposed to live there – excites such interest that even Lancastrians have begun to produce books about the right side of the Pennines. I report their success with a great deal of resentment.

I have always assumed that Peter Tinniswood (a Liverpudlian with a pathetic affection for Lancashire cricket in the age of John Ikin and Winston Place) set his stories of Uncle Mort and Brandon Carter in the West Riding. In *Uncle Mort's North Country*, the

Champion County is never actually confirmed as the location. But all the references place his stories firmly within the Broad Acres.

> *'How's the wife?' said the barman to the less toothless of the aged duo.*
> *'She's gone to Bridlington for the week.'*
> *'My condolences,' said the barman. 'And has she shown you how to work the mangle?'*

Add to that the inclusion of one of the other great names of Yorkshire folklore, when Uncle Mort visits Hattersley Main colliery, and philologists will confirm that the setting is within England's largest county.

The other quality which reveals Mr Tinniswood's work to be quintessentially Yorkshire is its gratuitous malice. It must have been his years working in Sheffield – when second-division full-backs always made sure to retaliate first – that developed in him the habit of tapping ankles just for the fun of it. For no particular reason we are suddenly told that 'Sebastian Coe's earned a stack since he became a professional amateur', and one character admits a long-established yearning to be a 'working-class equivalent of Clive Jenkins'. The admission of that dark desire comes from Dornford Scargill, Arthur's twin brother whose existence has up to now been kept as secret as Mr Rochester's first marriage. It is a good thing (not least for the security of Peter Tinniswood's front teeth) that an often overlooked Yorkshire characteristic is the ability to take a joke.

As a veteran of the Pennine Way and the Three Peaks Climb, I take it for granted that Mike Harding's *Rambling On* is set in Yorkshire. Its cartoons are funnier than the text which they illustrate. But Mr Harding (a professional comedian as well as president of the Ramblers Association) need not be unduly depressed by that. For the drawings are the work of the invariably hilarious Larry, who at least on this occasion wins the battle of ideas hands down. 'Fred Astaire and Ginger Rogers', we are told, once set out to dance the length of Yorkshire, 'but retired at Hadrian's Wall with third-degree blisters.' The Larry cartoon on the same page also pays tribute to the Hollywood immortals. It loses in translation from picture into words, but its flavour can be tasted in the sign which hangs on the wooden gate. 'Perpetual Youth Hostel. Wardens F. Astaire and G. Rogers.'

I am afraid that Mr Harding also comes off second best in *Walking the Dales*. But within its pages he is competing against an opponent even more formidable than Larry – Yorkshire itself. The three peaks of Whernside, Ingleborough and Pen-y-ghent and the county which surrounds them is the most awe-inspiring countryside in England. And within it, the high lake above Malham is as near to the landscape of heaven as we are likely to see this side of the Final Trump. Malham Tarn, Gordale Scar and Malham Cove are the places where J. M. W. Turner learned to paint light. And all those delights are confined in the north-west corner of the county. Mr Harding takes us on an illustrated hike through all of the Dales. The pictures are bound to come out on top of the words.

If Mr Harding suspects that I am prejudiced against him he is right. First, in *Rambling On* he is described as being 'born in Manchester where he still lives', thus encouraging my belief that he should mind his own business. In *Walking the Dales* he is said to be 'officially based in Manchester' although he 'has also lived in the Yorkshire Dales'. Why anyone whose primary occupation does not require residence somewhere else should choose to leave Yorkshire is a mystery. It is quite intolerable that persons of such execrable judgment should compete with native-born Yorkshire-men in the contest to make money out of the county.

Listener, 1 January 1981

'Whatever his Mood, Being in his Presence Always Gave me Pleasure'

I begin with what the members of my trade call a 'declaration of interest'. Tony Crosland was a friend of mine, and during the last ten years of his life I saw him more frequently than I saw any other politician. I remember him on holiday in Tuscany, at cabinet

171

meetings, at the EEC Council of Ministers, in the Sparkbrook Labour Club, in my house and in his – and even, though it was admittedly a rare sight, in the tea room of the House of Commons. To say that he was always the same, whatever the company or occasion, is grotesquely to over-simplify his complicated personality. But the pattern of paradoxes that made up his character never varied. He was loyal yet indiscreet, didactic but self-effacing, invariably kind and often inconsiderate. Whatever his mood, being in Tony Crosland's presence always gave me pleasure. In short, I admit bias about the subject of Susan Crosland's biography. And since its author remains a friend of mine, I write this review in the knowledge that I am something less than objective about the subject.

Even allowing for my proper prejudices, I have no doubt that Mrs Crosland has answered a publisher's prayer. She has written a political biography which deals seriously with serious subjects but enlivens the story of a great party's progress with anecdote and incident which will appeal even to readers who, being 'essentially frivolous', would have incurred her husband's deepest contempt. It is also essential reading for anyone who shares the classic Crosland conviction that those who love the Labour Party have a moral duty to abandon self-interest and self-indulgence in the cause of its electoral success. For as well as describing the object of his sometimes unrequited affection in all its infuriating, endearing, inspiring, frustrating, mean-minded, generous-spirited moods, it diagnoses the malaise from which Labour must recover if it is to become once more a party of mass membership, capable of winning the next election, and using its democratic power to change society.

During the weekend before his fatal illness, together we 'strolled through the greenhouses', as Susan Crosland puts it, in the gardens of Dorneywood, the Foreign Secretary's official country retreat. We had enjoyed a hilarious lunch, with the meticulously correct (but fundamentally iconoclastic) tenant mocking the temporary grandeur of his status, and the time had come for serious conversation. He 'talked about the need for a new book on socialism' – I still quote Susan Crosland – and said, 'We have got to keep making the point that the far Left are not the only people who can claim a socialist theory while the rest of us are thought to be mere pragmatists and administrators.' The distinction he made within the Party was between the radical thinkers and what he called the ameliorators of the Right. 'It's not enough to disagree with the Marxists *et al*. The Centre must remember and keep reminding people that we are ideologists too.'

In the five years that have followed that conversation, the Labour Party has all too often given the false impression that its members are divided between those who have an unattractively authoritarian view of the sort of society we want to build, and those who have no vision at all.

Crosland's own ideology was set out in *The Future of Socialism*, the only comprehensive statement of socialist philosophy to have been published in the last fifty years. Both his analysis and prescription proved 'over-optimistic about economic growth, as he admitted a few years later'. But the assumption that expansion would become an *automatic* feature of industrialised economies in no way invalidated his general thesis. If socialism is, as Crosland believed, about the pursuit of equality and the protection of freedom, *The Future of Socialism* is still the best blueprint for its construction that we possess. And Crosland was unusual amongst socialist philosophers in his enthusiasm for putting his theories into personal practice.

His devotion to public expenditure as an instrument of egalitarianism (like the conviction that Labour chancellors should struggle to create the economic growth which he once thought inevitable) was crucially tested during the IMF crisis of 1976. Many of the participants in those days of desperate cabinet meetings have given their own versions of that autumn's events.

Susan Crosland describes, with an accuracy that cabinet minutes will one day confirm, the case her husband made against that package of cuts and deflation. He argued his alternative with breathtaking confidence, and only gave up the struggle when his supporters deserted him and he became convinced that to fight on was to jeopardise the government he served. His instruction to abandon ship was, as far as I recall it, exactly as Mrs Crosland reports: 'Since I now propose to give my reluctant support to Jim, you must do the same. No time for heroics – or for you to think that your judgement is better than mine.' Tony's ability to be simultaneously infuriating and irresistible was, in my experience, unique.

Initially, Tony Crosland was a reluctant foreign secretary, and none of his friends was surprised by the enthusiasm with which he advanced his own remedy for the 1976 crisis. His willingness to go against his departmental brief originally worried his permanent officials. But some time between his final appointment and his death ten months later he developed an interest in his job that amounted to near obsession.

I watched in amazement as he turned his formidable intellect to the prosaic problems of the Cod War. This biography makes plain the courage required for the Member for Grimsby (with a deep emotional need for the love of his constituents) to compromise with Iceland and accept a reduced Humberside catch. It does not describe what the Foreign Office, at least, regarded as an equally extraordinary aspect of the affair. In the middle of a NATO meeting, fearful that the Norwegian mediator was losing interest in honest brokerage, he charged from Brussels hotel to Brussels hotel looking for the reception at which the miscreant could be found and returned to his exacting task. The dispute was 'ridiculous'. So he ended it.

A politician of pronounced opinions, who dies at the age of fifty-eight having written a famous work on the philosophy of his party, and while holding one of the great offices of state, provokes endless speculation about where destiny might have led him, if only . . . I have no idea whether or not Tony Crosland, had he lived, would have become leader of the Labour Party and prime minister. But Susan Crosland's book – not least when it faithfully reports his typical disclaimers – makes clear how much he wanted that ultimate chance to change the nature of society. That he remained genially joyous while wrestling with the often uncongenial obligations of pursuing that aim is a great tribute to his wife and biographer. Without her he would almost certainly have followed the same path. But he would not have enjoyed the journey.

Now she has produced a tribute to him, carefully researched and written, with an honesty that includes material that a second wife might have chosen to omit. I have only one major complaint about the whole book. As Susan Crosland knows, I believe it wrong to write down or remember once-private conversations and then publish them. Whether the dialogue is to the credit or discredit of the participants hardly matters. Unguarded casual comments should be kept secret. People ought not to feel a need to speak with caution when they go out to supper.

Of course, the tales of Tony Benn in his cycle clips and Roy Jenkins's attempts to assume Hugh Gaitskell's mantle add to the biography's attractions. But the book has qualities that transcend the gossip column. The childhood, the schooldays, the war, Oxford as undergraduate and don, Parliament in government and opposition, the hopes and agonies, fears and beliefs – it is a fascinating story of a fascinating man. Less biased judges than I will confirm that conviction.

Listener, 3 June 1982

Dragon-maker

Gilbert Keith Chesterton was an addicted essayist. Of course he was also a poet, a polemicist, a biographer, a historian, a perpetual chauvinist, an occasional antisemite, a professional journalist and an amateur theologian. But, his poetry aside, whatever he wrote turned out to be an essay or series of essays – narrative essays called short stories, biographical essays put together and called biographies, historical essays bound in the same volume and called histories. Each chapter of his longer books is complete, well rounded, discursive, didactic. Often he allows the essayist's personality to intrude in places where the historian or literary critic would never permit it to appear. Most significantly of all, he understands the importance of carrying his readers along on the strength of his language. Devotees of Father Brown will insist that the ingenuity of the plots and the subtlety of the characterisations hold them entranced. But when, in the mystery of *The Queer Feet*, we read that 'In the heart of a plutocracy, tradesmen become cunning enough to be more fastidious than their customers', we recognise an author who struck a proper balance between style and substance – the essential mark of the true essayist.

Chesterton was also a man of generous disposition, and usually his natural happiness was reflected in what he wrote – another essential attribute of the successful essayist. 'He seems', writes P. J. Kavanagh in his introduction to *The Bodley Head G. K. Chesterton*, 'always to be addressing a large and friendly audience.' That is something of an overstatement. But we ought not to complain when a Chesterton devotee exaggerates his idol's good nature. For when we read Chesterton's judgments on his own literary heroes, we applaud his affectionate reluctance to find fault. There is, in his assessment 'Browning as a Literary Artist', a passage in which the subject of the biographical essays is compared to Wordsworth and Shelley:

> The *Ode on the Intimations of Immortality* is a perfectly normal and traditional ode, and *Prometheus Unbound* is a perfectly genuine and traditional Greek lyrical drama. But if we study Browning honestly, nothing will strike us more than that he really created a large number of quite novel and quite admirable artistic forms.

Rivals for places in the pantheon of English poetry having been thus admonished for their comparative lack of originality, the panegyric sweeps on to applaud the personal as well as the poetic qualities of both the Brownings. I hope that it is more than my own admiration for that extraordinary couple which attracts me to Chesterton's account of their marriage. Even readers who are moved by neither the mystic wonder of Robert's poetry nor the strength of Elizabeth's character and the quality of her sonnets, must be recruited to their cause by the succinct brilliance with which Chesterton described the liberation of the sick daughter from her father's domination. After a slightly self-conscious sub-Freudian analysis of their relationship he moves on to stronger ground: 'She took a much more cheerful view of death than her father did of life.'

Not that Chesterton is invariably, and therefore tediously, in favour of everything and everybody. He asserts that 'what attracts Mr Kipling to militarism is not the idea of courage but the idea of discipline', and he clearly disapproves of such an attraction. He classifies the aphorisms of Oscar Wilde with ruthless accuracy into the work of 'the true humorist . . . the charlatan . . . the fine philosopher and . . . the tired quack'. The notion that 'Good intentions are invariably ungrammatical' he dismisses as 'tame trash'. Chesterton is instinctively against the popular and the fashionable, because he is on the side of the common man. Caught by 'two excited policemen' while 'throwing a big Swedish knife at a tree', he is gratified when 'the leading constable became so genial and complimentary that he ended up by representing himself as a reader of my work'. But he wonders 'how he would have got on if he had not been the guest at a big house'. It is the possession of such instincts which makes it easy to forget his excesses.

G. K. Chesterton overdid it – especially in support of favoured causes. In the excellent introduction we are reminded of the assaults on the Liberal Party establishment which he made on behalf of his dead brother, Cecil, who had sought to expose the corruption of the Marconi affair. In the text we are given an example of his absurd determination to defend the period of medieval history when the Catholic Church occupied the position in society to which he would have liked it restored. In his *Short History of England* – written as the kindly light was leading him towards Rome – he observed in apparent seriousness that

> torture so far from being peculiarly medieval was copied from pagan Rome and its most natural political science. Its application to others besides slaves was really part of the slow medieval extinction of slavery. Torture indeed is a logical thing common to states innocent of fanaticism.

From his more sensible writing we know that Chesterton could not have tortured a worm – indeed, rather, if its shape, size and religion had attracted him, he might have announced that in truth it was a dragon. Overstatement was one of Chesterton's greatest pleasures.

Times Literary Supplement, 12 July 1985

The Theory and Practice of Lunch

Keith Waterhouse was, for many years, Britain's foremost light essayist, the best comic columnist in Fleet Street, a wise (though unpretentious) commentator on important subjects and one of the very few working journalists who could be relied on to write a funny article every time that they sat down with that intention. For all I know, he may still be pretty good. But he has moved from the *Mirror* to the *Mail*. And I like to remember him as I last read him. In loving memory of the dear departed, I forgive him *The Theory and Practice of Lunch*. We should not begrudge him this act of blatant self-indulgence.

I do not believe that he would either resent or deny the description. Self-indulgence – indeed self-overindulgence – is the subject of the book. And Mr Waterhouse has chosen to write about it in a way which may amuse the reader and has certainly amused him. Part of its charm is that it has been written with so much obvious pleasure that the enjoyment seeps out of the pages and attaches itself . . . I almost wrote 'to anyone who reads them'. But therein lies my problem with *The Theory and Practice of Lunch*. I suspect that it will be generally incomprehensible to 95 per cent of the population.

The essayist's art is the description and discussion of inconsequential events in a way which makes them fascinating to readers who would not find such subjects even interesting were the triviality of the topic not submerged in the quality of the writing. It is a task which Mr Waterhouse performs superbly. But I am not sure that the technique travels from a 1500-word article to a hundred-page book.

In his luncher's guide, he employs all the tricks of the essayist's trade. We have the self-deprecatory joke.

> I use an invaluable little volume called the *Instant Menu Translation* . . . Say I fancy a light meal of (according to regional variation) *martedi, martes* or *mardi*, or *Dienstag* as some German menus call this interesting delicacy, I simply turn up the relevant initial under the relevant language to discover . . . that I was on the verge of ordering Tuesday.

And there is the mind-gripping opening sentence.

> I was in a Covent Garden restaurant once when a diner, to make a debating point with the management, rose to his feet, picked up his chair and smashed it to smithereens on the table.

Perfect in each case. But I quote from passages which conclude and begin individual chapters. I am not sure that even the Waterhouse skill can sustain the charm for page after page on the same subject. It is a book of lunches, by a luncher for lunchers. And I do not like the idea of lads from Leeds becoming so exclusive.

I have little doubt that, as a boy, Mr Waterhouse knew lunch to be the two slices of bread and jam which the pampered and privileged took to school to 'put them on' between breakfast and one o'clock dinner. I long for it even now. And I wonder what it was that the young Waterhouse used to eat when the dinner bell sounded. I had half a dozen favourites and they have now been combined into my ideal lunch. It has three courses, I have not eaten it for twenty years and, for reasons too personal to describe, I shall never eat it again. It is best consumed at home where it is possible to demand second helpings, unnecessary to make polite conversation and less than tragic if the tie is splashed and tablecloth stained. It consists of pea soup, haddock, chips and peas or steak and kidney pie with mashed potatoes and baked jam roll with custard. It would take a lot of lunches at the restaurants which Mr Waterhouse recommends to compensate for a life left barren of jam roll.

But then Mr Waterhouse enjoys eating in those places to an extent which is denied to most regular eaters-out. He benefits from a virtually unlimited expense account and the near nomadic life of a free (if not freelance) journalist. As well as choosing his restaurant, he can choose his companions. Let me assure him that if he went off, three days a week, to share a table with someone whom he barely knew (indeed, perhaps had never met) he would feel quite differently about the whole event. Yet that is the lot of a large number of the world's regular lunchers.

One day, he ought to sample a private room booked in the name of the well-known City company, Hoare, Capel, Phillips and Greenwell. The food will be as splendid as anything which is neither cod and chips nor steak and kidney pie can possibly be. But it will be consumed in such a concentrated determination to give an accurate description of the need for exchange controls that it will pass unnoticed over the tastebuds. I can only face my journeys to such assignations by thinking of the summer and the odd days when the diary is empty and a test match is on television. It is, I am sure, immensely damaging to the digestive system to crouch in front of the screen eating cheese and pickled onions or sandwiches hastily made from leftover cold beef. But it is pure pleasure. Too many lunches are work.

It may well be that I have written this review in a spirit of deep resentment – resentment that Mr Waterhouse enjoys what I, so often, dislike and resentment that he encourages the belief that what pains so many people is really undiluted pleasure. I hope he will forgive me and take me to lunch. They are clearly so much more fun with him than they are with most other people.

Listener, 21 October 1986

The Height of Impudence

I admire John Kenneth Galbraith to an extent that a man who did not possess his self-confidence would find embarrassing. My one reservation about his conduct and character concerns his contempt for athletic activities in general and ball games in particular – a crucial flaw which I am, nevertheless, prepared to overlook for as long as he confines his cultivated contempt to basketball and American football.

I do, however, understand why those who do not share what they would call his prejudices find his writing as insufferable as I find it enchanting. From evidence contained in this latest Galbraith anthology, it is reasonable to conclude that William H. Moore, chairman of the Board of Bankers' Trust, hates him.

The unfortunate Mr Moore was quoted in the pages of the *New York Times* as supporting the idea of a 'loan guarantee' for the Lockheed aircraft company. Professor Galbraith – whose compulsion to express himself extends through twenty-four books and innumerable essays and lectures into the correspondence columns of every serious newspaper – wrote to the editor on the day that the report appeared.

> He neglects to mention that if Lockheed suffers the normal consequences of its own mismanagement, his bank will take a substantial bath. He should, in truth, disclose interest. But he should also confess that he is the kind of free enterpriser who is steadfast in his faith up to the point where money may be made or lost. Then, like most others, he rushes hell-for-breakfast to the government. Wouldn't you prefer an honest socialist?

Professor Galbraith's combative style of disputation must, to his opponents, be offensive enough to make them lifetime enemies. But he adds to that primary offence a secondary misdemeanour. It is the effrontery of a man who is frankly unashamedly (and, in my opinion, wholly justifiably) pleased with himself.

Writing about Lord Louis Mountbatten – a subject upon which he possesses no special or professional expertise – he gratuitously refers to Philip Ziegler's 'excellent, ever fascinating but not flawless biography', and goes on to report, in passing, that Mountbatten once mistakenly believed that 'I was editing Randolph Churchill's collection of his father's papers.' The professor put him right at once. 'I told him I was not. I was merely reading the first two columns for possible correction of Churchillian economics.'

If the story contained a suspicion that Professor Galbraith was either bragging about the breadth of his social circle, or boasting about the width of the ground over which his academic writ runs, the story would be either pathetic or obnoxious.

He is, however, doing neither. He is simply entertaining his audience with an anecdote from the drama of a life filled with such supporting actors as Robert Kennedy, Lyndon Johnson, Archibald McLeish, John Kennedy, Muhammad Ali Jinnah and Eleanor Roosevelt. He writes about them all with an unselfconscious acceptance of the state to which he is called.

It is a role in society which imposes a special burden. For he is 'asked once a month, sometimes once a week, to introduce some writer's work – occasionally that of a friend, more often that of some would-be scholar of whom I've never heard'. Naturally enough, the list of those prefaces which Professor Galbraith agreed to write is simultaneously eclectic and discerning.

In ordinary men, the Galbraith style would be intolerable. But Galbraith is not ordinary. He is more literate, more learned, more erudite, more energetic, more amusing and (at six feet eight and a half inches) even taller than anyone else you are likely to meet this year or next. It would be wholly unreasonable to expect such an intelligent man not to admire his own attributes.

Professor Galbraith enjoys himself immensely. The pleasure is infectious and, as a result, almost everything he writes – economics, literary criticism, history, biography or polemic – is a delight to read.

The pleasure is heightened for those who enjoy effrontery. The Dean's circular on sexual harassment at Harvard is printed and elegantly ridiculed, and that and the fear that the illiteracy of advertising copy is indicative of the generally second-rate quality of industrial management are both vintage Galbraith.

Even the dust jacket is designed to make blood pressure rise. The author of an essay that lampoons the Harvard v Dartmouth football game is pictured stretched across three tiers of the Harvard football stadium.

Guardian, 13 February 1987

All his Yesterdays

Only the foolhardy write inconsequential memoirs. Generals, prime ministers and opening batsmen know that the tale they have to tell is, in itself, a justification for an autobiography. Indeed they made the history about which they write. If, on the other hand, an author chooses to describe the swings and roundabouts at the Holbeck Feast, Jack Lane Elementary School and Aunts Annie and Ethel, he must not expect their place in history to carry his narrative along.

Richard Hoggart's book is not simply the story of his early

years, nor 'an attempt to capture sentimental attention'. It is an account of life among the northern industrial poor between the two world wars – an account made all the more vivid by the emotion with which those years are remembered.

The story begins with Aunt Annie's death in St James's Hospital in Leeds. As we might expect, the author of *The Uses of Literacy* describes the sad event in the precise *patois* of his childhood. It was not any old Aunt Annie who 'got real bad in the night' but 'my Aunt Annie'. Not long after, 'she'd gone'. A more self-conscious family would have said that she 'passed away'. Twenty years later, and forty miles south, those who went genteel into the good night 'passed on'. There was a working-class disinclination to speak of death.

It was Aunt Annie who took young Richard to the Holbeck Feast, with its sights, sounds and 'unmistakable fairground smell – hot oil, clinkers, toffee apples, brandy snaps, mushy peas, cockles and winkles with vinegar'. What happened to chips? But then what happened to football (association or rugby league) and to cricket, those other indispensable opiates of the working-class boy?

I have a suspicion that Richard was always regarded as something 'a bit special'. That makes his story untypical. But without that early cleverness we would have been denied the story's brilliant perceptions: for example, on boots and shoes in the lives of poor children being 'particularly precise indicators of status'. Richard, it seems, hated having to wear 'a pair of public schoolboy's shoes [which] were sent to grandma'. His complaint was not that they pinched his toes, but that 'they *rightly* attracted vilification in the playground'. The emphasis is mine. The proper prejudice belongs to Richard Hoggart.

It belongs to a man with a remarkably sensitive ear and eye for time and place. Of course, those first twenty-two years from Hunslet to University impressed themselves on him with the force that is felt only by the young. But the talent to remember should not be underrated. Richard Hoggart describes the hopes as well as the experiences of a whole generation, the last survivors from the age before the Butler Education Act, free dental care and Ostermilk. The result is a joy as well as an education.

Observer, 25 September 1988

No-nonsense Jack

J. B. Priestley leapt into my life with two giant strides. First there were the postscripts – broadcast talks which followed the nine o'clock news on Sunday nights during the early years of the war. Winston Churchill complained that they 'expressed war aims which were in conflict with those of the Prime Minister'. But it was not the fine talk of change from 'property to community' which excited me. I rejoiced because the BBC – which I knew to be the glass of fashion and mould of form – had given official recognition to the Yorkshire accent.

After the war was won, the first pile of books which I was given at the Sheffield City Grammar School included *More Essays by Modern Masters*. It was my introduction to the inconsequential thousand words, written primarily to give ten minutes' pleasure but with a moral sometimes added at the end. I preferred J. B. Priestley to all the other authors – Chesterton, Belloc, *et al*. I still cannot sign the register in a hotel without wondering if it is Booked Right Through the Winter – according to my favourite essayist, the ultimate accolade of the trade.

Then, I moved slowly through *The Good Companions* ('to say that men paid their shilling to watch twenty-two hirelings kick a ball is merely to say that a violin is wood and catgut, that *Hamlet* is so much paper and ink') to *English Journey*. That account of a wander round this green and pleasant land ends with Priestley's joy at returning to blazing hearth and warm home. I thought of that final paragraph as epitomising Jolly Jack, the author who urged aspiring essayists to exhibit geniality. If Vincent Brome's biography is to be believed, Mr Priestley pushed open his own front door with, at best, ambivalent feelings.

His pursuit of a better companion (which did not end until his marriage to Jaquetta Hawkes in 1953 at the age of fifty-nine) is only part of the private life that belied the public persona: 'Protestations that his best plays were written in continuous bursts of inspiration are qualified by plays like *I Have Been Here Before* and *Johnson Over Jordan* with which he struggled over long periods.' It

184

is a very substantial qualification. Those plays attempted to set out the theory that time often stands still against the background of monotonous middle-class suburban life. He regarded them as his most serious work.

Priestley discovered Ouspensky's theory of time while he was on a lecture tour of America. With the exception of *An Inspector Calls* (which, until the very end, is a respectable social drama), I have always found the theory behind the time plays difficult to master. Thanks to Mr Brome's biography, I am comforted with the knowledge that J. B. Priestley also found it difficult: 'When we say the past exists it must exist along this [sixth] dimension. But what is this sixth dimension – the final dimension of what we call Time? Ouspensky does not give it a name but says it is the line of actualisation of other possibilities contained in any moment, but not actualised in our time.' All this was an aberration – the expression of an obsession which temporarily distracted the clearest and least pretentious writer of his generation from his true literary destiny. Mr Brome's biography proves it.

Descriptions of the plays are scattered throughout the book. One advantage of the disorder is the chance it provides to compare 'experimental' work with classic comedy. '*When We are Married* carries no particular moral message, but guilt riddles the play,' says Brome. The elders of the Chapel – pompous, overbearing and sanctimonious – are drawn from the men with whom Priestley was brought up in early-twentieth-century Bradford. The fear that their respectable reputations will be destroyed is clearly the fate which young Jack wished upon them. When he kept it straight and simple J. B. Priestley wrote with the vitality of genius.

Much of the vitality he owed to the other dominant characteristic of his life and work, provincialism. In this tight little, right little, metropolitan-dominated island the word 'provincial' now carries only pejorative overtones. In other countries writers enrich the nation's literature while still being associated with a single region. J. B. Priestley, lecturing in America, visiting Gracie Fields in Capri, chasing actresses in London's West End and living in the Isle of Wight or Warwickshire, remained an essentially northern figure.

The best of his work is part of what George Orwell called the 'cult of the north': the notion that 'the industrial work which is done in the north is the only "real" work, that the north is inhabited by "real" people, the south merely by "rentiers" and their parasites.' The whole idea may be nonsense. But it is a powerful image and Priestley recognised a powerful image when he saw one.

The essential J. B. Priestley is contained in a letter to Robert Robinson, written in 1965, when he had turned down a peerage but agreed to serve on the board of the National Theatre: 'If I should propose in the fairly near future that Tynan should go, I'll probably be told this is because he said "fuck" in public.' The reason, he went on to explain, would be quite different. 'He really doesn't care about the Theatre, which he uses as a trampoline for his ego.' Priestley's genius was built on the idea of 'no nonsense'. When he stuck to that principle he was one of the great writers of the twentieth century.

Observer, 16 October 1988

Not a Nice Man

When I first knew Bernard Ingham he was an amiable, though nervous, assistant labour correspondent with what was then the *Manchester Guardian*. He went on to spend several years as an affable though insecure press officer to Aubrey Jones's Prices and Incomes Board. A suggestion that he might become *alter ego* to the Prime Minister of Great Britain would have been treated as an unkind joke. Most people thought him a rather nice chap. His biography, *Kill the Messenger*, makes it necessary to reconsider that judgment. It is one of the most unpleasant books that I have ever read – coarse, bombastic, boastful and vindictive.

The account of Sir Bernard's relations with the late Lord Balogh – Minister of State at the Department of Energy when our hero was the ministry spokesman – is typical of the Ingham style, approach to biography and, I fear, attitude to life. 'I took the view that no one with a Middle European accent as thick as his was entitled to imply that he was more patriotic than the chap with an accent as thick as mine, especially when my accent is undeniably British.' Of course, John Bull confounded the knavish tricks of the lesser breeds without the law. The most spectacular confrontation ended, he tells us, with 'him ordering me from his room and me staring him out. I then left, slamming the door with such force that I could have done the hinges no good.' Sir Bernard seems to regard the incident as some sort of personal triumph.

The most revealing part of his narrative concerns the way in which he retaliated against those journalists who attempted to undermine 'the lobby' – the system of unattributable briefing by which Sir Bernard insinuated Margaret Thatcher's more unattractive opinions into newspapers. His battle with Peter Preston (whom he describes as 'the former gossip columnist editor of the *Guardian*') is recounted blow by blow. There are several paragraphs of bombast – 'all this made little impression on me . . . I am afraid that I was a little provocative' – before the reader reaches the crucial point.

> Members of the staffs of the *Guardian* and the *Independent*, and later the *Scotsman*, outside the lobby . . . were given the run around by my press officer. Before we had finished with them they very clearly understood that we were not to be mucked about by editors who arrogantly thought that they could have it both ways.

The idea that the Prime Minister and her servants had some sort of duty to inform the public of what was going on never seems to have entered Sir Bernard's head. He existed to manipulate the newspapers, and those who refused to be manipulated had to be bullied and blackmailed so as to ensure that a small revolt did not turn into a mighty revolution. I look forward to quoting from the Ingham memoirs during the debate which precedes the introduction of a Freedom of Information Bill.

I shall also report that, when it suited him, Sir Bernard Ingham did not hesitate to complain about the problems which the lobby system causes an honest, hard-working Downing Street press secretary. After John Biffen and Francis Pym had made injudicious remarks about Margaret Thatcher's popularity, Sir Bernard – at least, according to his autobiography – tried to pass off their indiscretions with a slight joke.

In the case of Mr Pym I said something like 'Oh, for God's sake, you lot, come off it, you know as well as I do that it's being so cheerful that keeps him going.' And in the case of Mr Biffen I said, 'I really am surprised at you lot. You all know as well as I do that John Biffen is that well-known semi-detached member of the Cabinet.'

These innocent comments were 'interpreted as a fierce attack by Number Ten upon the respective ministers . . . the circumstances in which they came to be made were never reported by the journalists. Members of the public might have imagined that I had deliberately attempted to denigrate them.' It seems that poor Sir Bernard was constantly misunderstood. He was, he assures us, a victim not a perpetrator of the Westland leak by which the solicitor general's letter, correcting 'material inaccuracies' in Michael Heseltine's version of the government's obligations, was sent to the Press Association. He admits to 'tacit acceptance' but insists that his only crime was a failure to 'object to a ministerial decision'.

Sir Bernard's problem was, in part, his absolute identification with the Prime Minister. His smallest aside was assumed to be her *ex cathedra* opinion. He became the extension of her will and wishes. Having read his book, I understand why they got on so well.

Literary Review, August 1991

Prophet of Hope

John Maynard Keynes made hope intellectually respectable. While professional economists argued about his claim to have filled the gloomy science's black hole with a plausible theory of demand, his lay audience rejoiced that, at last, someone had offered a credible cure for mass unemployment.

His prescription was constructed with a seductive, formal elegance. It was set out in flawless English and offered new remedies for old problems without frightening the property-owning middle classes. In the words of Keynes's open letter to President Roosevelt, he 'set out to mend the evils of our condition by reasoned experiment within the framework of the existing social system'. Because he offered the prospect of redemption without revolution, his theories were irresistibly attractive to the liberal establishment.

In the forty years which followed the publication of his *General Theory of Employment, Interest and Money*, Keynes's views on economic management dominated Whitehall and Westminster and spread, with varying degrees of acceptance, throughout the western democracies. Keynes was, Robert Skidelsky writes, 'a magical figure and it is only fitting that he should have left a magical work' to mark the apogee – though by no means the end – of his iridescent career. He is now the subject of a magical biography – comprehensive, fearless and written in a style which matches its meticulous scholarship.

An account of Keynes's life between 1920 and 1937, bearing the subtitle *The Economist as Saviour*, must raise in sceptical minds the prosaic question 'But was he right?' The undoubted answer is, 'Of course he was.' In the years when his theories went out of fashion – generally for reasons of political prejudice concerned with the role of government and the propriety of redistributing wealth – his detractors always pretended that he sought salvation through encouraging consumption.

'My proposals for controlling the business cycle' he wrote in the *American Economic Review*, 'are based on the control of *investment*'. The emphasis, Treasury officials should note, is his. He went on to insist that when a manipulation of interest rates fails to encourage economic expansion 'direct stimulation of investment by government is necessary'. Keynes is about to enjoy a second coming. There is much that present ministers have to learn from his views on coal production, foreign debts and fixed parities. But *The Economist as Saviour* is far more than a record of economic genius. The chapter that describes the contents of the General Theory will be a boon to indolent undergraduates. But readers who neither know nor care that M=kY, when the demand for money is a function of money income, will still find the whole book a delight. It tells the story of a life that was fascinating in every aspect.

Keynes was all of a piece. He was a product of the age of

Edwardian certainty and his belief in man's ability to solve the world's problems sprang from his unbounded confidence in the capacity of the human intellect. Society's ills were – he had no doubt – more likely to be created by ignorance and stupidity than by evil and malice, and he maintained the unshakable conviction that hard work and deep thought pointed the paths to redemption.

He could not, however, accept the conventional pieties of his age – among them, the sanctity of saving. In a single sentence, Skidelsky explains the psychological as well as the intellectual impetus behind Keynes's related theories of expectation and uncertainty. 'The clue to Keynes's attitude is that he linked part of the desire to save not to individual plans for a more secure and prosperous future, but to a general anxiety about the future, as well as a lack of capacity to excess. He even looked forward to long railway journeys. In an age of despair, he was the prophet of hope. When, during an Italian holiday, the lira – in which he had heavily invested – began to depreciate, he told his companions that spending had become a moral duty. His own purchases included seventeen pairs of gloves. His friends, who had contributed to the stake with which he gambled, took it for granted that given time, he would recoup their losses. Faith and patience were rewarded.

Keynes's optimism was infectious. One of his students described the General Theory as 'A Manifest for Reason and Cheerfulness'. Another thought it offered 'the opportunity to take part in a great adventure'. At a time when more and more thinking people had begun to fear that the only choice was between continual depression and Soviet communism, he 'supplied hope . . . that prosperity could be restored and maintained without the support of prison camps, executions and bestial interrogators'. By the beginning of the war, he had become the reasonable radical, whose ideas subverted the Tory Party barely less than they infiltrated Labour.

Although his ideas were claimed by Labour, he remained a semi-detached Liberal with an influence on all political parties, exerted through his writing, through his lectures, through his extraordinary range of acquaintances and through his City directorships. He remained, throughout his life, eclectic in his use of time and choice of friends. He could move easily between Cambridge and City boardrooms, from a committee to consider increasing the pension of retired professors, to Bloomsbury – a phase of Keynes's life that Skidelsky describes with a frankness that never turns into prurience.

In every aspect of his career Keynes's success was the triumph of intellect. It is only right that his definitive biographer – Harrod wrote too soon after his death to provide balanced judgment – is capable of reflecting his historic brilliance.

There is no literary equivalent to the congratulatory first. But I take my hat off to Skidelsky. It has been a joy to read his work.

Sunday Times, 8 November 1992

And When Did You Last See Your Father?

Men write about their fathers for many different reasons. Some seek catharsis from the pain of death. Others want to make a posthumous apology or convince themselves that, however they once behaved, they did (in their own peculiar way) show proper filial affection. A few believe that, if they write their father's story down, they will begin to understand their parents. Rather more hope that they will begin to understand themselves. I have no idea what compulsion prompted Blake Morrison to write *And When Did You Last See Your Father?* And I do not care. Whatever the cause, the result is a near masterpiece.

The publishers have chosen to call the book a memoir. That description does it far less than justice. For *And When . . .* is less the story of Dr Arthur Morrison and his young lad Blake than the autopsy of a relationship. At first it is told in two intertwining narratives – boyhood memories set against the story of the father's mortal illness and the son's attempts to adjust to the death. Described in two stark sentences, the idea seems pretentious and its execution certain to be sentimental at best. The fears are

191

groundless. There is not a maudlin page or a mawkish paragraph, and Morrison writes with a reckless respect for the sometimes unpalatable truth which elevates the narrative high above the usual run of rose-tinted nostalgia.

The text makes clear that Dr Morrison died less than two years ago. So the book must have been begun before his memorial plaque was unveiled in Earby town square. It may be the rush to write that gives *And When . . .* its spontaneity. The story spills out without pause or thought about if the anecdote will reflect well on his father or cause his mother grief. Indeed, Mrs Morrison is reported, in the final pages, as offering her son a typically mild rebuke for exposing his father's infidelities and describing his own early sexual encounters. At one point, Blake even hears his dad's voice inside his head, calling for filial piety. 'And leave Aunty Beaty out of it. It was a phase, no more. There are people who have to be protected.'

Clearly, Mr Morrison does not believe that protection is part of the writer's job. From the moment that we read of his father jumping the queue at the motor races – driving past the stationary cars with his stethoscope round his neck as a passport to the head of the line and then lying to the gateman about the colour of his ticket – we know that the picture is going to show all the warts which the memories of childhood retain. They are complicated blemishes. Dr Morrison calls his wife 'mummy . . . long after my sister and I have left home . . . not just in front of her grown-up children but in the company of friends and strangers in pubs'. Clearly, father is blamed for doing it, mother for allowing it to happen, and son for minding. If the relationship had been simple, it would not have been worth writing about.

The account of the early years is written with a passionate objectivity – determination to describe the nature and the extent of the ten-year-old's reluctance to go camping with his father in the Lake District, and an equal anxiety to explain the comic relief which was induced by the discovery that the tent poles had been left at home and the first night would have to be spent in an hotel. The realism of the story is enhanced by its essential simplicity, and the passages of introspective regret, which follow the narrative, are made all the more moving because we know that the man who mourns was once the boy who was embarrassed, intimidated and exalted in turn by a father whose character was too complex for a child to understand.

And When Did You Last See Your Father? tells us much about Dr Morrison and more about the son. But it tells us most about ourselves – especially the feeling of bewildered desertion that most men feel when their fathers die. It is (at least in part) ourselves we mourn for. But that makes the grief no less real. Blake Morrison has expressed that emotion with a candour and in a fashion which makes the story irresistible. Part of the compulsion is the desire to go on turning the pages simply in order to find out if he can maintain the quality of style and substance right up to the last page. He can and he does.

Guardian, 3 June 1993

Star Ahead of Her Time

Barbara Castle is a star. Her brilliance has illuminated politics for more than fifty years.

But stars, by their nature, are determined to shine. So – true to its author's character – her autobiography is not blemished by false modesty. The triumphs, great and small, are faithfully recorded.

I was her parliamentary under-secretary when she broke the government's prices and incomes policy by insisting that a group of underpaid women who sewed seats at Ford's Dagenham plant should be helped in their fight for a decent wage.

It was a minor dispute – but it ended with an historic agreement.

Not only was justice done, but Treasury intransigence was beaten, the Ford Communists were outmanoeuvred and – most important of all – the scene was set for the Equal Pay Act, which Barbara squeezed into the parliamentary timetable just before the 1979 general election.

Barbara will not forgive me for admitting it, but I felt nothing but irritation when I read, as her postscript to the Dagenham story, that she did not mind 'that her name had been tucked away at the back of the plate' on which the TUC commemorated the victory.

By drawing attention to the potter's idiosyncrasies – and convincing most readers that she minded very much – she diminishes her own achievements.

The achievements were extraordinary.

The title of her biography, *Fighting All The Way*, is (despite the overtone of self-admiration) wholly appropriate. Barbara's political life has been a battle – partly because of her combative temperament and partly because fate and Harold Wilson conspired to place her in the political front line.

At the Ministry of Transport – a job which she tells us was accepted with great reluctance – she stood up to the vested interests head to head.

The result was the motorway speed limit and the safety belt, now accepted as obvious commonsense but then bitterly opposed by the motoring lobby.

At the Department of Employment she was simply twenty years ahead of her time.

Reading her two-page résumé of *In Place of Strife* – her proposals for improved industrial relations – it is easy enough to argue with some of the details of her plan.

But the principles on which it is built – the strike as a last resort rather than a reflex response and the obligation of union leaders to consult their members – are so obviously right that it seems incredible that so many Labour Party members (me amongst them) ever argued against what she proposed.

Barbara recovered from the rejection of her policy to serve in Harold Wilson's 1974 cabinet and to lead the British Labour Group in the European Parliament.

She was a major figure in post-war politics and remains (even in retirement) the most loved politician in the Labour Party.

'There is,' one of her old friends said to me, 'much to be said for Barbara – and she says it all herself.'

History will be kinder even than her autobiography. And that is praise indeed.

Mail on Sunday, 13 June 1993

Digression Therapy

Memoirs of childhood have, historically, been divided into two classic forms. One tradition, exemplified by Richard Hoggart's *A Local Habitation*, makes a serious if slightly sentimental contribution to modern history. The alternative form, brilliantly represented by Blake Morrison's *And When Did You Last See Your Father?*, is a highly personal account of one man's life which teaches readers a great deal about their own emotions and relationships. Now, Alistair Horne has invented a third sort of boyhood reminiscence. Its most memorable characteristic is an obsession with parentheses.

Some pages of *A Bundle From Britain* convey the strong impression that the author has acquired a job lot of brackets and dashes and is determined to dispose of them as quickly as possible. Sometimes they are used in novel conjunction to bury one sentence inside another. The author recalls

> . . . the exotic off-key harmonies of Duke Ellington (even today I can never hear 'In My Solitude' – 'you haunt me with memories of days gone by' – without a frisson), or the long-drawn-out woes of 'Blues in the Night' ('My Momma done tole me . . .')

Were the reckless use of punctuation marks no more than the result of sloppy writing or the work of a crazed typographer, none of the brackets which close before they are opened or are immediately followed by dashes would be worth more than a belly laugh. But the style in which *A Bundle From Britain* is written reveals the book's basic and crucial fault. If the foreword is to be believed, Horne thought about writing 'a great big thank-you to the USofA . . . for many years'. Yet he never quite made up his mind about the form it should take. Memory is interrupted by hindsight. Reminiscence is disturbed by social commentary. The strength of stark facts is sapped by coy asides. As a result, one idea is confusingly embedded in another.

The problem is at its worst at the beginning of the book when Horne feels compelled to set the scene by telling the reader about his distant relations.

The last-surviving cousin of my mother, Victor Creer, vividly remembers being told by his mother, Veronique, about a bastard stepsister, and being taken – as a boy – to visit Grandmother Violet at Lord North's home in Oxfordshire. All his life he retained the image of two old lovers, respectively eighty and ninety, and manifestly in love with each other. (The love child eventually married a bank manager.)

That passage appears in the recollections of a young man who was sent to the United States, as a lonely evacuee, during the Second World War. There is a fascinating tale to be told of how this son of the upper, and mildly Bohemian, middle classes fitted into Washington and New England society during some of the most turbulent years in American history. From time to time, the facts and feelings of the period fight their way through the asides and disgressions. The combination of fear, anger and disbelief which followed the bombing of Pearl Harbor is described with vivid clarity. So is the feeling of failure which Horne experienced when, because of poor eyesight, he failed his air-crew medical and was detached from the Western Hemisphere Squadron. But the crucial faults persist.

A Bundle From Britain is young Alistair's story. But it is always told in the voice of old Horne. The experiences of youth are described with the understanding of age. Everything is reflected through a glass darkly rather than seen face to face. When the real feelings of the period break through, they are far too often qualified by reflections and information which bring the reader up-to-date with the later life of the characters. Up-to-date is the last impression that the book ought to create.

The America in which Horne spent four formative years changed from a mood of sullen isolationism, through its ambivalent role as 'the arsenal of democracy', to the saviour of the free world. It was, as *A Bundle From Britain* records, only when the United States entered the war that Churchill began to believe in victory and allowed himself to speculate about the future of Britain and the Commonwealth. Horne spent much of this fascinating time with fascinating people, not the least of whom was the prodigious Bill Buckley who, even then, was an articulate champion of the intellectual Right. It was, as he makes plain, all very different from

Stowe School where 'the numerous classical temples and copses . . . fairly vibrated with the love that dare not speak its name'. That is not how little boy Horne thought or felt about it at the time. That is big Alistair, the biographer of Harold Macmillan, being literary. An unaffected account of his youth ought to be a delight to read. *A Bundle from Britain* is not.

Sunday Times, 25 June 1993

Purely Fiction

I read *Phineas Finn* on my way back from Malaya and that is my only excuse for briefly believing that it is a novel of distinction. My father managed to be homesick with more discrimination. He opened *Bleak House*, with no great enthusiasm, during the hottest August that Rome had endured in more than fifty years. Before he had got to the bottom of page one – a slow process, because he was blinded by tears – he regarded the story of Jarndice versus Jarndice as the most beautiful novel in the world. He was overwhelmed by the description of the fog. When he got back to England – and coughed his way through real pea-soupers in every November – his literary judgment changed. He was a regular reader, but it was biographies that he borrowed from the local library.

My affection for Trollope lasted for several years and now I understand why. When I was a junior minister in the Ministry of Labour, I had a private secretary who, although normally a birdwatcher of academic disposition, rushed home twice a week to watch a television series called *The Plane Makers*. When challenged to explain this aberration, he reluctantly explained the programme's attraction. One of the characters was a private secretary. Trollope wrote about people like me – Members of Parliament with ambition that exceeded their talent and family affection. In 1974, still flattered by Trollope's attention, I prepared readers of the *Observer* magazine for the BBC's serialisation of all six (if you include *The Eustace Diamonds*) Palliser novels. After I had watched the series, I reviewed it for the *Listener*. My proposed title – 'Can You Forgive Them?' – was rejected by the editor. I have chosen to revive the benign analysis ('Trollope's Love Affair With Politics') rather than the more acerbic judgment.

Almost twenty years later, I described ('Party Poopers') the difficulties of writing a compelling novel of political life. High

199

quality novels of political ideas abound – as do glimpses of political life through the distorting mirrors of other sorts of fiction. But it is impossible to write convincingly about a fictitious prime minister's private life or public performance.

Some time between my philistine admiration for Trollope and the discovery that he was the novelist who is always quoted by people who do not read novels, I was standing proudly in the Members' Lobby of the House of Commons wearing my brand new, loud tweed 'weekend suit'. It had been paid for by Madame Tussaud's who, in exchange for the battered pinstripe in which they dressed my dummy, had provided me with a credit note with which I could have bought several suits of the type I normally wear. Lacking the nerve to order a full wardrobe, I told the tailor that I wanted the sort of weekend suit that Willie Whitelaw wore. On its first outing Denis Healey approached me and looked at me in the way that colour sergeants scrutinise soldiers who are about to parade 'on a charge' in front of the adjutant. 'You think,' he said, 'that you are Lord Marchmain. But really you're Rex Mottram.'

I was immensely flattered by Denis's assumption that I would understand his insult. I am perpetually perplexed by my admiration for *Brideshead Revisited*. Its values are no more my values than its world is my world. But it is a novel to which I return over and over again. Indeed I feel perverse attraction to all of Evelyn Waugh's work. The *Guardian* entitled my article on the subject 'Surrender to the Waugh Machine' and, despite the absurdity of the ghastly pun, that more or less sums up my attitude.

I admitted in the *Listener* ('The Book of the Film') that, although my parents had gently pointed me towards what they believed to be improving literature, it was J. Arthur Rank who arranged the love-match between serious novels and me. The day after I saw *Great Expectations*, I made a detour to the public library on my way home from school and started reading – 'My first name being Phillip . . .' – as soon as I sat down in the living room. The habit persisted. Sometime during the 1950s, I started to read *Anglo-Saxon Attitudes*. I was in my callow twenties, the one decade of my life when I felt no insurmountable shame in leaving a book unfinished. So I barely got to know Professor Middleton and Mrs Salad and was denied the pleasure of their company until the BBC broadcast its television adaptation. Instead of going to the library I bought a paperback. I have never enjoyed a novel more.

Anglo-Saxon Attitudes is one of the novels to which I came thirty years late – perhaps not thirty years *too* late, for it was only pleasure deferred and I would pay a considerable price for the joy of starting *Wuthering Heights* this evening for the first time. I did not read any of the Brontë sisters until I had escaped from the economic texts on which I could not concentrate at university. At school they were too *outré* to be included even in the lists of related reading and, being a conventional boy, I worked methodically through Dickens, Thackeray, Austen and (a cruel and unusual punishment) Walter Scott.

These days, I defend my own novels by citing – with reckless *lèse majesté* – the example of *Wuthering Heights*. When *The Maker's Mark* was being typed, the lady who had the task of deciphering my longhand innocently asked if it really was the first part of a family trilogy. When I proudly agreed that it was, she asked me how – since the first generation never touched each other – the second and third generations were conceived. Audiences of literary lunches and bookshop discussions – all of them accustomed to novelists who paraphrase passages from Masters and Johnson and the Kinsey Report – usually contain a bold spirit who asks the same question in the nicest possible way. My answer is always *Wuthering Heights*. It is the most passionate novel in the English language. But the reader has to imagine what Heathcliff does in bed.

At least, that was the case until Lin Haire-Sergeant wrote *Heathcliff – The Return to Wuthering Heights*. It was one of the few novels which the *Sunday Times* has allowed me to review ('Heathcliff! Cathy! Mr Rochester!'). I am steered towards biography, history and social commentary for reasons which are only marginally concerned with my critical judgment. My contract guarantees me a fee which is only paid for reviews which are published at the front of the book supplement – and that is where the non-fiction goes, because it makes up 90 per cent of hardback sales. Every time I review a novel, the literary editor's budget moves into deficit.

Do not tell me that a real lover of literature would volunteer to accept a reduced fee. I have tried that, and the *Sunday Times* accounting system cannot accommodate my sacrifice. These sordid commercial details are made public not because I hold the Auden-esque view that real writers are more interested in the money than in the plot, dialogue and characters. I want to make clear that my absence from the fiction pages of the *Sunday Times* is entirely unrelated to my condemnation of Sue Townsend's *The Queen and I*. Miss Townsend (a year in the bestsellers list) tells me that I am forgiven.

About which much rejoicing. For she is one of the few writers to whom I have sent notes of sycophantic admiration – not for Adrian Mole (who presumably made her rich) but for a Review Front she wrote for the *Observer* about being poor.

The hardest novels to write are those which describe being ordinary. Stories of infant Peruvian princesses – kidnapped whilst on a visit to New York, brought up by families of Mafia bosses, sent to Vassar, recruited by the SAS and dropped behind enemy lines, seduced by the richest man in Europe, converted to Catholicism by Franciscan abbots, told of their true origins by a cub reporter who turns out to be heir to the world's greatest media empire – hold no charm for me.

The true pedigree is by *Middlemarch* out of *The Old Wives' Tale*. Raymond Williams in *Realism in the English Novel* explains why that idea of fiction transcends all others. What matters is the extraordinary lives of ordinary people. When I wrote about his lecture ('True Stories from Fiction'), relating it to the work of Arnold Bennett, I constructed my first unlikely plot for the basis of a wildly successful novel. It was even more improbable than the tale of the Peruvian princess in that earlier version. The heroine meets Jeffrey Archer.

Trollope's Love Affair With Politics

In one sense British politics has hardly changed during the last hundred years. The great disputes that divide the nation are not the same as those that convulsed Parliament in 1874. The parties have established new allegiances and assumed new philosophies. But the trappings and the trivia of political life remain virtually unaltered. The postures struck by Members of Parliament and the manners they assume, the details of their daily lives and the peculiar pressures of their trade endure – and have been immortalised in Anthony Trollope's Palliser novels.

Strictly speaking the Palliser novels are not political at all. Politics is essentially about issues, the one thing Trollope does not and perhaps cannot provide. But more than any other writer he has captured the attitudes of politicians and the prejudices of people who support and sustain them, distrust and destroy them, and are never quite sure whether politics is a noble calling or a shameful trade. The attitudes and the prejudices remain.

The financial interests of MPs have become an issue of sorts during the 1970s. A hundred years ago in *The Prime Minister* (the fifth novel in the series), Trollope wrote that being in Parliament 'assists a man in getting a seat as a director of Certain Companies. People are still such asses that they trust a Board of Directors made up of Members, and therefore, of course, Members are made welcome.'

In an age of allegedly deepening disillusion with the party battle, we are constantly told that the conflict between government and opposition is no more than a fight to catch tomorrow morning's headlines. 'It became evident,' wrote Trollope in *Phineas Finn* during 1864, 'that in spite of his assumed fury, the gentleman was not irate. He intended to communicate the look of anger to the newspaper reports of his speech and he knew from experience that he could succeed in that.'

According to today's newspapers the stresses and strains of parliamentary life produce a risk of marital break-ups that rival the record of Hollywood during the jazz age. The reason for all the mayhem is the typical parliamentarian's priorities. Trollope described an attitude which persists until this day. 'Having been appointed to the Treasury bench he could easily accommodate the small everyday calamity of having a wife who loved another man better than she loved him.'

Trollope is the master of the brilliant glimpse. But although he provided flashes of light on political behaviour he hardly mentioned the great issues of conscience and conviction that lay at the heart of political life. That, Asa Briggs the historian believes, is because of the age in which Trollope's view of politics was formed – the period before the second great Reform Bill of 1867, when the lines dividing the parties were less sharply drawn than they were by the end of Gladstone's last administration. So, the Duke of Omnium is typical of both Trollope's political fiction and England's political fact in his insistence that

> when some small measure of reform has thoroughly commended itself to the country – so thoroughly that all men know that the country will have it – then the question arises whether its details shall be arranged by the political party that calls itself Liberal or by that which calls itself Conservative. The men are so near each other in all their convictions and theories of life, that nothing is left to them except personal competition for doing the thing that must be done.

That opinion of politics (developed during the age of Palmerston – who was, according to Trollope, 'by no means a man of genius and possessed of no more than ordinary gifts') is repeated again and again in the Palliser novels usually by politicians who know 'that a Prime Minister should be clever but need not be a genius'. It is a concept of politics that, although consistent with a political apprenticeship served during the 1850s and 1860s, shows a gross insensitivity to the massive radical programme launched by Mr Gladstone the year *Phineas Finn* was written, and which remained on the national agenda well after Plantagenet Palliser's old age was recorded in *The Duke's Children*.

Yet Trollope's political importance lies in his sensitivity to the parliamentary world around him. He knew that as he wrote the Palliser series the parties were becoming polarised, that party programmes and election manifestos were becoming important. His decision to immortalise the trivia of politics rather than the major themes of conviction and belief was, at least in part, deliberate. It had two main causes.

The first was literary necessity. Most of the readers of *Phineas Redux* knew perfectly well that the real First Lord of the Admiralty was Mr H. C. E. Childers. To believe in the existence of Phineas Finn, his fictional alternative, required substantial suspension of disbelief. The more Trollope pretends that Finn was the architect of Childers's policies (or for that matter the architect of policies Childers never espoused) the more difficult it is to believe that Finn ever existed. We can believe in him personally but not publicly. And what is more – with or without disbelief suspended – Trollope feared that, even in high Victorian England, he 'could not make a tale pleasing, chiefly or perhaps in any part by politics'. In his classic biography James Pope Hennessy says that politics went into the Palliser novels for the author's personal pleasure. He knew that his stories must contain 'love and intrigue, social incidents and a dash of sport'. But real politics had to be excluded.

But that is only half the story. Trollope was infatuated by politics. But his love deserted him at Beverley in 1868 when, at the age of fifty-two, he fought a bruising by-election and suffered painful, humiliating defeat. From then on both 'political' and 'non-political' novels contained obsessive accounts of corrupt canvassing and bribed electors, the degradations heaped on candidates and the malpractices of parliamentary agents. Trollope had written four years before his own campaign that it 'would be something to sit in the House of Commons, though it should only be for half a session ... for it is the highest and most legitimate pride of an Englishman to have the letters MP written after his name'. Yet fate and the electors of Beverley ordained that Trollope (unlike George Vavasour, the dissolute candidate of *Can You Forgive Her?*) would never be told, 'You have heard debates from the gallery. Now you'll hear them from the body of the House, and you'll find how very different it is.'

Trollope had told himself 'in anger and grief, that to die and not to have won that right of way [into Parliament] was to die and not to have done that which it most becomes an Englishman to have achieved'. He had, therefore, to construct excuse, justification and comfort. An explanation of sorts had appeared in *Can You Forgive Her?* – 'England does not choose her 654 best men.' That was as true in 1868 as it is in 1974. But it was written before the Beverley by-election. After his own defeat, that did not provide sufficient solace. Much as he loved the idea of Parliament and politics, he *needed* to find the reality hateful. So he turned to the prejudices of the people who, a hundred years ago, held politics in the same suspicion as the cynics and the worldly wise hold it today.

He reproduced their cynicism exactly. The young Phineas Finn is assured that aspirants to office succeed by making themselves 'uncommonly unpleasant to those in power, thus being taken to the Treasury Bench, not that they may hit others, but that they may cease to hit those who are there'. In *Phineas Redux*, Finn has himself come to believe the calumny that modern politicians still hear while canvassing: 'What does it matter who sits in Parliament? The fight goes on just the same. The same wrong falsehoods are acted. The same half truths are spoken. The same wrong reasons are given. The same personal motives are at work.' In the same book, Lord Brentford echoes the advice that the ambitious Phineas Finn had heard five years before: 'Most men rise now, by making themselves thoroughly disagreeable.'

It is worth noting that Lord Brentford inserts the adverb 'now'. He believed, as we sometimes believe, that the golden days were past. He was wrong then as we are wrong today. John Bright – in the real House of Commons – hit the Treasury bench hard and repeatedly. But he did not battle his way into the government. Nor does Enoch Powell who is, by any standards, 'uncommonly unpleasant to those in power'. Neither did Mr Turnbull, who was modelled on John Bright and attacked the cabinet with a Powell-like intensity. Trollope observed and recorded Bright's behaviour. But he was incapable of understanding Bright's motives, which were concerned with the issues of the day, not personal advancement.

For some of that, Trollope must be forgiven. 'No man', he wrote bitterly, 'can know what Parliament is who has never held a seat'. In politics, the spectator misses the best and the noblest of the game. From the Strangers' Gallery and club conversation,

Trollope could observe the patterns of political behaviour, the abiding trivia of parliamentary life, the postures men struck and the manners they assumed. But in terms of the burning issues that move most politicians he was simply the accurate reflection of prevalent inaccuracies.

Trollope's judgments of politics are the opinions of a man soured by failure to move out of the world of fiction to the reality of a seat in the House of Commons. But they represent a view of politicians that must come as a shock to those who think it has been all moral decline since the rigid party system invaded Westminster.

In the year that Mr Gladstone's first administration fell, the readers of the *Fortnightly Review* were told that 'loyalty in politics is simply a devotion to the side which a man . . . cannot leave without danger to himself and assures that most politicians would follow their leaders into the lobby like sheep. They have been so knocked about by one treachery after another that they care for nothing but their places.' As Benjamin Disraeli was planning to buy Suez Canal shares, Trollope was explaining that 'had some inscrutable decree of fate ordained . . . that no candidate could be returned to Parliament who would not assert the earth to be triangular, then would arise immediately a clamorous assertion of triangularity amongst political candidates'.

Those judgments are not presented as the aberrations of dispossessed and disenchanted place-seekers. They are offered as the *obiter dicta* of Liberal elder statesmen, ambitious government whips and the Prime Minister himself. Their weakness is that they were – and still are – wrong. Their interest stems from the simple fact that they encapsulate an image of politicians common in England even when giants canvassed the land. Their moral is that without dogma and theology, politics 'has to be practical. A party can only live by having its share of Garters, Lord Lieutenants, bishops and attorney generals.' We were not more respected before the party machines got up steam.

Yet, while Trollope is wrong about what moves and motivates politics, his powers of observation are impeccable, and they demonstrate how little parliamentary moves have changed during the last hundred years. It is still possible for 'the most unpopular man in the House to make himself liked by owning freely that he had done something he ought to be ashamed of'. When one of Lady Glencra Palliser's characteristic minor indiscretions seemed likely to be raised in Parliament, the Commons' reaction would have surprised neither Miss Christine Keeler nor Mrs Norma Levy: 'Had the welfare of the Indian Empire occupied the House, the House would have been empty, but the hope that a certain woman's name would have to be mentioned crammed it from floor to ceiling.' Phineas Finn was told, as others contemplating resignation have been told, that those who wished to go 'failed to comprehend the only way in which a great party can act together if it is to do any service in this country'.

Lord Farringcourt in *Can You Forgive Her?* rose to address the House immediately the major debate ended. Speaking above the hubbub of departing Members, he 'knew that the papers would not report one sentence in twenty of those which he uttered. He knew that no one would listen to him willingly . . . that he had worked for weeks and months to get up his facts and he was beginning to know that he had worked in vain.' That unhappy experience is not limited to the works of Trollope or his lifetime. Mr Quintus Slide, in *Phineas Finn*, was not the last journalist to say, 'If it is true, I have every right to publish it. If it's not, I've got every right to ask the question.' The Duchess of Omnium, in *The Prime Minister*, speaks for future generations of politicians' wives when, refused information on her husband's prospects, she bitterly agrees: 'Of course, you should keep the secret. The Editors of the evening papers haven't known about it for above an hour.'

Fortunate present-day politicians will find few other similarities between their wives and the Duchess of Omnium – one of fiction's silly women who infuriate more often than they fascinate. Having married Plantagenet Palliser out of duty rather than love, she is beset by recurring attacks of marital zeal that usually embarrass her husband more than her equally frequent fits of simple disloyalty. To beg Plantagenet's uncle, the Duke, to abandon his plans to marry Madame Max Goesler so that Plantagenet can be sure to inherit the dukedom is both absurd and impertinent. To encourage Ferdinand Lopez to believe that her husband would support him at the Silverbridge by-election was irresponsible and dishonest. To connive with her children in keeping their engagements a secret from their father was understandable but, by the standards of Victorian England, unforgivable. To believe that her husband's political fortune could be improved by lavish entertainment was wrong, but is also typical of a species of political wife that is not yet extinct.

It is because Trollope writes of incidents and characters that have obvious authenticity that the game of identifying real politicians behind Trollope's fictional characters began. James Pope Hennessy warns against the whole operation – but adds that Phineas Finn was almost certainly a portrait of his own grandfather. Trollope himself insisted that there was 'no distant idea in my mind of any living person'.

But one passage in the series is not, as Trollope claimed, 'pure creation'. In the opening chapters of *Phineas Redux*, the author turns unashamedly from fiction to a caricature of fact. Mr Daubney *is* Disraeli as he hangs on to office for six months after his majority has gone, sustained by the power of patronage and a willingness to abandon long-held beliefs.

The clergy were outraged by Daubney's proposal to disestablish the Church, for 'this was the man to whom they had looked for protection! This was the bulwark of the Church in whom they had trusted!' Disraeli's volte-face over electoral reform was no less abominable to his traditional supporters. Robert Lowe, the party's philosopher of autocracy and limited franchise, was convinced that 'never was there tergiversation so complete. Such conduct . . . merits alike the contempt of all honest men and the execration of posterity.'

In many ways the Daubney/Disraeli episode is the least convincing of Trollope's political vignettes. The confusion between image and reality must have bewildered contemporary readers. Having gasped at the audacity of Disraeli in 1867 they were asked to gasp again, seven years later, at a rather inferior version of the same incident. When they remembered Disraeli, Daubney must have been completely incredible. Then, because of the need for 'incident and excitement', the reflection of Disraeli's world is shattered when the President of the Board of Trade is murdered by an Armenian Jew turned Christian clergyman who had once been a suitor of Lizzie Eustace. When the issues are real, the people are not. When the excitement of politics is not enough, the political content of the novel is submerged in melodrama and novelette romance.

But although reflecting the great issues of politics and capturing convincing female characteristics was a task beyond Trollope's powers, reproducing common political events was not. At the Beverley by-election, he spent 'the most wretched fortnight . . . subject to bitter tyranny from vulgar, grudging tyrants'. The experience was faithfully recorded. In *Phineas Redux*, the agent at Tankerville urged on his candidate a policy that 'did not spring from his own convictions, but from the need to have a Liberal Candidate returned for the Borough'. In *The Prime Minister*, Ferdinand Lopez (although his prospects of being elected for Silverbridge had vanished) was assured 'that a good deal might be done by judicious manipulation' and told that 'another cheque for £500 . . . might be effective'. Trollope's personal disappointment had prepared him to believe that 'political cleanliness was odious to the citizen'. Fortunately, life had also equipped him to note – and wonder at – the ways of Parliament: 'We get men into the House now who are clever and all that sort of thing and who force their way up, but who can't be made to understand that everybody should not want to be Prime Minister.'

This is not Lord Shinwell's icy judgment on Parliament's new generation or Lord Salisbury damning with faint praise Iain Macleod and the 'One Nation' group of Tories whom he found too-clever-by-half in the 1950s. It is the judgment of Barrington Erle, the 'good party man' of the Palliser novels. And it seems impossible that Trollope's valediction for retired prime ministers was written for the Pallisers' Gatherum Castle rather than Churchill's Chartwell or Macmillan's Birchgrove – 'They sighed to be back amongst the trumpets. They had suffered much amongst the trumpets, yet they longed to return.'

The details are so much as they ever were that only one question persists. Should the enduring accuracy of Trollope's parliamentary observation provoke admiration for Trollope's perception or amusement at Parliament's inability to change and improve?

Observer Magazine, 20 January 1974

Surrender to the Waugh Machine

They say in Yorkshire that there is no accounting for taste. And for years – guided by this simple adage – I attributed my enjoyment of Evelyn Waugh to straightforward intellectual perversity.

I first read *Brideshead Revisited* whilst waiting to be told which Brightside and Carbrook Co-operative milkman was late enough to provide an opportunity for the employment of unskilled student labour. From the first page, I hated everything that Evelyn Waugh stood for and everything he wrote about.

But I loved the way he wrote about it. I am separated by birth, background and belief from the morals and mores of Waugh's society. If it ever existed I am glad that it has gone. If the men and women about whom he wrote did have some basis in fact, I cannot imagine that I would have welcomed their company. But all that I remember only when each novel is finished. As I read, I am so dazzled by Waugh's style that I hardly even notice the deficiencies in his substance.

No one writes more attractively about unattractive subjects than Evelyn Waugh. The characters in his early novels are wholly repulsive; those in his late books largely ridiculous. There is not a single redeeming virtue in the society he satirises and his parodies of London's louche establishment reveal an admiration for its social values that far outweighs his disapproval of its vices.

He is obsessed with the trivia of taste and the minutiae of manners. His hatred of the lower orders – especially when they have risen above their station – demonstrates the class consciousness of the insecure minor public schoolboy. The idea of redemption through the pursuit of a mystical yet military Holy Grail (which first appears in *Brideshead Revisited* and is the theme for the *Sword of Honour* trilogy) is silly as well as sad. Of course, it all turns into ashes.

In the trilogy, failure, despair and disillusion come in every shape and size. Guy Crouchback, committed by Catholicism to monogamy, attempts to seduce his divorced wife – and bungles it.

He takes a bottle of whisky to a sick friend. What was intended to comfort kills. And at the end of his three-volume crusade he discovers that the quest was not merely in vain. It was not even in a good cause.

A Jewish refugee reproaches him. 'Even good men thought their private honour would be satisfied by war. They would accept hardship in recompense for having been selfish or lazy ... Danger justified privilege.'

In *Men at Arms*, Crouchback would have defended his beliefs. Then he had only one fear, '*Domine non sum dignus*'. In *Unconditional Surrender*, Crouchback has another response: 'God forgive me. I was one of them.'

Being a gentleman, Crouchback is allowed to accept the death of his illusions with dignity. Less heroic heroes must see their dreams end in farce. Aimee Thanatogenos, mortuary beautician in *The Loved One*, is disappointed by one suitor and deceived by another. She chooses a professional suicide – a hypodermic of formalin. The more romantic of her two lovers takes the body to the animals' crematorium where the oven – although suitable for the disposal of cats and dogs – is really too small to accommodate larger mammals. Having recently incinerated a goat, he knows what to do. He pounds the skull and pelvis with a poker.

For Mr Waugh there is a worm in every bud. No one escapes. Even Lady Metroland, who foxtrots through *Vile Bodies* and *Decline and Fall*, is not spared. She makes a brief gratuitous reappearance in *Basil Seal Rides Again*. 'The room was in darkness save for the ghastly light of a television set. Margot crouched over it, her old face livid in the reflection.'

I never cared much for Margot even in the full flush of her Mayfair youth. Indeed the only Waugh character with whom I even remotely identified is the ambivalent college servant who welcomes the occasional five-shilling bonus, but welcomes the absence even more as it is paid in recompense for cleaning up young gentlemen's vomit. Yet I read his novels with genuine pleasure. They make me laugh. And I marvel at their careful balance, meticulous construction, and near perfect prose. Evelyn Waugh is master of the ugly thought beautifully expressed.

Take the episode of the Brideshead tortoise: 'It was a small tortoise with Julia's initials set in diamonds in the living shell and this slightly obscene object . . . swaying its antediluvian head . . . became a memorable part of the evening.'

It also became the vehicle for a little social commentary: ' "Dear me," said Lady Marchmain, "I wonder if it eats the same sort of things as an ordinary tortoise." "What do you do when it's dead?" asked Mr Samgrass. "Can you have another tortoise fitted into the shell?" '

The incident sets out society as Mr Waugh sees it. Rex Mottram, 'a lucky man with money, a Member of Parliament and a gambler', is guilty of vulgarity on the grand scale – the gift of the tortoise. Mr Samgrass, the 'dapper' don-on-the-make, is vulgar in a more venial but also more offensive way. Lady Marchmain is slightly fey and properly detached. In a decent world, she would be spared such company.

At least Lady Marchmain missed Lieutenant Hooper, a 'sallow youth with hair combed back without parting from his forehead and a flat Midland accent'. He was over familiar with other ranks and afraid of his batman, qualities which made Captain Ryder wonder if the war was really worth fighting. None of Waugh's heroes want to build a world fit for Hooper to live in.

That is the pathetic part of what Waugh wrote. The hilarious element is almost as prominent. Lord Copper, owner of the *Beast* and recipient of the Scoop, speaks: 'I never hamper my correspondents in any way. What the British public wants first and last and all the time is News. Remember that the Patriots are in the right and are going to win. But they must win quickly. The British public has no interest in a war which drags on indecisively. A few sharp victories, some conspicuous acts of personal bravery on the Patriot side and a colourful entry into the capital. That is the *Beast*'s policy for this war.'

The stories into which the hilarity, the class consciousness, the backward glance, and the sheer nastiness are woven are always meticulously constructed. Mr Joyboy, who 'had taken a baccalaureate in embalming in the Middle West and for some years before his appointment at Whispering Glades had been one of the Undertaking Faculty at an historic Eastern University', had a mother. From the moment she 'drew the fringe of a shawl and revealed the wire cage and in it an almost naked parrot', we realise that the bird is not a harbinger of hope. We know too that it is there for some purpose. Mr Waugh would not waste a near naked parrot.

Its death brings together the denizens of the human and animal crematoria. As a result of their meeting, complicated lies are exposed and the consequent disillusion leads to disaster – not an unfamiliar train of literary events. But in Waugh there is an almost exclusive difference. Usually when such things happen the gods weep. In the writing of Evelyn Waugh they snigger.

Their sniggering is superbly described. Having incinerated *The Loved One*, Dennis Barlow decided to complete all the procedures usual in the Happier Hunting Ground. 'He entered the office and made a note in the book kept there for that purpose. Tomorrow and every anniversary as long as the Happier Hunting Ground existed, a postcard would go to Mrs Joyboy. Your little Aimee is wagging her tail in heaven tonight, thinking of you.' It is all beautifully done. Hip, hip, hooray, and ugh!

Guardian, 19 October 1977

Tales of Espionage

During the last twenty years there has been a depressing improvement in the quality of British spy stories. I blame Mr Graham Greene. For years he has seen the 'agent's' secret life of doubt and deception as a paradigm for the sadder aspects of the human condition. And he writes about the same subject as Sapper in a way that Bulldog Drummond could never understand.

Perhaps a generation which learned to shave in the shadow of James Bond should be grateful that the profession which prompted Mr Ian Fleming's meretricious rubbish also inspired *The Human Factor*. Others will argue that anyone brought up on the halting prose with which Mr John Buchan described God popping out of the machine to rescue his old-fashioned hero, Richard Hannay – mining engineer, philistine, racist, temporary brigadier and permanent dunderhead – ought to be glad that the genre now includes such an ingenious stylist as John le Carré. I have my doubts.

When Richard Hannay arranged the slow murder of a prisoner ('I thought of the foul deeds that had made the German name stink by land and sea, a foulness of which he was arch-begetter'), or James Bond killed a young lady by knocking an electric fire into her bath, it was just good unclean fun. Buchan and Fleming did not write about real people in a real world. To be concerned about either their mores or their morality was about as sensible as worrying in case, next Christmas, the giant catches Jack before he gets down the beanstalk.

We rejoiced in our spy stories' invincible triviality. *The Secret Agent* we wrote off as hardly being a spy story at all. *The Riddle of the Sands* was very well written for a book obsessed with boats, but there were few interesting ideas submerged beneath the reef of anti-Hohenzollern patriotism, and when they came to the surface we put them down to the eccentricity of the author. Within the space of eight years, Mr Erskine Childers was successively a Clerk to the House of Commons, a lieutenant-commander in the Royal Naval Air Service with a DSC to his credit, a gun-runner for Sinn Fein, and a convicted traitor executed by the new Republic of Ireland which he had so recently served. He was entitled to take naval espionage seriously and to see some of the complications in the life of service which is only safe so long as it is secret.

John Buchan – in *Greenmantle* – saw life and loyalty in less complex terms:

> 'Three months ago, just before Kut, he staggered into Delamain's camp with ten bullet holes in him and a knife slash in his forehead . . . He told them nothing . . .'
> 'What a great fellow! What was his name?' I asked.
> Sir Walter did not answer at once. He was looking out of the window.
> 'His name,' he said at last, 'was Harry Bullivant. He was my son, God rest his brave soul.'

But Mr Greene and Mr le Carré (the latter no doubt relying for verisimilitude on the 'tradecraft' he picked up as a 'housekeeper', 'lamplighter', 'scalp-hunter', or whatever he used to be) have taken the innocence out of espionage and the frivolity from counter-intelligence. They have made it all real. The dog (wounded but not cleanly killed by the defector who must leave it silent in his cellar) and the Russian émigré (whose face was blown off by a 'standard Moscow Center assassination weapon') bleed real blood.

More important, the double agents (and sometimes the single agents, too) feel the terror and torment of lives that are perpetual lies. And they demonstrate all the moral confusion of men who have pretended to believe alien ideas for so long that they are no longer sure where conviction ends and conspiracy begins. Thus in *The Honourable Schoolboy*, George Smiley writes:

> I chose the secret road because it seemed to lead straightest and furthest toward my country's goal. The enemy in those days was someone we could point at and read about in the papers. Today, all I know is that I have learnt to interpret the whole of life in terms of conspiracy.

Most important of all, the Greene and the le Carré characters have freed themselves from the emotional certainties of the *Boy's Own Paper*. Maurice Castle is both redeemed as a man and destroyed as an agent by the human factor. His first loyalty is not to the service, but to the people who, long ago, rescued his wife; not to his own country but to the country from which his wife comes; not to the conventional judgments about that country's prospects but to the vision of the future cherished by his wife's people. Gerald Westerby, the honourable schoolboy, in a mad moment of quixotic absurdity, forgets the 'Sarratt rules' and tries to bargain with the 'Circus' that employs him for the safety of a blonde from Barnsbury who deserted her family in search of a disreputable fortune in Hong Kong.

It is the underlying theme of *The Spy Who Came in from the Cold* and it is the recurring dilemma in earlier novels and 'entertainments' written by Graham Greene. There are no – or there should not be – simple, uncomplicated loyalties. By its nature, the Secret Service faces each day Mr E. M. Forster's famous (though mercifully hypothetical) choice of betraying country or friend. Being human, the people about whom Mr Greene and Mr le Carré write agonise about the choice, postpone the decision for far too long and usually destroy themselves as a result.

A comparison between the love of Agent Castle for his wife and stepson and the strip-cartoon appetites of Agent 007 would be ridiculous. But in between the extremes of excellence and absurdity lie Mr le Carré and Mr Buchan. Mr le Carré chooses to face the personal problems of living in the half-world of doubt and deception. 'Control' created a second home with a second 'wife' which provided 'cover' for his confused personality as well as his complicated profession. Bill Haydon, treachery discovered and passage to Russia booked, leaves parting gifts for lovers of both sexes. George Smiley bears the burden of a constantly unfaithful wife whom he loves but cannot understand.

Compare all that with the courtship of Brigadier Hannay in *Mr Standfast*:

> Out from the shade came suddenly a voice like a nightingale. It was singing the old song 'Cherry Ripe', a common enough thing which I had chiefly known from barrel-organs. But heard in the scented moonlight it seemed to hold all the lingering magic of an older England and this hallowed countryside. I stepped inside the garden's bounds and saw the head of the girl Mary.

Reader, he married both of them – England and the girl. And they lived happily ever afterwards in a world of perfect public and private loyalty. It is more than the lost innocence of our age that makes me wonder how that novel ran to sixteen editions in fourteen years, more than the new sophistication that makes us now suspect that 'the intelligence community' live more complicated lives.

Indeed, we do more than suspect, we *know*. True stories about real spies appear in our newspapers and on our television screens almost every day. And we have been raised and reared in a world of incipient conflict which has taught us to believe that lies and deception are essential weapons in the defence of the values which we support. No doubt they are. But that does not explain why tales of espionage have been elevated to a level of literature which they did not previously occupy.

My fear is that we read superior spy stories because we suspect the spy to be a mirror of our time – morally insecure, emotionally uncertain, ambiguous in his personal relationships, and loyal and honourable only within his own limits. Richard Hannay was an intrinsically odious figure. He lived in a time which was in most ways inferior to our own. Yet, paradoxically, the world that could believe that he was a secret agent had something to commend it.

Listener, 3 April 1980

In Praise of Writing Women

I spent my youth in the Sheffield of the 1940s, surrounded by the symbols of male domination and female inferiority. Women slaving over hot ovens rarely started to cook Sunday's Yorkshire pudding until the public houses closed at two o'clock. For a man to travel 'inside' a tramcar on its non-smoking lower deck was to risk malicious gossip about his virility. We went to youth clubs to play table tennis and smash the furniture. Girls morosely dancing with each other at the far end of the old Nissen hut were treated with overt contempt and counterfeit detachment.

That I survived into manhood, spared at least the more gross characteristics of male chauvinism, is in part a tribute to my father's willingness to do the washing-up and my mother's management of the household budget. Dr Edith Summerskill and Alderman Mrs Grace Tebbutt of the Sheffield City Council helped to convince me that strength of character is not synonymous with wearing a waistcoat and braces.

Books were a more important influence even than politics and life under the partnership of equals which my parents strove to be. These days, the subliminal influence of early images is known to shape both temperament and character. I have actually attended a meeting at which a person complained about Puffin books in regular primary school use. According to her careful researches, in their pictures male characters outnumbered female by six to one – excluding the puffins, whose sex defied analysis. But the books which influenced me contained no pictures at all.

The books at which I marvelled most were written by women. As the greatest literary stylist of the nineteenth century was called

Jane, I felt little superiority over my female contemporaries simply because only men contended with Bruce Woodcock for the heavyweight championship of Great Britain. And since three novelists called Anne, Emily and Charlotte had gripped me with a quality in their writing which I suspected to be passion, I was reluctant to interpret all female emotions in terms of the young ladies waiting outside the Hillsborough Park Cinema for American soldiers from the Wortley Hall Camp. And that was before I had even heard of George Eliot.

I confess at once that I found Miss Evans much heavier going than the Misses Austen and Brontë. But I was encouraged – indeed impelled – to persevere by the clear moral imperatives that shine out of her every page. Her biographer, Mr W. Allen, retails the reminiscence of a young Cambridge don who 'walked with her once in the Fellows' Garden of Trinity on an evening of rainy May'. George Eliot 'stirred somewhat beyond her wont and, taking as her text the three words which had been used so often as the inspiring trumpet-call of men – the words God, Immortality, Duty – pronounced with terrible earnestness how inconceivable was the first, how unbelievable was the second and yet how peremptory and absolute the third.'

It never struck me that George Eliot was a 'woman writer' in anything other than the most fundamentally biological meaning of that term. To suggest that she wrote with special insight about women's feelings and dilemmas or, from the other side of the coin, dealt inadequately with male attitudes and emotions would be absurd. Being a great writer, she is as sexless as she is timeless. To imagine otherwise is as ignorant as to suggest that Thomas Hardy, being a man, could not understand the anguish of a woman whose husband sold her to a sailor, but that his male proclivities gave him a special insight into the psychology of country gentlemen who seduce their distant kinsfolk.

Yet, in these supposedly more equal days, people speak of 'women writers' as if they could or should possess some special virtue connected with their gender. Shusha Guppy (described by the *Observer* as author and critic) believes that *Wide Sargasso Sea* – the story of Mrs Rochester before Jane Eyre arrived at Thornfield Hall – is a 'novel that in its formal perfection, emotional immediacy, psychological truth and above all *feminine* outlook stands out amid the great novels of our time like a cathedral in delicate filigree gold'. The italics are, believe me, Shusha Guppy's, not mine.

Praise for Jean Rhys, the author of *Wide Sargasso Sea*, and her literary femininity is not confined to that single strange novel:

> While some of her famous contemporaries are beginning to 'date', to my mind Jean Rhys's work remains alive and of today – a mirror in which women can see their inner selves in moments of private truth (why, even Mrs Thatcher once confessed in an interview to weeping herself to sleep at times), and in which men can learn a great deal more about them.

I know very well that some writers cannot prevent their genes showing through. The more absurd episodes in Ernest Hemingway and the nastier aspects of Evelyn Waugh always seem to be essentially male creations. But that is a shortcoming in their work, not a reason for praise. Yet Miss Rhys and her ilk are congratulated for what their admirers see as essentially limited insight.

Let me say at once that if I am prejudiced about Miss Rhys, I am biased in her favour. The residual chauvinist within me admires anyone who looked as if she were the most beautiful member of the Dietrich family – the one who made Marlene jealous. The sheer effrontery of cannibalising *Jane Eyre* entitles her to a measure of grudging admiration. And the idea of taking a masterpiece and writing not a sequel but a prologue provides the inspiration for a brilliant parlour game. I have already seen *Heathcliff, The Missing Years* flaunting its pulp revelations in an Edinburgh bookshop.

But it is not bias alone that enables me to enjoy *Wide Sargasso Sea*. I genuinely admire that beautifully written, if slightly bizarre book. I even liked *Smile Please*, Miss Rhys's obviously unfinished autobiography. Even the minor works about seduction, betrayal and desertion have a sordid charm and titles that tempt the cautious reader to take a risk. Indeed, it is my respect for her writing that makes me resent the limited praise which she has drawn ever since Ford Madox Ford, her patronising patron, said that 'the instinct for form possessed by this young lady' was 'possessed by singularly few writers of English and by almost no English women writers'.

I am, in fact, wholly opposed to the idea of 'women writers'. Miss Rhys, and, for that matter, Margaret Drabble and Edna O'Brien, are 'writers' and should be spared the sexual adjective. When the description is apostrophised the insult is extended to half the human race. 'Women's writers' are presumably authors who meet a demand too illiterate to be satisfied by the usual run of literature – the sort of people who are advertised on containers of washing-up liquid by a picture of a rose and a promise of romance.

For one of the lessons that great writing should have taught is that washing-up liquid and literary inspiration can – metaphorically at least – go hand in romantic hand. Mary Ann Evans called herself George Eliot, but for twenty-four years she lived with George Henry Lewes, sharing the obligations, if not the formal status, of marriage. The Brontë sisters, also hidden under male pseudonyms, lived, like Jane Austen, constrained by conditions of extreme domesticity. Yet from Haworth and Hampshire burst forth novels of genuine imaginative genius.

I have no idea how many justified superlatives have been heaped on the words of those five ladies, or how many copies of their novels have been sold. The beneficial effect they have had on the human race is beyond calculation. The pleasure they have provided is too great to imagine. But to me in my selfish Sheffield male way, their most spectacular achievement was the penetration of deepest South Yorkshire in the 1940s. Had they not arrived, like a rescue column for our beleaguered citadel of sexual equality, I might still believe that a woman's place is in the home, and possibly the House of Commons, but certainly not in the library.

Listener, 17 July 1980

'The Book of the Film'

Sunday evenings at six o'clock have become immovable feasts again. *Great Expectations*, dramatised in twelve episodes by James Andrew Hall, is brilliant. Or so everybody tells me. I have seen, and much enjoyed, two episodes. But whatever critical faculty I possess was blunted by the alien appearance of the characters. I am bewildered by the casual casting, which I can only attribute to the immaturity of whoever was responsible. Everybody over forty knows perfectly well that Pip looks like the young John Mills, that Estella (in childhood identical to Jean Simmons) grew up to be indistinguishable from Valerie Hobson and that Joe Gargery *is* Bernard Miles. Even today, as I watch one of the relentless repeats of *Tinker, Tailor, Soldier, Spy*, I always recall that George Smiley operated, in his youth, under the name of Herbert Pocket: a pale young man with an enthusiasm for Handel and a propensity to be knocked down. No new image can obliterate or erase the black-and-white pictures that were painted on my mind in the Hillsborough Kinema some time during the 1940s.

In those days I went to the pictures at least once every week – 'first house' (starting at 6.15), 'upstairs' (which was more respectable), and a ninepenny ticket (for as long as I appeared to be under fourteen). I could manage ninety minutes' homework before I ran to catch the bus for Worrall. And if I ran out of the cinema the moment 'God Save the King' was over, I could be home again by half past eight. That was especially important on the nights that *ITMA* and *Take It From Here* were broadcast. On those evenings there was no loitering in or about the fish and chip shop. I often risked my life and the conductor's wrath by leaping on board a moving bus rather than miss the second part of my three hours' synthetic, sinful double-bill of pleasure.

Thanks to James Andrew Hall, I am beginning to believe that the guilt was inappropriate. At ninepence a night, neither my money nor my time was wasted. No doubt I sat through hours of rubbish. But before the Kinema was closed down, the Park Cinema became a bingo hall and the Phoenix was demolished (never to rise again) to make way for a car park, they provided more than evenings of simple pleasure.

Within twenty-four hours of the final, ambiguous shot of Pip either leaving or reclaiming Estella, I possessed the book on which the film was based. Of course, the Magwitch who leaped out of its pages was Finlay Currie, who sprang from behind the Pinewood gravestone. But thanks to him, and J. Arthur Rank, by the time that *Great Expectations* became required reading, I had read it. In thrall though I was to the whole film, I think it was the ending that made reading the real thing intriguingly irresistible. Had Charles Dickens chosen his hard-hearted alternative, and had it been faithfully reproduced on celluloid, the compulsion to unravel the complicated characters would not have been the same. Estella, married, embittered, married again and eventually reconciled to the harshness of life, would not have drawn me to the secondhand bookstall in the Old Market Hall. Neither would a frozen-hearted Pip, whose only good deed in 400 pages was his generosity to Alec Guinness. My enthusiasm to buy the 'book of the film' was a tiny justification for the faithful reproduction of the real plot and a confirmation that the happier ending was right, whether or not it was wholly consistent with the character that Charles Dickens had so carefully created.

I cannot recall if the postwar black-and-white film of *Anna Karenina* was similarly faithful to the novel on which it was based. For all I know, the natural integrity of the screenwriters was completely confounded by the necessity to compress all of Tolstoy's masterpiece into 139 minutes, thus allowing time for both Movietone News and the 'full supporting programme' in both of the 'houses' into which suburban cinemas divided their evenings. But whether or not Kieron Moore was a convincing Irish Vronsky, it was certainly Vivien Leigh casting herself under the bogie wheels of the snow-splattered railway train that made me plough my solemn way through the innumerable pages of the real thing. After all these years I no longer remember if the platform swirled with steam or mist. But the vivid picture of the tragic heroine – long-skirted, slim-waisted, and trimmed with fur round all her edges – remains the only vision of Anna that I shall ever possess. A sociologist should conduct an inquiry to discover how many middle-aged men who read *Anna Karenina* before they were eighteen owe their early enthusiasm for Russian literature to Vivien Leigh.

My literary debts extend across the Atlantic – Ingrid Bergman (with a toothbrush haircut that would not have looked out of place on top of a young American tennis player of the period) introduced me to Ernest Hemingway's *For Whom the Bell Tolls*. My brief acquaintance with Theodore Dreiser came about as a result of Elizabeth Taylor and *A Place in the Sun*, the film in which Hollywood drowned both Shelley Winters and *An American Tragedy*. And it was not just the beautiful heroines of my susceptible youth that lured me to the library. Gary Cooper and Franchot Tone set me searching the shelves for *Lives of a Bengal Lancer*, and I read it even when I discovered that it only had a title in common with the film. Alan Ladd was an improbable Jay Gatsby. But without him, I would have been denied Scott Fitzgerald for another five years – and I might have imagined Gatsby to look like Robert Redford, instead of knowing for ever that he is a small man with a snap-brimmed fedora.

It is, of course, the opening of youthful eyes for which I feel most grateful. But I continue to benefit from the publication of paperback reprints described as the 'book of' a recent Hollywood release or television series. Lucky is the nation that is about to experience a boom in *Brideshead Revisited* sales. And the one service that the BBC performed by serialisation of the Palliser novels was the popularisation of the real *Phineas Finn* and the true *Prime Minister*. I had read neither *Love in a Cold Climate* nor *The Pursuit of Love* until I was encouraged to brave a station bookstall by Judi Dench's husky squeak. Now I shall ease myself gently towards the *The French Lieutenant's Woman* in print via the film of the same name – not least because the constant public discussion of what Harold Pinter has done to John Fowles will make it increasingly difficult to pretend that I have already read the novel.

I cannot recall a single occasion when seeing a film has either dissuaded me from reading the book on which it was based or diminished the pleasure I enjoyed from the real thing. Errol Flynn as Soames Forsyte left *The Man of Property* unscathed. And dozens of other novels which would have passed me by, had it not been for their conversion into 'major motion pictures', have opened innumerable enjoyable pages. My only real regret is the failure of the post-war British film industry to produce tantalising adaptations of *Daniel Deronda, Rasselas, Lavengro* and *The Magic Mountain*. If only I had seen such pictures at the Kinema and the Phoenix, I would be twice as well read as I am now. And I would know what their characters looked like.

At least, the magic imprint would have been stamped indelibly on my memory if the films had been shown at some 'first house' before 1948. After my sixteenth birthday, I started painting mental pictures of my own. Wendy Hiller remains *Major Barbara*, but she is no more Mrs Morel than Trevor Howard is her misunderstood husband. But, then, I saw *Sons and Lovers* when I was too old and wise to sit back and let the shadows sink in. I had ideas of my own about what Nottingham miners looked like and how they behaved when they were frightened and sad.

But because I saw *Great Expectations* in my fifteenth year to Heaven, I have no ideas of my own (and not so many of Charles Dickens's) about how the characters ought to look. And any image that conflicts with the original imprint automatically registers as wrong. That is, I hasten to add, not an argument for preventing the young from sitting down quietly in front of their television sets on Sunday evenings. Indeed, I urge quite the opposite. If it is as good as my less mature friends claim, it may well rescue a whole generation from the awful fate of not reading the book.

Listener, 22 October 1981

Idylls of Arthur and Martha

I am reading yet another version of the Arthurian legend. My fascination with the goings-on in Camelot began on the day when I first realised that the immortal chronicles were very little to do with knights in armour, jousting tournaments and damsels in various forms of distress but were, in truth, an elaborate way of describing original sin. The rise and fall of King Arthur is less concerned with the sword in the stone and the hand in the lake than with the worm in the bud. The story holds us in thrall because it charts a path to the final battle which – thanks to the irresponsibility of Adam and Eve – we all one day must fight and all must lose.

There are, of course, subsidiary fascinations. The legend was taken up by the Victorians as an anachronistic sideshow of their Gothic revival and as a theologically lunatic collaboration of the notion that the True Church found its natural home in the England south of Watford. Of course, they vulgarised the story with the special combination of philistinism and self-confidence which characterised that vital age. It was sentimentalised into an idyll of merrie England by the very people who had driven the agricultural labourers from the land and herded them into rows of hovels around the iron foundries and weaving sheds.

Although – in the words of E. V. Lucas – Tennyson 'turned Mallory's lance into a china shepherd's crook', the Victorians made sure that every schoolboy knew about Lancelot and Guinevere. The dream endures. Three years ago, I read Rosemary Sutcliffe's enchanting *Road to Camlann* as if it were a new story with an unknown ending. This summer, I found (rather belatedly) *The Mists of Avalon* by Marion Bradley. *The Mists*, as I shall affectionately call it, is different from the rest. For, according to its flyleaf, 'The Arthurian world of Avalon and Camelot . . . is seen from the perspective of its heroines.'

Before I am the subject of attack from those admirable organisations which espouse and entrench women's rights, let me repeat my long-held conviction that the three greatest English novelists are called Eliot, Austen and Brontë. And I have – as this essay will gently reveal – only admiration for women writers who tell women's stories. But the description of Guinevere, Islaine and Morgaine as 'heroines' does seem to me a special extension of the English language. It is, I suspect, all part of the fashionable compulsion to tell old stories in new ways.

It is the extension, rather than the adaptation, of a great work which contains the dangerous element of *lèse-majesté*. I make no complaint about amusing novels concerning the life of Flashman after he was expelled from Rugby. Anyone who has actually read *Tom Brown's Schooldays* is unlikely to think of it as a work of literature so perfect that no second-hand sequel could possibly do it justice. On the other hand, I am affronted by even the idea of someone attempting to describe the happy married life of the second Mrs Rochester.

The suggestion that anyone might have dared to write about the marital problems of the first Mrs Rochester before she moved to Yorkshire, took up residence in the attic and so frightened the governess with her goings on would have seemed simply shocking had I considered it before I read *Wide Sargasso Sea*. It is a mark of Jean Rhys's genius that she performed the sacrilegious act and escaped without being struck down by a thunderbolt. Although, when I read her biography, I could not altogether suppress the thought that it was her attempted theft of Charlotte Brontë's fire which provoked the gods into punishing her so savagely for so long.

It is important that writers of lesser talent should not imagine that they can follow the dangerous road that Miss Rhys trod. In theory the possibilities are endless. For the treasures of English literature seem to invite the presumptuous and the gullible to write books which are both preface and prelude to well-known works of genius. Consider the possible titles – *Brideshead, Brave Old World, 1983, Mrs Tanqueray, Paradise, The Fairie Heir Presumptive*. The list is endless and even Shakespeare would not be wholly safe – *Eleventh Night, An Autumn's Tale*, even *Beth*.

However, I am not sure that even the presumption is as great as re-writing works of genius 'from a new perspective' – the Stoppard Syndrome as it shall be called in future in grudging tribute to *Rosencrantz and Guildenstern are Dead*. Hamlet was as Shakespeare made him and as a character (as distinct from a man) cannot therefore be improved upon. If *Sons and Lovers* reappears in the bookshops with Walter Morel portrayed as an NUM official and his stifling wife as an allegory of the National Coal Board, it may teach us something about the pit closure programme. But the author will have no right even to claim acquaintance with D. H. Lawrence.

In *The Mists*, Miss Bradley has not strayed quite so far from the real Arthurian legend – as she makes plain in an introduction which lists her scholarly research. But if the diversely wicked women of Avalon are to be allowed the expression of their point of view, she is telling a different story. They exist to cause trouble, not to be understood. If we are to reassess the role of Eve, the history of our whole civilisation has to be re-written. Though I admit that in the story of the Fall, re-assessment may be easier than describing the years which preceded the previously published work. No one could invent a title for the book before Genesis.

Guardian, 11 August 1984

Let Other Pens Write Jokes

For years I believed myself to be a Jane Austenite of the sort described by E. M. Forster in *Abinger Harvest*. Proclaiming his devotion, he admits to being 'slightly imbecile' about his 'favourite author' and confesses that 'I read and re-read, the mouth open and the mind closed ... The Jane Austenite possesses little of the brightness he ascribes so freely to his idol. Like all regular church-goers, he scarcely notices what is being said.'

Until this week, I thought that E. M. Forster spoke for me. Now, thanks to *The Jane Austen Companion* – an American work of popular scholarship – I wonder if I am a Jane Austenite at all.

Having read, for example, the essay on 'Jane Austen and Contemporary Feminism', I realise that (if Nurse Cavell will forgive the plagiarism) infatuation is not enough. Without understanding the underlying meaning of Jane Austen's 'obscure joke about *Corinne*' and the reasons for her refusal to meet the author of that work, I shall never fully appreciate why Sophie Croft in *Persuasion* 'does not represent Rousseau's restricted view of female nature'. It is difficult adequately to describe the pain I feel at the exposure of such ignorance. The realisation that I have never really understood Jane Austen is even more distressing. Since I was sixteen I have thought that Jane Austen's genius lay in the elegance of simplicity. Because of the way in which she wrote, she seemed able to anaesthetise a small part of the mind whilst, at the same time, making the rest abnormally sensitive. Her novels describe the lives of silly girls and their worthless relations in a way which makes what is foolish sound attractive and what is inconsequential sound important. For four decades I have thought of Jane Austen's novels as the triumph of style. Now I must learn that their importance lies in social commentary.

I say in my own defence that E. M. Forster seems to have made the same mistake. Indeed, in his description of the behaviour of the true Jane Austenite, he gives examples of the textual errors which the genuine acolyte should not even notice.

'When is your next ball to be, Lizzy?' asks Kitty in *Pride and Prejudice*. It is important, Mr Forster tells us, not even to consider why she should ask a question to which, if previous paragraphs are to be believed, she already knew the answer. No doubt when he first heard that mistake, he was, like me, still enjoying the previous passage of dialogue: ' "Kitty has no discretion in her coughs," said her father. "She times them ill." "I do not cough for my own amusement," said Kitty fretfully.' I cannot say for certain that *The Jane Austen Companion* does not deal with Kitty's (or is it Jane's?) lapse of memory about the social season. For I have not yet had the pleasure of reading it from cover to cover. But I fear that if the topic is examined at all, it is most likely to appear under a heading, The Treatment of Mental Disorder in the Major Novels or, Revelations about Attitudes towards Amnesia in Georgian Hampshire.

My loathing for that particular school of literary criticism is absolute and irrevocable. But the confidence with which I assault it is undermined by another revelation from *The Jane Austen Companion*. Having studied 'Jane Austen and the Consumer Revolution', and 'Jane Austen on the Military (Army and Navy)', I turned with some relief to 'Influence on Later Writers'. Unless the author of that analysis does E. M. Forster an injustice, the high priest of Jane Austenism was far more intellectual in his worship than he ever admitted. 'Influence on Later Writers' gives chapter and verse. When Forster, for instance, begins chapter six of *Howards End* with the words, 'We are not concerned with the very poor – they are unthinkable and only to be approached by the statistician or the poet', he seems to be echoing and relying on his reader to recognise the opening of a chapter in *Mansfield Park*. 'Let other pens dwell on quiet and misery. I quit such odious subjects as soon as I can.'

I am still trying to decide whether that item of analysis is best described as transcendental brilliance or pretentious tripe. Whatever my eventual conclusion, I propose to put it out of my mind. For as well as being an Austenite, I am a Forsterite. And I think far too highly of that novelist to harbour the notion that he was relying on his readers to recognise the allusion. Even T. S. Eliot thought it was possible to appreciate his poetry without hearing the echoes. And Forster wrote for the enjoyment of others. True, it was that exclusive group of others to whom he refers in the introduction of *Howards End*. But I doubt if even the Apostles of King's College Cambridge – with so many other things on their minds – could be relied upon to make the connection between statisticians, poets and odious subjects.

My diatribe ends with two intimately related questions. The first is whether or not the word diatribe ought to be replaced by polemic or philippic. The second is why is all this detailed contextual stuff so infectious? *The Jane Austen Companion*'s approach to literature also fills me with apprehension about an episode in this column's past. About a year ago, Endpiece was devoted to the question, Could Hamlet Swim? My work of scholarship provoked dozens of letters, most of which argued about the evidence on which my conclusion was based. At the time, I thought that the correspondents were joking. Now, I feel a need to emphasise that, even if they were not, I was.

Guardian, 15 April 1989

True Stories from Fiction

I honestly believe that I read *The Old Wives' Tale* sometime between the autumn of 1952 and the high summer of this year. But although I remember opening *Brideshead Revisited* in the Co-op dairy canteen, enduring *Crime and Punishment* on a Norfolk beach and bumping my way through *Tess of the D'Urbervilles* on the wooden benches of a third-class German railway carriage, I recall neither the time nor place at which I met Constance and Sophia Baines.

There have been moments during the last month – after I bought the Penguin paperback in Waterstone's splendid Bath bookshop – when I feared that all I know of Bennett's monumental novel was learned from a television serial. And purchasing my second copy of the book for no better reason than attraction to the jacket says very little for my literary credentials. But that is what I did. *Old Woman Reading a Newspaper*, by Norman Garstin, seemed to me to typify life in the nineteenth-century Five Towns.

Having judged the book by its cover, I became joyously re-acquainted with the circus elephant that ran amok, the signboard which scandalously read 'S. Povey, Late John Baines' and the bull-dog which was on sale for 150 sovereigns. I was astonished to discover that a Victorian dog could cost so much and I am sure that I felt that astonishment before – felt it and pondered upon its implications in a way which would not have been possible if the fact only flashed across a flickering screen. But the price must be right. *The Old Wives' Tale* is the shining example of realism – the novel which, in Raymond Williams's words, neither idealises nor caricatures. I swear I have known the fact, if not the definition, for thirty years. You do not learn that sort of thing from television – not even Channel 4.

I was given Williams's essay on the subject of the Chester Literary Festival after I had spoken, in not altogether adulatory terms, about the sort of novel that describes the life of a New York orphan who turns out to be heir to a White Russian dukedom, comes to Europe with General Pershing, meets and falls in love with a Marseille flower seller, discovers that she is the estranged daughter of a millionaire, reunites the family and sires a long line of merchant bankers – including a Fellow of All Souls who goes into politics and meets Jeffrey Archer. The novels I like are the antithesis of that. Although I learned, from the Williams essay, that there are two points of view on the subject. In 1881, the *Daily News* denounced Zola for his 'unnecessarily faithful portrayal of offensive incidents'.

There are few offensive incidents in *The Old Wives' Tale* – except for a young girl being seduced and initially abandoned by a scoundrel who, having been forced to marry her, thereafter treats her with callous contempt. If I have made that half of the story sound melodramatic, I can only say in my own defence that I am not called Arnold Bennett. Such catastrophes are commonplace in all our neighbourhoods. What he wrote about happened then and happens still. But he told more than a single story. Raymond Williams leaves no room for doubt. The realist tradition in fiction 'creates and judges the quality of a whole way of life in terms of the quality of the persons' who experience the everyday triumphs and tragedies.

Williams argues that true realism – a whole society revealed by the descriptions of its individual members – has little or nothing to do with the 'detailed stock-taking description of shops or back parlours and station waiting rooms'. But in Bennett the lists do not distract attention 'from the people to the things'. The description of the Baineses' kitchen tells us almost as much about the family as the room.

> Forget-me-nots on a brown field ornamented the walls. Its ceiling was irregular and grimy and a beam ran across it. On this beam were two hooks. From these had once depended a swing much used by Constance and Sophia . . . A large range stood out from the wall between the stairs and the window . . . Opposite the bottom of the steps was a doorway without a door, leading to two larders . . . Vague retreats where bowls of milk, dishes of cold bakes and remainders of fruit pies reposed on stillages.

Some readers will not be surprised that a woman who hoards yesterday's bones and half-eaten pies drives her daughter to seek false romance in the arms of a commercial traveller. Others will take it for granted that such paragons of prudence breed children who marry sensibly and help their husbands to manage the family businesses which they inherit. The details all contribute to our understanding of what made Constance and Sophia what they were and why they went their separate ways.

The Old Wives' Tale is the novel which any decent tyro novelist aspires to write. That is why I cannot imagine why I have not ranted and raved about its virtues for the last thirty years. Perhaps I took it all for granted – not the square and the shop, not France in 1870, not the furniture, the manners or the mores of the time, but the people. Bennett wrote about real emotions and that is all that is really worth writing about. It does not matter when the story was written, only when it was read.

Guardian, 14 September 1991

Noble Ideas Lost in a Splutter of Four-letter Words

Can anyone tell me why we have had so much D. H. Lawrence recently? I ask in a spirit of enquiry rather than of complaint. But – for reasons which are quite different from those that motivate the Viewers and Listeners' Association – I do wonder why the BBC chose *Lady Chatterley's Lover* as its spring *Book at Bedtime*. Perhaps the same mysterious influence encouraged the Cambridge University Press to publish its new edition of *Sons and Lovers* and persuaded the gossip columnists in otherwise serious newspapers to start writing D. H. Lawrence 'items'. A month ago, one 'diary' announced that it had discovered the identity of the real-life, though long dead, rude mechanical on whom gamekeeper Mellors was based.

I searched the *Oxford Companion to English Literature* for an anniversary or book or author which might justify all this activity. And, although I searched in vain, I did find out that Mellors was christened Oliver. Before that revelation, I had always assumed that he had survived on family name alone as a symbol of his servant status. The reason for my ignorance is that forty years ago I was lent a copy. It had been printed in Sweden on thick fawn paper and the Scandinavian typesetters had confused the letter F with the letter S: an error which, for all its Elizabethan antecedents, did make that particular work of literature occasionally hard to follow. I read it for the wrong reasons and I was hugely disappointed. The passage which excited me the most was Mellors's proud claim that he had been educated at Sheffield Grammar School. Much of the rest of the book made me laugh with incredulous embarrassment. My problem was not the behaviour but the language.

Ten years later, despite only passing acquaintance with the novel, I rejoiced – as did all men and women of progressive inclination – at the outcome of what was called the 'Trial of Lady Chatterley'. When Penguin Books published an edition on normal paper with all the letters in the right places, they were prosecuted under the Obscene Publications Act. At the time the victory seemed a vindication of liberal values. Today – having read both *Lady Chatterley's Lover* and the book-of-the-trial which Penguin subsequently produced – I am not quite so sure. Of course the novel should be in our bookshops and libraries. And the humiliation of the Philistines who tried to suppress its publication makes wonderful reading. But they were humiliated by witnesses whose view of the reading classes was profoundly patronising.

At the time of the trial Mr Griffiths-Jones (Senior Treasury Counsel and, like the Mellors of my imagination, a man whose Christian name does not appear in print) received much deserved ridicule for asking various distinguished literary figures if *Lady Chatterley's Lover* was the sort of book which they would want their servants to read. Unfortunately, the replies leave no doubt that many of the experts would not have hesitated to impose their views on the labouring classes. I could imagine Dr John Robinson, then Bishop of Woolwich, insisting that a working knowledge of the 'book which all Christians should read' was a minimum entrance requirement for appointment to his service. The witnesses all thought that one way or another, *Lady Chatterley's Lover* was 'a good book' and therefore suitable reading for those less educated than themselves.

The summing up of the case for the defence was explicit on the point.

> There is one thing that I want to make quite plain because in my submission it is of some importance not only that you (the Jury) should realise it. No one should think that if the use of these words for this particular purpose, by this particular author in this particular book is legitimate it will follow these words can be used by any scribbler writing any kind of novel.

I know that the 1959 Obscene Publications Act required the tendency 'to deprave and corrupt' to be balanced against literary merit. But to me, the idea of a judge and jury deciding which authors are allowed to lapse into Anglo-Saxon is both offensive and ridiculous.

Now, having read *Lady Chatterley's Lover* properly, I have a second complaint to make about all those high-minded opinions which were expressed so eloquently in the trial. The book's supporters said, time after time, that Constance Chatterley was in the dock not because of what she did, but because of the way in which Lawrence described her behaviour. 'She was distinguished culpably from Cleopatra and Madame Bovary by her lover's four-letter words.' To defend the literary merit of the novel, it became necessary to defend its language which, we were told, was intended to equate purity and simplicity and argue against the corruption of inhibition. Perhaps. But that is not the result which the language achieved.

There are, in *Lady Chatterley's Lover*, noble ideas about human relationships and the condition of England. It contains views of society which follow exactly the tradition of Robert Owen. Lawrence had something important to say about the values that this country espoused between the wars. But for the generality of readers, all that has been obscured behind a splutter of four-letter words and a number of risible pet-names for private parts. Anyone with even a vestigial understanding of the real world would have realised that the language would obscure rather than illuminate the meaning and that, in consequence, the noble ideas would be lost. If you doubt it, ask the next person that you meet what they know about *Lady Chatterley's Lover*. A 'good book' ought not to need people like those who defended Connie Chatterley, to explain what it is really about.

Guardian, 7 September 1992

Heathcliff! Cathy! Mr Rochester!

It is not even possible to congratulate Lin Haire-Sergeant on her courage. Any writer who aims to fill the gap which an author of genius has left in a novel of uncontested brilliance must possess a reckless daring. But her *Heathcliff: The Return to Wuthering Heights* is the product of a bravery which was best illustrated by the soldiers who survived the Charge of the Light Brigade at Balaclava and chanted, 'Go again! Go again!'

Haire-Sergeant sets out to tell the story of how Heathcliff spent the three years that followed his sudden departure from Wuthering Heights – years about which Emily Brontë chose to tell her readers virtually nothing except that her flawed hero made a fortune. Any attempt to remedy the Brontë omission would be a daunting task. Attempting to achieve that result in the Brontë manner was bound to end in disaster.

Writing of Heathcliff's hope that his rival Edgar Linton might become 'the perfect third in his shining communion with Catherine', debases the style as much as it misunderstands the character. Brontë would never have allowed him to say anything as banal as, 'the fact that only one of us could marry Catherine Earnshaw divided Edgar Linton and me, but something further did too; the great gulf between our births, our temperaments, our essences'. The crude language is matched by the confused thought. Our complaint should not be that Haire-Sergeant fails to get inside Emily's head. Her mistake was the impertinence of thinking that such a trick was possible.

Wuthering Heights is built around an extraordinarily complicated structure which Brontë manipulated with extraordinary skill. It is, in effect, a double flashback. Mr Lockwood, a travelling gentleman, tells the story but in part he is reporting what was told to him by Mrs Dean, sometime housekeeper to the Earnshaws of Wuthering Heights. The plot moves backwards and forwards through time without ever confusing the attentive reader. Haire-Sergeant copies the technique. Charlotte (yes, Charlotte) Brontë meets Lockwood on a train. He possesses a letter in which Heathcliff describes the events of the missing years. Mrs Dean, with whom the letter was left, takes up and complements the narrative. The result is not so much confusion as chaos.

The problems of coherence are compounded by Haire-Sergeant's determination to pack the story with what are essentially extraneous items from the Brontës' collected works. Heathcliff is befriended (implausibly, some readers will think) by one Mr Are, who makes him his servant and protégé. A mysterious hooded woman is seen wandering in the house. Mr Are is wounded by the unidentified assailant and insists on keeping his injury secret. He eventually proposes to marry his children's governess, but as they stand at the altar a Mr Mason cries out that the groom is already married. There are no prizes for guessing that the governess is called Eyre.

At least Haire-Sergeant deserves credit for not attempting to become Jackie Collins in a crinoline. There are no graphic descriptions of sex among the heath and harebells, and it is reasonable as well as charitable to assume that the one passage which might qualify as pulp-sensation was included not so much to titillate as to respect the gothic tradition about which the author had read.

Heathcliff decides (for a number of improbable reasons, including fear of offending Catherine) not to kill Edgar Linton. Instead, he determines to frighten him into abandoning his wedding plans. He therefore operates on his rival with the gelding tackle that he finds in the stable. He is careful to remove only one testicle. The second, he warns, will go, unless the proposed marriage is abandoned. Of course, were the castration complete, the unfortunate Linton would not be able to fit back into the end of *Wuthering Heights*.

Such contrivances are, we must presume, intended to provide

consistency with the original novel. Unfortunately the image that they leave in the reader's mind is not so much a portrait of convincing characters, as a picture of an author who is struggling to fit her story into a strait-jacket.

It is possible for an author of talent to produce a successful addition to a great work, as Jean Rhys proved with her re-casting of *Jane Eyre*, *Wide Sargasso Sea*. But it is a rare achievement. The penalty of failure is immense. For we ask with every justification 'What made her believe that she could stand comparison with genius?'

Haire-Sergeant teaches nineteenth-century literature at the University of Massachusetts. No doubt she knows about the Brontës. But she cannot write like Emily. She should not have tried.

Sunday Times, 4 October 1992

A Voyage Round My Father

I was forty and he was dead when I found out that my father had been a Catholic priest and had left the church for love. I felt immensely grateful to Bishop William Ellis, the man who had told me about the heroic moment in my father's generally cautious life. Gratitude turned into affection which easily survived my mother's reaction to the news that I was going to see him. 'Bill Ellis! He was the man they sent to take your father back.'

Ten years later – when I began to write a novel around the story of the priest and the parishioner – I needed a character who regarded the obligations of faith as more important than the responsibilities of friendship. All I knew of Father William Ellis made him the obvious candidate for that role. It was the natural, indeed the proper, reaction of a normal priest. And he did go on to become a bishop. But what had really happened was of no consequence. I was building a fiction around fact and I felt no compulsion to make my inventions a replica of the truth.

Nor, despite my gratitude and affection, did I feel a duty to protect the bishop's posthumous reputation by describing his early years in the priesthood as if he were a candidate for canonisation. Once I began to write, he belonged to me. The real man was God's creation – given, according to his own beliefs, a free will with which to choose between right and wrong. The false friend was made by me. He acted – for good or evil – according to my instructions.

I developed exactly the same strange relationship with the characters which were based on my parents. By the end of *Skylark's Song*, it was difficult to think of the hero and heroine as my mother and father. They shared the same names. And half a dozen turning points in the lives of the real Rex and Enid were identical to triumphs and tragedies experienced by my reflections of reality. But as I struggled to maintain a consistent (or at least credible) pattern of behaviour, I never thought 'my mother would not do that' or 'that doesn't sound like my father'.

The people with whom I had to keep faith were not my true begetters. I was theirs.

It was I, not the vicar general of the Nottingham diocese, who decreed that Rex (as a penance and punishment for his first and unsuccessful attempt to turn his back on Rome) should be sent as one of the courier-priests on an Easter pilgrimage to Lourdes. My father never made that harrowing journey. But there is nothing fictitious about the description of the conditions on the train as the sick and dying made their slow and painful progress across France. That is based on a dozen careful accounts provided by pilgrims. So is the explanation of how pious Catholics feel when Saint Bernadette fails to perform her promised miracle. Those facts – like the sights and sounds of the 1930s in which the book is set – are sacred. Only the characters and their conduct belong to me rather than to history.

Perhaps it is possible for some authors to write a novel which is consistent with the truth in every detail. For years I believed that *Sons and Lovers*, like *The Way of All Flesh*, was an accurate – perhaps even literal – description of the relationship between author and father and, in the case of D. H. Lawrence, something like a record of how his parents (one so brutal and the other so emotionally demanding) had made him into the strange fellow that he became. Now, I have my doubts.

Perhaps, moved by the memory of some ancient passion or

adolescent drama, Lawrence and Samuel Butler set out to work childhood traumas out of their system. They may have even wanted to exorcise family ghosts. But my guess is that, after the first few chapters, they were no longer interested in auto-therapy. Walter Morel and Gerald Pontifex became the characters which their authors needed for the story.

I am perfectly prepared to believe that Mr Micawber is a caricature of Dickens's father and that his unsuccessful struggle against insolvency illustrates why young Charles was sent to work in the blacking factory which eventually employed David Copperfield. But nobody treats that relationship between fictional father and real son with inappropriate solemnity. There are aspects of Dickens's life which are most easily understood after reference to Freud. Yet few people suggest that Wilkins Micawber – either waiting for something to turn up or confronting 'Heep the liar, Heep the coward' – is resolving a conflict within the author's subconscious. He is, like any other character, a product of experience and imagination.

We are told that, long after *Sons and Lovers* was published, Lawrence began to regret that he had written so savagely about his father's brutal personality. If that is true, I feel little sympathy for the sorrowing son. He should have thought of Morel as no more than a shadow – inspired by, based on or by courtesy of the real tyrant who made his boyhood terrible. But he is no more entitled to say that his novel proved his father to be a villain than I am justified in claiming that my story demonstrates that my parents were hero and heroine. Nor should we write with the intention of either vindicating or vilifying those we once loved. We should write for writing's sake. If our parents help us in that difficult task, they are doing no more than their duty.

Every part of a writer's life ought to be available to them, when the time is right. Often we absorb the material on which we depend without realising that it is seeping in through the pores.

Two years ago, reading from *In That Quiet Earth* to an audience assembled in a Bath bookshop, I suddenly realised that my account of harvesting in Victorian England was (wholly unconsciously) by *Lark Rise to Candleford* out of *The Once And Future King*. In *Skylark's Song* there is a minor pit accident that turns out not to be a colliery disaster, but a triumph for family affection. As I corrected the proofs, I realised that the spirit (although not the details) of the incident could be traced back to the collapse of the printing works in Clayhanger. I have never been sure if we are what we eat. But we certainly write what we read.

We also, if we are wise, write what we know. The plot of the turbulent priest (and the even more turbulent woman with whom he ran away) seemed to me too good to miss – particularly since life had provided art with the dramatic turning points at which boy, having met girl, worries about losing both her and his immortal soul. I could, of course, have changed the names. But I was proud of their small part in the creation of the story.

That is not, however, why I wrote *Skylark's Song*. The peculiarity to which I confess is not ancestor worship. It is the need to write.

Sunday Times, 9 May 1993

Where the Heart Is

It was just the right house. The survey was depressingly ambivalent about the wiring and, worse still, totally unequivocal about the roof. There were only three rooms downstairs but the washhouse could have been converted into a study and, Peak Park Planning Board permitting, a second bathroom might have been built on top. Even if the date, 1904, had not been carved over the front door, it would have been instantly recognisable as Edwardian, heavy rather than elegant and without even the hint of decoration on either lintel or gable. Yet it was just the right house for us.

For we imagined ourselves inside the house looking out, not outside wondering if the drainpipe could be moved to the side and wishing that the roof had a steeper pitch. From the front windows all that we could see were hills – hills rising up from the river at the bottom of what should have been our garden, hills which because they were made out of limestone and millstone grit rose one above the other, like steps up to the clouds, hills which were greeny brown in winter and browny green in spring, hills of the sort I used to walk when I was a young man.

There was also a stream. It ran down one side of what the estate agent called 'substantial land' and was well out of view of the road. I could have dammed it with stones and turf in the way I dammed the stream at Sowerdyke on the day, in 1944, when I found the dummy hand grenade that the Home Guard had left during their weekend manoeuvres. It was the stream that made me weep at the thought of what buying the house would mean. 'If I owned this,' I said, 'I would have come home.'

So we offered the asking price and, when the estate agent said that four other potential buyers had done the same, we told our solicitor that, when our sealed envelope was opened at noon on Friday, our bid should be the asking price plus ten per cent. He did not comment directly, but I realised that his reassuring judgment that I 'ought to be all right unless somebody goes mad' contained a gentle rebuke. He found it difficult to identify with somebody who was prepared to pay over the odds for anything as intangible as a view. Somebody went mad. One sealed envelope contained an offer of the asking price plus 25 per cent.

I have tried, ever since, to convince myself that buying the house would not have been going home at all. The postal address was Sheffield but the Ordnance Survey confirmed the message of the council tax assessment form. The house was in Derbyshire. And Derbyshire was *terra incognita* until I was in my teens and allowed to join the youth club ramblers on Whit Monday. These days, I always talk (and often feel) that we visited Haddon, Hardwick and Chatsworth on every one of my boyhood summer weekends. But the Derwent Valley was two tramcar rides, two bus journeys and a long walk away from the house where I was born. We went to Castleton on the day that Neville Chamberlain told us that 'a state of war exists' and we walked from Fox House through Longshaw Park some time during the year of my eleven-plus. But the moorland villages of Derbyshire had to wait until 1955 when my father bought a lime-green Austin Cambridge.

Home was the border county before Derbyshire began, Yorkshire's southern boundary. During thirty years of exile I have never felt that I belonged anywhere else. Certainly not London. Even if I had admired *Rasselas*, regarded the dictionary as a work of historic scholarship, or found the slightest amusement in Boswell's journals, I would still have regarded Doctor Johnson as an idiot simply because he claimed that 'anyone who is tired of London, is tired of life'.

In my more rational moments I realise that my affection is built on emotion rather than reason. Sheffield was the first hen that this chicken saw when it hatched out of its egg. Sheffield was not the New Jerusalem. But it was the place in which I first felt the arrows of desire and held the bow of burning gold – as well as discovering the joys of cricket, the splendours of football, the pleasure of reading and the agonies of political hope and ambition. I was born a Sheffielder. But I also had Sheffield thrust upon me.

I went back to work there because I hoped for a seat on the local council. My ten months in the steel industry were even worse than 'Likely Lad' – published in the *Spectator,* almost ten years after I had escaped – reveals. As 'The Name on the Knife Blade' made plain, coming face to face with the reality of Sheffield's basic industry destroyed some of the romantic illusions but did not diminish the family feeling.

That feeling – belonging to one place – is not easy to disentangle from other loyalties. One infallible creed. One tightly knit family. One football team to follow. One cricket team to mourn. The word to describe all these peculiarities is 'tribal'. I have no idea whether or not that is an admirable emotion. But I do know that the attachment is permanent. I am no more capable of abandoning my allegiance than I am of changing my vowel sounds. Part of my attachment to the place where I was born was the direct result of what I can only describe as my peculiar upbringing. My father had been a Catholic priest and left the Church in the hope of marrying my mother. The book which described the bumpy progress of that true love also explained the consequences for the product of that union.

> They had formed themselves into a psychologically self-contained community – protecting each other from the world and locked together by a secret which, although it was not shared by me, still held the whole family together.

It is because I understand at least the origins of my family and territorial affections ('In Search of My Father') that I have never feared that I was becoming a 'professional Yorkshireman'. The feelings that I express, perhaps too often, may be sentimental. But they are certainly genuine. If I ever doubt that I turn to the chapter in *Yorkshire Boyhood* called 'Pulling up the Drawbridge' and realise that emotionally I am still inside the walls of the citadel.

The Name on the Knife Blade

On the day that I was born my grandmother wept to think that she should have a grandchild who would never see a green field. An invalid, she had travelled by closed car from Nottingham and all she really knew of Sheffield was the walk, last made thirty years before, from the Victoria Station, through the Pond Street slums to the Edwardian shops on the Moor.

The Pond Street slums were demolished in 1930 during one of the earliest and most imaginative slum-clearance programmes in English history; the Edwardian shops were flattened by a ruder hand during two December nights in 1940; even the Victoria Station will soon be swept away. But one thing about Sheffield never changes. It is still the unknown city, the name on the knife blade and no more. The real people remain hidden behind a pall of now imaginary smoke. Most of Britain knows as little about Sheffield as my grandmother did.

History is to blame. It set Sheffield at the foot of the Pennines on the millstone grit which made its grindstones and near to the water that drove them. Coal confirmed its place at the heart of nineteenth-century England, but made it an industrial city where people work, not a commercial city that people visit. In consequence, Sheffield has fewer hotels than most towns half its size and hardly any of the goodwill that replete salesmen and satisfied representatives carry home from Birmingham and Manchester.

But Sheffield has hills (more than Rome) and rivers (more than Venice), and although they are no longer the tools and the power of the city's trade, they have an abiding influence on the character of the place. Sheffield is divided by them into suburbs as distinct and separate as the cutlery processes in which they each once specialised. The people of Walkley, Woodseats, Firth Park and Wadsley still talk of 'going into Sheffield' as if it were some friendly but distant place. Sheffield is less a unified city than a federation of sovereign suburbs which owe guarded allegiance to the Labour local government that has ruled from the Gothic town hall for over thirty continuous years.

246

It is almost as long since one of the Sheffield football clubs won either the Cup or the League. Although the city has no time for any other winter game (Rugby League is unknown, Rugby Union has a precarious toe-hold on the southern Derbyshire boundary), only grandfathers can remember the last time a local team came home to a civic reception and was carried through the cheering crowds on a be-ribboned bus. Supporters of United and Wednesday eye each other warily across the city lest, by some freak of chance (merit being out of the question), 'the other side' wins the Cup or League first. The rivalry between them is of the fratricidal, not the fraternal, sort. As a boy, I genuinely believed in the man who never ate bacon because its red and white stripes reminded him of United – indeed, I supported and applauded his loyalty. But although I despised Bramall Lane in the winter, in the summer it was the only place I wanted to be. When Worcestershire beat Yorkshire for the first time in the history of the County Championship, I suffered every ball that was bowled.

Bramall Lane seemed to me the only flat cricket ground in Sheffield. I played my youthful strokes on pitches cut into hillsides where, on one side of the wicket, uppish shots hit the ground a yard above the batsman's head, and on the other, fielders waited for catches, eyes on a level with the batsman's boots. Gradients like that broke fielders' hearts, but they made the reputations of several architects. Most of the virgin land available for housing after the war had been rejected twenty years earlier as too steep for practical building. Yet houses have been cut into, hung from and stuck on to the steep slopes of Gleadless, Woodside, Stannington and Netherthorp. The maisonettes and the town houses, the point blocks and the flats have extended and elaborated the city skyline and provided a thousand new vantage points from which the city can be seen spreading out from the factory roofs of the East End to the Victorian suburb of Broomhill in the west.

Men who spend their lives working with hot and sharp metal acquire special virtues. Twenty years of bending and breaking steel will convince any man that no task is beyond him, given the tools and given the time. It will convince him, too, that caution as a virtue is second only to courage. When, as the bloom or billet goes back from the hammer to the furnace, one of its masters spits on it with unerring aim and precision, it is not a sign of contempt for the cooling steel. It is an admission that even now it possesses hard, hot strength. It is an indication that although he will shape it in the end, if he approaches it too rashly its value and his bonus (and possibly the hand or eye of one of his mates) will be destroyed as quickly as his spittle vanishes from the hot ingot.

So Sheffield men are both cautious and cocky, and they are sceptical, too. They are especially sceptical about the proposition that outside Sheffield there are places with ideas or habits or neighbours as good as theirs. Because of this, they have preserved pieces of the nineteenth century unspoilt by improvement. The Whitsuntide processions of Sunday School queens and captains that sing in the public parks, the typically Sheffield suit, broad-shouldered, narrow-waisted and bell-bottomed, the pipeclayed steps and window-sills are part of an earlier, less sophisticated age. Sheffield kept its trams longer than any other English city. It kept them for good practical reasons and parted from them with solemn and formal regret. 'The Last Tram' drove ceremoniously to the town hall to the tune of 'Auld Lang Syne' and, in the square where the unemployed rioted in 1926, the assembled corporation bade it a last sad farewell.

Sheffield is a booming city. Although the craftsmanship of its cutlers will soon be swamped by the new techniques of European mass production, its engineers, its rollers, its turners, its coggers, its stampers and its pressers still exert a great influence on the life of the nation. But despite its new (and doomed) enthusiasm to take its place as capital of one of Britain's new regions, despite the success of the campaign to convince the nation that within five miles of the city hall is some of the most beautiful country in Britain, Sheffield will remain a city to itself.

Three years ago, a party of Russian visitors was astounded to hear the Lord Mayor explain that within the city boundary it is possible to shoot grouse, tickle trout and sail a yacht. Most Sheffielders prefer pleasures other than these, but they believe that all that they need can be found along the banks of the Sheaf, the Porter and the Don. Oscar Wilde believed that 'when good Americans die they go to Paris'. There is no doubt where the good Sheffielders go. They go to Sheffield.

Spectator, 7 May 1965

Goodbye to All That

When I was twelve I was desperate for the ownership of the steel industry to pass into different hands – mine. I was not moved by the national interest, filled by a desire to stimulate production or fired by a determination to rationalise investment. I just wanted to own some of those big black chimneys and deep golden furnaces.

I compiled an envious list of the great names of Sheffield steel – Osborne, Doncaster, Vickers, Tozer, Firth, Peach and Tyzack. I knew the gaunt grey houses they had built in the smoke-free southwestern suburbs. I could recite lists of their overlapping directorships and recount which grandfathers had played baccarat with Edward VII at Tranby Croft.

During the annual taxi-ride which completed my summer visit to Mablethorpe or Bridlington I travelled from the station with my nose pressed against the window, intoxicated by the billets and blooms in the stockyard below the station approach and hypnotised by the red glow that hung over the Wicker and Shaksmoor. I was in thrall to the steel-masters, to their steel and to the huge corrugated-iron sheds in which they broke and bent it.

When I am old I shall certainly pretend that at twenty-one the finger of fate beckoned me home to Sheffield, and that replete with a new and shiny BSc (Econ.) I determined to become, if not a captain of my native industry, at least a corporal. But it will be an old man's fantasy. I returned to home and steel simply because I was not sure of where else to go. My boyhood love affair with cogging and stamping had been eroded by youthful cynicism and overlaid by an all-consuming passion for politics.

Throughout my finals year I had toyed with the nation's great manufacturing companies hoping – irrationally and vainly – that an academic miracle would free me from industry altogether. The miracle mirage faded, the Ford Motor Company lost patience and five weeks before finals and seven before my wedding day I was still potentially unemployed. Then it happened, the 'makers of high quality steel pressings, forging, extrusions and drop stamping; established 1781' came into my life. Undeterred by the unfavourable omen of appearing for interview at the Efficiency Department on the wrong day, I gave the managing director a short lecture on mobile lifting gear (having seen an advertising film the day before) and offered my services. The lecture apparently forgotten and the confusion of dates overlooked, incredibly I was offered the job and began to re-create the relationship that steel and I had once enjoyed. Having returned from the Trojan War I found my old love still waiting, weaving her endless tapestry of crankshafts, propeller blades, car valves and steel balls.

Sometimes it was easy to re-live the old emotions. At six o'clock in the morning it was the most romantic place in the world. The furnaces glowed a friendly red instead of the fearful white that they shone later in the day. The hammer drivers struck speculative blows and there was so much rolling of sleeves and flexing of muscles that it was possible to forget the holes in the roof and the oil on the floor and believe that every day brought a new technical breakthrough.

But for the rest of the day it was simply purgatory. For one thing, nobody really believed in graduates. There was a grudging acknowledgment of their existence, but an outright rejection of the notion that they could be helpful. I was a concession to modernity and no one was going to waste time or money pretending anything else. In the early fifties some firms wasted their graduates' talents by flinging them into management innocent of any experience of the way their industry worked, believing that they had nothing more to learn. It was not so with me. I was taught nothing, not because I already knew enough, but because I was adjudged industrially ineducable.

There was the occasional period of character building, usually a painful lesson in humility. One morning an Oxford historian and I poked about in a blocked-up drain with pieces of ineffectual wire. Most of the time I stood about watching other people work. Occasionally I held a stopwatch in my hand as part of an elaborate, but ill-fated, campaign to convince the workers that piecework rates were based on a more rational calculation than a shrewd guess at how little the management could get away with.

For long periods I did virtually nothing. I arrived each morning a little late but appreciably before other employees of my grade.

The day began with tea made by an ex-submarine officer who, splendid in flat cap and long brown dust coat, then went off to fulfil his duties as heir apparent to the manager of the saw shop. I then read the previous day's *Express* and awaited instructions.

Sometimes they never came. Sometimes I did simple calculations with all the complicated precision of a totally unnecessary slide rule. Sometimes I looked at stock cards and sales records, seeking to understand them in order that they might be improved. If they are better now than they were ten years ago, no credit is due to me. The secrets of only a few were vouchsafed to me. The occasional improvements that I recommended were invariably turned down. Often I just talked to the 'lads', elderly employees past hope and retirement, who shuffled about sweeping floors and making tea if there were no graduate trainees about to do it. We shared the despair that comes from inactivity. The fearful prospect of becoming a 'lad' myself seemed at times to stare me in the face.

But it was not the sheer indestructible hopelessness of it all that finished me. I could stand the refusal to employ engineers because of their tendency to agitate about new machinery, and I could survive in offices kept down to a dingy overcrowded minimum to ensure that executives were encouraged to 'get out into the works'. It was the uncongeniality that was beyond endurance. I was in daily contact with people who really did believe that art galleries hung Picassos upside down and no one knew the difference, who really did suspect that all poets are homosexual and were certain that 'politics is a dirty business'.

And then came Suez. The moralists, who usually confined their wisdom to the proposition that all decent men and women are at home by half past ten, found a new scope for their virtuous advice. One morning as I read *Unconditional Surrender* (carefully keeping it free from the bacon grease that ran out of the sandwich I was eating) a phone call told me of a job in adult education. I lost a hundred pounds a year but gained for almost the first time the approval of the management. 'You have made,' they said, 'a wise choice.'

I left with no regrets and little experience but two things remain. The first is the absolute conviction that something must be done about the steel industry. The second is the imperishable feeling that as far as I am personally concerned the steel-masters can keep it.

Spectator, 17 December 1965

Band of Hope

The history of British socialism is more than a chronicle of great events. It is a story of countless working men and women whose lives turned into the folklore that helps to hold together a party of diverse background and belief.

I met three of the men who made the movement – Gladstone Mather, George Stevenson and Willy Brookes – in Denby Dale at the Labour Party fair. They came neither to jostle for bargains nor to enjoy the lethally substantial Yorkshire tea, but to hear the speeches. I have no doubt that they were disappointed by what they heard, for they remembered the party in its more eloquent days. But when the opening ceremony was over they stood together with the calm certainty of men who know that styles may change, but conscience and conviction endure.

They had lived through all the great events of the Labour Party's past, experiencing, not just observing, its changing fortunes. On the night of Ramsay MacDonald's desertion, 'it was all despair and disillusion in the Skelmanthorpe Labour Club'. The members were not merely witnessing a tragedy: 'We were taking part in it.' Nearby in Colne Valley there was support for the National Government. For them 'Philip Snowden was king'.

But 'we kept loyal all the time'. So when, in 1945, Mr Attlee 'did the impossible', the same club members knew that the victory was theirs as well as his. For 'we were always Labour'.

They were always Labour. In 1911 George Stevenson, aged eight, marched behind the band that led Keir Hardie to the Primitive Methodist Church and the audience which expected his speech to be more revivalist than revolutionary. It was a romantic introduction to Labour politics, but no more important a part of the movement's heritage than his encounter with public assistance twenty years later. George Stevenson was a musician, a member of the Huddersfield Choral Society. Before he received his benefit, he was asked the classic question that apologists pretend is a parody of the poor law: 'Have you a piano you can sell?'

Gladstone Mather, aged eighteen, was in the audience at Keir Hardie's meeting. It was an age when speeches no less than sermons had texts – 'Can a man be a Christian on a pound a week?' In those days 'it was easier to preach socialism than now. Nobody expected you to go into details.' Innocence and idealism went hand in hand. 'We believed that once we had abolished poverty we would have solved all our problems.'

Gladstone Mather discovered that people are more complex and politics is more complicated than the ILP believed. But to him, that is a reason for reasserting, not rejecting, the old virtues. We ought 'to go back to preaching the need for services. The Labour Party has too many economists and not enough evangelists.'

Willy Brookes was a miner for over fifty of his eighty years. One month before the General Strike he was promoted deputy and spent the bitter six months keeping Emley Moor Colliery free from flood, fall and fire, ready for the day when the miners went back. He has no false or foolish regret about missing the conflict ('The strikers did not want us to do anything else') and no sentimental illusions about the pits. He became a miner because 'there was nothing else to do' and is glad his sons 'have more sense' than to follow in his footsteps.

The mutual love of walking brought Willy Brookes and Gladstone Mather together. George Stevenson and Gladstone Mather are united by a less muscular but equally robust passion: both are children of the Methodist Church and their lives have been formed by its testament and teaching.

Today they attend, but are not members. The schism stems from increased rather than diminished conviction. Gladstone Mather rejects the doctrine of personal salvation and prefers 'something like the view of Dr Soper that service is the most important thing'. Their deepest beliefs have not changed since they were formed. Principal amongst them is the certainty that socialism and Christianity are indivisible in practice as well as in theory.

They have had plenty of opportunities to put their theories to the test. In 1914 the 'No Conscription Union' boasted forty members in Skelmanthorpe, for 'we had been taught peace in the churches'. When the campaign failed, Gladstone Mather registered as a conscientious objector and travelled via Halifax Barracks, Durham Gaol and Wormwood Scrubs to the national tribunal which inevitably 'adjudged him to be genuine'.

He found the early months of solitary confinement agonising. For the camaraderie of common principles kept the COs' morale high when they were together. In Durham when the governor's daughter was away on holiday, the voluntary organist from Quaker Mirfield lifted the prisoners' spirits by ending the Sunday service with two unauthorised verses of 'The Red Flag'. A man who has sung 'The Red Flag' in Durham Gaol is really the socialist word made flesh.

The socialist word as spoken in Emley Moor, Denby Dale and Skelmanthorpe was intended to improve and uplift. In the 1920s the Skelmanthorpe Labour Club boasted eight chess sets, met regularly for talks, discussions and debates, and strictly observed the rule that no alcohol was to be sold or consumed on the premises. But there was nothing austere or bitter about the socialism of its members. They believed theirs to be a joyous cause and liked nothing better than a rousing speaker. Snowden, before his defection, Jowett and Lansbury were their favourites. In later years only Jim Griffiths 'painted the picture of socialism that we hoped to see'.

They certainly had cause for the bitterness they never felt. George Stevenson started half-time work at the age of twelve and spent fifty-six hours each fortnight at what he insists 'was not hard physical work'. As a youth he became a trammer and hauled 6-hundredweight tubs from the coalface to the pit-shaft bottom. To his regret, he grew to six foot six, no longer fitted into the low galleries, and was forced to return to less well paid hand-loom weaving.

Perhaps he was lucky. In 1921 a shot exploded in Emley Moor Number One and Willy Brookes was carried to the hospital for the first time. Thirty years later he had his third accident in a roof fall which, according to the surgeon, 'knocked his head square'.

Before the First World War, Gladstone Mather started work as a hand-loom weaver. But in 1918 there was little love for the returning conscientious objectors of Skelmanthorpe, a village described in the text of a visiting patriotic preacher as the place afraid to come to the help of the Lord. Gladstone Mather eventually found a sympathetic employer, but his brother was less lucky. So together they set up a small poultry farm and, for fifty years, poultry farmers they remained.

Throughout all these vicissitudes, the three old men were borne up by the absolute conviction that if you 'alter conditions we will have better men and women'. The world has not changed as fast as they hoped. Willy Brookes fears that 'some people are never satisfied'. Gladstone Mather believes that there is 'too much emphasis on receiving and not enough on giving'. George Stevenson recognises that there is 'more selfishness in man than we once supposed'.

But they are neither disillusioned nor depressed. Once they believed that the walls of Jericho would fall down at the first blast of the trumpet. Now they are wiser as well as older and know that the great work on conversion has only just begun.

Guardian, 2 October 1978

Off the Edge

I confess that I am biased about Bramall Lane. It is the only *real* cricket ground on which I have played. And while I have warm affection for the places where I have spent sunny Saturdays in happy observation, my feelings for Headingley, Lord's and the Oval can hardly compare with my emotional attachment to the only county pavilion steps down which I have walked and the only first-class wicket on which I have taken guard.

It was not one of the major fixtures in the cricket calendar for 1948. Sheffield United Under Sixteens were at home to Wadsley Church Youth Club – a team for whom I usually opened the batting in a style which I believed to be identical to Len Hutton's because we both touched our caps nervously between balls.

The secretary of my team, a rotund retired civil servant (who did not understand the command over opening bowlers that my cap-touching signified), believed that my technique would not withstand the opening onslaught of United's pacemen, whom he wrongly thought to be Yorkshire 'colts'. So I was demoted to number three, and left with the terrible dilemma of deciding whether to imitate Bill Edrich (who, the previous season, had scored almost ten times as many runs as the whole Wadsley Church Youth Club team) or Harry Halliday, who had ended 1947 lower in the averages but went in first wicket down for the county of my hopes and dreams.

I had just decided to shrink by three inches, and to be bow-legged and carry my head slightly on one side when, to my delight, Brian Stevenson, the red-headed left-hander who had usurped my rightful place, was bowled first ball. So there I was walking out *virtually* to open the batting at Bramall Lane.

My nerve held all the way to the gate which divides pitch from pavilion – the gate that had been held open for half a century of Yorkshire heroes as they hurried back to the dressing-room anxious not to milk the applause that celebrated yet another century. As I passed through it and on to the outfield, which was flatter and smoother than the pitches on which I usually batted, I could see, out of the corner of my eye, my mother and father on the seats below the scoreboard, conspicuous in the solitariness of the deserted enclosure. My only consolation was that the humiliation would not last for long. The demon bowlers were well known to me. We all played for the Sheffield City Grammar School and I batted against them in Wednesday afternoon nets. But clothed in the raiment of Sheffield United they assumed a new and terrifying persona. McDonald and Gregory, Larwood and Voce, Martindale and Constantine, even the bowling sensations of the season, Lindwall and Miller, seemed as nothing when compared with Cotterill and Oakes.

I asked, as always, for 'middle and leg'. No doubt as a help to my cricket education, the umpire replied 'two leg' in mild reproof and correction. And that was only the beginning of his unintentional intimidation. He was an elderly member of the Bramall Lane staff who had been relegated to supervision of the young. As part of his coaching duties he instructed the bowlers in setting of fields. There is something particularly unnerving in preparing to take strike and suddenly noticing that the *umpire* is reinforcing the slips.

In the hope of avoiding total humiliation I promised myself that somehow I would get into the line of the ball and trust that the lifting, swinging bouncers would hit me rather than the edge of my bat. It was cowardice, not courage, that made me pray that the only rattle I would hear would be the rattle of broken teeth, not falling bails. With any luck there would be a happy ending, 'retired dead, 0'.

If life were anything like an adventure story I would either have been bowled for a duck (as punishment for my pleasure at Brian Stevenson's dismissal) or scored a century to prove that guts and determination triumph in the end. Fact being duller than fiction, I scored 10 or 12, an achievement somewhere in the same limbo between success and failure as 33 in the county championship. Most of the runs I forget. The first I shall always remember.

Oakes was a bit too fast for me and I played back late. So although I got him in the middle of the bat it ran down through the slips. As I ran past the other batsman in undisguised relief I whispered that 'it wasn't off the edge'. Did my parents realise this important fact, I wondered. It really matters very little. For most of the rest were.

A few years earlier I had seen Keith Miller in the Victory Test drive a fast bowler back over his head for six and crash the ball against the pavilion clock. Compared with my first single it seemed as nothing. Nor, two years later, did Everton Weekes hooking over long leg on to the concrete terraces of Spion Kop. For Len Hutton I made an exception. In my time no cover drive has been like his. For a decade I consistently awarded it the highest accolade – a stroke fit to compare with the shot that scored my first run at Bramall Lane.

Listener, 22 November 1979

God Bless Us, Every One

Each December the Hattersleys of Airedale Road bought what we proudly called a 'real' Christmas tree. More up-to-date neighbours owned complicated constructions of cardboard and green celluloid, with wire branches that could be collapsed for convenient storage after Twelfth Night. But our sapling made a gradual departure from the festive season. A few more needles fell from its atrophying boughs with every day that the Magi journeyed on, confirming our annual suspicion that the rapacious greengrocer had tampered with the roots to prevent us from transplanting the fir or pine from living room to garden until it was needed again next year. So, at the time of our Saviour's birth, we were constantly amongst death. Perhaps the desire for a real, but withering, tree was the product of some sinister folk memory that lay buried in our pagan subconscious alongside holly, ivy, mistletoe, and all the other fruit and vegetables of the Old Religion. Or perhaps it was the result of 'real' trees costing less than imitations, even though (greengrocers being what they are) the artificial variety are the best long-term investment. But whatever the true reason for our prejudice, we took great pleasure in sticking coloured paper on an old biscuit tin filled with damp earth, ramming in the attenuated tentacles, and pricking our fingers on the work of God rather than man as we tied the glass baubles in place.

After sixteen years in Parliament, I have still to endure a more tedious activity than running cotton through the wire loop that is insecurely attached to the neck of a tawdry glass apple and then attempting to knot the near-invisible thread around the very tip of a conifer's branch. In novels, 'dressing the tree' fills the evening with joy and the house with the laughter of excited children. Certainly, for me, the ceremony of decoration always began in that spirit. But it always ended in disaster as the floor – which was later to be littered with pine needles – was gradually covered in a light, seasonable sprinkling of broken glass. The cotton invariably slipped out of the wire loop at the top of the silver star, and the wire loop itself always worked loose from the golden bell just as I was about to complete the reef-knot that every Wolf Cub knows is the only way to tie together cotton of equal thickness. In wartime Sheffield there was a certain bellicose pleasure to be had from watching tinsel-covered apples fall with Newtonian certainty, bounce like the bombs that Wing Commander Guy Gibson dropped on the Möhne Dam, and explode exactly as Barnes Wallis intended. But as we had too few decorations to cover the tree even before the blitzkrieg began, every detonation extended the areas of unadorned branch. Attempting to avoid mounting carnage placed an intolerable strain on the infant eye and youthful arm. Halfway around the tree, I always insisted that my father climbed down from the chair on which he was standing and finished the job for me.

My father, I ought to explain, only stood on chairs immediately before Christmas and even then limited his levitation to the time it took to festoon the living room with paper streamers. Forty Advents on, the ways in which the northern working class used to prepare to celebrate our Redeemer's coming seem too bizarre ever to have been true. Perhaps we were really celebrating the coming of Charles Dickens. For the Christmas we all attempted to re-create happened not in Bethlehem at the moment that BC turned into AD, but in the Victorian England of our imagination. We bought packets of synthetic snow from Woolworths and scattered the powder on our window-sills, received Christmas cards decorated with stagecoaches carrying merry gentlemen who looked remarkably like Mr Pickwick, and turned to *A Christmas Carol* as surely as cold chicken follows hot.

Before I was old enough to read it for myself, my father read it to me. When I had reached the age of supposed literacy the same volume was taken out of the Hillsborough branch of the Sheffield City Libraries and left lying about the house, first as a suggestion and then as a reproach. On Christmas Eve, the paper streamers being hung and the tree decorated, my father would offer to read the last triumphant chapter aloud. The final conversion of Ebenezer Scrooge merges into my memories of half-forgotten Christmas past, alongside G. K. Chesterton and Gillie Potter. Chesterton's hope that both ox and ass really do kneel down in their stalls at midnight was usually the last idea that pious parents put into my head before

I fell asleep. But if I woke before the early-hour coming of Santa Claus, it was Gillie Potter whose words rumbled around in my mind. Perhaps Mr Potter broadcast on other nights of the year. If so, I do not recall them. No matter, for his place in history is secured for me at least by the Christmas Eve message he invariably sent from Hogsnorton to the anxiously waiting world.

I was in hysterics from the moment that he welcomed his audience with the courteous 'Good evening, England'. I particularly enjoyed the descriptions of life in the city state he had invented. In the baronial hall there hung, I recall, two pictures: the Fifth Earl (after Constable); and a constable after the Sixth Earl. Gillie Potter was the humour of Christmas Eve. But, as I remember it, the BBC always provided some suitable seasonable pathos. *Children's Hour* was invariably sentimental, though not always uplifting. It must have been Zane Grey who first told the story of the cowboy who fought his way through Sioux and Apache to deliver Christmas presents to a sick child who – because he possessed no toys – was unable to accept the message of Redemption. The tale pointed a dubious moral and underlined the commercialism of Christmas. But in the early forties I was untroubled by such subtleties. I still remember the closing line. The dying cowboy (looking more like St Sebastian than St Nicholas) was asked by his bunkhouse compadres if he had a last message for the boy he had befriended. His voice wheezed out of the old Marconi: 'Tell him that Santa Claus has come to Sampson's Bar.'

When Santa Claus came to Airedale Road, he brought so many gifts that they filled a pillowcase that was left, conveniently, at the bottom of my bed. In those hard times, everybody else in the family was given presents which were both cheap and useful. My grandma once got half a dozen pencils with which to write her weekly letter to the Worksop relatives. Young uncles simulated joy and counterfeited gratitude as they opened little parcels of handkerchiefs or socks. In later, more prosperous, years my father claimed that he was once given a cobbler's last (known in Sheffield as a hobbin' iron) to symbolise both comfort and joy and the need to economise during the following year by mending his own shoes. But I escaped the austerity. The great year was 1940, when some unexpected bonus provided a plywood fort and boxes of lead soldiers. But there was never a Christmas Day when the pillowcase did not bulge. As I tore open the last package, I was always told of something which, though bought for me, I would not receive as my father had given it the previous day to one of the mendicant families he had met at the Assistance Board office. I fear that I felt as wounded as the Sampson's Bar cowboy.

On Christmas Day itself, there was always the itinerant Salvation Army band in the morning and a roast chicken halfway through the afternoon. The chicken was, I am sure, a prince among birds. It is not only nostalgia that makes me remember it as tasting quite different from the frozen, prepacked, vacuum-wrapped, eviscerated specimens that are common today. It really was a superior breed. It was also the only chicken we had throughout the year. Over the years the quality and the rarity of its taste has enabled me to evolve a 'chicken theory' of human development. Sometimes more does mean worse. But if the quality has to be reduced so that the quantity can be spread around, those of us whose Christmas stockings and bellies were always full ought not to complain.

Listener, 18 December 1980

Pennine Mist

I had forgotten that the early morning fog clings to the Pennine foothills even in August. So my journey to Buxton took almost twice as long as I expected. On the other side of the concentrated mist that ran in irrational rivulets across my windscreen the gorse, grass and heather covered all of the known world. The sheep crouched sensibly in the shadows of the wet dry-stone walls, and the occasional rowan tree looked as if it too had lost its way on a journey to more hospitable country. From time to time, I came to crossroads and an emphatic signpost which should have been accompanied by a highwayman standing in his stirrups to catch an early sight of the approaching Royal Mail. The wooden fingers all pointed to a place called Strines.

Until last week, Strines meant only one thing to me. It was the place in which my mother fell off the footbridge and tore her cartilage – an injury which improved my standing with my friends as it was associated with professional football. But although Strines has passed into family mythology, five pilgrimages in a single morning did not produce a state of grace. The road to Ladybower – squashed between a ridge of dark grey stone and a trickle of dark grey water – is instantly recognisable. When, thanks to good luck and incompetent navigation, I suddenly saw it ten yards beyond my front bumper, I felt the combined relief and astonishment that John Hanning Speke must have experienced when he eventually beheld the true source of the Nile.

Ladybower is a dam which used to be a village. Forty years ago, when it was first decided that the valley would be flooded, the conservationist movement was still in its infancy. But even then, there were country critics who claimed that the Peak District was being defiled. Perhaps I am prejudiced by my upbringing. My school stood in the rain to cheer King George as he made his way to the ceremonial sluicegate opening and I have eaten a hundred ice-creams at the spot where the memorial plaque now stands. But I believe that the reservoir has done the hills a good turn. They now rear up behind the tranquil surface, looking twice as high and alpine as they did when a friendly village littered their gentle lower slopes.

I spent weeks of my youthful summers looking for the lost Ladybower village. We used to believe that beneath the water which was directly connected to our taps the relics of a whole community still stood like a cross between Pompeii and Atlantis. The myth continued with the conviction that in a scorching, searing, rainless August the water level fell and the old church spire suddenly appeared above the surface like a hand waiting to clutch Excalibur. Ladybower was not like that last week. Morgan le Fay would have worn her mackintosh. And Arthur would have worried about the condensation turning his sword rusty.

At the far end of Ladybower the mist began to clear. Derbyshire gets soft as it moves south. Indeed, by the time it reaches Ashbourne it has turned into the Midlands and bottles and sells its water as if it were some cissy French town. But the Cavendish villages of the north – Hathersage and the alliterative townships of Bamford, Bakewell, and Baslow – retain a rugged northern, if slightly feudal, character. No one who notices the names and the coats-of-arms which hang outside hotels and public houses could possibly doubt that the Chatsworth writ runs throughout the whole area. North Derbyshire is Devonshire country, a great tribute to the family that took the title of a southern county but had the good sense to build its great house on the banks of the Derwent.

The ten miles between the point where the Snake Pass comes down to earth at Ladybower and the spot where the last of the Derbyshire villages is left behind, crosses some of the most colourful country in England. It is all green, but green in a thousand different shades. There are lush low fields where the green is thick and dark, high patches of twitchgrass where the sheep root for stubble which is almost khaki, water meadows where the weeds are near to yellow, and clumps of gorse and bilberry which look at a distance to be battleship grey. There are great dock leaves the colour of spring pea-pods and ash trees with leaves like the Rifle Brigade's best uniform. Even on a damp August morning, Derbyshire is irrepressibly green.

The road that actually leads into Buxton is, or ought to be, one of the most romantic highways in England. It is the A6 that runs from Manchester (where friendly fires were lit in the streets to welcome Charles Edward Stuart) to Derby, which (since its glum burghers rejected him) became the place at which the Young Pretender turned and headed for home. Assuming that the Bonnie Prince kept up his subscription to the AA, the road through Buxton must have been the recommended route to glory. On the southern side of the town it runs along the floor of a valley with sides almost as steep as those which hid the secret approach to the Kingdom of the Doones. You are, the road insists, on your way to something special.

The road does not lie. Buxton was one of those unfashionable northern spas created to accommodate the Tony Lumpkins who felt out of place in Bath or Brighton but had grown weary of a trip to Scarborough. It has had two renaissances. One created the opera house in what, today, would be called a comprehensive redevelopment incorporating tropical plant-house and tearoom.

The second made the opera house the centre of an annual festival and caused a notice to be pinned to its stage-door announcing that 'Napoleon's Marshals must wear wellies'. In August the town is alive with concerts and exhibitions and well worth a visit on that account alone. But try also to sample the subsidiary joys of Derbyshire. Set off early on a foggy morning, without an adequate map.

Guardian, 14 August 1982

In Search of My Father

My father was buried according to the rites of the northern Labour Party establishment. The hearse and coffin came from the Co-op and, on the day of his funeral, the great green and blue city flag flew at half mast over the town hall. The clergyman who conducted the service was a devout party member and when he invited us to sing 'Jerusalem', he knew nobody in the congregation would need to read the words from the hymn sheet.

It was a family occasion which ought to have provided the consolation that comes from the sympathy of friends. So as we filed out into the cold sunlight, I should have asked, 'Death, where is thy sting?' But as my mother led the family mourners home for a modest tea, I felt none of the catharsis which funerals are supposed to provide.

Although it failed to comfort me, my father would have been more than satisfied with the ceremony. He was a modest man who had entered what we then called 'public life' for personal rather than public reasons. A seat on the Sheffield City Council was the best – perhaps the only – way of spending his retirement in my mother's company.

By the time that he died, he had become a successful chairman of the health committee. Throughout his brief period of office, he was genuinely surprised that he had been entrusted with such great responsibility. If, on that morning in December 1972, he had known that the Lord Mayor of Sheffield was sitting in the front row of his funeral service, he would have felt immense pride – assuming that such profane emotions are possible in heaven.

I knew at the time of his death that he had been a Catholic. But I believed that he had been no more than a Catholic layman and I was certain that he had abandoned all the convictions which might have called him to a Roman resting place. Indeed, I had recent evidence of his preoccupation with this world rather than the next.

After his fatal illness was first diagnosed, a second (and theoretically more thorough) examination changed the prognosis. My father was not, we were told, going to die. The new hopes were quickly confounded. But for a week or two we experienced the elation of reprieve. I was confident enough – and close enough – to ask him how he felt when he was told that he had only a few months to live.

He assured me that, at first, his brain filled with a blur of fear and disbelief. 'Then,' he said, 'I felt pleased that we had bought that little Wolseley.' I was puzzled about how so prosaic an achievement might have smoothed his path to eternity. 'For a couple of years,' he told me, 'your mother would not have had to worry about repairs.' It was not the reply of a man who believed that being buried according to heretic rituals would send him to an apostate's hell.

The bishop's letter arrived three weeks after the funeral. Beneath the mitred coats of arms, there was a printed message of condolence to which my father's name had been added in careful copperplate. Below the signature, the personal message had been appended in the same ancient hand. 'You may not know that as well as being with him at the English College in Rome, I was priest in the next parish to his.' At the time, I did not even notice how the postscript began. But during the years which followed, 'You may not know' pushed itself to the front of my mind, time after time. It became a challenge and a reproach.

At first reading, I assumed the letter to be an old man's mistake. Then I realised what I should have known for years. Each detail suddenly fitted into place like a jigsaw puzzle that had been blown together by the wind. My father could read Latin at sight – a comparatively rare talent among Ministry of Pensions employees. He hated Oliver Cromwell, loved Charles Edward Stuart and knew that the Young Pretender's brother – the cardinal Duke of York and Archbishop of Frascati – should have been Henry IX of England. It seems barely credible that I had failed to understand for so long.

I felt neither betrayed nor deceived. Rome was my parents' secret. If they wanted to keep it from me, that was their business. My only feeling was regret that I had not known the one important part of the story before he died. That my father had been a Catholic priest was a matter of interest but no great consequence. That he had left the priesthood – with its comforting certainty, its status and its security – for no more than the hope of marrying my mother was a glorious part of his past about which I should have been proud while he was still alive.

My father and I had a relationship which we described as 'getting on very well'. From the day when he first watched anxiously as I paid my sixpence at the juveniles' turnstile to the afternoon when I helped him home from his last football match, we looked after each other. 'Looking after' was one of his preoccupations. He was a kind, thoughtful, self-effacing and, above all, gentle man. I loved him for all that. But I never thought of him as a hero. Yet – back in 1929, when abandoning the priesthood was not the everyday event which it is today – he had been as brave as Hector or Lysander.

The day that I found out – less than a month after the funeral – did not seem the moment at which to tell my mother about my discovery. Indeed, we did not speak of it for almost a year. Then, on a return journey to London from a Blackpool Labour Party conference, an elderly priest introduced himself as 'an old friend of your father's'. It was Monsignor Wilson, a veteran of the First World War who had gone from the trenches to Rome. I suppose that he mentioned our meeting to Bishop Ellis, for the bishop invited me to tea at the convent which had become his retirement home.

I combined my visit with a political meeting in Mansfield. A member of the audience told me that my father had taught him everything he knew about the Holy Trinity and even more about cricket. When, during the subsequent general election, Catholic educationalists attacked me for my opposition to private education,

Archbishop Dwyer of Birmingham organised my defence. He sent me a note saying that he had done it because of his 'affection for Rex'. My father had been called Rex in Rome. The time had come to tell my mother that the secret was out. She accepted the news with absolute equanimity.

Only when Bishop Ellis's name was mentioned did she show any emotion. 'That was the man they sent to take your father back.' The amused contempt with which she described the mission indicated how little hope it had ever had of being successful.

I had just started to write *A Yorkshire Boyhood*, an account of life in a northern family during the extraordinary years of the war and the social revolution which followed. The book, I decided, should begin with a preface which described how the family, which typified the emerging working classes, came together. For too long my father's years in the Church had been treated like a disgrace to be kept secret. My account of the brief courtship and flight from Shirebrook to Sheffield was a proud son's boast about his father's achievement.

For years I had been fascinated by the story of my forefathers. Paradoxically, while my parents were keeping their own past from me, they were telling me incessant tales of ancestors whom I had never known – nineteenth-century patriarchs, ne'er-do-well grandfathers, uncles who emigrated to Canada and aunts with ideas above their station. When a publisher suggested that I should write a novel – a novel in the Victorian style – I already had the outline of a plot and half a cast of characters in my mind. What I wrote was fiction. But it was fiction based on fact.

I searched for the family in parish records, business directories, electoral registers and catalogues advertising the goods which they made and sold. I became, briefly, an expert on industries in which they worked, the hobbies which they pursued and the religion which they followed. I learned how spades were made in Victorian England, the way in which the Sunday School Union organised its Whitsuntide picnic, and what life was like in a touring theatrical company. I read the proceedings of the Liberal Party Assembly of 1890 which – since it was held in Sheffield – was much influenced by Nonconformist opinion and reacted with suitable righteous indignation to news of Parnell's adultery.

Sometimes the facts had to be changed for the sake of the

story. Some characters – like all the dialogue – had to be invented. But the skeleton was there waiting for me to provide the flesh. Its backbone was folklore – the supposed facts and perceived truth that had been passed on to me since I was a child. *The Maker's Mark* is a legend – history passed on (and improved) from generation to generation.

A couple of chapters contain a truth on which fiction could not improve. Herbert Hattersley, Private 2042 of the 1st/7th Battalion, Sherwood Foresters, was killed on the first morning of the Somme. He joined the territorials when he was sixteen and died in France, shortly after his eighteenth birthday. All he left behind was a cheap notebook (turned into a crude diary) and half a dozen letters from home. With the help of the regimental museum, I discovered how he spent his last forty-eight hours. The account of his death (apart from the description of the moment when he fell) is incredible, but true.

The most extraordinary letter which he left in the trenches was from Roy, his little brother. If Private Hattersley was irritated by its contents, no one could have blamed him. It was filled with assurances that life was not as bad as it seemed and promises that everything would be all right in the end. Roy was thirteen when he wrote his last note to Bert. The handwriting was almost identical to that in which he wrote his last letter to me fifty-six years later.

The school to which that little boy was sent – having been rescued from labouring in a hosiery factory by the Bishop of Nottingham – closed down between the wars. So, in the novel, my father went to Ratcliffe College, the institution to which the same bishop sent his two younger brothers. During the day that I spent there, I tried to imagine what life was like for a workman's son who was taken out of a Nottingham terrace and sent to public school. The only record of the years which my uncles spent there is an entry in the *Ratcliffian* for 1927. Hattersley, C. S. came second in the junior sack race. Academically, they must have done better than that. Like my father, they were both sent to superior seminaries.

I followed my father to the English College in Rome and saw again that distinctive handwriting in the *Liber Ruber* for 23 October, 1920, the day on which was entered *Venerabili*. College scrapbooks were full of his pictures – Rex Hattersley (as he had become) in the garden of the British Embassy on the afternoon of King George's State Visit, playing football during the annual St George's Day picnic and walking in the Via di Monserrato. He was almost always in the company of men who became cardinals or bishops – Ellis, Cashman, Dwyer, Heenan and Monsignor Hinsley, who was then Rector of the College – and he always looked like a schoolboy playing Father Brown in amateur theatricals. The pince-nez, which were just visible in the shade of his shovel hat, survived for over a decade. I broke them when, at the age of two or three, I snatched them from his nose.

I had no doubt that my father loved the ancient serenity of the English College. He held the past in sentimental awe and he must have gasped with wonder every time that he remembered that he walked on flagstones which had been trodden by four centuries of saints and martyrs.

He never talked to me about the college. But he did tell me about Rome – where, I believed, he had worked for Thomas Cook in Termini Station. Thirty years before I saw the panelled roof of Santa Maria Maggiore, I knew that no other church in Christendom had so magnificent an interior. I cannot imagine how he reacted to the theology which he was taught. But I know how he responded to the sounds and sights around him.

Some of his happiest bank holidays were spent in museums and art galleries. Living in Rome must have been like one long day out. The excursion which he undoubtedly enjoyed most was the annual retreat to Lake Albano in the Appian Hills – a social rather than spiritual occasion made necessary by the summer heat in the Eternal City. Late at night, two years ago, I drove round the lip of the lake, looking between the pine trees for Palazzola, the Cistercian monastery which became home to my father during five hot Italian Augusts. When I found it and pulled on the rusty bell chain, schoolboys looked out at me through a peephole in the door. Palazzola had become a holiday home for Catholic tourists. Sister Assumpta took me on a guided tour – cells, garden and chapel, sixteenth-century frescoes just visible on the walls. What I remember most are the fireflies; shining golden like stars in the black night. Ancient Romans, the sister told me, wrote about the fireflies when they came to use the lake as a reservoir. The fireflies must have sparkled during my father's summers there.

My father was ordained in the Cathedral Church of St Barnabas in Nottingham. Thanks to the help of the present bishop, I met the man who lay face-down by his side as he was ordained at the same ceremony. Monsignor Atkinson recalled the parishes in which my father had served. In March I met an athletic young man in a sports jacket who was my father's lineal successor as curate at St Philip Neri in Mansfield. In Shirebrook, Father McSpirit took me through the old parish records at St Joseph's and I saw again that distinctive handwriting, carefully arranged along the lines of baptisms, burials and weddings. 'This house,' said the priest, 'must have been too big for your father. He'd have a problem affording the coal.' The local coal merchant was Ernest Brackenbury. The priest with the cold presbytery ran away with his daughter.

Observer, 27 May 1990

Limestone Country

I read *Fame is the Spur* when I was about thirteen, wrote pencil messages in the margins of *Lycidas* a couple of years later, and spent last Wednesday campaigning in the Ribble Valley by-election. The connection between these three milestones in my life will be clear enough to anyone who is capable of taking John Milton's poem a little further than it usually goes. My day in Clitheroe was certainly not laborious in anything except the ideological misuse of that word. But the scorned delights were advertised on every signpost.

The Ribble rises in Yorkshire and then, perversely, turns and runs disloyally to the sea down the wrong side of the Pennines. At or about its source are Whernside, Ingleborough and Pen-y-ghent, the three great summits of north-west Yorkshire. Somewhere between them is Malham Tarn. If heaven is clear and clean and cold, it will be an imitation of that high, mountain lake. Malham Tarn is the most serene sight in England.

Its serenity is emphasised by the glorious chaos of the landscape that surrounds it. Twice, before the Pennines were hunched up along the backbone of England, the land split open along the Craven Fault and acres of primeval Yorkshire sank towards the warm centre of the earth. Then wind and water began to wear down the jagged edges, and the caverns – cut by water in the lower levels of soft rock – collapsed. So Malham Tarn is surrounded by sheer escarpments that would serve as a backdrop to King Solomon's Mines, broken crags and outcrops which look as if they have been scattered across the countryside by the haphazard hand of an untidy god. Sometimes the millstone grit and the Bowland shale show through the thin covering of soil. But it is the limestone that the visitor remembers, white as bleached bones against the dark green of the hard grass.

Limestone, ridged and fissured like gigantic blocks of white chocolate waiting to be broken into convenient squares, spreads across the foothills. Limestone is built into the walls which mark the boundaries of fields with a crazy irregularity of triangles and polygons. Limestone provides north Yorkshire with its mysteries: potholes which reverberate with the murmur of water a hundred feet deep, and subterranean streams which suddenly surface and just as quickly disappear back into the earth.

W. H. Auden gave an accurate but strangely scientific explanation of its fascination:

> If this
> Is the landscape which
>   we, the inconstant ones,
> Are constantly homesick for,
>   this is chiefly
> Because it dissolves
> In water.

Malham Tarn has neither soaked into the earth nor dissolved the land on which it stands for the simple reason that Providence provided the lake with a waterproof lining. Its floor is a massive slab of slate, and the water is held back by a dam of grit and gravel that the glaciers deposited on Malham Lings. It has always seemed to me that really there are eight proofs of the existence of God: the seven the Catholic Church once talked about, and Malham Tarn.

I first saw Malham Tarn forty years ago when I went north on a geography expedition and wrote an essay about scree and moraine in an exercise book with a green cardboard cover. I was there again during the next summer on the day when Len Hutton scored his hundredth hundred, and I returned in my romantic twenties and imagined a hand reaching out of the water to catch and keep Excalibur. In the early sixties, I persuaded easily led comrades to desert the Labour Party conference and drive me east from Blackpool.

These days, equipped with a car of my own and an increasingly irresponsible disposition, I get there more frequently and join the company of determinedly expert walkers.

They wear knee-breeches, hiking boots, extravagant woollen socks, and carry haversacks with cantilever frames and exotic alpine names. But Malham Tarn never changes. I knew last Wednesday, as I drove down from the press conference to the fire station, that it would be just as it was when first I saw it.

It was, I suppose, because I could not see the places that I began to think of the names and their admirable simplicity. The bare rock-faces are called scars: Gordale, Highfold and Great Close. The holes that the rain has bored into the ground are puts: Jingle and Hurtle. At God's Bridge, just below Chapel le Dale, the river Twiss rushes out into the sunlight and hurries, with a noise like laughter, to join the Greta. But at Gaping Gill it disappears and flows on underground.

The names are just as exciting as the elusive water that sinks and surfaces at will. If Stephen Vincent Benet hears about Arncliffe Cove and Fountains Fell, he will regret his decision to be buried at Wounded Knee.

As I hurried south, from the fire station to Preston and from Preston to Euston and home, I should have worried about how many more visits I would make north before Milton's blind fury came with abhorred shears and slit my thin-spun life. I shall never again walk the three great peaks in a single day, and wisdom has combined with age to ensure that I have scrambled down the water face at Gordale Scar for the last time. But I was not in the mood for bitter restraint and sad occasion. The only poem that ran through my mind ended on a strangely theological note:

> When I try to imagine a
> faultless love
> Or the life to come, what I
> hear is the murmur
> Of underground streams,
> what I see is a limestone landscape.

Guardian, 9 March 1991

The Family of Football

I no longer remember the year of the great revelation. But the time, the place and the day of the week are all etched on my memory by indelible gratitude. It happened at five minutes to three on an autumn Saturday afternoon at the Boothferry Road ground of Hull City Football Club. The light was not blinding. At football matches, myopia is the prerogative of referees. But the conversion was total.

A moment earlier I had been overcome by my first experience of real despair – brought on by the profound conviction that I was about to fail my degree and pass my National Service medical examination. On the heels of those two disasters, a whole series of other catastrophes lurked ready to come rushing into my life. Despite my charcoal grey suit and near-white Bri-Nylon shirt, the Ford Motor Company, Unilever and ICI would pass me over. I would become a traffic apprentice with British Railways with a lifetime's ambition of managing a rural goods siding. I was attempting to reconcile myself to the fate usually reserved for KGB generals when the two teams ran out into the pale sunlight. Life was good again.

As I recall, Sheffield Wednesday lost by two goals to one, playing in the distinctive style – 'being robbed' – which has become their hallmark. Inside my little partisan cocoon I felt the disgrace of defeat right up to half past five. But the pleasure far outweighed the pain. I was so engrossed in my little passion that I had no room in my heart or mind for the great emotions of the world beyond the turnstile. I left the ground full of confidence in my uncertain future.

I still feared that I had made the wrong choice between healthy mind and healthy body. And I certainly did not look forward to eighteen months as a clerk-typist in the Royal Army Ordnance Corps, followed by an indeterminate period as a trainee shunter at Wath-upon-Dean. But I had no doubt that – whatever the trials and tribulations of my working week – I would be happy on Saturday afternoon as long as I could afford the price of going to a football match.

As I walked back to my lodgings, I was downcast for a moment by the fear that my prospects were so bad that, on some weekends, I might not have one and ninepence in my pocket. Then I remembered that, during the dark days of the great depression, my father and uncles waited outside the ground at Hillsborough until the unemployed were let in free at ten past four. The guarantee of thirty minutes' sanctuary from the world, provided on every other weekend from September to May, seemed one of fate's better bargains. It still does.

What happens now seems better still. On two dozen Saturdays each year – not to mention half a dozen weekday evenings – nothing matters except what J. B. Priestley called the 'conflict and art' of association football. These days I can even hide my troubles behind a wholly trivial encounter – say Spurs against Manchester United or Arsenal versus Liverpool. But real nirvana only engulfs me when the team that I support, *my* team, is straining every nerve and sinew on the pitch whilst I am fighting off a heart attack in the stand.

Last Saturday – watching Sheffield Wednesday revive their traditional style of 'giving it away' – I began to realise how the spell is cast. It has taken me almost forty years to understand that the joy of being a football supporter comes from one of the better atavistic instincts. Football is a family affair.

That does not make football an invariably admirable activity. But few families invariably behave with the constant virtue attributed to that institution by sentimental novelists and carpet advertisements. However, being like a family, football does radiate the feeling that anyone who is held in its sometimes violent embrace is secure in the close company of real friends.

Arriving, absurdly early, for the first match of the season, I walked into the Wednesday ground as if I were arriving home after a long exile. I took it for granted that I had been at school with the older supporters and I assumed that all the half-price juveniles had learned, at their fathers' knees, about the old heroes – Albert Quixall, Redfern Frogatt and Jackie Sewell. It was a place for men who were boys when I was a boy to sit and drink with me. Or it would have been, had there not been restrictions on the sale of alcohol.

It was not necessary to proclaim my allegiance any more than it was necessary for an affectionate son to tell his mother that he loves her. And I complained about Wednesday's mistakes in the way I might complain about being locked out late at night or allowed to oversleep the next morning. Such grumbles may be reasonable or ridiculous. But they hardly matter because they are not a preparation for leaving home. Wednesday's midfield can spend the rest of the season walking the pitch with the detachment of Carmelite nuns and I will still turn up to cheer them right up to May.

Football makes people believe that they belong to something. It is an insoluble bond and an indestructible comfort. For ninety minutes on most winter Saturdays I shall belong to something for the rest of my life.

Guardian, 24 August 1991

The Shaming of Our People

The Prime Minister has misjudged the mood of the British people. Nothing – at least in my political lifetime – has produced an outburst of national resentment to match the spontaneous explosion of angry disbelief which has engulfed the government this week. The pit closures – sudden, savage and economically indefensible – have done more than touch a raw nerve. They have cut deep into the country's conscience.

Despite the excesses of Arthur Scargill, the British miner, earning a hard living at the dark and dangerous coalface, still commands a special place in the country's affection. The miners have been betrayed, and all over Britain men and women who believe in justice and honest dealing feel deeply ashamed of what has been done in their name.

The destruction of the mining industry typifies all that is worst about the John Major administration. It illustrates the whole government's contempt for manufacturing industry. It confirms the Chancellor's obsession with inflation and his bone-headed disregard for investment, output and employment. It underlines the whole cabinet's callous disregard for the human misery that many of their policies cause.

Perhaps most tragic of all, it highlights the inability of the whole Tory leadership to take a long-term view of Britain's future. And it proves that the Prime Minister is incapable of decisive leadership. The Conservative Party conference ended less than a week ago. Few of the 30,000 miners who will be on the dole in the next few weeks will be consoled by John Major's Brighton promise that there will be more lavatories on the motorway.

Coal has a special place in British history. Without the pits, Britain would not have led the industrial revolution and enjoyed the years of Victorian prosperity. During two world wars, miners – working double shifts and reinforced by National Service volunteers – kept the factories busy without massive increases in imported fuel. A nation in balance of payments crisis should not be destroying one of its great national assets. By closing the pits we are mortgaging our future.

Risking dependence on foreign energy, when the oil has finally run out, is a madness that no previous government would have contemplated. Who doubts that one of the reasons for the cabinet's folly is pure spite. At the height of the miners' dispute, I made plain my belief that Arthur Scargill should have balloted his members before he called them out on strike. But it is impossible, morally or economically, to justify punishing the men who followed him by sentencing them to a lifetime's unemployment.

Michael Heseltine, who looks more shifty with every television broadcast, has changed his propaganda tactic. The crocodile tears – 'The most difficult decision I have ever made' – have been wiped away. Yesterday, on *Newsnight*, he blamed the miners for the whole catastrophe – their productivity record, their restrictive practices and their militancy.

The country is not in a mood to believe that sort of nonsense. They know that some of the collieries which are to be closed are the 'super-pits' which use the latest technology and are manned by miners who rejoiced at their industry being brought up to date. Many of those men moved home and job on the promise of permanent employment. That promise has now been broken.

And Michael Heseltine – once the super salesman of Conservative policy – defends the decision with double-talk which would drive his audience to hysteria were it not describing a tragedy. He warns the miners not to adopt wrecking tactics. The men and women who will be on the dole before Christmas know that their industry has been wrecked already – by Michael Heseltine and the government.

In Nottinghamshire, members of the Democratic Mineworkers' Union must have listened to Michael Heseltine's *Newsnight* performance with bitter incredulity. They broke away from the NUM and worked on through the year-long strike. They, for a moment, were the government's darlings, and believed that they would have special negotiating rights and special compensation for the services they had rendered. They have been betrayed. No one should rejoice at the bitter lessons they have learned. Like miners in other parts of Britain, they are the victims of the government's perfidy.

The price that they will pay can only be understood by people who know the mining communities. There are villages in every coalfield where the pits are everything. They provide the jobs – every penny is earned by miners or by men and women who make their livings from the services which miners' wages buy. The social life of the whole area – football, brass bands, cricket, evening classes – is built around the collieries. So is much of the health and welfare which sustains the families. Close the pits and those communities collapse.

Kenneth Clarke talks about finding new employment for the miners in his constituency who will soon be out of work. A few of them may travel to nearby towns. But in Yorkshire and Scotland, Wales and the North-east, Lancashire and the Midlands, government policy will create ghost towns – no jobs, no amenities, no prospects and no hope.

The despair will not be confined to the coalfields, where they are used to hard knocks and will struggle as best they can to make decent lives for their children. We will all pay the price of the government's vandalism. Today the electricity generating companies think of cheap energy from gas-powered stations.

How long will the cheap gas last when there is no longer competing coal to keep the prices down? And who will pay the redundancy bills, fund the unemployment benefits, and meet the cost of rebuilding the mining communities? The answer is the British taxpayer. Politicians with a modicum of common sense would use the money to keep the miners cutting coal. Unlike Germany and Japan, we still have not learnt the lesson that paying men to do nothing is the biggest waste of all.

For all of our industrial history, British miners have been expected to risk their lives to contribute to this country's prosperity. Now that the private electricity industry believes that it can make a faster buck without them, miners are being given a couple of weeks' notice and told that market forces are too tough for them to beat.

The government either does not care or dares not act. The British people know that the attack on the coal industry combines economic folly with callous disregard for human misery. The Tories will not be forgiven.

Evening Standard, 16 October 1992

Strictly Personal

Endpiece readers are compulsive writers and a fair proportion of their letters are reproofs. Many of them concern the rules of formal grammar and advocate a discipline so rigid that I am able to reply with quotations from Fowler which insist that the cadence of the language is more important than classical construction. A similar response goes to those correspondents who complain about trivial errors of fact. Sometimes 'seven' (having two syllables) maintains the rhythm of the sentence far more satisfactorily than monosyllabic 'three'. So I was always prepared if necessary to write about the Seven Kings of Orient, the Seven Men in a Boat and the Seven Musketeers.

The kindly folk who write to remedy my ignorance are always firmly told that working for the *Guardian* means never having to say that you are sorry. Another category of complaint I deal with more cautiously. They are people who disapprove of my jokes. To those who claim that the jokes were not funny I send a guarded reply – '. . . not possible to answer all letters individually . . .' For I lack sufficient conviction effectively to defend my sense of humour. But to the critics who claim that the jokes should not have been made at all because they are unfair to their favourite authors, politicians, and television personalities, I give shorter shrift. Since, in so much of what I write, the joke is on me, John Major, Kenneth Branagh, Anthony Clare and Joan Collins ought not to complain if, once in a while, I try to raise a smile at their expense.

It may be that I am humiliated more frequently than is the lot of the average middle-aged man. Or it may be that – being, as my mother readily explains, highly sensitive – I recognise shame in situations in which cruder intellects would not detect even a hint of embarrassment. Anyway, it all happened. I *was* assaulted by a demented bird ('Goose Encounter at New Street'). After I flew with the Red Arrows, I *was* too debilitated to grasp the tie with which I was presented ('Per Ardua Ad Astra'). I *did* fall off a ladder in the House of Commons library ('Through New Eyes'). I *do* use a bottle of Tipp-Ex a day and I *am*, in consequence, often asked by people who note the white streaks on my finger if I am white-washing the coalhouse.

The best humiliation of all – not included in this anthology of shame because my brief account of the incident was no more than a prelude to a threnody for the old sort of county cricket – I experienced at Lords. I was hanging about behind the pavilion when the Yorkshire team climbed out of their coach. As I discussed the technicalities of the game with those players who were prepared to talk to me, a small boy with a miniature bat approached our group and began to ask for autographs – Old, Sharpe, Carrick, Bairstow. His mother – who I can only assume to have been a Labour Party member – told him to make the same request to me. With the modesty which has characterised my life, I told him that I was not a cricketer. He took his bat away. I do not know if the mother was motivated by courtesy or real enthusiasm. But, what-ever her reasons, she told him to ask me again. He refused. She hit him.

She hit him hard. So I was not surprised when he began to howl. It was the nature of the howl that caught me off guard. Running hysterically amongst the MCC members who were making their stately ways to their seats, he begged them to save him from the terrible fate which his mother had decreed. 'I don't want his autograph,' he shouted, pointing at me as if I were forcing it upon him. 'He's not a cricketer,' he added, as if I were pretending that I was. I think that Yorkshire lost the one-day match, but after the mother led the screaming boy away, the afternoon became a blur in my mind.

Some of the pieces which follow are accounts of humiliations endured with dignity. I did, after all, decline the barber's offer of an introduction to a hair transplant specialist ('Mortality in the Barber's Chair'). And for several years I steadfastly rejected his suggestion that I should move my parting from the left – 'the girl's side' as we used to call it. Three years ago, bored witless by his constant assertions that I was combing against my crown and nature, I made the switch during the trim I always have in preparation for Labour Party conference. Standing at the back of the Blackpool platform, Tony Benn looked at my head and asked me, 'What's happened?' I told him, 'Everything, this year, is moving to the right.' When an account of our conversation appeared in one of those posh-paper gossip columns which call themselves diaries, I assumed that we had been overheard. I had certainly not reported my indiscretion and I know that Tony prides himself on not co-operating with the capitalist press.

I wrote about 'The Man Who Lived in Railway Trains' for a double pre-Christmas issue of the *Listener* and the children's fairy tale style seemed appropriate to the season. I no longer recall the Sunday journey to which agonised reference is made in the last two paragraphs. Its horrors have been obscured, since 1971, by the traumas of a thousand other 'unavoidable delays'. I wrote about one or two of them and produced a lexicon of British Railway patois which included an apology for late arrival 'consequent on the prior occupation of the line' which the guard (I beg his pardon, senior conductor) subsequently translated as 'train in front, broken down'.

The essay on exercise ('Jogging Along') appeared towards the back of the last issue of the *New Statesman* which was edited by Tony Howard. I think that he wanted something more serious. But I was a member of Jim Callaghan's cabinet and there was no time to go through the complicated procedure which might (or might not) have resulted in prime ministerial approval of an article on the theory of socialism or the management of the economy. In those more disciplined days, we all took the Rules for Ministers very seriously and journalists in the government reminded each other that Attlee had prevented John Strachey (then Secretary of State for War) from publishing a poem on sunset in the Malay Straits. Strachey took his case to Downing Street. 'What,' he asked, 'is the possible objection? It's not as if it contained classified information or publicised some internal Labour Party argument. What's wrong with a ten-line poem?' The Prime Minister puffed on his pipe before he answered. 'Doesn't scan.'

If there is a poet in the modern Parliamentary Labour Party his work too is unpublished. And I see no sign of dangerous literary tendencies in John Major's administration. My occasional references to Mr Major's own turbulent relationship with the English language numbered amongst the little jokes which caused most offence. So most of the articles which included them have been omitted from this essentially benign part of *Between Ourselves*. I think that the only apology which is required of me is due to my 'sort of god-daughter'. She has been bored for more than twenty years by the constant repetition of the story about her around which 'Sort of Related' is built. I can only tell her, as I have told her brother, that such treatment is the inevitable penalty of being the child of my closest friends. Anyway, good and authentic stories are too rare to waste.

Jogging Along

I am delighted to discover from the pages of the *New Statesman* that the Deputy Commissioner of Police for the metropolis believes that middle-aged men running through the streets of London 'dressed as athletes' should be treated with the utmost suspicion. Anyone concerned with the moral welfare of the capital must rejoice that its elderly degenerates have been driven to such reckless desperation. And, since few potential victims will be seduced by breathless blandishments wheezed out of paunch-distended tracksuits, it is comforting to know that ageing roués have forsaken collapsible top hats and silk-lined opera coats and now stalk the West End with ADIDAS written on their backs.

But my greatest joy is purely personal. I am no longer alone. So many other middle-aged men are making a similar (if you will excuse the expression) exhibition of themselves that their portly image has imprinted itself on the mind of the perceptive Deputy Commissioner. The discovery that the rest of the daily runners are not all young and lithe is worth the risk of arrest. And if I am taken in charge by one of the assiduous young constables of South West 1, I shall simply place the blame where it rightfully belongs – on E. R. T. Dexter and Leo Tolstoy.

In 1976 I gave to Mr Dexter a piece of information that the Foreign Office had taken thirty seconds to collect. Being a man of extreme courtesy, he invited me – as a symbol of gratitude – to spend a day at Lord's during the Second Test against the West Indies. To West Indians, Mr Dexter is a particular hero and as we walked round the ground, men from Kingston and Georgetown pressed all sorts of alcohol upon him in memory of centuries he had scored and they had witnessed. Being a man of extreme courtesy Mr Dexter never refused their salutations. Yet at close of play he was as upright and lucid as he had been before the stumps were pitched. In wholly unslurred speech he told me how he triumphed over such adversity: 'I run every day.'

I was ready to receive the word. It was the summer of *War and Peace* and Napoleon's army marched out of my television set twice each week. The retreat from Moscow had begun and Russian peasants staggered west, weighed down by the loot and luggage of the Grande Armée. The least fit and most feeble collapsed in the snow and were dispatched by a single thrust from a long French bayonet. I knew that, had I been there (I always identify with peasants), I would have been among the first to go, victim of the fate that destroys those who take too little exercise.

So I followed Mr Dexter's example and most of his advice. But for some weeks I ignored the instruction to buy proper shoes. The effect on my feet was spectacular. The blisters I anticipated, the swollen ankles were to be expected. But I was not prepared for the toenails. Each one grew to look exactly like the flag of Imperial Japan. Despite ten identical suns, rising blood red at the end of my feet, I ran on.

I ran on, but at first not very fast and not very far. 'Start gradually,' Mr Dexter told me, so I began by running a hundred paces and walking a hundred paces, running a hundred and walking a hundred. I hit the pain barrier after fifty, but the tendency to collapse almost immediately my feet hit the ground proved a remarkable advantage. From the earliest days I enjoyed the double fantasy of being Emil Zatopek and David Coleman simultaneously. Through the purple haze and the high-pitched buzz the unmistakable voice drove me on: 'His legs have turned to jelly – only courage keeps him going now.'

Fantasy is absolutely essential. One touch of cold physiology and the senior or mature runner is finished. Reading *Running* – the American runners' bible – I became so disheartened that I had to choose between the book and the activity. I reached page 300 before I could run the distance recommended on page 19. Now I avoid all medical advice. Prognoses that step from the promise of twenty extra years to the threat of sudden death are difficult to reconcile. So I pushed them all to the back of my mind where they rattle about as I run.

Yet I run with increasing enthusiasm. Instead of boring people with stories about Sparkbrook Labour Party, Sheffield Wednesday and the Retail Price Index I now bore people exclusively about running. I pity men who do not run and in their presence smile the secret self-satisfied smile exclusive to the elect who look out on life from inside a Marks & Spencer's tracksuit.

Of course, it is still an effort to start and a relief to finish. But once I have forced myself over the first few yards real enjoyment sets in, and there is a special satisfaction in lying back, submerged in hot water and the knowledge that I ran again today. I still pant when I walk upstairs or pick up small parcels. But I can run for two uninterrupted miles. And on good days with the wind behind me I sometimes manage three.

Most important of all, I have regained the sensations of my youth – aching muscles, sweat running down the small of my back, and the special abandon of being out in the rain and not looking for shelter. Now the police, after all these years, have become suspicious again. Deputy Commissioner, it's great to be young.

New Statesman, 21 March 1978

Goose Encounter at New Street

Believe it or not, Clive Jenkins was the star of the Monty Python sketch that brought down the curtain on the first half of the recent Amnesty International charity gala. He played the 'mystery guest' on an imaginary television quiz show in which bound and blindfolded contestants won handsome prizes if they guessed the identity of a visiting celebrity who kicked, punched and generally knocked hell out of them.

Apparently, Clive performed superbly. Carping critics may say that his triumph was no more than the outcome of shrewd typecasting. But when I saw pictures of Mr Jenkins putting his polished and pointed Chelsea boot in I could only feel regret that I had refused an invitation to do the same on an earlier night.

I had no sense of guilt. The gala was a sell-out, with or without my trivial participation. I had no feeling of lost opportunity. I learned many years ago that politicians who do ridiculous things in public with the hope of appearing warm and lovable never look warm and lovable but only ridiculous. But, as I looked at the pictures of the willingly pinioned victims awaiting with obvious pleasure the collision of Mr Jenkins's pointed toe-cap with the tender parts of their anatomy, I was overcome with a single simple conviction: into each life some farce must fall. And how much better if it can be exorcised on stage in aid of a good cause rather than in real life, on, say – to take a single humiliating example – New Street Station, Birmingham.

I have alighted on New Street's concrete platform (remembering 'to take my hand baggage with me') at least once each week since the lovely red brick of Snow Hill was pounded into the ground to make a smooth surface for a car-park. And my problem has never been leaving luggage behind but bringing too much with me.

During the transient days of ministerial office I travelled between London and Birmingham loaded down like a nineteenth-century Kowloon coolie. I could only manage it at all if every bag and parcel was suspended from me with the precision of a Guggenheim mobile.

My right elbow I kept close to my side, bent in an exact right angle so that my forearm stuck out precisely parallel to the ground. A suit-bag over my shoulder and hooked to my right hand pulled my forearm upwards. But a ministerial red box clutched tightly in the same fist pulled my arm down and kept the Euclidian aberration in perfect balance.

In my other hand I carried a suitcase, the weight of which kept my left arm rigidly and vertically by my side, ensuring that the briefcase of constituency correspondence squashed between it and my rib-cage could not escape. My ticket I trapped between thumb and suitcase handle.

It was quite impossible to lift it to the level of the ticket-collector's outstretched palm. But most NUR members were kind enough to reach down and take it from me, and all preferred the thumbtrap technique to the alternative – carrying the ticket in my mouth and either blowing it to them as I passed their box or offering it from between my lips like a bird returning to the nest with a worm for its fledgling.

I tried to reconcile myself to the weight, inconvenience and risibility of my complicated load by thinking of the whole procedure as a health-giving combination of Canadian Air Force callisthenics and Tibetan yoga. But I could never complete the exercise with the degree of casual nonchalance that ought to typify the behaviour of a man with a Harvard suit-bag. Frankly, I had to concentrate very hard to move at all. No doubt it was the effort of moving forward that prevented me from noticing the packing-case that was rattling and shaking at the other end of the platform.

It was when the shaking turned to a shudder and the planks that made up its front and sides collapsed that I first became aware of the goose. But by the time it stepped out of the debris my attention was fully engaged. My first, distant thought was that there was a man inside. As a child of the twentieth century, I suspected a publicity stunt. As a child of Yorkshire, I wondered if geese travelled more cheaply than people and if this was an elaborate way of defrauding the railway. Then it drew near and I realised it was the work of God, not man; a goose's goose, the sort of goose that sensible swans would like to be.

The goose walked towards me, perfectly goose-shaped, like a four-foot pear covered in feathers. It was a well-adjusted goose that walked calmly and with self-possession in regular paces, not high stepping idiotically like a German soldier. It looked neither to left nor right, but moved with enviable certainty towards the first-class waiting room.

I have always thought of the goose as a benign bird that lays golden eggs, flies up suburban sitting-room walls and saves the

Capitol. A small boy, attempting to smash a chocolate machine, must have been to the wrong pantomimes, subscribed to a more sophisticated school of interior decoration and lacked a classical education. He was terrified by the goose, and ran screaming to his mother, colliding in his flight with a massive tin tumbril used by British Rail to carry Red Star parcels from train to post office. By unhappy chance his impact released its brake. The juggernaut began to roll slowly towards me down the platform incline. It quickly gained pace.

By this time my hands were totally atrophied, approaching the stage when failure of blood supply produces either gangrene or frostbite, or both. But I did not lose my nerve. Lifting my left foot I diverted the rogue wheelbarrow into a pile of mail sacks where it no doubt remained for several days. But my pleasure in the passage of athletic, indeed balletic, self-defence was dimmed by my failure to keep hold of my ticket. It spun from my right hand and landed on the line between train and platform.

But I was, after all, in Birmingham, the city I had represented in Parliament for well over a decade. If I could not talk my way through the barrier here... So I advanced to the ticket collector and boldly announced, 'I am Roy Hattersley.' His reply – 'Well done' – was less than encouraging, but I pressed on. 'I have no ticket,' I confessed. The subsequent long silence destroyed my remaining confidence. I rushed in to fill the verbal vacuum.

'London train... platform six... weighed down with luggage... packing-case shaking... split open... great big goose... three feet tall... grey... four feet tall... perfectly amiably... five feet tall... little boy... very frightened... screamed and shouted... crashed into lorry... released brake... at least forty miles an hour... nasty accident... stopped with foot... look at mark on shoe... ticket fell on line. Recovering it would be both dangerous and illegal.'

The ticket collector was a reasonable and compassionate man. In any case, the queue building up behind me had begun to turn ugly. 'OK, squire,' he said. 'On your way this time. But if it happens again you'll have to pay.'

Listener, 20 September 1979

Per Ardua ad Astra

I gave up ministerial machismo on a sunny May morning back in 1969. I was in an aeroplane somewhere over Anglesey, though it is uncertain whether or not I was technically flying at the time. The precise height at which I determined never again to pretend that I was healthy and brave is also in doubt. The decision took me several seconds to make. And during that time the projectile into which I was strapped fell from a few feet below the clouds to a few inches above Beaumaris Castle. Fell, but not like a stone; for as we spun to earth we turned in a tight spiral as if the pilot hoped to bore us into the ground like a jet-propelled corkscrew.

The day had begun pleasantly enough with a slow ride in a plane which possessed propellers – visible means of support in which I always take comfort.

The first sign of trouble was on the runway at RAF Valley. From the air it looked like a gigantic scarlet ball-point pen with wings. It was a Gnat. But it was no ordinary Gnat and it had no ordinary pilot. It and he were both members of the Red Arrows Acrobatic Display Team.

Refusing 'a little ride' required a kind of courage which I did not possess. And, anyway, nothing very terrible could happen. When I first became Minister of Defence (Administration) I had endured a medical examination which, after subjecting me to ingenious indignities, had pronounced me fit for supersonic flying. A few minutes in the wide not so far blue yonder and I would be back leaning on the bar in the Officers' Mess learning about the strategic importance of stationing more of Strike Command within bathing distance of the then peaceful Cyprus beaches.

I was not even really worried by the rubber suit – which I assumed from the trailing tubes was meant to be plugged in to the plane's central heating. I had just begun to explain that I would be perfectly satisfied with a gentle jaunt near enough to the warm Welsh earth to make frostbite impossible when a young man began to inflate the suit with a giant bicycle-pump. 'It is not,' the pilot explained, 'for insulation. It is to help with g-force. It stops your blood and guts slopping about at high speed.'

Dignity is difficult for anyone dressed as a Michelin man, but encapsulation in pneumatic swaddling-bands does help to disguise the palpitations. I walked, stiff-legged, towards the crimson bullet and was hoisted to my place in the *front* cockpit.

Then I heard the hissing and blowing. At first, I feared that the blown-up suit had exploded and I had visions of my intestines swaying about under my rib-cage like offal hanging in a draughty butcher's shop. Then I realised that as I was still being split up the middle like a defective clothes-peg the suit (unlike me) must be in good shape. Something was clearly escaping from the engine – undoubtedly inflammable, combustible and likely to catch on fire.

I spoke calmly into the microphone that wound round my face from the American-football helmet into which my head had been jammed. There was no immediate reply, evidence I initially took to point to the pilot's death. But in my agitation I inadvertently moved the switch marked 'receive' and I began to ponder the calming advice, 'Not to worry!' A man has the right to prepare himself for death so I demanded a fuller explanation. I was spared nothing. 'A lot of people are frightened at first. The intercom exaggerates the sound of nervous breathing. Nothing to be embarrassed about.'

Had we not, at that very moment, turned upside down, genuine shame might well have compelled me to counterfeit composure. But the full effect of the g-force hit me just as I was about to ask a series of inconsequential questions as a mark of my insouciance. G-force – for the information of those who have never been fired from a gun or dropped from a balloon – creates a feeling like red-hot cannon-balls rattling about in the large intestine. When we had slowed down, straightened out, rolled over or done whatever brought me back to consciousness, the sheer joy of being alive encouraged me to respond to the cheerful message that Caernarvon Castle was just below.

By the time I replied we were fifteen miles away and I saw Beaumaris – 'a lovely little castle' I had not visited for twenty years. 'Want a close inspection?' my pilot asked, and down we dived – the kamikaze end of the tourist trade. By then I knew that I was not going to die. I had infinite faith that my captor would do no more than inflict pain and suffering. I swore never to do it again as we turned for home.

Back at the airfield, the RAF public relations department had been hard at work. As I climbed out of the cockpit the station commander stepped forward to present me with my Red Arrows tie. As the assembled photographers raised their cameras I held out my hand to receive the polyester proof of my daring. I clutched but could not hold, and it fell symbolically to the tarmac. Three or four times I tried to grasp the cellophane package. Three or four times I dropped it. 'Cramp?' asked one photographer. 'Fear,' I told him. I was liberated at last.

Listener, 4 October 1979

The Man Who Lived in Trains

Once upon a time there was a Man Who Lived in Railway Trains. He did not live in railway trains out of choice. If he had chosen to spend his night lying on narrow bunks insecurely fastened to the walls of sleeping-cars and his days inhaling smoke in non-smoking carriages, and his winters attempting to make the heating work and his summers attempting to stop it from working, he would have been the Stupid Man Who Lived in Railway Trains.

No. He did it because he had no choice. And, since the reason why he had no choice points a moral for us all, I shall tell you about it. So, if you are sitting uncomfortably in Euston station waiting for the departure of the 15.10 to Birmingham which had been delayed because of unavoidable engineering works at Bletchley, I will begin.

Long, long ago, when a crossed knife and fork in a timetable meant that a restaurant car was available on that service and it was still possible to travel between one great city and another after ten o'clock at night, the baby who was to grow up into the Man Who Lived in Railway Trains was visited by a Good Fairy. And, as is the habit with Good Fairies on such occasions, she offered him One Wish. Not for the last time in his life the baby who was to grow up into the Man Who Lived in Railway Trains replied without pausing for consideration.

'Please,' he said, for he was a very well-mannered as well as articulate baby, 'please, when I grow up I want to be a politician and never go home on Fridays and Saturdays and stay up all night in the House of Commons and be hectored by Robin Day.' (The reference to Robin Day is not an anachronism. As is well known, in the presence of Good Fairies, babies develop the gift of prophesying disasters.)

'Your wish is granted,' said the Good Fairy with boring predictability. And, mouthing the magic words that made the promise stick, she disappeared. The magic words were not abracadabra or fee-fi-fo-fum or any of that foreign nonsense, for this was not any old Good Fairy, this was the Yorkshire Good Fairy and she cast a Yorkshire spell. 'Nothing is for nothing,' she said. And being Yorkshire she meant it.

The nasal emphasis on the second vowel in the second 'nothing' had barely reverberated into silence when a second mysterious figure appeared. If this were a stereotyped fairy story the new arrival would have been a Bad Fairy or – if the depths of northern humour were to be plumbed even deeper – the Lancashire Fairy. But this fairy story is far more original than you yet realise. In proof of which there suddenly arrived beside the cot of the baby who was to grow up into the Man Who Lived in Railway Trains not a Bad Fairy at all but a Bad News Fairy.

Her job was to tell people the price they had to pay for the promises that the Good Fairy had lightly given and they had unthinkingly accepted. The Bad News Fairy did not appear to enjoy much job satisfaction. She spoke to the baby who was to grow up into the Man Who Lived in Railway Trains with such gratuitous aggression that, although he was only a few weeks old, he instantly recognised a defence mechanism which revealed fundamental insecurity.

The Bad News Fairy could hardly have been more frank. Indeed, she told her tale with the glee some people seem to think appropriate for warnings of catastrophe. The price to be paid could be simply described. The parts of his life not occupied in all-night sittings and being hectored by Robin Day would have to be spent in Railway Trains.

The baby who became the Man Who Lived in Railway Trains could hardly believe his luck. Dining cars with Tiffany lamps. Thin bars of chocolate from automatic machines. Deep, brocaded seats with antimacassars. Pictures of Scarborough and Brighton flanking tasteful mirrors frosted with mystical symbols like GWR and LMS. Guards who never woke sleeping first-class passengers. It seemed a shame to take the Good Fairy's money.

When he grew up, the baby who became the Man Who Lived in Railway Trains (or to put it more briefly, as we had now better begin to do, the Man Who Lived in Railway Trains) often thought of the Bad News Fairy with kindness and concern. He thought of her particularly during the days when his colleagues in the govern-ment – for his wish really was granted – went around the country, promising reductions in the inflation rate. He had to follow after them, telling the trade unions that nothing is for nothing and if their wish was to be granted the increase in earnings that year could only be six pounds or ten per cent or whatever had been decided was the current magic spell. But as he had grown up to be excessively loyal (though he was probably less articulate and polite than when a baby) the Man Who Lived in Railway Trains never even allowed himself to think who played the part of the Good Fairy in all these goings-on.

But I digress. Having become a politician, as he had hoped and wished, the Man Who Lived in Railway Trains was obliged by the magic spell that had elevated him to the 'acme of every Englishman's ambition' (Trollope in one of those Palliser novels) to pay the price the Bad News Fairy had stipulated.

At first the Man Who Lived in Railway Trains did not mind. He had seen Marlowe's *Dr Faustus* and felt rather flattered to be associated with one of the 'legends that recur throughout Western Literature'. Anyway, he thought he had struck a rather better bargain than the Doctor. Being a Member of Parliament was far more fun than watching Helen of Troy walk pointlessly from one side of the stage to the other or turning invisible and playing public-school japes on the Pope. And eternal damnation seemed a great deal more unpleasant a price to pay for the granting of a dearest wish than travelling on British Rail all the time – travelling to make speeches in other people's constituencies, travelling to Annual Dinners and to Annual Meetings, travelling to appear on obscure television programmes.

For years it was all accepted with fortitude. Euston to New Street, Birmingham, late seven times out of ten hardly seemed to matter. Hull to Edinburgh and King's Cross to Cambridge completed in calm despite the need to disembark and drag bags and baggage overland like Indians whose canoes are incapable of navigating unexpected rapids. Preston, reached in grave dignity despite vandalism to overhead wires that required five journeys through Crewe – three going north and two going south. Engine failure at Milton Keynes. Signal failure at Watford. Points failure at Honor Oak. It was a small price to pay.

Then came the experience on the '125' from Swansea on a wet Welsh Sunday morning. It was an early start, but late due to the need to change an engine unit as a result of a fault being detected in a wheel. The Man Who Lived in Railway Trains waited patiently.

The news that the promised restaurant-car would not be available caused neither horror nor surprise. It was Sunday and British Rail expected total abstinence on Sundays. It was a religious obligation, the only reason that Sabbath services were called fast trains. So the news that there would be a new super-dooper grill and griddle serving a variety of hot snacks and toasted sandwiches was received with surprised delight.

The Man Who Lived in Railway Trains opened the copy of the *Listener* that he took with him wherever he went and read one of its fine articles while he worked up a really fierce appetite. The words 'no food after Newport' will, when he is dead, be found engraved on the flywheel or whatever the Man Who Lived in Railway Trains has in place of a heart.

He looked out of the window at the countryside moving slowly past (for on Sundays the 125 does not travel at that number of miles per hour) and cursed the Bad News Fairy. He even cursed the Good Fairy. His wish had come true. The price had to be paid. It was still worth it. But, at that moment, only just.

Listener, 20 December 1979

Mortality Met in a Barber's Chair

My barber is a muscular man with a better beard than W. G. Grace. He spends his lunchtimes at art galleries and his evenings in philosophy seminars. So, until last week, I naturally accepted that, despite the heavy hand with which he occasionally tugs at my forelock, his recreational activities marked him out as a man of sensitive understanding. I was wrong.

Last Tuesday, seizing a hank of my hair in either hand, he pulled outwards as if to demonstrate how wise I was not to plait a pair of pigtails. In the mirror over the washbasin, it looked as if two Comanches were fighting over the same scalp. The effect on my previously adequate hair was miraculous. The waves parted and left a gap with which Moses would have been satisfied. Despite the pulling and tugging, the demonstration was entirely painless. The implications were not.

The accompanying advice was even more painful. The suggestion was simple and undoubtedly made in my best interests. Before it was too late I should have roots of my hair dug from the back of my neck and planted, like seedlings, in the part of my scalp that was beginning to show through. Six 'plugs' – at about ten pounds a cut and thrust – would do the trick. Once the tentacles had spread beneath the skin, the tell-tale flash of flesh would disappear from human view for ever.

He grew more enthusiastic with every gruesome detail. A local anaesthetic, a day in bandages. A week or two of careful combing to make sure that the saplings were not disturbed until they had taken root and I would grow old hairily. The important thing was catching it early. If I struck now, at the first sign of creeping tonsure, I would go to my grave as hirsute as in the days of my Brylcreemed youth.

No other solution was possible. Seborrhoea and Alopecia Scalp Lotion ('will destroy scurf and dandruff and stop falling hair. Contains no oil or grease') might be advocated by less scientific barbers. But for all the good it would do, I 'might as well rub my head with ...' He paused to allow my imagination to wander

294

over the whole range of absurd and disgusting substances that the disreputable side of his profession had once pretended were remedies for a condition so horrible that its name never passed his lips.

An early holding operation was, he insisted, a public relations as well as a zoological necessity. Too many sufferers postponed the decision until their baldness was the talk of polite society. Then, when they reappeared as hairy as Esau, cosmetic surgery was suspected. Do it at once and no one would notice. In any case, he added, sensing my scepticism, no one would care. And, proving that he did not spend his evenings with Russell and Whitehead for nothing, he moved in for the intellectual kill. Could I provide a real distinction between the constant vanity of regular haircuts and a single act of surgical narcissism? 'I do assure you,' he said, 'there is no real difference.'

I offered him one. Haircuts, I admitted, provide no pleasure. But at least the *thought* of a visit to the barber does not make my eyes water and my knees shake. My hands moved instinctively to comfort the agonising pain in my head and neck. As I contemplated the landscape gardener in mask and rubber gloves tilling away at my skull with tiny trowel and miniature rake, the bottles of shampoo began to tremble on their glass shelf.

What is more, I added – willing even to risk his derision in order to divert my own attention from the drilling and hoeing which was going on in my scalp – haircuts are normal. Hair transplants are deviant. Fearing being trapped into a discussion about the nature of what is natural, I quickly switched from philosophy to sociology, in which, as far as I could remember, he was untutored.

No doubt, I conceded, somewhere there is a group of noble savages who regard the constant use of the comb and clippers as flamboyant folly. But I had been brought up in the decadent tonsorial values of South Yorkshire – short back and sides. We boycotted the barber's shop at the bottom of Wadsley Lane when the proprietor's wife was employed to sweep the floor. Mounds of shorn hair lying underfoot were infinitely preferable to a female invasion of an exceptionally masculine world. At school, I had once been ironically offered the alternatives of an immediate haircut and the enrolment for violin lessons. Perhaps the threat said little for the aesthetic standards on which I had been raised. But the story proved that I had not been prepared for cosmetic surgery.

'Consider, at least,' my barber implored, 'changing the position of your parting.' And, so saying, he held a hand mirror up to nature, pink in skin and scalp. I promised to consider moving the demarcation line that my mother had drawn on my head long before I understood the difference between left and right. It had survived the 'D.A.' of the forties and the crew cut of the early fifties. Was it now, I wondered, to fall victim to the Bobby Charlton and the Arthur Scargill? Like J. Alfred Prufrock, I considered one of the desperate expedients of impending middle age. 'Shall I part my hair behind?'

He shook the few clippings of what remained of my hair from the mauve shroud in which he had wound me when the world was young at the beginning of my haircut. I had never noticed before so many silver threads among the gold. The till bell clanged like the manacles of Marley's ghost. The brass taps gleamed like coffin plates. I had met mortality in a barber's chair.

Listener, 21 February 1980

Mightier Than the Sword

Last week a red ballpoint pen exploded in my back pocket. I felt the plastic casing crack as I sank, exhausted, into my seat on what British Rail call the 2200 hours from Birmingham International to London. But I had no idea that the cartridge had erupted and spread its sticky lava halfway up my back until the train pulled into Euston at what normal people still call twenty minutes to twelve. As I tottered to my feet and turned to pull on my coat in protection against the cold night air that comes rolling up like thunder out of Bloomsbury 'cross the road, the lady in the opposite seat turned as grey as a carriage headrest and pointed to the spot on my back where, whenever I have a cold, I anticipate that the lumbar puncture will go in. The vermilion stain was still spreading.

I am, by nature, inclined to fear the worst. For a moment I really suspected that a foreign assassin had passed undetected between the seats of the open carriage, umbrella in hand. I then realised that a nervous system so sensitive that it feels the dentist's hypodermic long before it reaches the gum would have noticed as the thrust went home. It was, I decided, my long-awaited kidney haemorrhage.

After ten years of false starts, dismissed by unfeeling relatives as mild lumbago, it had happened at last – massive enough to seep through jacket, pullover, skin, muscle and bone. Fortunately, before I called for either the police or an ambulance, the truth dawned. The curse of the pens was upon me once more.

I have been in trouble with pens all my life. Indeed, ever since I was given my first thick cylindrical Waterman's almost forty years ago, they have seemed to conspire to stop me putting words on paper. Yet, like democracy – to paraphrase Winston Churchill's defence of that underrated institution – pens possess the single virtue of being infinitely preferable to any of the alternatives.

Typewriters – more particularly electric typewriters – interpose machinery between the ideas in my head and the words they ought to form on the page. I want nothing to come between my sweating hand and the paper on which I am trying to inscribe my thirty-fourth attempt at an opening sentence. The careful crossings out, the tea stains, the thumbprints, are all indispensable. Curled round the rubber roller the paper stays, literally, at arm's length. With dictating machines the problem is even worse. I find it impossible to lavish care and attention on a roll of magnetic tape. Writing it all by hand was good enough for Shakespeare and it is good enough for me.

On the dust-jacket of his autobiography, Field-Marshal Viscount Montgomery assures his readers that 'every word in this book was written in pencil in my own handwriting'. I can only conclude that the victor of El Alamein enjoyed with his secretary a relationship very different from the one I have with mine. For years I used an austere 3H for engraving faint but precise characters on what I have called, since childhood, 'striped paper'. For anyone who holds a pencil so tightly that he seems fearful it will be snatched from his grasp, and presses on the page so hard that his fingers have grown corns that would make a spin bowler envious, the familiar HB is useless. Unless it is sharpened after every fifty words, it produces letters that look as if they have been scratched in sand with a stick.

I need to produce a neatly written, if less than pristine manuscript. Yet I am tyrannised into giving legibility preference over precision. Narrow-lined foolscap and 3H pencils have only to appear in my desk drawer for the conversations to turn to detached retinas, the Monopoly Commission's report on the cost of spectacle frames, and the Shops and Offices Act.

So I am driven back to pens. And I do mean pens in the plural. Partly because, for one reason or another, I write so many words each day I buy about four pens each week. I also lose about four pens each week, so one rarely expires in my hand.

Whenever I get an idea about next Thursday's article, I discover that my pockets are ominously empty of everything with which it can be recorded for posterity. So I rush out to the nearest stationer's and reach me down a couple of little cellophane cartons which tantalisingly reveal the means by which my inspiration can be shared with the waiting world. By the time I have torn the tough transparent box from its half-inch-thick cardboard backing, the muse has flown. As my mind turns blank, I am forced to take refuge in clichés like 'muse has flown', 'take refuge' and 'mind turns blank'.

It is not simply improvidence or poverty that prevents the bulk-buying of pens in dozen bundles or gross lots. If I bought a hundred a week, a hundred a week would lose themselves or invent some other way of causing me embarrassment and inconvenience with all the ingenuity known only to malign pens.

I find it impossible, for example, to clip one on to the inside of my jacket – their only possible resting place since my days at the Sheffield City Grammar School, when I actually rejoiced at decorating my breast pocket with little bits of plastic and tin. Separated from my heart by no more than the thickness of a shirt and suit-lining, pens always fall apart, leaving me to pull out the empty cap when I have an important document to sign. If the implement in question is full of real ink, the whole humiliating business ends in soggy disaster.

I have now given up ink altogether and try, like a recently redeemed drug addict, to avoid all thought of it. I really did become the man with the writes-blue/dries-black arm. Others I know can fill a pen without getting a drop of the azure liquid on their fingers. I am lucky if I end the operation with my elbows unmarked. No doubt it was because of customer resistance to looking like an over-made-up ancient Briton that somebody invented little plastic tubes of ink, complete with a partially punctured end, ready to receive the sharp little pipe that connects them to the nib like a docking space-station.

With me, the partially punctured end usually becomes totally punctured before the operation is completed, and once again I look like the man who fished the murex up after an industrial accident.

For some time I was driven back on ballpoints. I admit it with shame because my attitude to 'Biros' (like my regret at the passing of the Gentlemen v. Players match at Lord's and my nostalgia for Tiffany lamps in dining-cars) is probably ideologically unacceptable. But I really do find it difficult to believe that very much of value can be written by anything so flimsily disposable and so insubstantial that no sooner is one stolen from a friend than it disintegrates and ruins your suit.

In my ministerial days, ballpoints were left lying around my department like cigarettes at a Foreign Office party – for use on the spot but not to be taken home. It was not the broad arrows, crowns, royal ciphers and other marks of public property that kept me honest; writing with ballpoints, all my infinitives are split and all my sentences end with prepositions.

Had it not been for the sudden appearance on the market of a happy compromise between new ballpoint and old fountain-pen, I might well have had to resign from the NUJ. But now it is possible to purchase a thin barrel that gently trails liquid across the page but keeps the reservoir of wilfully ubiquitous fluid secure within its plastic bowels.

I would have regarded it as the most important contribution to the technology of writing since Caxton, had it not coincided with another major literary discovery – trichlorethane. It is almost impossible to estimate the contribution made to our civilisation by the opportunity that creamy liquid offers, literally, to cover up our mistakes. I would write this minute a hymn of praise to Tipp-Ex and a love song to Liquid Paper had I not lost . . .

Listener, 6 November 1980

Through New Eyes

I have begun to wear spectacles. Friends who have witnessed me poring over the 'close work' for which optical assistance is now necessary have all reacted in the same way. Had I, they asked, any idea of writing about the most recent physical catastrophe to overtake me? Before I had time to reply, they all offered the unsolicited advice they thought an appropriate response to the anticipated affirmative answer – 'Forget it'. The onset of myopia was not, they said, a suitable subject for Endpiece.

It was not that they thought my affliction should be kept secret, like one of those socially unacceptable diseases of profligate youth or debauched manhood. They were not so prejudiced against astigmatism sufferers that they suspected anyone who squints of being louche. Nor did they fear that every politician with Daltonism leaks Budget secrets. Quite the contrary. According to my friends (some of the best of whom wear spectacles), half the world looks at the new moon through glasses, and it would be a positively unlucky – not to say unwise – politician who antagonised so many potential voters by making weak jokes about how shortsightedness comes about and why it affects so many football referees.

After my friends' first half-dozen warnings, I developed a perverse attraction to the idea. I even tested out a few titles. 'My light is spent!' seemed a shade too dramatic though there is no doubt that Milton quotations always go down well with *Listener* readers. 'Ol' Four Eyes is back' had a swinging contemporary attraction, but I discarded it because it was even more irrelevant to what I had proposed to write than it was offensive to the subjects of my essay. My final choice, tried out on a few discerning colleagues, produced a pressure to suppress which was, at the time, irresistible. 'No specs, please, we're British' seemed to my bifocaled friends to call into question the patriotism of everyone who had ever entered an optician's consulting room. So I agreed – with some reluctance – that at least that title would never appear in print.

The second argument in favour of overlooking my glasses convinced me, temporarily at least, that the subject of my spectacles ought to be taboo. Far-sightedness (alas only in the literal sense) came to me during my forty-seventh year. It *is* unseemly for middle-aged men to rail against death and decay – even if they have got to the point where they can only see it all around them with the aid of contact lenses. I would, as in earlier accounts of my physical disintegration, overstate the speed at which senility is setting in. Try as I might to describe without exaggeration the latest manifestation of incipient infirmity, the phrase 'middle-aged' would sneak in somewhere. So I abandoned the whole idea and tore up the introductory paragraph which explained that I had decided to have my eyes tested after I had attempted to become a cornea donor, but found myself unable to fill in the form because I was incapable of reading the small print.

I changed my mind for wholly tactical – some people may even say cynical – reasons shortly after falling off a ladder in the House of Commons library. I was ten rungs up, looking for the collected works of Alfred, Lord Tennyson – daunting task, for the Palace of Westminster, although long on Central American econometricians, is short on English poets. Peering at the faded gilt titles that were engraved on the crumbling leather spines during the century that Tennyson typified, I needed my spectacles to determine where the Ss ended and the Ts began. Unfortunately I forgot to remove them before I began the perilous descent – during which I dropped Francis Thompson who had caught my eye as I searched in vain for older and better poetry. Attempting to catch him as he fled down the Victorian-Gothic arches of the House of Commons bookshelves, I tried to focus on an object six feet away through lenses intended to concentrate my attention on pages of fine print twenty-four inches from my tortoiseshell-type plastic rims.

No damage was done either to me or to the carpet that so

faithfully reproduces the Pugin patterns. But I did hit the floor with something of a bang, awakening several of those Members of Parliament who are so modest about their ceaseless pursuit of knowledge that the long hours they spend in the library are passed in the pretence that they go there to sleep. I also dislodged my spectacles, which bounced several times and lodged themselves behind one of the radiators that keep the library cool in winter.

Prescription charges being what they are, I naturally did all that I could to retrieve them. Colleagues distracted from their scholarly labours by the noise of my fall noticed that, instead of rising at once, I remained on my hands and knees. The speed with which they rushed to my side signified either comradely compassion or a morbid desire to be in at the death. Fortunately, none of the young ladies who staff the library was nearby. In their presence the explanation would have been a double humiliation. Elderly gentleman on library floor, groping blindly to find his glasses, is not how I mean to be remembered.

However, it suddenly struck me that there are worse possible reasons for my recently acquired habits – falling down, missing when attempting to shake hands, failing to acknowledge old friends in the street, pouring tea into plates rather than into cups, taking other people's coats from cloakrooms. They are all the problems of adjusting to wearing spectacles – or, to be more precise, the difficulties of wearing spectacles occasionally and forgetting when, and for what reasons, I need to wear them.

The rule is simple enough. The distant prospect of Eton College is as clear as it ever was. However, I can no longer easily read the poem unaided. It seems difficult to believe, but if the injuries to our West Indies touring team continue at their present rate and I am eventually asked to join the party, I will see Joel Garner's bumper perfectly clearly as it leaves his hand, but it will gradually disappear as it approaches me at ninety miles per hour. The sheer irrationality of my eyesight makes it impossible to take the condition seriously.

So, I often begin to read or write without the aid of spectacles. After half an hour the lines of print or manuscript begin to undulate like a demented snake, or gradually fade like the Cheshire Cat, leaving behind the blank, bland grey page. It then takes me ten minutes to find my glasses, by which time the pain in my head has subsided and what little inspiration or interest I previously possessed has disappeared. Thinking of the muse as Aladdin thought of the genie within the lamp, I attempt to release it by pouring boiling water on Co-op 99 and waiting for signs of its existence to be manifested in steam coming out of the spout. These days the task is beyond me. Normally I simply scald my feet or scour the kitchen table, because I have forgotten to remove my glasses. I ought to remember to remove them with regularity – even panache. Bifocals only institutionalise the problem. Half-glasses are still damagingly associated with the defeated Sir Alec Douglas-Home.

All I need to do is remember – remember that I need them for reading and that for the rest of my days they will be a bulge in my breast pocket. But remembering is a confession. If the poor eyesight had always been with me, I would not have cared a jot.

Bill Bowes – whose burly fast bowling my father always urged me to emulate – wore metal rims from early childhood. P. A. Gibb, who scored a century on his début for Yorkshire, did the same. My father wore pince-nez clipped to his nose and secured to one ear by a safety chain that (I am assured) was used by the infant me as a convenient way of pulling the whole apparatus from his face. But such men were born myopic. For them it was not a sign that youth had fled, that Cupid had become Pandarus, that Diana now follows the hunt in a closed carriage. There is much to be said for reaching an age when it is clear that every goose is not a swan and every lass is not a queen. What a pity some of us can still only tell the difference as long as we remember to wear our glasses.

Listener, 19 March 1981

Song of the Shirt

Just before Parliament rose for the summer recess, both Commons and Lords presented the Queen with a Loyal Address which congratulated Her Majesty in suitably archaic language on the marriage of her 'dearly beloved son, the Prince of Wales – etc, etc, etc', rather as another monarch (the King of Siam) would have said, at least according to Oscar Hammerstein II. With initial reluctance and eventual enthusiasm, I took part in the event. Anyone who has any feeling for either history or England finds it difficult to resist an antiquarian excitement at the prospect of climbing inside the time machine of royal ceremonial. The bearers of last month's formal, but affectionate, message were greeted on their arrival at Buckingham Palace by a piper whose presence was clearly a relic of Queen Victoria's Highland obsession. From then on the clock moved backwards until I felt like a page out of a textbook of Tudor history – or an extra from *The Six Wives of Henry VIII*.

My Privy Councillor's oath prevents me from describing all that took place. Indeed, it probably prohibits me from using the Privy Councillor's oath as the reason for not describing all that took place. So abiding, as I must, by its secrecy clause (the existence of which I neither confirm nor deny), I am unable to reveal that the Lord Chancellor shamelessly hammed up his part in the proceedings. Nor can I give a full account of the way that fragments of gold embroidery fell from the Speaker's robes. Anxious, as always, to ingratiate myself with authority, I picked up the gleaming desiderata and handed them back to their temporary owner. As I did so, I felt that my role had changed. The peasant from the wild North Country who goes to court, sees the Queen and recovers the gold that has fallen from the wise man's raiment is clearly a character from Hans Christian Andersen.

If the word 'peasant' implies a life deeply rooted in the soil, it may not be the most technically precise description of my origins – although, during the war, my father did briefly rent an allotment. However, the more accurate phrase 'industrial proletariat' (which, now that I have thought of it, I propose to insinuate into *Who's Who*) does not fit into a fairytale. And in the middle of all those City of London aldermen in their red robes and bearskin caps, with the gentlemen ushers ushing away like mad, and ladies-in-waiting about all over the place, a fairy story it was. And I, for reasons that my Privy Council oath in no way prevents me from explaining, had the momentary feeling of a mendicant at court. The reason concerned my shirt.

I make no proletarian claims concerning my shirts in general. Indeed, I admit extravagance in every particular – capital cost, frequency of maintenance and speed of turnover. The problem on the day of the Loyal Address was specific. It first appeared that (as a result of summer holidays at the laundry) two weeks' supply languished in some Kentish Town depot. Then hope was revived by news that a van had arrived at the Horseferry Road shop. But, instead of containing boxes of carefully ironed cotton Oxford and Bengal stripes, complete with little cardboard bow-ties to keep the collars straight, it was filled with coat-hangers from which were suspended crumpled pieces of cloth. The presser had missed his flight back from Tahiti or some such holiday resort.

There will be those who say that I should have slipped into a heavy brown check or the little white sleeveless number with the crocodile on the breast pocket. My argument with them will have to await my years of political re-education in the jungles of Barnsley, or the time when the cultural revolutionaries require me to contemplate past sins in a Lambeth cowshed.

I could have carefully pulled on a bright blue confection with dazzling white collar and cuffs. But, apart from being out of fashion, my Jermyn Street rhapsody on an original theme by Everton Football Club had a small tear under the left arm. It was the sort of tear that would have easily survived a normal day's wear but which might well have extended itself across the front of the shirt if provoked by violent movement; like, for instance, a low bow. Since I was preparing for the only day in my life when a low bow might have been required of me, wearing a shirt which would fall apart at the moment of obeisance seemed at best perverse and at worst treasonable.

So I got the ironing-board out. I have no social or sexist

objections to ironing. I send my partner (as Councillor Valerie Wise would call her) out to work as an indication of my enthusiasm for equal opportunities. And although she has not (unlike Councillor Wise herself) signed over all the property to the better half of the partnership, I try to accept some share of domestic duties. This highly moral attitude is reinforced by my actual enjoyment of ironing. Smoothing out the wrinkles and making straight what previously was crooked seems to me a rewarding way to spend a Sunday morning. With a little Rodgers and Hart on the gramophone and the smell of Sunday dinner coming round the door, it is possible to think great thoughts while flattening the final crease out of a sleeve or into a trouser leg.

Indeed, I have been accused in the past of being an ironing obsessive. I possess a travelling iron which I take wherever I go. And I pride myself on my hotel bedroom technique – folded towel on the dressing-table to provide a suitable surface, clean handkerchief soaked in water to protect the wool, knob turned round to 'v. hot' and the Hattersley auto-valet service is in action.

I even own that special mark of ironing class, a sleeve-board. When Sarah Wilson – my agnostic equivalent of a god-daughter – was a child, she mistook it for 'an ironing thing made for little girls'. If she had asked me for the dining-room table to make into a 'Wendy house', I would have found it difficult to deny her request. But I put the sleeve-board on a high shelf, well out of her reach.

I have loyally maintained my affection for ironing through every vicissitude. Humiliating phone calls to hotel receptionists, asking for a quick check on the room to which I will soon return, 'to make sure that the iron is switched off', have done nothing to cool my ardour for applying hot pressure to bent lapels and crushed pocket flaps. The briefcase that marked my first ministerial promotion is scarred for life with a horseshoe-shaped scorch mark. But my search for suitable portable surfaces on which to make the whole world flat continues.

I did not become an ironer, or have ironing thrust upon me. I was born to it. If I am not very careful, I will draw psychological conclusions about my enthusiasm. They concern the Levellers and the pursuit of equality.

Despite all that, I could not resist wondering if any of the

other men at the auspicious Buckingham Palace gathering had done
any ironing that day. The Speaker wore beneath his velvet suit a
riot of ruffles which, if they were prepared by mortal hand, must
have been the work of a team of professionals. There was no way
of knowing what state shirt (or, indeed, if any shirt at all) was
concealed by the Archbishop of York's stock and clerical collar.
Loyalty prevented my mind dwelling on either the Duke of Edinburgh's or the Prince of Wales's laundry. But I did speculate a little
about the Lord Chamberlain. As Chief Scout, he must often have
started fires by rubbing two twigs together and tied securely pieces
of rope of unequal thickness. But I was unable to envisage him
doing his good deed for the day, stooped over some old lady's
ironing-board.

I drew no conclusions from my musing, except the obvious
one that ironing is, for better or worse, a wholly working-class
occupation. But then, so is bricklaying, and Sir Winston Churchill
boasted of that as an achievement as well as a hobby. Perhaps I
should include 'ironing' in *Who's Who* when I change the entry to
include a reference to my industrial proletarian origins. Of course,
I could not tell the truth and put my pastime as *ironing exceedingly
well*. Thinking of that in Buckingham Palace, I looked down at
my shirtfront and felt with pride that, thanks to my own efforts, I
was the smoothest man there.

Listener, 27 August 1981

Sort of Related

My relationship with the young lady is most accurately
described by a definition of our condition which she herself
created. We were walking hand in hand towards the House of
Commons at the time and our reverie had just been interrupted by
Richard Crossman. He had borne down upon us, collar flying and
wearing both his floppy Fellow of New College suit and his taut
Fellow of New College expression. Crossman's conversational

technique was a compromise between cross-examination and inter-rogation. Instead of saying 'hello' he demanded to know if 'this' was my daughter.

I confessed that 'this' was not. 'Is she,' he asked in a tone of friendly accusation, 'your godchild?' The suspected godchild answered, 'Sort of' and the author of *Plato Today* staggered back in shock from the impact of such improper language. He repeated her six-year-old confession in a way that made the two-word sentence end with both question and exclamation marks. 'What,' he asked, 'does sort of mean?' emphasising the 'does'. The irony was totally lost on the object of his interest. 'If,' she explained, 'we went to church, he would be my godfather. But because we don't he's only sort of.'

Dick Crossman smiled the smile of a man who knew when he was beaten and we went, hand in hand, on our way towards the Houses of Parliament. When we arrived she seemed to enjoy feeding the photocopying machine and talking to herself on the two telephone extensions. I hoped that the pleasure of the unaccustomed gadgets made up for the horrors of the previous day.

We had travelled by Thames steamer to Greenwich and back, and she had sat in the stern of the boat shivering inside her little double-breasted tweed topcoat. For me the most painful aspect of the journey was the way in which she kept trying to smile.

She is smiling now. Or at least she ought to be. For in two weeks' time she is off to university, bound by extraordinary coincidence and the vagaries of the admission clearing house system to Hull, the alma mater of her sort of godfather. As a sort of godfather I have not always been a conventional success. No leather-bound complete works of Jane Austen has ever passed between us. The uplifting and improving advice which is supposed to play so prominent a part in the relationship between sort of godparents and sort of godchildren has been noticeably absent from our friendship. But in mitigation of my offence, I make this plea. The discovery that she was on her way to Hull gave me the kind of palpitation that owes more to pleasure and pride than to indigestion.

She will not go to Hull quite as her sort of godfather went. He travelled by train with his trunk and his bicycle in the luggage van, and she will be driven up the M1 and along the M62 by her mother with her coffeemaker and cassette player on the back seat. Her portable property is the product of a year's hard labour as waitress and scullery maid. But whoever paid for the consumer durables they are a symbol of a new age. These days there are no Nissen huts on the campus at Hull. In my time, we lived and learned under corrugated iron.

Professor Jessop, who was gassed in the First World War, will not be there to wheeze to all the assembled freshmen that 'learning must be followed to wherever it may lead'. Indeed, I suspect that these days the new recruits are not even called freshmen. And it is not only the exclusively male suffix to which my academic heirs take exception. Not for them the language of the ancient universities. For they do not regard their elders as betters, and would no more ape the patois of Oxbridge than call students undergraduates.

They do not, I understand, buy long striped scarves to ensure that when they walk the streets of the East Riding nobody mistakes them for anything other than seekers after truth. I hope that they still send Student Union Christmas cards to their elderly friends and relations though I doubt if they troop off en masse to Beverley at Advent to hear the *Messiah* performed under the echoing arches of the Minster. However, I suspect that the early awe remains. Anyone who is calm and composed on the first day of a great adventure ought not to be allowed participation in the enterprise.

Thirty years ago we were engulfed in awe for a full three years. Universities were not the sort of thing that the likes of us attended. So we decided to make the most of every unexpected minute. After she comes up for air my sort of goddaughter will feel more free to pick and choose. Her mother and father, and a few thousand of our contemporaries all helped to break the academic ice. I hardly dare ask her if she will join Film Soc and Soc Soc for I fear that she will explain that she proposes to watch the movies of her choice in the city's cinemas and pursue her political interests in the local Labour Party.

But she will, like her sort of godfather so long ago, begin to buy and read all of those books – and a few of them connected to the course, but the best concerned with subjects which she reads for pleasure. Just to think of it makes me irrationally ambitious for her younger brother, my sort of godson.

Years ago, when he first began to show an interest in science, I wrote about my hope that one day he would repay my many kindnesses by discovering the elixir of life. Today, as his sister packs her bag, crosses her fingers and holds her breath, I wish him a slightly less successful future. I will be satisfied if he unravels the secret of eternal youth. And when, as an act of gratitude, he mixes me the first dose of his potion, I would like to be kept for ever at nineteen and on my way to Hull.

Guardian, 5 October 1984

Upstaged By a Tub of Lard –
Allegedly

It is now more than a month since the tub of lard was placed on the table in front of the chair on which I might have sat during a recording of *Have I Got News For You*. So I hope that I can write about that milestone in broadcasting history without appearing to seek catharsis for a heartbreaking experience. For any readers who persist in identifying tearstains between the lines, I ought to explain – since their powers of comprehension are obviously limited – that when I wrote of a broadcasting milestone I intended irony. The only interesting aspect of the episode is the way in which people reacted to it.

First of all the facts. I agreed to take part in the programme about a month before the transmission date. When I was told that it would take a whole evening to make a programme which lasted for less than thirty minutes, I almost pulled out straight away. Then I remembered that, in television, the illusion of spontaneous wit is created by recording hours of garbage and then extracting the good bits. Anxious for my reputation to be enhanced in that way, I decided to turn up late as usual. Once upon a time, I tried to calm frenzied producers with Stephen Sondheim's aphorism, 'the hero always comes in the nick of time'. But, for reasons which I have never understood, it made them even more angry than my last-minute arrival.

I was considering how late I could be when the hinge of fate swung in Bolton. Winston Churchill made a speech on a subject which he called 'immigration'. In fact the children of whom he spoke were not immigrants, but the black and Asian British who – being born in this country – are as British as he is. Certainly some had colonial parents. But politicians with an ethnic obsession may regard that as an improvement on the nationality status of little Winston's grandfather. His mother was American. And without his grandpa, where would little Winston be? Certainly not in a position to provoke me into cancelling television engagements.

Enter the *Sunday Times*. Months ago I agreed to write an article about the Muslims in Britain. My handler on the paper believed that the Churchill diatribe was a perfect curtain raiser for its publication. She thought the piece was topical. I regarded it as a chance to contradict dangerous nonsense. So I set out to talk to families which had made a contribution to British life that not even a Tory backwoodsman could deny. I had to choose between supporting the multi-racial society and laughing at bad jokes about the Duchess of York. It was not a difficult decision.

It was a man from the *Daily Mirror* who passed on the good news about the tub of lard. Until he telephoned my office, I assumed that the cancellation was of no consequence – the sort of thing that I do, and is done to me, most weeks. But he told my secretary that he wanted to give me a chance to tell my side of the story. That is the sort of message which is usually shouted through letterboxes at bankrupt businessmen who have just been visited by the Fraud Squad. But I still did not take the crisis seriously. Even when I received the anonymous, warning telephone calls – a man who claimed to work for the *Sun* and a breathless lady who said she was employed by the production company – my complacency remained invincible.

I was writing on the night of the broadcast and forgot about the repeat until the last thirty seconds of the programme. Admittedly, the little plastic tub was a great disappointment. I had hoped for an obese barrel with wooden staves which bulged inside cast iron hoops. But I still assumed that the producer's intentions were entirely honourable. My absence provided the chance to promote valuable pre-broadcast publicity and the opportunity for Paul Merton to perform without the handicap of partnering a visiting old codger. I took it for granted that, far from being outraged, the programme wanted to behave outrageously. No complaints about that. Anyone who agrees to take part has accepted all of the rules.

Yet people persisted in taking the affair seriously. Some of my friends did not talk about it – conspicuously. That nice couple on ITV's *Good Morning* (who had once cancelled my appearance on their programme because they could not find anyone to challenge my pretentious claims about *Coronation Street*) asked me about the incident in tones which are usually reserved for burial services. Ed Doolan – a Birmingham chat show host – offered me the opportunity 'to tell the truth about what went wrong'. They all seemed to think that it mattered.

As a result, I have begun to harbour a terrible suspicion. Perhaps the people who make *Have I Got News For You* really were offended – affronted in the way that the Queen would be affronted if somebody failed to turn up at an investiture. Part of me faces that prospect with equanimity. But another part minds very much indeed. It is not possible for any programme that takes itself so seriously to be genuinely funny.

Go on! Invite me back next year. Then I shall be reassured that it was all done for the best – that is to say most cynical – of reasons.

Guardian, 5 July 1993

Heroes and Hero Worship

Heroism comes in different shapes and sizes. So I have no doubt that Joan of Arc rests in peace within my pantheon alongside Hattersley, Private Herbert; 2042; 1/7 Sherwood Foresters, killed in action on the first day of the Battle of the Somme, six weeks before his nineteenth birthday and after almost two years' continuous service in the trenches. Nor do I find any contradiction in placing Ronald Reagan and John F. Kennedy side by side. President Reagan was, and remains, a hero of middle America. My own distaste for his style of politics ('Wanting in Imperial Graces') is no more than the expression of surprise that he was held in such high esteem. The reputation of President Kennedy has, on the other hand, been tarnished with the years – not least by professional detractors. Perhaps in 1971 ('The Torch-bearer') I overstated his achievements. But he remains the prophet of hope, the politician who believed (or convincingly pretended to believe) in man's ability to improve the condition of the whole hemisphere. If that does not make him an authentic hero, heroism needs a new definition.

Like President Kennedy, Clem Attlee was a war hero before he became a politician. But his heroism was of the modest sort. He was wounded in the backside by Turkish shrapnel so he crawled out into no man's land to act as an 'artillery marker', planting flags to guide range and trajectory. Typically he was engaged in the meticulous work which is the key to victory. On modest men like him the world has hung suspended. As prime minister, he changed history by the assiduous application of high principle and steadfast determination. It was not until I wrote and presented the BBC's centenary tribute (and complemented my programme with 'The Man Who Was Attlee' in the *Radio Times*) that I realised the full extent of his achievement.

Mr Attlee (as we always called him) was the senior member

of the Trinity that I almost worshipped as a boy. His two unlikely companions were J. B. Priestley and Len Hutton, who burst into my life during the last year of the war. Both, as I later discovered, were (in their different ways) very unheroic heroes. So my admiration for them is a confirmation that, although I have stolen my title from Thomas Carlyle, I do not share the Promethean view of leaders and leadership that he advanced with such ponderous logic. The people I admire most are 'ordinary' (my father's warmest compliment) in appearance and behaviour until they begin to demonstrate their particular genius.

Hutton and Priestley – two such men – were the infatuations of my twelfth and thirteenth years to heaven. Joan of Arc (so ordinary in speech and appearance that her claims to be the instrument of God were dismissed as madness) was a later passion. I had barely heard of her before, in the sixth form of the Sheffield City Grammar School, I read Bernard Shaw's *St Joan*. Her fake Yorkshire accent ('Be ye, bastard?') first embarrassed and then annoyed me. Now, she is almost the only thing connected with GBS that does not cause me intense irritation. I was captured by a single sentence. 'Nothing counting under God save France free and French.' That expression of total commitment redeemed the play and almost made up for all the tosh about the beginning of nationalism that was talked by kings and bishops.

According to Anatole France's version of the Orleans' story, the Inquisition had been inclined to take a lenient view of the maid's heresy on the grounds that she was mad rather than possessed of devils. They based that view on her behaviour at the battle of Compiègne when she threw turnips at the advancing Burgundians. Joan refused to accept the plea in mitigation. Turnips were the only weapons to hand. So she did her best with the resources at her disposal. When I read that story, I was lost forever and I still feel the need ('Plausible Miracles') to reaffirm my admiration. I avoid the word infatuation in case its carnal association results in me being struck down in the manner of Foul Mouth Frank.

Since the only other woman included in this section is Jean Rook, late of the *Daily Express*, some explanation of her presence is necessary. It is a mark of my admiration and gratitude.

Half way through my years with *Punch*, I decided that my

Press Gang column should occasionally include profiles of famous Fleet Street figures. My first, and only, subject was Jean Rook ('Express Delivery'). I spent a whole day with her and wrote my column the same night. When I saw the proof, I feared that one paragraph was gratuitously offensive and struck it out. Sub-editors put it back in. To my horror, the day after publication, I recognised a famous neck-to-ankle mink coat preparing to climb into a taxi which I was about to pay off.

Miss Rook waved the taxi away and *thanked* me for my article. The offensive passage had, she said, 'summed her up to a tee'. From then on her column contained the occasional compliment. When my second novel was published she *offered* to write about it. She telephoned me (I later discovered from hospital) to apologise that her article only appeared in early northern editions of the paper. 'It's never happened to me before,' she said. 'Wait till I get back to the office.' She never did.

Ian Botham I include amongst the immortals because, although all heroes are flawed, some are more flawed than others and I wanted to make an invidious comparison between the tawdry icons of our age and the more austere objects of veneration who were worshipped in my youth.

Some of the gods who inhabit my Valhalla – Stephen Sondheim, Arnold Bennett, E. M. Forster, Thomas Hardy, George Eliot – are celebrated in other parts of this book. Priestley appears here ('A Great Writer from the North') and in the collection of book reviews. Shakespeare – as befits the greatest hero of all – dominates the section which is devoted to plays and playwrights. Its title ('Living at this Hour') is meant as a tribute not to Milton but to him.

The article on Hugh Gaitskell ('Hugh Gaitskell's Legacy') possesses no literary merit and is included here for two equally sentimental reasons. Anything which I put together under the title Heroes and Hero Worship would not be complete unless Gaitskell was included. And the tribute (published in the *Sheffield Telegraph*) was the beginning of my serious journalism.

It was written, in 1965 at the height of Harold Wilson's popularity, because I believed that Gaitskell's contribution to Labour's long-awaited victory had largely been forgotten. For an ambitious young backbencher – desperate for promotion into the Wilson government – touting such an article round Fleet Street was an act of mindless irresponsibility which I cannot explain. Nor can I excuse the conceit which made me believe that a national newspaper might consider publishing such a piece. I do not pretend that I was undaunted by universal rejection. But I was sufficiently resilient to send the returned manuscripts to the serious (some people would say intellectual) weeklies. The *Listener* was not interested. The *New Statesman* did not reply. Neither did the *Spectator*, but Iain Macleod, then titular editor, stopped me in the library corridor of the House of Commons. 'Are you,' he asked in that strange sharp voice, 'the man who sent me the Gaitskell article?'

Before I had time to feel false hope, Macleod embarked on a detailed explanation of why the article was not worth publishing. He then added menacingly that Alan Watkins (now columnist on the *Independent* but, at the time, the *Spectator*'s political correspondent) had told him about me. 'Would you,' he asked in an infuriatingly casual aside, 'like to work for the paper regularly?' Before I was capable of giving an answer, he explained his idea. I was to write 'A View from the Left' to counterbalance the Tory bias in the magazine's general tone and would take my turn with Endpiece. When, ten years and several Labour governments later, Tony Howard asked me to write a column for the *Listener*, I stole the name. I have been writing Endpiece for somebody or other ever since.

Which leaves Tony Crosland. Our relationship is best illustrated by an incident which I recorded in the *Listener* on the fourth anniversary of his death.

> . . . On the day that Harold Wilson announced his intention to resign the Labour Party leadership, I was in Bulgaria. When the Ambassador told me that the impossible had happened, it took me some time to recover from the sort of bewilderment that must have overcome the ancients when they discovered that the world was round. After equilibrium was restored, my single obsession was to prevent Tony Crosland from contesting an election which could only result, for him, in a damagingly small vote. An attempt to telephone the Department of the Environment only produced the Victorian message that the Secretary of State 'had already left

for the Palace'. Unfortunately, he had not been summoned to form a new administration but was attending a royal reception for sporting personalities.

I struggled through the first 48 hours of a five day visit and then decided that duty called me home. I went straight from London airport to the Marsham Street monstrosity that perversely houses the Environment Department. The Secretary of State would see me at once. I decided that it was not a moment for prevarication. It was, I told him, my clear and unequivocal judgement that he should not stand. Would I, he asked, vote for him if he rejected my advice? 'Not' had barely followed 'certainly' when Tony Crosland replied in a single sentence that led me to believe that the conversation was over.

A porter was waiting for me when I got out of the lift. Could I, he inquired, spare a moment for the Secretary of State? Having confirmed that there was no mistake and that he had a second spare moment in mind, I made the long, apprehensive ascent. Once again I was ushered straight into the presence and once again I was asked a single direct question – was I free for lunch on Sunday? Of course, I was. We ate in the kitchen, the rest of the house being occupied by young men who were promoting the interests of a candidate whom I did not support. I knew them all. But Tony Crosland insisted on formal introductions. 'This is Roy Hattersley. He's going to vote for Callaghan and is going round forcing people to listen to the hard truth as if he were a member of the Oxford Movement.'

Two articles about him appear in this anthology. But they both only really add up to what he said at the dinner to mark the tenth anniversary of Hugh Gaitskell's death. 'Had he lived, all sorts of things would have been better. I miss him.'

The Gaitskell Legacy

On 15 October 1964, less than two years after the death of Hugh Gaitskell, twenty-one of his most committed supporters became new Members of Parliament. At least twice as many hard core 'Gaitskellites' returned to the House for a second or third time – many of them not simply as supporters but as members of the Harold Wilson government.

Under any conditions sixty or seventy like-minded Members could exert a substantial influence. In a parliamentary majority of five their pressure and persuasion could have a crucial effect on government policy. Yet no attempt has been made to marshal these forces.

Three years ago it would have been beyond belief, four years ago beyond hope that the contending armies of Brighton, Blackpool and Scarborough would come together in a united and unified Labour Party. Superficially it seems that the old battles are forgotten and the old wounds healed.

Of course, the atmosphere of the new Labour Party is all against corporate action by any faction. The frustrations of opposition bred dissent and disagreement. Talents once wasted on fratricide are now admirably employed running ministries.

The chance, after thirteen years, of putting promises into practice, preoccupies most MPs, and the tiny majority by which the government is maintained has engendered an enthusiasm for self-preservation which Conservatives always enjoy but which Labour often lacks.

Elder-statesmanship has spread like a contagion, and yesterday's dissidents are the first to warn tomorrow's rebels of the consequences of public disagreement.

But there is more to it than simple survival. When the Campaign for Democratic Socialism quietly did itself to death (notifying potential mourners by a brief news item in one or two newspapers some days after the corpse was securely interred) it was acknowledging that at least some of the objectives for which it once struggled were achieved.

It was also admitting that the price the party would have to pay to obtain the others was too great. The Labour Party is a gigantic compromise; its strength has always been in the reasonable men who know where the compromise must be made.

How such a solution came about can only be understood if the unhappy battles of the early sixties are seen as political (which they were) rather than personal (as they are often portrayed).

Many of the people who stood vocally and persistently behind Hugh Gaitskell hardly knew him. Only a few were his close friends; many he would not have recognised had he met them.

They supported his leadership because he seemed the best hope there was of reinvigorating and reforming the Labour Party. He stood for a party committed to pragmatism rather than ideology and he accepted the overriding importance of gaining power. At a time when the Labour Party desperately needed, and many of its members desperately wanted, rationalism, radicalism and reason, Hugh Gaitskell appeared rational, radical and reasonable. He also seemed a good party leader.

He seemed a good party leader – indeed a great one – because he spoke with authority, courage and conviction. He inspired confidence in the general public and affection in his supporters. He was the right man leading the party in the right direction.

At the numbing news of his death, it seemed inconceivable that another leader of his kind and calibre could be found. In fact his successor possessed very different but equally compelling talents. The election of Harold Wilson marked one of the turning points in Labour Party history.

In 1960, the main opposition to Harold Wilson's bid for the leadership of the Labour Party came from people who believed (almost certainly incorrectly) that he supported 'the wrong policies'.

He won in 1963 because some of the people who had opposed his policies three years earlier decided that he was 'the right man'.

Over the three years a significant number of Labour MPs had stopped thinking about the place a potential leader occupies in the political spectrum.

Hugh Gaitskell was the overwhelming choice of the parliamentary party both because of his political point of view and his personal attributes. The crucial votes that made Harold Wilson leader were influenced by ability alone. This fundamental change in attitude was very largely the work of Hugh Gaitskell himself.

For three years after the agonising self-criticism of the 1959 Blackpool conference, Hugh Gaitskell urged the Labour Party to think in terms of 'issues' rather than of 'slogans'. His own willingness to judge single cases on their apparent merits was emphasised by his opposition to British entry into the Common Market.

The philosophy of his general political position and the persuasion of his friends and supporters must have urged British membership. But having considered the arguments, he accepted the case for staying out and chose to ignore both his allies and his general philosophy. Europe was considered like all other things as an 'issue' – a vital, relevant, perhaps moral issue, but an issue to be judged by the available empirical evidence.

Six months after Labour had apparently turned its face against Europe, the election of Hugh Gaitskell's successor faced the party. The lesson had been well learned. Members of Parliament based their decision on the empirical evidence of personal ability rather than pre-conceived ideas about personal ideology. Harold Wilson was elected.

Had there been any turning back from the new empiricism the lesson might have been forgotten again. In fact the leadership of Harold Wilson convinced the pragmatists of the early 1960s that their victory was won.

The new approach dominated the election manifesto of 1964. Earlier promises to 'take into public ownership the road haulage industry' were replaced by the undertaking that British Road Services would expand their activities. This sort of adjustment is typical of an approach which relies more on common sense than on ideology.

In some fields rationalism has taken over where even under Hugh Gaitskell emotion reigned. The reiteration of support for free entry into Great Britain by Commonwealth immigrants has given way to precise proposals for helping those who are already here, those who are likely to come and those among whom they live, to enjoy the amenities of normal twentieth-century life.

The first fifty of 'the hundred days' have seen a score of decisions based on the same empirical methods – many of them proving that rationalism is not necessarily the enemy of enlightened, humanitarian government.

Pensions increases (paid the moment the economy can stand it) and the supply of military aircraft to South Africa (embargoed after the present obligations have been met) have proved that government action can be based on the highest principle, yet applied with reason and restraint.

It was the battle for the acceptance of these beliefs that Hugh Gaitskell fought and it is upon this framework that Harold Wilson has brilliantly built Labour victory and Labour government.

It is his acceptance of this, more than admiration for the Prime Minister's talents, more than gratitude for his genuinely representative government, that has ended the conflict within the party.

Perhaps the new order would have never come about under Hugh Gaitskell. Perhaps his fight to establish the sort of party and the sort of leadership that wins elections and governs nations made him too many irreconcilable enemies.

But the new order would have never come about without him. Had he not flown the kite of 'Clause 4' in 1959, defied conference in 1960, won again in 1961, the new strength and the new tranquillity would have been out of the question.

In his eloquent memorial essay, Roy Jenkins asks what Hugh Gaitskell left behind. The answers that he gives include 'a Labour Party with both the will and the capacity for victory'. It was a great, and at times apparently unattainable, achievement. It is his greatest and most permanent memorial. Those who fought with him to build the new Labour Party will not, because of minor disagreement or personal dissent, see that work destroyed.

Sheffield Telegraph, 18 January 1965

The Torch-bearer

'Let the word go forth from this time and place, to friend and foe alike, knowing that the torch has been passed to a new generation of Americans.'

On the morning of 20 January 1961, John Fitzgerald Kennedy, thirty-fifth President of the United States, was proclaiming in his Inaugural Address that the new men were taking over. The youngest president in American history had replaced the oldest, and hope grew in young men everywhere. The ancients of Europe seemed invincibly immortal no longer. The young and the bold could inherit the earth.

Of course, the prospects of the young and the bold are much improved if their fathers are multimillionaires utterly and ruthlessly committed to their son's success. But in the first flush of the new president's victory, that was easily forgotten. Nothing – not even the compromise with Joe McCarthy in 1954 – seemed as important as what John Kennedy could offer. The prospect was intangible, but to many people it really seemed that he might bring a new quality to American politics.

Most of his eventual support came from the hard core of traditional Democrats who would have voted for any candidate their party chose – and he lost votes in the south that virtually any other Democrat would have held. But part of his strength sprang from his ability to inspire men and women who wanted politics to be a crusade. Kennedy talked about principles and was not embarrassed by ideals. In an imperfect world, that made him as good a leader as a practical crusade can find.

Perhaps the reputation was little more than the ad-men's varnish, invented and superimposed by Madison Avenue, but if it was no more than tactics, it proved the right stratagem. Opposed by Richard Nixon (who in 1960 seemed at home only in smoke-filled rooms), labelled with his own Catholicism and his party's growing support for civil rights, he had to appeal to those Americans who hate machine politicians, loathe religious bigotry and despise racialism.

So it might have been principle or it might have been expediency that guided his strategy. In one sense the motive hardly matters. A campaign that calls on the people to lift up their eyes to the hills has at least one virtue – a few eyes are uplifted. And if the campaign is successful, a suspicion begins to grow that politicians who talk about principles sometimes even win.

Not that, as some disciples now pretend, President Kennedy followed truth and justice with a self-destructive passion. He was, and had been for fifteen years, a professional politician who knew that the wheels of government need oiling with patronage and compromise. But partly by choice, partly because of the necessities of his campaign, Kennedy became the champion of most Americans who wanted to improve the quality of American government.

Quality in government is dependent on the quality of the men who govern. From the day after his election, Kennedy sought to recruit men of experience and ability to his administration. Ten years later, not all his appointments seem the result of the methodical search for excellence. Some were made out of gratitude for past help or in the hope of future favours. The reputation of some who served him has been prejudiced by their continuing involvement in Vietnam – the policy which he began but which death prevented him from carrying through. A few were, or became, so devoted to one president that they adopted a view of the White House that was more dynastic than Democratic. Some simply failed to live up to their early promise. But most of them were there simply because they were thought to be good – usually very good – at their jobs.

By the time of the inauguration they had imprinted their indelible mark on his speeches. The style is now amicably theirs and his – the call to arms sounded with the imperious instruction 'Let . . .': the harsh vocabulary of new professional America, where 'surveillances' and 'capabilities' are understood. They shared his total commitment, his willingness to 'pay any price, bear any burden, meet any hardship, support any friend, oppose any foe, to assure the survival of liberty'.

In his inauguration speech the unquestioning belief in America's duty to the world appears again and again. To his audience ten years ago it seemed a simple statement of American idealism. Today, to a new generation of American liberals it appears only the strident rhetoric of ill-thought-out imperialism. In fact, it was something of both.

The message could hardly have been more clear. 'In the long history of the world only a few generations have been granted the role of defending freedom in its hour of maximum danger. I do not shrink from this responsibility. I welcome it. I do not believe that any of us would exchange places with any other people or any other generation.' With Shakespeare to write his speeches, Henry V could hardly do better when he addressed his troops before Agincourt. That philosophy sustained the war against the French for a hundred years. Kennedy's declaration was no less a genuine statement of the duty he believed he must do. The inevitable outcome – for better or for worse – was the Bay of Pigs, the

Cuban missile crisis and Vietnam. The Bay of Pigs was a clear disaster but quickly over. The Cuban missile crisis was a brilliant victory for nerve and judgment. Vietnam festered on, providing every day more opportunities for recrimination, reproach and retrospective wisdom.

To argue, as apologists have tried to do, that but for his death in Dallas Kennedy would have brought the war to an end is to replace logic with loyalty. 'This hemisphere,' he told his inauguration audience, 'intends to remain master in its own house.' He meant it, so neither the prospect of international condemnation nor his contempt for the regime he proposed to re-establish prevented him from helping the Bay of Pigs invaders. Five years later, his reaction to another squalid government in Saigon would have been much the same. 'We dare not tempt them with weakness' was his inaugural conclusion on foreign affairs. He meant that, too.

It was that philosophy that drove him on during the Cuban missile crisis. When he could, he shortened the odds. When possible, he minimised the risks. Then he gambled. Had he lost, what was left of the world would have thought him less than a hero. As it happened, he is entitled to the credit and that alone provides him a place in the pantheon of American presidents.

But it is not the Cuban missile crisis for which he will be remembered. He will be remembered because his three-year presidency promised so much. Lyndon Johnson did more for the Black American than Kennedy ever did, yet it is Kennedy who gave hope that the hundred-year promise of emancipation would be honoured. The war against poverty moved faster and further in the years that followed Kennedy: but what Kennedy said helped to dispel the despair of the poor. Later statesmen carried *détente* further, but Kennedy provided the first hope that the cold war need not last for ever.

Indeed, hope remains the word that best characterises the presidency of John Kennedy. Perhaps if Lee Harvey Oswald had missed, hope would have died in the war in Indo-China. But by the time Kennedy was killed it had become a respectable political emotion again.

That is why most people over twenty-five remember where they were on 22 November 1963 – not the date, but how they spent the day that Kennedy died. It is hope that makes the Camelot legend live on – belief that somehow the good days can be unearthed and recreated.

In a way, it was all foreshadowed in the Inaugural Address. 'All this will not be finished in the first hundred days. Nor will it be finished in the first thousand days, nor in the lifetime of this administration, nor even, perhaps, in our lifetime on this planet, but let us begin.' Kennedy began by giving hope and reviving optimism. It was a good beginning.

Guardian, 20 January 1971

The Grandeur of R. H. Tawney

Last Sunday was the hundredth anniversary of R. H. Tawney's birth and his centenary was suitably celebrated by the unveiling of a plaque on the house in which he lived and worked, followed by a modest Fabian Society reception. Mecklenburgh Square – with its overtones of European aristocracy and its heavily prosperous nineteenth-century architecture – always sounds too grand an address for the author of *Equality*. But, according to Hugh Gaitskell, the author of *The Acquisitive Society* was not conspicuously a man of property:

> I remember our first meeting. It was in 1926 during the General Strike when I was taken by Margaret Cole to meet him in Mecklenburgh Square. There he was sitting surrounded by that appalling muddle of books, papers and used matches that his friends knew so well and wearing his sergeant's jacket from the First World War.

It was the jacket which impressed Gaitskell most – 'the greatest socialist philosopher of his generation' not only having 'a sergeant's jacket, but actually wearing it'. The future leader of the Labour Party saw the jacket as a symbol of the austere life he led. 'Yet he never sought to make other people live as he did. It was just the way of life Tawney chose for himself.'

Though Tawney lived humbly, he wrote with a grandeur that no other twentieth-century political philosopher can match. George Orwell believed that political writers should 'let the meaning choose the words, not the other way about' and warned against 'all stale or mixed images, all prefabricated phrases, needless repetitions and humbug generally'. Orwell was particularly severe on the modular sentence constructed piece by piece before the idea is completed in the author's head and 'tacked together like sections of a hen-house'. Tragically, Mr Orwell's criticism is wholly appropriate to half of the political philosophers who ever lived and wrote. Take even a brief definitive statement from *Das Kapital*: 'The production of use-values of goods is not affected in respect of its general nature by the fact that it is undertaken for a capitalist and under his control.' It is sentences like that which get Marxism a bad name. Tawney was incapable of such a construction. His disciples can rejoice in their prophet's style as well as in the content of his work.

Tawney wrote in a way which brought joy to millions of men and women who, although unsympathetic to his philosophy, took pleasure in the English language. His style has a colour and opulence which, in a writer of less rigorous intellectual discipline, might lead to the occasional act of verbal self-indulgence. But Tawney always knew exactly what he wanted to write before his pen touched paper, and his images always illuminated rather than obscured his meaning. 'How infinite,' wrote Winston Churchill, 'is the debt owed to metaphors by politicians who want to speak strongly but are not sure what they are going to say.' Tawney never had any doubt of his intention. His metaphors clarify the concise meaning of complicated concepts, illustrate involved ideas and (not unimportant in works of scholarship) make his readers laugh.

Twenty years before Mr R. A. Butler made equality of opportunity fashionable, in his 1944 Education Act, Tawney leapfrogged the notion of a benignly competitive society and asserted that 'only the presence of a high degree of practical equality . . . can diffuse the general opportunity to rise. The existence of such opportunities in fact, not merely form, depend upon not only an open road but upon an equal start.' After twenty years of 'compensatory education' and 'positive discrimination', no one has constructed a sentence that more succinctly sets out the simple truth that the eleven-plus is not the same examination in Brixton as in Bournemouth, even if the children from those dissimilar boroughs are invited to answer the same question paper.

That truth is still not universally accepted. But, then, Tawney never expected that it would be. He knew that a competitive society would construct a theory of social evolution that provides moral justification for those who find room at the top and comfort and consolation for the majority of their contemporaries who either fail to rise from their original condition or actually fall further behind in the competition for wealth, power and respect. Readers on the way up and on the way down must both recognise themselves in Tawney's duckpond and marvel at the clarity of his images.

> Intelligent tadpoles reconcile themselves to the inconvenience of their position by reflecting that, though most of them will live to be tadpoles and nothing more, the fortunate of the species will one day shed their tails, distend their mouths and stomachs, hop nimbly on to dry land and croak addresses to their former friends on the virtues by means of which tadpoles of character can rise to be frogs.

That paragraph might have been written as an epitaph for selective secondary education. Tawney also provided the perfect opening paragraph for one of the numerous (but invariably inconclusive) volumes that the late Labour government produced on the subject of 'industrial democracy':

> It is idle for a nation to emblazon Liberty, Equality, Fraternity and similar resounding affirmations on the façades of its public buildings, if to display the same motto on its factories and mines would arouse only the cynical laughter that greets a reminder of idealism turned sour and hopes unfulfilled.

Such paragraphs have been seized on by Tawney's critics as examples of the windy generalisations that they believe his work to be. The sentiments may inspire, their argument runs, but the real content hardly provides a blueprint for the construction of a new system of industrial management. In one sense that is entirely true. But it is not the job of the philosopher to design complicated formulae by which noble ideals are turned into normal practice.

327

It is part of Tawney's extraordinary attraction that, even as he speaks in the emotive language of a moral crusade, he warns those who travel to fight with him against being carried along by no more than the romance of rhetoric. He is the critic of unsubstantiated assertion and unthinking affirmation. He wants to inspire his readers, but he wants to inspire them for a carefully thought-out cause. Tawney, on public ownership, is a pragmatist:

> Whether in any particular instance it is desirable or not is a question to be decided in the light not of resounding affirmations of the virtues of either free enterprise or of socialism but on the facts of the case.

Nobody should rally to Tawney's standard just because they have discovered by the time of his hundredth birthday that he was a practical philosopher. Tawney was all of a piece. His radicalism cannot be separated from his realism. His idealism is irrevocably tied to the determination to turn principles into policies and policies into practice. He stated simple philosophic truths with a clarity that has rarely been surpassed.

> It is still confidently asserted by the privileged classes that when the state holds its hand what remains as a result of that inaction is liberty. In reality, as far as the mass of mankind is concerned, what commonly remains is not liberty but tyranny.

But, more important, he constantly called upon the party he supported to lift up its eyes to the hills. He knew, since he was a man of charity, that sometimes it would fall. For,

> That movement is liable, like all of us, to fall at times below itself and to forget its mission. When it does so, what it is apt to desire is not a social order of a different kind ... but a social order of the same kind in which money and power will be somewhat differently distributed.

But he knew that his party, and indeed all parties, should struggle to recall their mission. It is not a bad thing to remember on the centenary of his birth.

Listener, 4 December 1980

The Man Who Was Attlee

On the day that Clement Attlee resigned the leadership of the Labour Party, the shadow cabinet assembled in his House of Commons room for a dolorous farewell meeting. Many eyes were moist. But only Edith Summerskill – in her time the most formidable woman in British politics – openly wept. And even she half hid her tears behind a large handkerchief. It was a short meeting. 'Offered an earldom,' Mr Attlee announced. 'Shall I accept?' Dr Summerskill briefly lowered the damp white linen and murmured, 'Of course. Of course' – her voice breaking with emotion. 'Right,' the departing leader said. 'Then that's agreed.' The meeting was over and twenty years of Labour history had ended in characteristic style. The democratic proprieties – so important to the party – had been observed. Attlee's will had prevailed. And the whole operation had been conducted with a minimum of fuss and without the waste of a single word.

In 1935, when the two decades of his dominance began, nobody believed that the meticulous little man in the waistcoat and carefully brushed Homburg hat would become the twentieth century's greatest peacetime prime minister – the man who presided over the creation of the mixed economy, the dissolution of the Empire and the development of the modern welfare state. Indeed, few of his House of Commons colleagues believed that his leadership would last out the year. Yet fifty years on, and at a centenary of his birth, he is now thought of as the model Labour Party leader – the man who could keep the socialist coalition in one piece, convince the electorate of its virtues and carry out the policy included in its manifesto. It was an extraordinary achievement, the result – as is often the case with political success – of good luck as much as good judgment.

Having survived the slaughter of 1931 when the established leaders (Morrison, Dalton, Clynes, Greenwood and Henderson) were all cut down, he became deputy leader virtually by default. Most of the forty-odd MPs who made up the parliamentary Labour Party believed that his task was to support George Lansbury until the real heroes returned. But fate or fortune decided otherwise. First, Lansbury resigned the leadership; forced out by age, illness and the rejection of his pacifist policy. Then, only a fortnight later, Stanley Baldwin dissolved Parliament. Attlee was the obvious temporary choice to see Labour through the general election. But not even the leader himself expected he would be confirmed in office when Parliament reassembled after polling day.

The assumption that he would return to the ranks of worthy mediocrity was based on what seemed to be a major character weakness. Some of his colleagues found him aloof. Others accused him of nothing more reprehensible than reticence. But there was virtually unanimous agreement that he lacked the capacity to communicate with either politicians or real people – an indispensable quality in the successful leader of a democratic party. At meetings, he often chose to sit silent, biting on his pipe. When he spoke at all, he usually produced staccato monosyllables, enlivened by the one flight of rhetorical fancy in which he seemed at home – the patois of the Victorian public school. When he sacked the Viceroy of India, replacing Wavell with Mountbatten as proof of Labour's commitment to independence, he talked of 'changing the bowling'.

It is impossible even to guess why Clement Attlee chose to live in a protective cocoon of verbal incapacity. What is certain is that the taciturn replies and delphic half-sentences were only one – though much the most common – of his forms of expression. When a newsreel interviewer asked him why he had decided to call a 1951 election, he answered, 'Because the time seems right.' And his reply to a second question became a classic example of missed opportunity. 'Is there anything else you want to say, Prime Minister?' moved the party leader, on the verge of a titanic campaign, to answer, 'No, thank you.' No other politician, even of that period, could have missed the chance to justify his own policies or denigrate the programme of his opponents. It remains one of the mysteries of politics how Attlee would have fared in a television age – admired as uncompromisingly honest or ridiculed as virtually inarticulate. But there were moments when he adopted a defiant style. In 1945, provoked to real resentment by Winston Churchill's claim that voting Labour was like voting for the Gestapo, he issued an elegant and crushing rebuke: 'The Labour party is the one party which most nearly reflects in its representation and composition all the main streams which flow into the great river of our national life.'

In fact, Clement Attlee's character was made up by a complicated pattern of paradoxes which the combination of invariable clear thinking and occasionally blurred expression typified. He was the humble autocrat and the reasonable revolutionary. And that was exactly what the Labour Party needed.

Attlee's character was, in essence, all of a piece. But different facets shone on different days, creating the superficial appearance of contradiction and inconsistency. Thus Lord Longford's well-known story of the Prime Minister's reluctance to pay by cheque in a restaurant where the waiter did not know him is matched by Jim Callaghan's less commonly repeated account of his reputation and bearing in the House of Commons Members' tearoom. Mr Attlee's tray was always carried from counter to table by his parliamentary private secretary, walking one pace behind a leader who enjoyed more than the superficialities of social respect. One day when a bitter argument broke out round the table at which Welsh Labour Members congregate, Aneurin Bevan gave a young colleague a stern warning. 'Say that again,' he threatened in a voice consistent with the deployment of the ultimate deterrent, 'and I shall take you to see Attlee.' Those stories are not in conflict with each other. In the Labour Party an authoritarian leader – who openly rebukes erring ministers when they first offend and sacks them for their second failure – is much more likely to be accepted by the comrades and friends if he travels, unrecognised, on tube trains.

The fortunate possession of balanced and balancing characteristics enabled Attlee successfully to lead the most radical government to hold office this century. Unlike the great Gladstone ministry of 1868, the Labour administration of 1945 was led by a prime minister who actually believed in the transformation of society on which it was engaged. His commitment to opinions which today would be called at least 'soft left' was genuine and long-standing. In one of the letters to his brother Tom (which Kenneth Harris quotes with such revealing effect in his recent biography), Attlee offers an opinion of the economic failure of Ramsay MacDonald's Labour government. It has been unknowingly paraphrased in a hundred recent Tribune meetings: 'The real trouble to my mind has been the failure of Snowden all through to face the financial situation. He has always rather slavishly followed City opinion while JRM has been far too prone to take his views from bankers and big business.'

But Attlee had a facility for thinking of later Labour governments' programmes in terms of public need and practical necessity. He saw socialism as the political translation of common sense. That approach made him a leader to be trusted rather than feared. Despite the plans for nationalisation and the prospect of an end to Empire, there was nothing wild about the prime minister who proposed such a brave new world.

His background and opinions, his early history and his essentially middle-class appearance all equipped him for the role of the reassuring radical, a man who could change society without frightening its members. The son of a modestly successful solicitor, he was educated in the Church of England tradition at Haileybury College and in the comfortable scholarship of Victorian Oxford. He might well have himself become a London lawyer with a comfortable practice and steady habits had he not, in October 1905, accompanied his brother Laurence on a visit to the Haileybury Club in Stepney. Moved by both the poverty and dignity of its young members, he became involved in the club's organisation and, within a year, became its manager. The Haileybury Club made him a socialist. 'From this it was only a step to examining the whole basis of our social and economic system. I soon began to realise the curse of casual labour. I got to know what slum landlords and sweating really meant. I understood why the Poor Law was so hated. I learned also why there were rebels.'

Attlee was not himself a rebel by nature. When war broke out in 1914 his brother Tom followed the Labour Party line and registered as a conscientious objector. Clem thought it his duty to fight. And, at the age of thirty-one, he enlisted (with difficulty) as an elderly infantryman. He was twice wounded – first in Mesopotamia, while prophetically attempting to plant a red flag as a marker for the artillery bombardment, and then in France. It was while he was still a soldier, awaiting demobilisation, that he met Vi Millar. Douglas Jay, who was to become first a member of Attlee's Downing Street staff and then a minister in his government, believes he was at the Millars' when the future Mrs Attlee met her eventual husband. Young Douglas was playing tennis in Hampstead with the daughters of the house and was invited home to tea with Major Attlee. The veteran was wearing full service dress, with Sam Browne gleaming and sleeves which proclaimed he had reached field rank. At the approach of the children he clicked his heels to attention, touched his cap with his cane and barked, 'Afternoon, little boys.' Major Attlee was, by nature, a good regimental officer; a believer in teamwork and discipline, loyalty and healthy exercise.

During the next two decades Attlee became Mayor of Stepney, Member of Parliament for Limehouse, minister of the Crown and leader of its opposition. He behaved in complete character at every stage and his progress was marked both by good fortune and general surprise that he had travelled so far and acquitted himself so well. As Mayor he led a deputation of the unemployed to see the Prime Minister, and when violence threatened 'ordered the column to halt and turn about . . . thus avoiding broken heads'. As MP he captured a constituency that held to Labour even in the slaughter of the 1931 general election. As Ramsay MacDonald's Postmaster-General, his departmental duties kept him well clear of the economic agonies which preceded the collapse of the second Labour government and the Prime Minister's apostasy and the formation of a coalition with the Conservatives – described by Attlee as 'the greatest betrayal in the political history of this country'. By the time of the 1935 election he was the obvious interim leader. But the caretaker – to general surprise – was confirmed in office. When the new parliamentary party assembled to choose its champion, Attlee led on the first ballot and won by almost two to one on the second. Hugh Dalton (who had backed Herbert Morrison, the London Labour leader and putative heir to MacDonald's crown) observed with fine disregard for the scriptures 'a little mouse shall lead them'.

Attlee won the leadership election largely because he retained the support of the trade unionists who had held on to their seats after 1931. They were men who felt an instinctive loyalty to any incumbent. But they were also the Members of Parliament who knew Clem best. They knew that the mouse could roar, that he worked unceasingly for the cause and that his unfortunate manner hid a first-class mind – a quality that the group of socialist intellectuals around Hugh Dalton had totally failed to recognise. Douglas Jay recalls the surprise of his second meeting with the Labour leader. Jay had joined one of the innumerable sub-committees that discuss party policy and had produced a discussion paper which, he hoped, would improve the understanding of those of his colleagues who had not been Fellows of All Souls. The group was to consider economic imperialism under the unlikely chairmanship of Leonard Woolf. When it assembled, the author of the day's document found Attlee sitting in the next chair. 'He tore it to pieces,' Jay confesses.

The party of which he became leader in 1935 (offering in his acceptance speech to stand down on request) was in deep intellectual and moral confusion. A passionate and genuine opposition to fascism was matched, and partly undermined, by a passionate and genuine horror of rearmament. So Mr Attlee visited Spain and incurred the wrath of the *Daily Mail* and *Daily Express* by giving 'the Communist salute' to the battalion of the International Brigade which bore his name. He was also cheered in the Commons by Conservatives who saw his uncritical acceptance of Hitler's promise to abandon the invasion of Czechoslovakia as an endorsement of appeasement. But once war broke out, Attlee and Labour had no doubts. Their only criticism of the war effort was the infirmity of Prime Minister Neville Chamberlain's purpose. By 1940, the opposition was ready 'to take its share of responsibility' under a new prime minister. It is still not clear if Attlee favoured Churchill or Lord Halifax. What is clear is that he was determined to bring about a change. Asked if Labour would join a coalition under Chamberlain or under an alternative Tory leader, his famous taciturnity came into its own: 'The answer to the first question is, No. To the second, Yes.'

The change came and Attlee became deputy prime minister in the Churchill coalition. Ernest Bevin (the secretary of the Transport and General Workers Union), Morrison and A. V. Alexander, First Lord of the Admiralty in Ramsay MacDonald's government, joined him. And together they established the reputation for patriotism and prudence that proved invaluable during the election campaign of 1945. Attlee was anxious for their joint participation in the coalition to continue until Japan was beaten. But the architect of victory – confident of the love and loyalty of a grateful people – insisted on calling an election immediately the war in Europe was over. Churchill, campaigning as if he had not just ended five years of victorious co-operation with his principal opponent, constantly accused Attlee of latent extremism. Attlee behaved like Attlee, reminding the incorrigible warrior that 'socialist theory was developed in Britain long before Karl Marx by Robert Owen'. Labour won a majority of 173 over the Conservatives.

The administration that Attlee formed was probably the most talented government this century. It contained Stafford Cripps, Dalton, Bevin, Bevan and Morrison; five men of diverse political genius. It also included politicians of long experience, impressive durability and occasional ambition – Emmanuel Shinwell, Lewis Silkin, Alexander, Arthur Greenwood and George Isaacs. There were even new recruits of conspicuous talent on the bottom rung of the ministerial ladder, Harold Wilson and Hugh Gaitskell among them. They made up a difficult team to manage. Indeed, the trouble began even before portfolios were distributed. Herbert Morrison – still certain that ten years before the leadership had been let on a short lease – would not even agree that Attlee was entitled to accept the King's Commission. Supported by Harold Laski, the party chairman and that least admired breed of Labour politician, a professor at the London School of Economics, he demanded a poll in the parliamentary party to decide who should be prime minister. 'If the King asks you to form a government,' Attlee observed, 'you say Yes or No, not "I'll let you know".' The people's Clem said Yes.

He was supported in his determination to go ahead by Ernest Bevin, who warned Morrison: 'If you go on mucking about like this, you won't be in the bloody government at all.' For the next four years, Bevin supported 'his little man' against all the attacks of the latter-day Adullamites, the distressed and the discontented. Without Bevin's strength and authority behind him, Attlee would still have survived. The survivors of the 1945 Parliament all insist that the plots and counter-plots were hatched, developed and abandoned in the upper reaches of the party, and that the innocent Labour lobby fodder would not have contemplated Attlee's removal. Neither would the party in the country. For although, then as now, there were charismatic leaders of the left who were more loquacious than loyal, 'Mr Attlee' was confirmed in the affection of the rank and file by their enthusiasm for the policy which he was implementing.

Much of the policy which made up the huge legislative programme of the 1945 Parliament now seems no more than part of the compassionate consensus. That is in itself part of Attlee's achievement. And the Acts of Independence for India and Burma appear in retrospect to have been overdue not premature. The same can be argued for the nationalisation of the ailing railways and the antiquated pits. But in their day they were giant steps towards the sort of society which Labour Party members worked to create. The Hattersleys, direct beneficiaries of the health service and the determined application of the 1944 Education Act, cycled to Barnsley to see a notice tacked to a coal-mine gate. It read: 'This colliery is now managed on behalf of the people by the National Coal Board.' We were more than content with the party leader who brought that about.

However, the cabinet was not quite so easily satisfied, not least because of the temperamental brilliance of some of its members. 'For Minister of Health,' Attlee wrote, 'I took a chance in appointing Aneurin Bevan. He had the ability, but he might not have the judgment while his ability as a minister has not yet been displayed.' That chance paid off and demonstrated the wise willingness to stretch his cabinet across the full spectrum of the party.

He was never a friend to any of his colleagues. There was no kitchen cabinet or late-night discussion with cronies in Downing Street. Arthur Moyle, his parliamentary private secretary and for years his political body servant, confessed: 'I have worked for that man for twenty years yet still know nothing about him.' Geoffrey de Freitas, who accepted the same position ten years earlier, told a story about the strange convolution of the PM's relationship with his colleagues. When the lowly PPS said that he was too busy to take his children to the Trooping the Colour, the Prime Minister of Britain seriously offered to go in his place. But de Freitas still did not think of him as a friend. That may have been because of the strong Christian ethic that dominated his character long after the theology had disappeared. Hugh Dalton, having technically breached the security rules which traditionally surround a budget, offered his resignation and had it instantly accepted. John Belcher, a parliamentary secretary accused of accepting bribes, was remorselessly pursued through a public tribunal. Attlee was a man who inspired more admiration than affection, a loner who chose to be on his own. That characteristic must be held responsible at least for some of his success. For it made him the honest leader without fear or favourite. It may also have led to his undoing. When he decided that Hugh Gaitskell was the natural candidate for Chancellor of the Exchequer he followed the promptings of his intellect. This led to Aneurin Bevan's resignation and the disintegration of the government. A more emotional (or even a more corrupt) man would have seen the storm clouds over the horizon.

It is never possible accurately to apportion individual credit for the success of a government. When prime ministers fail, judgments about their administration are usually based on the superficial appearance of success. The flamboyant and visible end as heroes. The reticent and retiring are assumed to have been carried to their achievements by more colourful colleagues. So for thirty years Attlee was relegated into the category of honest nonentity by the public. Even the moments of decisive action – the insistence to President Truman that atomic weapons would not be used in Korea – were quickly forgotten. All that remained for decades was the memory of a little man in a moustache surrounded by more spectacular figures. Now Attlee has achieved a unique distinction. He is the only prime minister this century whose reputation has improved with the years. His role as reasonable revolutionary and humble autocrat was decisive in the success of the party. If one of the alternatives had led Labour, the government of 1945 might well not have been the most successful administration of the century.

Observer Magazine, 3 September 1983

Express Delivery

Jean Rook is the by-line made flesh. Her conversation is her column come to life. Not for Jean Rook one personality at home in Kent and another on the pages of the *Daily Express*. She is, as they say in her native Yorkshire, 'all of a piece'. It is an attractive characteristic which confounds at least some of her critics. She cannot be accused of counterfeiting brash materialism as a publicity stunt. For she really is brash and materialistic. And she is proud of it.

It was those characteristics which carried her into journalism. At the end of a slightly improbable academic career ('They rang the church bells in the village' when she won a scholarship to Whitby County School), Miss Rook (having 'missed a first by two marks') wrote an MA thesis entitled 'The Impact of T. S. Eliot on the Drama of his Time'. Her mentors expected her 'to be a headmistress or something academic'. But young Jean 'wanted a car and a house' and thought that journalism would provide them more quickly. She blames it all on her 'lousy commercial mind'. The disapproval of commercialism is wholly ironic.

At first, the frankness is astonishing. I knew, of course, that Miss Rook was billed as 'First Lady of Fleet Street' – an accolade which its recipient disarmingly described as being 'dreamt up' by the *Daily Express* when she first joined the paper. But her even more unofficial title of 'First Bitch' on the same public highway was unknown to me until the owner of that sobriquet referred to it – on the first of the five occasions when she introduced it into our sixty-minute conversation. Vinegar was gladly accepted as the best word to describe the taste of her column. 'Never bland,' she said, and intoned the promise three times as if the words had mystic significance.

Lack of sincerity was, the First Something-or-Other explained, the downfall of her imitators – none of whom she was bitch enough to name. Indeed, the suggestion that Lynda Lee-Potter (her successor at the *Daily Mail*) might have copied her style provoked outrage. Any comment from her on that lady would be 'indefen-

338

sible'. But she did speak of an anonymous contributor to a northern newspaper who 'did a straight copy' which, for all its brilliance, was a failure. The reason, Miss Rook insisted, was that the plagiarist did not really feel what she wrote. And the readers could tell.

One recent editor of the *Daily Express* believes half the same thing about his ex-First Lady. He insists that the rage is all synthetic, but – thanks to years of practice – the readers are always deceived. The ex-editor is wrong. Asked to justify the more offensive items in her column, she defends the paragraphs of prejudice with transparent conviction. Mark Thatcher gives her 'the screaming abdabs ... He has done nothing. He is nothing. Who is he to go swanning around in cars and saying that he is this, that or the other?'

Princess Diana excites similar passions. This year, the press has called the Queen-apparent 'everything from God Almighty to the fairest English rose', yet she could not raise a real smile for the cameramen who had assembled (by official invitation) at the bottom of the Liechtenstein ski slope. 'Fair comment,' asserted the author. And more important, the judgment was endorsed by the readers. Rook *aficionados* had long been suspicious about the Princess of Wales's character. Nineteen letters expressed the fear that Diana could be 'rather sulky'. Saying what her readers feel is the secret of Jean Rook's success – that and an insatiable desire for money and success.

She always wanted the top job and the top salary. And she set her mind on both from the day on which she joined the *Sheffield Telegraph* as a trainee. From then on, the path always led upwards. Sometimes progress seemed intolerably slow. But she climbed: first, to *Flair* magazine, then on to the *Sun* (when it was the old *Daily Herald* in disguise), then the *Sketch*. When it amalgamated with the *Daily Mail*, Jean Rook moved with the furniture; still contemptuous of conventional women's journalism – 'the sort of thing the *Daily Telegraph* still does now ... how to weave a rush basket and play the Celtic harp.'

Miss Rook would perform neither task with pleasure or distinction. Such folksy pursuits are incompatible with the six gold rings, the double-banked ear-rings, the gold snake bangle and the gold watch of a sort which most people only see in the Christmas advertisements at the back of glossy magazines. Nor, I imagine, could she pluck or plait whilst wearing a fur coat. And on the evidence of the column the First Lady and her fur coats are insepar- able. On the morning of our meeting, it was the wolf that hung from the back of her chair. Having read so many of her columns, I would have felt just as much at home with the mink.

Enthusiasm – 'not for money, but what money can buy' – took Jean Rook to the *Daily Express*. The passion links writers to readers. All the editors who have employed her believe she is indispensable to her present paper and that 'anyone who let her go would be in trouble'. But they all suggest or concede that she sells into a limited market. Perhaps the *Daily Mirror* feeds similar tastes – the haves or the would-haves-given-half-a-chance whose vision of the good life owes more to Tony Bennett than Thomas Aquinas. But their natural paper is the *Daily Express*. It is Jean Rook's natural home. No other job appeals. Stories of editorial ambition are denied. Her husband ('absolutely no ambition. That is why he works for the Press Association') is praised as a far better reporter than she could ever be. The occasional profiles are rewarding. But it is the column which really counts. Criticise it, and she reacts as if there has been an assault on Gresby – the only son whose exploits are a legend in the *Express* building, not because they are interesting, but because they are so frequently described in loving detail.

We examined together the final paragraph of her attack on 'double-barrelled standards', the willingness to condemn or con- done cruelty to animals according to taste:

> As a meat-eater and fur-wearer, I don't fire the first cartridge at Philip. But I would suggest, now that Sandringham has been flushed of photographers, that he puts a safety-catch on his lips as World Wildlife spokesman. Even the Queen's husband can't have his pheasant and shoot it.

Hearing the words made Miss Rook smile with undisguised joy and helped me to imagine the pleasure of the men and women who share her values every Wednesday morning. Like the author, they find the style clever rather than convoluted; strong, not stri- dent. They are excited by the idea of reproving royalty and comforted by the reassurance that double standards are widely held and commonly accepted. The Sandringham story was supplemented by three other items: a defence of 'proper' accents, a reproof for Billy Connolly and an attack on *Dallas*. She is not just a by-line made flesh. Jean Rook is the *Express* personified.

Punch, 1 February 1984

Ronald Reagan Is Wanting in the Imperial Graces

The British people are predisposed to dislike American presidents. The chief executive of the United States embodies the national power and imperial glory that we loved and lost. Often he behaves in a way we regard as wholly inconsistent with the reticence and dignity proper to a head of state: campaigning for votes, holding his hands above his head like a triumphant prize-fighter and speaking in public about his devotion to the First Lady. As the Victorian theater critic said of *Macbeth*, 'How unlike the home life of our own dear Queen.'

Some presidents won their way into our reluctant hearts. Roosevelt (eventually) helped us beat Hitler. Truman behaved with a humility we thought wholly appropriate in an American. Eisenhower had contributed to victory in Europe, and we did not know that he liked his driver too much, and Field Marshal Montgomery too little. Kennedy was young, handsome, heroic and vaguely related to Harold Macmillan. But they had to win their way into our affection.

There was never any hope for Johnson, Nixon, Ford or Carter. President Reagan was first treated with a mixture of suspicion (from the radicals) and hope (from the reactionaries). He is fast becoming a figure of ridicule and contempt. I report the fact with no pleasure. For I am a devoted supporter of the Atlantic Alliance and it cannot prosper if one of the partner nations regards the leader of the other as absurd. And that is, increasingly, the judgment made in Britain of Ronald Reagan.

Prime Minister Margaret Thatcher has helped create the image. Her ideological commitment to both Mr Reagan's vision of the free economy and his views of the Russian threat to world peace is total. But Mrs Thatcher describes the president's economic policy as if it were a whole series of mistakes made by a well-intentioned but badly informed country cousin. Mr Reagan's reputation cannot easily withstand the patronizing head-patting of the lady who is supposed to be his greatest international friend. But that is only the beginning.

His natural opponents cannot take his simplicities seriously. They hear him speak, with apparent conviction, about the global Soviet threat, the inherent evil of Soviet Communism and the glory of American life as personified by the US Olympic team, and they marvel at his lack of intellectual sophistication. They ask themselves, who is really running America? And they worry about the hard men who, they assume, are persuading the president to talk implausible nonsense about a democratic crusade in Latin America while they pursue some Hispanic objective of their own.

The typical Briton judges the president by less convoluted criteria. They read of the 'gaffes.' The *London Times* reports that 'in a rare retraction the White House Chief of Staff, Mr James Baker, seeking to minimise the political damage, explained that President Reagan did not mean . . .' They recall the argument about whether or not the US administration regards a theater nuclear war in Europe as a strategic option. And over the last month they have seen and heard for themselves the president of the United States behaving in a way that seems totally out of place in a man who claims to be the leader of the free world.

Naivete is an admirable quality in teenage daughters. In presidents, it is less of an advantage. In monks, simplicity is a virtue. In commanders in chief of the US armed forces it is not to be encouraged. It is not just the hair and the suits and the never-to-be-forgotten Hollywood past that make the British skeptical about his capabilities. It is his demeanour. Even the one-liners which have won him applause at home grate on the Anglo-Saxon ear.

It is impossible to imagine Charles de Gaulle or Winston

Churchill surviving an assassination attempt with the apology, 'Sorry, honey, I forgot to duck.' And the mawkish sentimentality that characterizes so many of his speeches causes literal embarrassment in many of the British homes to which television has replayed them. In Britain we take D-Day and the liberation of Europe seriously. Until the Allies landed the German enemy was only twenty miles away. To many of us it seemed that President Reagan's contribution to the anniversary ceremonies diminished and demeaned the whole occasion.

We heard the part of his Normandy speech that dealt with the dead veteran who had asked his daughter to take his place on the anniversary beaches. The president spoke the words of the promise she gave in reply as if he were auditioning for the part of Sergeant York. After a performance like that, it is virtually impossible to imagine Mr Reagan's successfully surmounting the complex subtleties of government. The prince, said Machiavelli, must be both lion and fox. Mr Reagan as fox is beyond belief. And Mr Reagan as lion roars like the introduction to an MGM film.

Even before the Republican convention in Dallas, that was the increasingly accepted opinion. What happened in Dallas was so alien to the British experience and so antipathetic to the European view of statesmanship that the judgment of the president changed. Instead of being seen as amiably risible he became dangerously ludicrous. This man, the television news seemed to say, cannot possibly be running the US.

Much of the bizarre behaviour in Dallas, of course, did not involve the President. He was not down there on the convention floor twirling the pompons with the majorettes. But the shots we saw of Ray Charles singing 'America the Beautiful' in an unhappy compromise of styles that embraced rock, country and western and Deep-South revivalist had Ronald Reagan in full supporting role. None of this, however, could match the acceptance speech for crass insensitivity. And the film that preceded it made the acceptance speech seem something written by three aides called Thomas Jefferson, Benjamin Franklin and Daniel Webster. No British politician could tell a story about 'God sitting on his shoulder' and survive. No doubt the good Cardinal Cook did put the notion of intervention into the President's head. And I am sure that Ronald

Reagan does believe that he was saved from assassination by a Grand Old Providence. But national leaders should not say that sort of thing – even in election year. Emotional reticence is a quality leaders of the democratic West ought to cultivate.

It is a quality President Reagan appears entirely to lack, and its absence is regarded in stuffy Europe as a major handicap. There is no direct connection between the absence of inhibition and the absence of judgment. But in the experience of the older democracies, politicians who employ no sensitivity over private matters are likely to be equally insensitive in their handling of complicated issues. We do not doubt that Mr Reagan loves his wife and his country in equal measure. Indeed, we so take it for granted that the hairs stand up on the back of our collective neck whenever he finds it necessary to remind us of his affection.

We are equally uneasy about the President's easy relationship with God. For we see politics as a profession that concerns morality, not theology. The President at prayer – like the President standing to attention with his hand across his heart – seems to the British a Hollywood version of politics.

Of course, performances of the sort we have seen on British television may contribute to his reelection. But if he achieves a second term they will leave him with a legacy he will not find easy to overcome. America will have a president whom Europe in general – and Britain in particular – finds the greatest difficulty taking seriously. Some critics will believe that someone else governs the US. Others will fear that no one governs it at all. That cannot be good for the Atlantic Alliance.

Wall Street Journal, 4 September 1984

A Great Writer from the North

I could recognise J. B. Priestley's voice long before I had read a word that he had ever written. I was reared by hand during the Second World War, and his radio *Postscripts* were exactly the sort of middlebrow broadcasting which my parents both enjoyed and regarded as required listening for a little boy who would one day get a job-with-a-pension in the Sheffield Town Hall.

In 1945 – as the first step towards that secure condition – I became a pupil at the City Grammar School, and began to work my weekly way through a little anthology called *More Essays by Modern Masters*. I read of Robert Lynd buying a Savile Row suit, G. K. Chesterton playing croquet and E. V. Lucas eating lunch in a restaurant car. But towards the back of the book there were essays concerned with the life we led in the north.

> It is a country, whether it expresses itself in fields or streets, moors or mills, that puts man on his mettle. It defies him to live there and so has bred a special race who can live there, stocky men with short upper lips and jutting long chins, men who roll a little in their walk and carry their heads stiffly, 12 stones of combative instinct. If you have never seen any of these men, take a look at the Yorkshire cricket team next summer. Or come to t'match.

Inevitably I moved on to *The Good Companions* and, before I had even heard of the word, came to the conclusion that Priestley was the great vernacular writer of the north. I was, of course, only partly correct in my impertinent adolescent judgment. He was a great writer *from* the north – so great, so prolific and so wide in the range of his talent that no adjective should circumscribe his genius.

The genius lay in the quality of his writing. It would be absurd to suggest that he never constructed an ugly sentence. Anyone who over almost sixty years wrote 27 novels, 36 plays and 33 volumes of biography, criticism and essays (apart from the weekly journalism that was not reprinted in collections) must have written thousands of imperfect lines. But his ratio of excellent to imperfect was infinitely higher than most of the highbrow critics who complained that he wrote too much.

In *The Good Companions*, he wrote an explanation of Association football – 'conflict and art' – which remains the classic definition of the game's appeal. And his description of the Bruddersford Town Hall is something to be avoided by writers who contemplate making comments of their own on the startling appearance of

Victorian Gothic in the centre of industrial cities. For to read it is to realise that it cannot be bettered.

A Priestley revival – of a sort – has already begun. And it will no doubt be further encouraged by the perverse paradox that makes writers briefly more interesting immediately after their obituary notices have appeared. *An Inspector Calls* has been televised, and its ending (which turns it from a whodunnit into a morality play, with the inspector himself becoming Everypoliceman) gives a warning about the penalties of the divided society which are as appropriate now as they were when the play was written. *When We Are Married* at the National Theatre was a perfect example of the meticulously constructed comedy. The *Spectator* complained that the National Theatre should set its sights higher!

Last year not even the literati of that small-circulation magazine managed a sneer at *English Journey* when the fiftieth anniversary of its publication produced the inevitable crop of reassessments and replicas. Not surprisingly – for it is one of the most *agreeable* books which have ever been published. It is agreeable because it is so well written and, therefore, so easy to read. It is agreeable because it describes the sights and sounds of England with such obvious and uninhibited affection. But above all, *English Journey* conveys to the reader the pleasure with which it was written – the pleasure of travelling and the pleasure of coming home. 'I would rather spend a holiday in Tuscany than in the Black Country, but if I were compelled to choose between living in West Bromwich or Florence, I should make straight for West Bromwich.'

The geniality which characterises all of his writing was an essential ingredient of both Priestley's personal popularity and the massive success of his published work. He spoke of himself as a 'grumbler'. But his public thought of him as 'Jolly Jack'. An instinct for happiness is an essential characteristic of the essayist. And despite the popular success of his novels, the ingenuity of his plays and erudition of his literary criticism, it is almost certainly the quality of his essays which will mark him out as an historically important figure in English letters.

Almost sixty years ago Priestley described the essential relationship between an essayist and his readers and the grey area of literature where writers and journalists are indistinguishable: 'Not only did periodical writing encourage the essayist to feel that he was addressing a company of friends so that he lost his self-consciousness, it also encouraged him to focus his attention upon little passing things that he might have disdained were he not writing for next week's paper.'

The willingness to write about 'little passing things' was one of the characteristics which prejudiced the pompous and pretentious against Priestley – that and his own self-deprecating jokes about being the highbrow for the lowbrows and vice versa. Self-caricature was one of his great liabilities. The last time I saw him was at a party to launch a First World War biography, *With Machine Gun to Cambrai*. In his speech he could not resist explaining that his presence was all a terrible mistake as he had been at a different battle several miles away.

His great advantage – indeed his virtue and genius – was the ability to write simple English of unusual beauty. He, above all other twentieth-century writers, proclaimed the connection between the beauty and the simplicity of our language. We owe him our gratitude.

Listener, 23 August 1984

The Unheroic Hero

Lucky is the man who finds in middle age that the heroes of his youth were even more admirable than he realised when he was young. I have just made such a discovery and I rejoice. When I was sixteen my feelings about Len Hutton were only just on the respectable side of the line which divides admiration from adulation. Now I have revised my opinion not so much upwards as sideways. I still think of him as the best batsman in the post-war world. But, because of what I have read about him since he died, I now believe him to be a thoroughly nice man with a character of fascinating complexity. Forty years ago, those qualities would not have seemed half as important as scoring 364 runs against the

Australians in 13 hours 20 minutes. Sometimes age does bring wisdom.

I knew that the war had harmed his career. But it was not until I read the obituaries that I realised how great the damage was. It was a subject he never mentioned. Indeed, when I spoke of it at a cricketers' dinner, he reminded me that not only cricketers lost six of their prime professional years and came back with half their youth gone. But there is something particularly poignant about a young batsman – at the height of his powers – going off to join the army and breaking his arm in a gymnasium.

There are no pictures in the Imperial War Museum of rear-guard actions fought around a vaulting horse or of battle-scarred veterans raising the union flag after the capture of parallel bars. So young Leonard did not go to Buckingham Palace for a medal. But he did return to Pudsey with one arm shorter than the other. The triumphant resumption of his career was a remarkable physical and mental achievement. If we believe those who wrote about him when he died, it was also an extraordinary emotional victory.

Before the war, he enjoyed his cricket. He was a young batsman who could do everything – score quickly, improvise, bat all day without feeling much strain or fatigue. He always concentrated hard. It was one of the secrets of his technical perfection. But concentration came easily to him. Walter Hammond captained England and took the difficult decisions about who would bat first and how to change the bowling. Hutton had mastered Tiger O'Reilly's fizzing venom. He was all set for a contented, as well as a hugely successful life. After the war, cricket was less of a joy and more of a burden.

Perhaps Hutton was never quite the happy warrior whom every boy in pads would wish to be. But in 1946 – having adjusted to the short left arm and learned how to play with a bat of a size usually only to be found in youth clubs – the whole burden of English cricket was piled on his shoulders. He had to open the batting against Lindwall and Miller. He had to hang on whilst more glamorous batsmen got themselves out with flashy shots.

Then he had to take on the England captaincy and win back the Ashes. He did it all with professional dedication. But, since he was not a roisterous man or noted for the wit of his after-dinner speeches, we are entitled to ask ourselves how funny he believed his most famous – indeed his only publicised – joke to be. Whilst resisting one particularly savage spell of pace and lift, he walked down the wicket for what commentators undoubtedly called 'consultations' with Dennis Compton. 'There must,' said Hutton, 'be a better way of earning your living than this.'

He was a quiet man – occasionally called taciturn and often described as remote by his fellow professionals who believed that after stumps were drawn it was a cricketer's duty to enjoy himself. Hutton read in a profile that he was not 'likeable' and was as surprised as he was wounded. But he did not change his ways. He scored a hundred centuries, amassed more runs in a single month than any other cricketer in history, became the first professional to captain England, beat Australia and was knighted. He remained reticent.

It is suggested that he was instinctively opposed to glamour. And if that is true, his judgment on the subject was greatly to his credit. I suspect that he thought that walking down pavilion steps wearing a Yorkshire and England cap was glamour enough. Whatever his attitude, it caused him to turn down all sorts of offers for advertisements and personal endorsements. He did not regard them as beneath his dignity, but simply feared that he would not feel happy at personal appearances or seeing his huge portrait staring down from hoardings.

It is no longer fashionable to admire reticence in sportsmen. But admiration for physical courage remains. It comes in different shapes and sizes – Dennis Compton coming out to bat after being felled by Ray Lindwall, Terry Butcher playing on with head bandaged and his shirt soaked in blood, and Roger Bannister collapsing exhausted after completing the first four-minute mile. Len Hutton had courage of an essentially Len Hutton sort. He was frail. And life for a frail professional cricketer is very hard.

I know that he took his health seriously. The last time that I met him, I asked him how he was, and he told me in considerable detail. A few months later he was dead, having completed barely three score years and ten. I hope at the end he had put all the nonsense about being cold and aloof out of his mind. If St Peter did hold that against him, I know what his reply should have been.

I hope that he described how he gave an awestruck admirer a lift to Headingley and talked not about runs scored and matches won but of how nervous he was when he watched his son play and how sorry he had been that his wife – working in the fur department of Swears and Wells – was not able to get to as many matches as she would have liked. That is far more likely to have got him through the pearly gates than the simple announcement that he had scored 364 runs in 13 hours 20 minutes against the Australians.

Guardian, 17 November 1990

Hero and Friend

I had been a Member of Parliament for more than a year before Tony Crosland spoke to me, and the idea that I might speak to him – without serious cause or invitation – had never entered my mind. Even in those more deferential days, young backbenchers often engaged in casual conversation with cabinet ministers. But Tony Crosland was different. He was the author of *The Future of Socialism*.

Our first exchange was typical of the friendship which followed. He asked me – peremptorily and without any explanation – a detailed question about Sheffield's plan for comprehensive education. I did not give a satisfactory answer and when I was told that I would be required to do better that evening, I offered what I believed to be the perfect excuse. My father was in London and we were having dinner together in the House. Tony announced that he would join us.

Had I known then – as I learned to my cost during the next ten years – that Tony Crosland bored was Tony Crosland intolerable, I would have counterfeited a heart attack. In my ignorance, I simply assumed that the occasion would end in disaster. It turned out, at least for one of us, to be a delight. Tony treated me like an intruder and my father as if he were an expert on South Yorkshire schools. That night Tony Crosland became my father's hero as well as mine.

Tony and I remained friends until he died. It was not a friendship of equals. For both of us thought of him as superior to me in every particular. But he always expected me to stand my corner during the arguments which were his alternative to small talk, and only a saint or a masochist would have accepted his intellectual tyranny without retaliation. Whatever his mood, being with him made me happy. What I recall now with most pleasure is not our brief and unsuccessful alliance during the International Monetary Fund crisis of 1976 or his infuriating agnosticism about Britain's entry into the Common Market. I remember the acts of friendship – all of them heavily disguised for fear that they would seem silly or sentimental.

In 1966, when I was not included in Harold Wilson's first reshuffle, Tony telephoned me immediately after the names of the new ministers were published. For ten minutes we had a pointless conversation about his difficulties in finding a suitable parliamentary private secretary. Then he added, as an afterthought, that only an idiot would think that the Prime Minister had promoted on merit.

My hero worship was able to survive our friendship because the better I knew him, the more clear it became that he genuinely possessed the virtues which I had admired from afar. He believed passionately in equality – socialism's historic 'big idea'. But he had no romantic illusions about either its achievements or its consequences. It had to be pursued methodically and with calm determination. And it had to be achieved the hard way – free from the deadening by-product of dull uniformity. Sloganising about great ideals he regarded as 'frivolous' – the ultimate political condemnation. But he often hid the strength of his convictions behind a pretence of flippancy. Pomposity he found genuinely funny. His response to the French foreign minister's lecture on Cartesian logic almost broke up the European Community.

His faith in the power of education to heal, improve and redeem combined with his passion for equality make him the natural heir to Matthew Arnold. But if anyone had accused him of believing in 'sweetness and light' his response would have been unprintable. Although he took ideas seriously, he regarded the rest of life as a joke. One minister – fearful of being dropped from the cabinet – called to canvass his support. Tony told him that his survival was essential to socialism. He was the only minister with a moustache. A totally clean-shaven government, he said, would not be taken seriously by the floating voters.

During the weekend before his fatal stroke in 1977 my wife and I spent the Sunday with the Croslands at Dorneywood – the foreign secretary's official residence. Susan Crosland has described in her biography of her husband what he said that day about freedom and equality. He also repeated his constant regret that those of us who shared his beliefs had failed to convince the Labour Party that we possessed a coherent ideology. We were good at getting individual items into manifestos. But we failed to inspire the people for the pursuit of real equality.

The day ended with talk and drinks and jokes – mostly about our colleagues. Tony found the mock grandeur of Dorneywood ridiculous and was particularly amused by the size of the television set thought appropriate to the foreign secretary's viewing. Even on the great screen he was unable to identify a former girlfriend who had a bit part in the afternoon film. He pretended to be sad about time and age and decay. Ten days later he was dead. The idea that socialism is the gospel of equality almost died with him.

Independent Magazine, 22 June 1991

Uncle Bert and the Ultimate Price

Bert was sixteen when he joined the territorials. His mother – who was musical and religious – told him that he had taken the King's Shilling under false pretences and that he must admit his deception and return his uniform. But his father – who was a bar-room patriot – said that he was proud to have a soldier for a son and promised to clean the buttons and badges on the faded khaki tunic.

The belt buckle would not respond to brush and Brasso so he took it secretly to the polishing shop at the Raleigh Cycle Company and buffed until it shone like silver. When Bert saw it, gleaming on the kitchen table, he wept and called his father an old fool. Next day it was taken back and repainted regulation light infantry black. Bert had enlisted in the 1/7th (Robin Hoods) Battalion of the Sherwood Foresters, the Notts and Derby Regiment.

Despite his mistake with the belt buckle, Bert's father retained his reputation as an expert on the army – a status which he had enjoyed since, at the age of twenty, he had spent a whole day in the 11th Hussars before being bought out for five guineas and returned to his apprenticeship. So, when he assured his wife that territorials were not allowed to serve outside the British Isles, she believed him.

For three months, Private 2042 paraded at Derby Road Drill Hall on Tuesday and Friday nights and counted off the days until the summer. He had been attracted to the Robin Hoods by a poster which promised a Fortnight at Fascinating Filey. Bert was the only boy in the packing department at I. and R. Morley's hosiery company who had never seen the sea.

The whole Notts and Derby Brigade pitched tents in the field behind the Hunmanby sand dunes on Saturday, 25 July 1914 and, according to the official history of the regiment, 'the European situation was constantly discussed'. If the account of life in camp is true, the territorials exhibited a concern for international affairs which was not shared by the Kaiser (who was on a yachting holiday in the Norwegian fjords), the commander-in-chief of the German Army (who was taking the waters in his favourite spa) and the British cabinet, which met in emergency session a week after Archduke Ferdinand was assassinated at Sarajevo, and discussed the risk of war – in Ireland.

The mock battles and bathing lasted for eight days. Then, on Bank Holiday Monday, the brigade was ordered to strike camp. The local papers had printed special editions which announced the time at which the Robin Hoods would arrive back home in Nottingham and a great crowd had assembled outside Victoria Station to cheer them off the train. Three days later, the crowd returned to cheer them on their way south. Bert's parents waved their paper Union Jacks and shouted good luck as the column moved off. They never saw their son again. He was killed on the first day of the Battle of the Somme.

Throughout August, the Robin Hoods trained for battle with

nothing to relieve the tedium of drill, route march and firing range except enteric fever injections, but on 1 September they were addressed by the divisional commander himself, Major General the Honourable E. J. Montague-Stuart-Wortley. He reminded the battalion that the territorial obligation required no more than service at home in Britain.

Then – having vindicated Bert's father – he offered the Robin Hoods a choice between courage or cowardice. Volunteers for active service had to do no more than stand fast. Men who chose to remain non-combatants would, on the word of command, take one pace forward. A quarter of the battalion took the single prudent step. Bert was not among them.

There was no embarkation leave for the East Midlands Brigade, so Bert wrote home with the news that he had volunteered for France. His father bought drinks all round in the Grove Hotel while his mother stayed at home and wrote the first letter in her long and ineffectual campaign to obtain his discharge.

His sister Augusta – the practical one in the family – bought a cheap leatherette wallet with a penny notebook inside and sent it to him in anticipation of his seventeenth birthday. Bert used the notebook as a diary. For the first six weeks he made a careful entry every day. Then he recorded only the grief and the glory. On the day before he died he made a list. Ploegstreert. Kemel. Houge and Sanctuary Wood were bracketed together as Ypres. Loos (the Hohenzollern Redoubt). Vieille Chapelle. Mont St Eloy. By the side of his battle honours he wrote '15 months'.

The diary began as English adventure stories had begun for 600 years: 'February 24th. Embarked for France. Sailed three miles out.' It was a false start. The battalion embarked again three days later and on the 27th the SS *Trafford Hall* did not turn back. On 5 March they 'went to trenches with 1st Hampshires. Relieved after twenty-four hours duty. C. V. Shepherd killed by accident.' After that the diary became a litany of death.

The official history of the regiment records that on 4 October 1915, 'orders were received for the battalion to proceed to the Loos trenches ... The German barbed wire on the West side of these trenches held a considerable number of British dead ... some hundreds of men were passed who had been laid out for burial. It was a gruesome sight and not very cheering to the Robin Hoods.'

Bert's diary records no emotion: 'Went up to trenches in motor buses, went to place where big advance was made, hundreds of dead lying on the ground.' Nine days later his entry was equally laconic.

> Our Division made an attack on the Hohenzollern Redoubt, Jack Burton was killed on the same day, we were relieved from the trenches, then went for a rest.

They fought for and in the redoubt for almost a week – capturing the trenches, being driven out and recapturing them so often that one assault was led by soldiers singing, 'Here we are, here we are, here we are again.' They fought for five days – the last two without food – and when the fighting was over Major General Montague-Stuart-Wortley addressed what was left of the brigade to 'express his congratulations'. When the parade was dismissed, Bert completed his account of the battle.

> Jack was killed on 13–15, he was killed in a bayonet charge, I think that he was hit in the head by a piece of shell. Jack was eighteen and he was seventeen and a half when he first came to France. The trench where we were attacking . . . was a very strong German position. Pt H. Timson was killed at the same time trying to bury Jack.

It was the last entry before the eve of the great offensive. That afternoon – 30 June 1916 – Bert wrote the list of his previous battles, folded three letters inside his leatherette wallet and left it in his billet at Bienvillers. One letter was from his mother: 'Goodnight and God bless you, may He send you safely home.' The note from his little brother was philosophical: 'I expect that you are sorry you haven't had leave before now but your turn will come before long.' Augusta – his practical-minded sister – told him that another brother, Leslie, 'was giving Alice Smith the glad eye'.

When the diary was sent home, the entries – all made in indelible pencil – had been blurred purple by damp. That was the legacy of a week at Bienvillers – behind the front line but within range of the German guns. The rain, like the artillery, was unremitting and, as the battle turned out, equally lethal. The official history is explicit about both the conditions and their consequences: 'In the Communication trenches and the Fire trenches, it was difficult to find a place where the muddy water came below the knees and, for long stretches, it was up to the thighs.' The 'disastrous weather' was 'a deciding factor in the failure of the attack'.

For more than a week the Robin Hoods remained at Bienvillers trying, unsuccessfully, to rebuild the trenches which rain and bombardment had combined to demolish. During the days they dug. At night they sent out patrols beyond the front line and, in turn, rushed to the firing step to drive German reconnoitring parties back behind their own barbed wire.

The continuous downpour was more difficult to bear than the continual shelling. They were wet in the trenches and wet in their dugouts. But the drenched and waterlogged soldiers had one consolation. After seven soaked and sleepless days and nights, they felt sure that at least they would not be chosen to lead the battalion for the attack. They were wrong.

At two o'clock on the afternoon of Friday, 30 June 1916, the Robin Hoods were ordered to parade by platoons and marched from Bienvillers to Fonguevillers. There was no gunfire in the early evening and the soldiers sat in the ruined village eating bacon sandwiches and cleaning their rifles.

At seven o'clock the padre conducted a brief service among the scarred trees of a devastated orchard. Bert – with the letters 'RC' engraved on his identification disc – did not attend. The first prayer began 'Lord God of Battles . . .' The last would have ended with a blessing. But the bombardment began again and his voice was drowned by the noise.

A cadre of officers and NCOs was detached from the battalion and told to remain at La Baseque Farm, behind the lines, for unspecified duties. They had been chosen to re-form the 1/7th Sherwood Foresters after the battle. The general staff anticipated that it would be virtually wiped out. In that, at least, their judgment proved correct. Almost 600 Sherwood Foresters went into action. Ninety came out.

The Robin Hoods moved off at nine o'clock, carrying – in addition to their normal equipment – barbed wire, spades, pick-axes and sand-bags. It took three hours to file along 600 yards of communications trench. At each step the men sank up to their knees in mud. Often a soldier sank so deep that the column behind him came to a dead halt while he was pulled clear. It was never possible to set down the loads for fear that they would disappear under the brown slime.

The journey ended in the front line, 600 yards to the right of Gommecourt Wood. The battalion was packed so tightly in the trench that it was impossible to sit down and almost impossible to move. Nobody slept. They leant against the sand-bags and waited for the German bombardment to begin. When it did, neither stretcher-bearers nor medical orderlies could pass along the line. So the wounded were left slumped against the firing step.

At 7.27 precisely on the morning of 1 July, the smoke bombs exploded in front of the German trenches and A Company – the first wave of the attack – crawled through gaps in the British barbed wire and dropped into a shallow ditch which had been dug just beyond the front line. At 7.30 the flares were fired and, to the accompaniment of subalterns' whistles, the first wave advanced, with B Company making up the second wave, filing through the British barbed wire, 20 yards behind them.

Bert, in C Company, was part of the third wave to go over the top. Before he was out into open ground, the German machine-guns were all trained on the gaps in the British wire. The official history describes the third and fourth wave as being 'virtually annihilated'.

The first and second waves pressed on. Smoke bombs were exploded in no-man's land, but the wind blew the smoke back over the British trenches so that, instead of protecting the Robin Hoods' advance, it cut them off from their own reserves and reinforcement. A and B Companies walked on towards the machine-guns which, augmented by heavy artillery, built up a fire curtain between them and the German front line.

A journalist described the advance in the romantic language of popular newspapers. 'Through all those barriers of intense fire our men marched quite steadily as if nothing was in their way, as if they were under review. At every step men fell.'

The battalion's war diary, written by the adjutant on the night of the battle, describes what happened in soldiers' language.

> They moved out from the fire trench, but found when reaching the new advance trench the smoke had cleared and (though a number of men attempted and a few succeeded) it was practically impossible to advance owing to Machine gunfire... The smoke was quite clear between the German 1st Line and our new advance... Efforts were made to get the remaining portions of the 4th wave and carrying companies to advance on the expected resumption of the smoke, but no more was sent over.

The German barbed wire still lay ahead.

According to Martin Middlebrook in his book *The First Day of the Somme*, the worst of all the errors made on that day was the assumption 'that a week-long artillery bombardment would destroy all the German defences – the trenches, the dug-outs, the wire and the Germans themselves... Unfortunately neither the guns nor the shells were appropriate to their allotted task...' The plan was to cut the barbed wire with 18-pounder shrapnel shells, but 'the margin for error was so slight that great stretches of the German wire still faced the infantry when they attacked'.

What remained of the 1/7th Sherwood Foresters advanced into a barrier of unbroken barbed wire; though, paradoxically, their small part of the front line was one of the few places at which the British bombardment had succeeded. The war diary of the German Second Guard Reserve Division for 1 July explains why the Robin Hoods were caught like fish in a net.

> The wire was unable to withstand the systematic bombardment. But all damage caused by the bombardment during the day was repaired during the night.

Only twelve Robin Hoods struggled clear of the wire and reached the battalion's objective – the German second line of trenches. A few struggled back to their own trenches. The initial count recorded 46 killed, 33 missing believed killed, 10 missing believed wounded, 117 missing, 235 wounded.

That tally was taken on the night of the battle and, like most regimental roll-calls made on 1 July, underestimated the slaughter. Most of the missing men – Bert among them – were dead. Some bodies hung on the German barbed wire. Many more had sunk into the no-man's land mud. Fifty of the wounded men died before the end of the year.

Despite the final toll – almost 200 dead, nearly 200 wounded and 50 taken prisoner – the 1/7th Sherwood Foresters' casualty roster was light compared with some of the losses which were suffered on that single day.

The big battalions of Kitchener's New Army were hit hardest. The 10th West Yorkshire lost 710 men killed and wounded, the 4th Tyneside Scottish 629 and the 1st Tyneside Irish 620. Four territorial battalions had suffered more than 500 casualties. Less than half of the men in the attacking battalions returned unharmed to the British trenches. In a single day, 19,240 British and Empire soldiers were killed, 35,493 were wounded, 2,737 were listed as missing.

It was because the slaughter was so great that, back home in Nottingham, Bert's family enjoyed five days of false hope.

The local papers reported the battle as a great victory. 'Heavy Fighting to our Advantage,' announced the *Nottingham Express*. It went on to quote Sir Douglas Haig's communiqué as if it was all the public needed to know about the big push: 'Several thousand of Prisoners Captured by the British and French. Number of Villages Taken. German Casualties very High.'

The absence of any reference to the British losses did not convince Bert's parents that the allies had won the battle unscathed. But after five silent days they reassured themselves that Bert was safe. Soldiers' parents knew the routines of death. Casualties were announced by telegram. No news seemed good news. In fact, the bad news was delayed because the War Office had so many condolence messages to despatch.

The telegram arrived on 7 July 1916.

Deeply regret Hattersley Private Herbert 2042 1/7 Sherwood Foresters killed in action 1.7.16. Army Council expresses sympathy.

Bert's mother drew the front-room curtains, as a sign of mourning. When his father got home from the Raleigh Cycle Company he noticed that every house in the road had done the same. At first, he thought it was a mark of respect. Then he realised. The Robin Hoods were the City Battalion, born and bred in Nottingham. Every family in the road had lost a relative on the Somme.

The telegram was not quite the end of the story. Bert's diary – and the letters which he had folded in it – were returned to

Nottingham. Then came a letter promising posthumous campaign medals (which were never delivered) and printed notices announcing the inclusion of Bert's name in the Book of Remembrance in St Mary's Church and on the memorial at Thiepval to the 'Empire's dead who have no known resting place'.

Bert's father was invited to take part in the Victory Parade. On the strength of his day in the 11th Hussars he chose to march with Cavalry Old Comrades rather than Parents of the Fallen.

Then, in 1922 the War Office reached out to Bert's family for the last time. A quartermaster sergeant called one evening and asked if Bert had been issued with a black light-infantry busby. The records showed that some territorials had received best uniforms, but they did not name the lucky recipients of Lincoln green tunics and suitable accoutrements. The Robin Hoods were reforming. It was thought that a band was necessary for recruitment. Old busbies were being collected to give the musicians some swank and style.

Just to show willing, Bert's father agreed to search the attic. All he found to remind him of his soldier son was a poster which promised a Fortnight at Fascinating Filey.

Observer, 30 June 1991

Plausible Miracles on a Yank and a Prayer

This is the third time within a year that I have written about Saint Joan. So some readers may fear that I have begun to hear voices which are inaudible to those around me. But this week I have an excuse for my decision to return to La Pucelle. I have visited the castle at Chinon in which she performed one of her plausible miracles.

All that remains of the Throne Room is one gable end. But it is impossible to look up at the great fire – suspended half way up the wall where the first floor used to be – without thinking of the decadents who dominated the French Court and their attempt to make an ass of the country girl from Domremy. Perhaps it was no more than good luck that enabled her to identify the Dauphin, masquerading as a count or duke or something equally trivial, whilst an impersonator sat on the throne and waited for the Maid to make her mistaken obeisance. But I always hope that Joan's immediate recognition of Charles VII was the triumph of simplicity over sophistication. After all, Saint Joan – at least according to Bernard Shaw – spoke with a Yorkshire accent.

My favourite Saint Joan is Anatole France's cheerful fanatic who talked her way into death and excommunication by giving obvious answers to complicated questions. Only a lunatic, her counsel argued, would have fought the Burgundians by pelting them with turnips. Not at all, Joan insisted under cross-examination. Turnips were the only weapons which she had at her disposal. Better to fight with the inadequate weapons in your possession than not to fight at all. The memory of the Maid's turnips has helped me through several general election campaigns. Often, as I hurled my ineffective missiles, I prayed for one of the practical miracles in which my heroine specialised.

When we performed *Saint Joan* at school, we had a terrible problem with a mystical happening in Act III. According to Bernard Shaw, on 29 May 1429 the French army was encamped on the south bank of the Loire, waiting impatiently for a west wind to blow its boats down river for an assault on the rear of the English forts. For several days the wind had blown from the east – as witness the 'streaming pennon' which appears in the stage directions. But soon after Joan's arrival – striding across the stage like a pantomime principal boy – the flag began to furl and flutter in the other direction. Dunois, Charles's commander-in-chief at Orleans, is described as 'looking at the pennon' before he offers his marshal's baton to the strapping eighteen-year-old girl.

> *The wind has changed – God has spoken.*
> *You command the King's army – I am your soldier.*

For some time, the woodwork department insisted that they could make it happen. All that was needed was a plywood pennon

361

hinged to a brush-handle and connected to the wings of the stage by an invisible wire. At the announcement that the wind was about to obey God's will, a yank on the wire would dramatise the change in the weather. It all seemed so simple. But what Saint Joan had achieved by prayer, the woodwork department was unable to accomplish with pulleys.

When the wire was too thin, it broke at a touch. Thick wire uprooted the broom-pole flagstaff from its hole in the stage. Dunois's page – a myopic youth – was almost decapitated by running between the pennon and the boy who was supposed to make it wave. At some rehearsals, Dunois announced that the wind had changed after a dramatic glance at a flag which remained pointing stubbornly in the wrong direction. In the end, we decided that the miracle would occur off-stage. It was the moment when I discovered what obscene really meant.

Like Saint Joan, we made the best of what we could lay our hands on. And, like her, we were offering to those who watched us, a practical miracle – a mystical experience which they could believe or not according to taste. All the best miracles can be explained away as chance, coincidence, auto-suggestion, or the consequences of an original misdiagnosis. If they were indisputably miraculous, there would be no virtue in accepting their provenance.

During the school play, the mother of the girl who played Saint Joan had no doubt that the pennon was blowing west, somewhere out of sight. It helped to increase her enjoyment of the evening. On the banks of the Loire, in 1429, they believed that the wind had changed, not because of moving depressions and colliding isobars, but because Joan had persuaded God to puff out his cheeks. The French soldiers fought all the harder as a result of their faith that they were reinforced from heaven.

Joan is the saint of the almost credible.

All that happened to make her the most potent icon in European history had a perfectly rational explanation. But when all the individually mundane episodes are added together, the inventory adds up to indisputable sanctity. She had one foot on earth and the other in heaven. It was not, as Shaw argued, the irresistible force meeting the immovable object that caused the combustion by which she was burned. She just ran out of good luck and fortunate coincidences.

Guardian, 5 October 1992

Old Men Forget

According to Tony Benn's diaries, I made 'a bit of a fool' of myself at the press conference which launched his campaign as candidate in the Chesterfield by-election in 1984. And so I did. I was asked to set out both the policies that united Mr Benn and me and the issues over which we were divided. The agreed strategy was to make the candidate appear as reasonable as his record allowed, so I began to race through a list of subjects on which our opinions coincided. As I charged on – comprehensive education, health service funding, higher pensions – I began to consider the couple of trivial disputes which I would mention in the hope of improving my credibility. As a result, I began to say 'disagree' when I meant 'agree' and 'oppose' when I intended 'support'. The triumph of my subconscious was broadcast on every news bulletin that night.

That, however, is not the example of my idiocy to which Tony Benn's diaries refer. Indeed the incident – which might well have prejudiced his whole campaign and resulted in the suicide of the deputy leader of his party – is not even mentioned. The foolishness which Mr Benn records was my defence of Neil Kinnock's gradual conversion to the idea of nuclear deterrence.

I describe the greater shame which he overlooked neither in the hope of catharsis for me nor in praise of his compassion. The illustration simply demonstrates that recording the day's events each night is no guarantee that the tapes will form the basis of an accurate or objective book.

Having preached, at least by implication, the importance of objectivity, I admit the various forms of bias with which I read *The End of an Era*. I find it impossible – and I have tried very hard – to dislike Tony Benn. To those with a sense of humour much is forgiven. On the other hand, I detest the way in which he has regarded his own reputation – and his half-baked ideas – as more important than the party which he claims to serve. More important, I loathe the revelatory memoirs, the private confidences published as if some sort of public service is done by betraying a friend.

Take the case of poor old Michael Meacher. For years, while Benn was out of the House of Commons, Meacher was known (as the diaries faithfully record) as Benn's 'representative on earth'. Nothing could be more natural than for Meacher to tell his hero that he was agonising about leaving the far-left Campaign group. The anguish was immediately recorded and casually reported, together with occasions on which the disciple 'wrung his hands' in despair. Whatever Benn's view on liberty and equality, his enthusiasm for fraternity is limited.

Characters as diverse as Anne Leslie and George McGovern are dismissed in a single patronising sentence. Neil Kinnock, the undoubted villain of the diaries, is vilified page by page. There is, however, an authentic hero. It is Tony Benn – congratulated by even Roy Jenkins for his oratorical powers and incisive judgment. Clearly, the author of *The End of an Era* believes himself to possess so much integrity that he fears there is none left over to redeem anyone else.

The reader must decide whether it is guilt, self-deception or something worse that makes him return, time after time, to the claim that comradeship always characterised his campaigns. He never wanted to drive anyone out of the party. But it seems inconceivable that he did not know how his supporters behaved. I have always despised those Social Democrats who left Labour not for reasons of ideology but because they were intimidated by Bennite abuse. But it took nerve to stand up to the intimidation. The diaries record with triumph the humiliations imposed on trade union leaders who robustly criticised Benn.

The most sanctimonious passage of all concerns the way in which Denis Healey – at the time, Benn's rival for deputy leader of the party – was shouted down at a rally in Birmingham. Ever pious, our hero reflects that 'all candidates should be listened to respectfully'. What a pity that discipline was not imposed on his supporters. They went on shouting Denis down and, even after he was re-elected, publicly excoriated those who had voted for him.

Old men forget. But Benn remembers with the advantages of shameless selectivity. He tells us that the speech which he made at the 1979 Labour Party conference – proposing that the national executive should assume exclusive responsibility for preparing the election manifesto – was one of the best of his career, but he does not mention that, after the resolution was defeated, objective commentators pointed out that most of the promises which he had described as broken were either kept or never made. His inability to consider the possibility that he did major damage to the Labour Party explains why he and his supporters continued for so long in their destructive way. They had no real understanding of the world outside Tony Benn's head.

The End of an Era also reveals how lacking in ideology – at least, one with any intellectual content – Bennism was. It relied not on ideas but slogans. The announcement that 'the right wing of the Labour Party' (in which Tony Crosland is included!) 'have made R. H. Tawney their apostle . . . whereas, when you read what he has written, he turns out to be an intensely radical man' is the judgment of a politician who relies on the selected essays rather than the complete works.

Of course, Tawney was a genuine radical, which is why he believed that socialism was concerned with equality, not state ownership and trade union powers – the two objectives to which, as the diary makes plain, Benn devoted much of the decade which they cover. When, one morning, in the national executive of the Labour Party, I quoted Tawney on the failure of state monopolies, Benn denounced me as a latterday social democrat, believing the judgment to be original. If the diaries are to be believed, that was after he determined to save the old man's reputation from contamination by the likes of me.

There are a few redeeming passages. The account of Benn taking his mother to tea with the Speaker (naturally enough, after that dignitary had congratulated him on his parliamentary performances) is genuinely endearing. So is his real affection for his numerous grandchildren. But the best thing about the book is its title. The days of destruction are over. The Labour Party paid a terrible price for the absurdities of Bennism at the beginning of the 1980s. The cost was not electoral defeat alone. Benn and his associates gave genuine socialism a bad name and there is still much work to be done to redeem its reputation. But at least the Bennite era has passed. That is real cause for rejoicing.

Sunday Times, 27 September 1992

Goodbye to Beefy

Botham has been the most exciting cricketer of his generation – and in many ways the most frustrating. He is one of those rare players whose achievements cannot adequately be described in the statistics of runs scored and wickets taken.

He was a flawed hero, but a hero nevertheless. Right up almost to the end of his career, whenever he walked out to bat or came on to bowl, the ground buzzed in anticipation of great deeds.

Sometimes, he did not live up to expectations – often because the expectations were unreasonable. Occasionally he caused great offence by his demeanour and behaviour. But he possessed a genius which was denied to most of his contemporaries. He frustrated his admirers by what looked like the wilful refusal to exploit his great talent to the full.

With Botham, glory and disaster have always gone hand in hand. He is undoubtedly a figure of his modern time – charged with smoking cannabis, betrayed by kiss-and-tell revelations and involved in late-night altercations.

Cricketers of an earlier age could not have survived such a charge list, but he has also been a victim of the standards which debase the time in which he played. Most of his misdemeanours were not unique. Similar ones were committed during pre-war cricketing tours, but in those days we did not hear so much about the indiscretions of sporting heroes.

But that does not excuse some of the more unhappy episodes

in Ian Botham's career. He was never the player whose conduct (any more than his haircut) provided an example for little boys to copy.

His brutal strength, aggression and towering will to win all contributed to his greatness. But they also combined to make him appear graceless, and occasionally boorish, in competition. One could always admire his skills, but not always his attitude.

Yet even the most unforgiving of his critics found it hard not to rejoice at the way in which he recovered from his self-inflicted wounds.

In 1986, after his cannabis confession, he was banned from county cricket until the season was two-thirds over. By August, he was back in the England team. On his return, he took a wicket with the first ball he bowled, and broke the record for the greatest number of Test wickets taken in the history of the game.

That was perhaps the most dramatic moment in his nineteen-year career, but his story is a saga of glorious episodes created off his own bat. At Headingley in 1981, everyone else (including Botham's colleagues in the Test team who had checked out of their hotel in anticipation of an early finish) took Australian victory for granted – but not Botham. He scored 149 and saved the day for England.

His tragedy is that the moments of triumph are not all that history will record. Had he concentrated on his cricket, he might well have become the greatest all-rounder the game has ever known.

But batting and bowling was never enough. Like so many icons of this materialistic age, he always wanted more – more glory, more fame, more money. And the way in which he pursued those dubious objectives often diminished him in the eyes of the sporting public.

His reputation has been enhanced by his prodigious feats of fund-raising and his amiable and witty performances in *A Question of Sport*. But the same cannot be said about his appearances in pantomime or his ill-fated expedition to Hollywood which, his publicists explained, would make him a second Errol Flynn.

Had he kept his swashbuckling for Test matches and county cricket he might, single-handedly, have made the game so attractive that the crowds would have been encouraged through the gates without the need to dress up players in pyjamas on Sunday afternoons.

As a captain – both of his county and his country – Botham was not a success and his last years with Somerset, the team for which he made his first-class debut in 1974, were an unhappy mystery. The three greatest players in the world – Joel Garner, Viv Richards and Botham himself – were all in the side. Yet Somerset finished bottom of the county championship in 1985 and only one place better in the following year.

The county, sensing dressing-room disharmony, got rid of Richards and Garner, and Botham reacted by walking out in protest. Was he being disloyal to his employers, as his critics said, or simply loyal to his friends? Whatever the answer, there was no doubting Botham's response on the playing field. He helped his new county to the championship, staged another international comeback, and briefly looked indestructible.

When he moved on to Durham, as one of the highest-paid county cricketers ever, one wondered if he could repeat the heroic feats. But time catches up even with Beefy, Guy the Gorilla, Rambo or whatever nickname you think appropriate to Ian Botham. His years up north, despite a regularly repeated preference for that part of the country, were a disappointment.

Age, a chronically bad back and the generally poor performance of the fledgling team all combined to sap his zest for the day-to-day grind of the first-class season. Botham was a star, and denied even the hope of shining in a Test match, it was inevitable and right that he should bring his cricketing days to an end.

For a man of less resilience, 1993 would have been a sad summer. But Botham will console himself with more than memories. In June, he scored his last first-class century. It was against Worcester – the team that had given him a second lease of life.

The sport has lost one of those rare players who make things happen – who take wickets when they are most needed, score runs when they seem most unlikely and attract catches like wasps to jam.

But the end of the Botham era will be only one reason for the sadness. We will all remember how good he was, but we will also imagine how much better he might have been.

Goodbye to Beefy

He is, indisputably, one of the great cricketers of his age – but he might have been the greatest of all time. It is difficult not to be sad about the chances missed, but impossible not to be grateful for all the pleasure given.

Daily Mail, 19 July 1993

Out and About

I like England best. That does not mean that I am never happy away from home. As I hope the articles which follow prove, I have been enthralled in Edinburgh, exhilarated in Lahore and ecstatic in Florence. And I have felt all those emotions simultaneously in Rome. But Rome is different because Rome was enchanted. That is why I still think of it in the fairytale language of a fictional broken heart. Whenever I remember the Spanish Steps, Santa Maria Maggiore or, above all, the Pamphili Gardens, I give a silent cheer for Audrey Hepburn, the wayward princess who returned to respectability and royal duties after a brief taste of freedom.

Her European tour ended with a press conference at which she was, naturally enough, asked which capital she had most enjoyed. She began to read from the prepared text. 'All of the cities which I have visited have possessed an individual charm. It would be invidious . . .' Then all reticence and responsibility was swept away by the memory of the glorious four days. 'Rome,' she said. 'Definitely Rome.' If the Pope will forgive me, Amen to that.

For years, the Italian joke which the British newspapers made about what is laughingly called the Labour Party leadership, always concerned Tuscany where we were said to spend half of the long parliamentary recess. Certainly the best summer holiday of my life was spent in the rough vicinity – a hundred miles further north in a village (and railway siding) called Aulla. The *fortezza* was one of the castles in Italy that the Waterfield family owned, wrote about and lent (almost free of charge) to deserving cases. Amongst the deserving cases which shared the idyll with me were Brian Walden, Shirley Williams and Tony Crosland. They read and I wrote. In the afternoon I had to retreat from the roof garden, which had been built between the battlements, and spread my pens and rulers on the table in the cool, white library. If I stayed outside the sun dried my Tipp-Ex before I had painted out my mistake.

I always write my way through the summer. Ira Gershwin said that 'the best holidays are working somewhere else' and I have followed that creed for thirty Augusts. Afterwards, I write an essay: 'What I did on my holidays'. Often it is even more like the old primary school exercise than even the title suggests.

My account of a weekend spent in Dublin has been omitted from this anthology only because of the fury that it caused amongst Dubliners. In the new General Post Office, the Easter Rising of 1916 is commemorated by a bronze statue of a man who is chained to a rock with an unpleasantly aggressive bird hovering over his shoulder. In an eloquent passage about the years of Irish enslavement, I (not surprisingly) described the local hero as Prometheus. Wrong. By coincidence the same thing had happened to an Irish patriot. Most of my correspondents said that in this case the vulture was English. I wrote letters of cringing apologies to all of my complainants – except those who added that Aeschylus had stolen the idea from Celtic folklore.

My articles on revolutionary landmarks seem rarely to succeed. After a visit to the bridge at Concord, I wrote a moving piece about 'the shot that rang round the world' – which, according to an immigrant from Massachusetts, contained seventeen errors of fact. Although, when challenged, he could only substantiate his charge in twelve cases, I decided that 'Tales of Old New England' – carefully constructed on my return from the Institute of Politics in the University of Harvard – should not be preserved for posterity. Harvard's Kennedy School is just a blur in my memory. To be frank, it was a bit of a blur in my mind at the time when I was there. Parliamentary duties called me back to England so often that my boss, Professor Richard Neustadt, suggested that the year book describe my association as No-Time Visiting Fellow.

When I first went to America, two of the Kennedy brothers were still alive and the Democrats were still the party of the New Frontier. Now Senator Edward Kennedy is about all that is left of that time of hope. In 1980, at the New York Democratic Convention, he made the best platform speech that I have ever heard and, twelve years later, again in New York, he was still bravely expressing the aspirations of liberal America. His was a lonely voice. Madison Square Garden was packed with Democrats who wanted to win and feared that the old liberal values might stand between their party and power. The article that I wrote on my return ('Politics of Naked Fear') was a lament for the New Frontier which fear of a fourth consecutive Republican victory forced the Democrats to abandon.

Back in 1970, I was about to write 'The New Frontier, Ten Years After' for the now defunct *Today* magazine. Unfortunately, the editor (Julian Critchley) was sacked by the proprietor (his friend Michael Heseltine) just before I left for the United States. His successor wanted to make a clean break with past commissions. So the idea hibernated for a decade and came back to life ('The New Frontier Twenty Years On') in the *Observer*. My views on President Bush – and particularly the sudden illness which struck him down in Japan – are reprinted ('Feeling Bushed at the Passing Out Parade') in part because of my happy memories of his 1981 visit to London. The political establishment were summoned to lunch at the American Ambassador's Residence and as we filed into the dining room, each of us was photographed shaking hands with the Guest of Honour. The pictures were developed and printed whilst we ate, and solemnly distributed, table by table, as we drank coffee and workmen erected a podium which was decorated with the 'Crest of the Vice President of the United States of America'. Mr Bush spoke for fifteen minutes. Before he sat down he offered to answer three questions.

'Good,' said Denis Healey, who was sitting on the top table. 'I've got three questions to ask.' The first concerned the iniquitous behaviour of some of the regimes which the Reagan Administration supported. When Mr Bush insisted that America's only objective was the 'extension of global democracy', his tormentor warmed to his theme. 'When you're tied down in a cell, you don't worry about the motives of the man who's fitting the electric terminals to your testicles.'

Despairing of an adequate reply, Denis moved on to his second point. It concerned warheads, throw weights and multiple entry systems.

When Denis Healey had completed his demonstration of intellectual superiority, Peter Shore drove me back to the House of Commons. 'Sometimes', he said, 'Denis goes too far. If the

Archbishop of Canterbury hadn't been there he wouldn't even have said testicles. He would have called them balls.'

I first met Senator Robert Kennedy in the dining room that was the scene of George Bush's bewilderment, and I marvelled that so small a body could support so much hair. I last saw him in his Washington Senate Office. He apologised for keeping me waiting. 'We always', he explained, 'give priority to nuns.' We agreed to meet again on my next visit. It was postponed for three months and by the time I returned to Washington he was dead.

My visit to Pakistan – 'going home' as many of my constituents call it – was postponed seven times in five years. Sometimes it seemed that every time plans were made and dates decided, the President dissolved parliament and declared martial law. Once, the Speaker of the Pakistan Parliament sent me a telegraph cancelling my invitation and asking me to break the bad news to his ambassador. Sind, Kashmir, the Punjab and the North-West Frontier were worth waiting for. I left full of doubt and apprehension and returned to record ('East of Suez') my infatuation with Karachi, Lahore and Peshawar. Romania ('Death Throes of a Pathetic Empire') was, on the other hand, even worse than I had feared.

I wanted to end my tribute to Pakistan with the confirmation that 'When you've heard the East a callin' you don't ever hear naught else'. But then I recalled that Kipling wrote those words about the Road to Mandalay, and that is not to be compared, for splendour or historic importance, with the Khyber Pass.

My fascination with old India is part of an obsession which has excited Englishmen for three hundred years. There were Scotsmen who were infatuated with old India too. One of them, Sir David Baird, with the dead Tippoo Sahib at his feet, stares down from the wall of the National Gallery of Scotland. I stare back every time I visit Edinburgh. But Scotland is a different country and, despite the annual delight of the Festival (about which I have written year after year), home is where the heart is. For me if not for Peter Mayle, that is the place where I was born. What I wrote about *A Year in Provence* ('An Expedition to Oblivion') is not really about France at all. It is about the love affair between England and me.

The New Frontier Twenty Years On

Accordingto the legend, it was both duty and destiny that called John Fitzgerald Kennedy to the presidency of the United States. The myth-makers, who at first did so much to establish his reputation and then so much to damage it, nominated exact times at which the blinding light struck.

The sentimental suggested that as soon as his elder brother was reported missing, presumed killed, young Jack accepted the obligation to fulfil the hopes that his father had originally reposed in Joe Junior. The romantics insist that sometime during the hours spent in Ferguson Sound, fighting to keep himself alive and a wounded comrade afloat, he determined that if he survived the war in the Pacific, he would dedicate himself to the service of America.

Political success is rarely built on moments of sudden spiritual revelation. The evidence suggests that John Kennedy, like other mortals, developed his ambition gradually and made virtually imperceptible progress from casual, almost indolent, Congressman to determined presidential candidate. Certainly by 1952, two years after he ignored the advice of his elders and betters and successfully challenged Cabot Lodge for a seat in the Senate, the idea of the White House was in his mind.

The early fifties were years of continual pain and prolonged illness for Kennedy – conditions which might have convinced a less resolute contender that he was disqualified from running for an office which Woodrow Wilson said was only open to 'wise and prudent athletes – a small class'. Yet in the 1955 Senate campaign (according to Jacqueline Bouvier Kennedy, 'the toughest ever – just running, running, running') he achieved the biggest majority in the history of Massachusetts elections.

In 1956, he determined to add the title of 'national figure' to the accolade of 'proven vote-winner', and pushed himself forward as a potential Vice-Presidential running-mate to Adlai Stevenson. But the liberal Democrats, led by Eleanor Roosevelt, did not trust Kennedy, while the 'professionals', led by Truman, were equally sceptical about his abilities and intentions. Factions usually implacably opposed to each other united to rebuff him.

It was a fortunate defeat. It left John Kennedy free to fight for the next nomination as the candidate of the new Democratic era. It also convinced him that the new candidate could only win if he played according to the old rules. John Kennedy was the grandson of two of Boston's most formidable political manipulators. To the guile he inherited from them he added a special gusto of his own.

They were four years of virtually continuous campaigning – subsidised by his father's fortune and the financial ingenuity of the men who surrounded him. In state after state he did favours for party bosses that they would feel obliged to repay. He established outposts of his empire across the Union.

No presidential candidate has pursued the nomination with such uninhibited vigour. The official biographies abound with accounts of how he outsmarted and outmanoeuvred the 'ward heelers' of New York and New Jersey to ensure the support of Tammany Hall and the associated lodges. A staff-officer in the Kennedy army remembers how the undetected wrongdoings and misdemeanours of the bosses from the Bronx, Queens and Newark were laid out menacingly before them, and recalls how one of them reacted to the implied threat of exposure: 'Mr Senator, for a Harvard man, you play awful rough.'

When the nomination was secured, the election itself was fought with the same devotion to victory. If a single issue swung the narrow balance of advantage away from Nixon it was the 'missile gap' – the notion that an ageing and negligent President Eisenhower had allowed the Soviet Union to achieve a dangerous nuclear supremacy over America and her allies.

Within weeks of taking office the new administration insisted, with breathtaking cynicism, that there was no significance in the discrepancy between the nuclear weapons NATO *possessed* and those that the Warsaw Pact was *capable* of manufacturing.

Today, some of the men who created the counterfeit crisis admit that they always knew that the nuclear balance was not in danger. But the idea fitted the scenario of vigorous youth ready to remedy the failures of indolent age. It was a bad beginning for Camelot.

After eight years of Eisenhower, the American people were looking for a young, energetic president. Indeed, they were so anxious to obtain one that obstacles which, in a normal year, might have proved insurmountable did not, in that special year, block the path of even a Roman Catholic, provided he had the qualities for which they yearned.

In his brilliant polemic, 'The Kennedy Promise', Henry Fairlie argued that 'the politics of expectation' prejudiced the prospects of the United States for a generation and more. The Kennedys, he claimed, led the people to believe that under their leadership anything was possible – and then attempted to satisfy the expectation that their rhetoric aroused. Undoubtedly, the heroic view of politics – 'bear any burden, meet any hardship, support any friend, oppose any foe' – has its penalties. One is the disillusion that follows frustrated hopes. Another is the despair that comes from the discovery that, in a complex world, the simple remedies often create worse problems than those they claim to solve.

But when, twenty years ago, John Kennedy decided to lift the tone of the political debate he did something for the profession of politics. Whether or not the decision to follow the high moral road was a conscious stratagem, calculated to increase the size of his popular vote, is still a matter of dispute. But, without doubt, the idea of politician as hero was more than an electoral bonus. For a time it elevated politics from the level of 'what have you done for me recently?' and 'think of what I might do for you soon.'

Even though it was this idea which propelled him into politics that ended with the war in Vietnam and the slaughter of Cambodia, it also produced the real legislative drive towards civil rights. It saw America through the Cuban missile crisis. And, to a very real extent, however misleading or inappropriate to the times, it lives on today.

John Kennedy was ideally suited to the role of politician as hero. At least since PT 109, the idea of heroism had infatuated him. In 'Profiles of Courage' written (undoubtedly by him) in 1955, when the presidential idea was beginning to burgeon, he offered America both a promise and a reproof: 'A nation which has forgotten the quality of courage which in the past has been brought to public life is not likely to insist upon or reward that quality in its chosen leaders today – and in fact we have forgotten.'

Courage in public life – 'grace under pressure' – was only one of the political themes which both genuinely attracted Kennedy and provided him with the opportunity to exploit the nation's mood and the public persona he had so assiduously cultivated. Equally important was the notion of duty. He brought to the presidency what at least appeared to be a high sense of patrician obligation and he was anxious to portray the White House as a place of service and sacrifice. He never pretended that the burdens did not bring with them compensating solace and satisfaction – though perhaps he obscured some of the less decorous of these advantages.

But so far as his public life was concerned, he chose the hard road of politics in preference to the delights of rich idleness, because 'from those to whom much is given, much is required'.

'We must always consider,' said John Winthrop, the first Governor of Massachusetts, 'that we shall be a city that is built on a hill. The eyes of the people are upon us.' Those were President Kennedy's last words to his home state as he left to take up his new office.

The attraction to such grandiloquent language was always a dangerous catalyst for John Kennedy. It bound together other dangerous tendencies in his government – belief in the infallibility of advisers, the passion for activity, determination to act the hero as well as speak in the hero's voice. These attitudes he imprinted on the whole administration. They contributed to his successes as well as his failures.

On 17 November 1960, almost two months before the Inauguration, Alan Dulles, then head of the CIA, told Kennedy of tentative plans to arm and train exiled supporters of Cuba's deposed President Batista. We will never know if the President-elect really thought that when the ragged army landed on Cuban soil there would be a spontaneous mass uprising and an irresistible clamour for the return of the overthrown dictator. According to Arthur Schlesinger, he let the 'preparations go ahead for the time being, because they could always be cancelled later'.

The attitudes struck and the promises made during the cam-

paigns for the Democratic nomination and for the presidency itself
were already becoming a burden on the new administration.

A president who had promised, 'We shall pay any price, bear
any burden, meet any hardship, support any friend, oppose any
foe to assure the survival and the success of liberty' in his inauguration speech could hardly desert a battalion of desperate volunteers
who had been trained and equipped by American agents, and
promised – with his acquiescence if not real approval – that they
would be launched on a war of liberation.

It was perhaps the problems of publicity more than anything
else that finally trapped a reluctant president into the abortive
Cuban adventure, despite the obvious probability that the Batista
Battalion would be defeated and America would be disgraced. If
it was cancelled, a thousand disappointed desperadoes would sit
on bar stools in Florida telling anyone who cared to listen that the
President who had promised to 'oppose any foe' had lost his nerve.
If the raid went ahead without overt American support, the
wounded would return to the same bars with stories of how
the President who promised to 'bear any burden' had left them to
die on the Cuban beaches. Faced with such a risk, the understanding with the Chiefs of Staff – that the President reserved the right
to cancel at any time – was meaningless.

The Bay of Pigs fiasco was the result of President Kennedy's
unwillingness to compromise with his public persona. It was the
failure of muscular politics, an object lesson in the dangers of
politicians building myths and then trying to live up to them.

In the more prosaic field of health and welfare even the President who had to be a hero was able to compromise and make
progress – as he did with his Medicare Bill, which was finally
guided into the statute book by Kennedy's successor, Lyndon
Johnson.

But it was in the global arena that Kennedy faced his crucial
test as hero-President. Kennedy had come to office committed to
closing the 'missile gap' that he claimed President Eisenhower had
allowed to divide the United States and the Soviet Union.

Within weeks of arriving at the Pentagon, Defence Secretary
McNamara began in private conversations and unattributable brief-
ings, to dismiss fears of an adverse nuclear balance. McNamara

confessed distaste for the whole political stratagem and did all he could to distance and dissociate himself from the fraudulent claim. The falsehood was finally and officially interred at Hot Springs, Colorado, on 21 October 1961. McNamara's deputy, Ross Gilpatrick, spoke of a 'sober appreciation of the military power of the two sides. . . . The total number of our nuclear vehicles, tactical as well as strategic, is in terms of thousands.'

So the 'missile gap' was closed in the way it had been opened – by a series of public speeches. That was a domestic political necessity, for if America remained vulnerable to Soviet attack, only Kennedy would, in future, be to blame. But while an announcement of nuclear strength was the least expensive way to remedy the imbalance, it carried international penalties. Khrushchev had never doubted America's nuclear superiority. But a sudden announcement that Russia's supposed advantage had disappeared put special pressure on a Praesidium already divided over defence.

Khrushchev, anxious to save money, had proposed a reduction in Russia's standing army from over three and a half million to two million men. It was a bad moment to read the American declaration of invincibility. If his policy was to survive, he needed allies. One possible recruit to his cause was General Biryuzov, the commander of the recently formed nuclear rocket force. There is no doubt that Khrushchev had domestic politics in mind when he decided to install in Cuba forty-two medium range and fifty-two intermediate range missiles. Once in position, they would double Russia's first-strike capability and outflank the United States's early warning system.

Of course, to attribute the stationing of rockets at San Cristobal solely to concern at the creation, and subsequent destruction, of the 'missile gap' is to oversimplify a complex decision. That was only one of the reasons hidden under the pretence that Cuba feared a second American invasion. But one source of the Cuban missile crisis can be traced back to the President's campaign and the assertion that the old men had let America down and the promise that the new generation would re-establish political and military supremacy.

There was no natural reason for the rockets to be sent to Cuba. Kennedy and his advisers considered every possible cause. It was not rational to risk global war to placate critics in the

Supreme Soviet. It was not rational to provoke a possible nuclear conflict simply to ensure the removal of the obsolete Jupiter rockets from Turkey. It was certainly not rational to 'test the President's nerve' with an adventure which might bring the whole world to an end. Yet Khrushchev did it. And because of the total irrationality of the enterprise President Kennedy was slow to perceive the danger and slow to react to the threat.

On 12 September 1962 an American agent actually saw a missile on its way from Havana to the rocket site at San Cristobal. It took nine days for a verbal message to reach the Pentagon. The message was incredible and no one took any action until the 'hard' copy of his report reached Washington. Because of bad luck, bad organisation and bad weather, a U2 surveillance flight that should have overflown Cuba on 4 October set out ten days late. It eventually took off on 14 October, sixty-three days after the first ship with Russian missiles on board docked at Havana, and seventeen days after a CIA agent had actually seen rocket parts sticking out from under the tarpaulins on a Cuban lorry.

During the days between the rockets' unloading and their discovery, America was inundated with rumours about Russian missiles. The administration was incapable of believing them. The political intelligentsia recruited by Kennedy into the State and Defence Departments had carefully calculated how they would behave if they served Soviet rather than American masters. They concluded that Russia 'would feel the risk of retaliation from the United States too great to take'. Whatever the Cuban refugees in Florida might say, there were no missiles in Cuba. It made no sense. The President could be assured that Castro 'would not acquire an offensive capability.' Robert Kennedy admitted that they were 'deceived by Khrushchev, but we also fooled ourselves'.

It was the year of the mid-term elections and President Kennedy was on the stomp, paying debts, winning friends and hoping for a more sympathetic Congress. The 'threat' from Cuba was an unavoidable issue. Reassured that no real threat existed, the President reverted to the unqualified heroic language of his own election. He promised the removal of 'any offensive build-up from Cuba' and undertook 'to do whatever needs to be done to protect our security'.

The discovery that the highly developed intellects of his

advisers and the incompetence of his handpicked bureaucracy had combined with the legacy of his election campaign to push America to the brink of disaster damaged Kennedy's faith in neither the style nor the substance of his administration. The tactics and the technique would be the same. A climbdown was inconceivable. This was the 'supreme probe of American intentions'. He wondered why 'if they doubted our guts – they did not try Berlin'. But it was a moment for the firm response. There were no more attacks on 'armchair strategists who would send other people's sons to war'.

The temptations of heroism can never have been stronger. Kennedy became the authentic hero of the Cuban missile crisis by resisting them. The Air Force urged a 'pre-emptive strike', but Robert Kennedy (knowing 'how Tojo felt when he was planning Pearl Harbor') begged the President to consider every other alternative. He too was conscious of the judgment history must make of the President's performance. An illegal attack on a tiny neighbour who claimed to be doing no more than protecting herself from a second invasion would change the world's judgment of his brother for the rest of time.

If the President ever considered an air strike during the early days of the crisis, the incompetence of the Air Force prevented him from accepting their own recommendation. Asked to prepare a 'surgical strike' that would clinically cut out the missile sites and damage little else, they simply presented the President with a previously constructed contingency plan to which they had made minor amendments. To provide a 90 per cent chance of destroying the silos the Air Force would need to make 500 sorties. There would be much 'collateral damage'. The casualties would number tens, perhaps hundreds of thousands. A more limited operation could have been mounted and might have been approved but the Air Force offered a blitzkrieg. President Kennedy was not in the blitzkrieg business.

He chose instead a naval 'quarantine', a blockade which by naval standards was at first a fiasco. There was indecision about where the line should be drawn around Cuba. Two Russian ships were allowed through rather than precipitate an early confrontation. Confusion about the tactics to be adopted towards Soviet submarines resulted in the Navy actually forcing several to surface while the President agonised about whether or not they should be harassed. There was fear in the White House that Khrushchev must share the US Navy's opinion that this was 'one hell of a way to run a blockade'.

But somehow the message got through to the Kremlin that Kennedy's willingness to wait was a sign that his nerve was holding. He was running away from neither the Soviet Union nor the Joint Chiefs of Staff. As the work on the missile sites continued, the generals could barely believe that he would not agree to a nuclear attack. On the morning of 27 September, a single Soviet ship detached itself from a convoy that was sailing in parallel with the quarantine line and headed straight for Havana. During the afternoon an American reconnaissance plane was shot down. It seemed to be the day of the final challenge. Time was running out. 'There was near-unanimous agreement that we had to attack early next morning.'

The attack was never made. Robert Kennedy proposed one final attempt to convince the Soviet Union that it was also 'the day of ultimate decision for them'. A public tirade, written by the Chairman on behalf of the Praesidium and released to the press before it reached the White House, would be ignored, but a private conciliatory note would be acknowledged with gratitude. That would be the final sign of grace.

It would be balanced by a formal warning to the Russian Ambassador delivered by the President's brother. 'The point of escalation is at hand. The United States would proceed towards peace or we would take overwhelming retaliatory action.' Of course, he added, this is not an ultimatum. And by the way, 'there could be no *quid pro quo* ... however, the President had been anxious to remove the missiles from Turkey and Italy for a long period of time.'

It worked. And because it worked we are all here today to make a judgment about Kennedy's achievement. Harold Macmillan told the House of Commons that the moment that the Russian convoy stopped was 'one of the great turning-points of history'. Kennedy himself believed that 'future historians, looking back, may well mark this as the time when the tide began to turn'. The popular press hailed it as a victory for the Kennedy style. It was, in fact, a vindication for the substance of the administration.

President Kennedy – and the men who surrounded him – had made a mistake. But the discovery of the errors did not shake their confidence in themselves or in their established technique of government. Having been proved wrong, they were properly reluctant to assume that the Chiefs of Staff were right. His nerve was tested by both Russian and American generals. He capitulated to neither. Nor did he expect them to capitulate to him. The end came with a compromise. The Russians were offered an opportunity to save face in a way that the Kennedy of 1960 would not have contemplated. He had become interested in results rather than gestures. He was turning from the presidency of promise to the presidency of real power.

He never quite achieved that status – a condition probably beyond any president until his second term. He was robbed of that reputation by death and by posthumous disaster. His memory was damaged both by the devotees who tried to deify their lost leader and by the detractors who seized not only on his policy failures but also on the vulgarities of the publicity that surrounded him.

The arguments about the war in Vietnam are pointless. Certainly Kennedy initiated American involvement in South East Asia. But it is impossible to guess whether or not he would have ended escalation before a handful of 'advisers' grew into an army of half a million men. If he is to blame for the napalm, the defoliation and the anti-personnel bombs, he must also be given credit for Lyndon Johnson's unique record in social welfare and civil rights. For the Great Society Programme also began under President Kennedy.

On the evidence of a thousand days he was a good, potentially great, president – learning as he grew in office as good and great presidents have always learned. The legends do no service to his memory. For legends are barely distinguishable from folklore and folklore is closely related to myth. The Kennedy people created many of the myths themselves. Camelot was their own embarrassing invention. When Lyndon Johnson nominated young Jack for Vice-President back in 1956, it was actually a Kennedy aide who asked him to 'proudly cast the vote of Texas for the fighting sailor who bears his country's scars'.

The myths do the man less than justice. But that they are still potent today remains Edward Kennedy's best hope of following his brother into the White House.

Observer, 2 March 1980

Happy Endings

If I could smuggle a single treasure out of Florence, I have no doubt what I would bring home under my coat. I would steal Donatello's statue of David from the Bargello Palace. I would take it in preference to any of the adorations, annunciations, and ascensions. And I would certainly rather own that simple sculpture than all the della Robbias in Tuscany.

Indeed a room filled with della Robbias is too awful a prospect for decent fantasy. Living surrounded by such a collection would be like squatting in the Best of Burslem Exhibition, with the finest flowering of vitreous sanitary enamel on blue and white display.

Of course if it were beauty that I was after, I would have one of Botticelli's long-nosed, fair-haired, straight-backed Uffizi ladies standing beside my television set. But I choose Donatello's David, not for what he looks like but because of what he does. Having him in the living-room would be like owning a science fiction hope machine which radiated optimism waves into every head within reach of its irresistible beams. I do not believe that it is possible to be in sight of that statue without believing that things will get better (in the case of nature's optimists, even better) tomorrow.

The David in the Bargello is not the young king and clear-eyed father of his people carved out by Michelangelo and now in double vision in the Galleria dell'Accademia and the Piazza della Signoria.

It is boy David wearing a silly hat, carrying a sword which is several sizes too big for him and smiling from the contented conviction that everything will turn out for the best in the end. It is, I suspect, that naïve belief in the inevitability of happy endings – as much as sharp light and cheap wine – that has attracted generations of Englishmen to Italy.

Robert Browning thought it the most likely place to provide a cure for Elizabeth's bad back. John Ruskin believed it would inspire him to kindle the seven lamps of architecture. D. H. Lawrence was less miserable in Italy than he was in either Mexico or Australia. Perhaps we should not be wholly surprised by that. But he actually seemed to find positive pleasure in exploiting his rich hosts and rowing with Frieda – as long as it happened in Italy.

The tourists assembled in Florence by E. M. Forster for the opening chapters of *A Room with a View* were all touched by the same Italian spirit. There was not one of them – no matter how absurd, pathetic or insensitive – who was not better for having spent some of the summer on the banks of the Arno.

Italy in August is a conspiracy to make men lift up their eyes to the hills. It is impossible to travel in Tuscany or Lombardy without staring at the skyline. Sometimes it is broken by the great spectacular silhouettes of the tourist posters. Siena shimmering golden in the sunlight with its great towers pointing to heaven and its little houses overflowing down the side of the hill. More often the horizon is disturbed by a church that has become a barn, a monastery that is being converted into an hotel, or a village that has not changed in a thousand years. But the focus of attention is always what Browning called 'just under the stars'.

Almost three hundred years ago John Winthrop of Massachusetts told the people of his state that politics was a 'conspicuous condition' and that government should be 'like a city built on a hill'. His image was meant to argue for the election of heroes; men of unyielding principle and unflinching resolution who led rather than followed the common will.

When I sat across the river from the Massachusetts Statehouse arguing about whether such a patrician philosophy was consistent with popular suffrage, I could never concentrate on the simile. I always thought of terracotta-tiled roofs and vine-covered walls, olive trees, and lights that sparkle in the sky like glow-worms after dark.

Sometimes the optimism that Italy engenders is immaterial to the point of absurdity. Last week, driving from Siena to Florence, I was held up by what I was assured translated into 'essential roadworks'. Had my progress been halted in England I would have cursed fate and the Environment Department. But in Tuscany, I stared benignly at the raw cliff-face that the Italian bulldozers had cut into the once gentle slope and gradually became convinced that I would suddenly spot an unearthed, but unnoticed, Etruscan treasure.

So certain was I of my impending discovery that I began to ponder the moral implications of my find. Was it my duty to report it to the authorities or was I justified in taking it home? Would a Medici sword fit into my suitcase? Could a hole be cut into my bathroom tiles to accommodate a della Robbia Madonna?

I first had that feeling of abandoned good fortune when I stayed in the *fortezza* at Aulla and stared at the Ligurian Hills through which Napoleon marched – promising his soldiers spoils from the richest plains in Europe. In the library of the castle which the Turks could not capture, I found the complete works of Robert Graves. Sandwiched between a poem describing a Master of Fox-hounds pursuing his quarry in heaven and a verse concerning the ghost of a Welsh Fusilier walking the streets of a Flanders village, there was an account of David's battle with Goliath.

David, brash and over-confident, loosed his sling and flung his pebbles. But the giant did not fall. Then, with a single swish of the Philistine sword, the history of the Jewish people was changed. If you believe in Donatello's David you dismiss the Robert Graves story as rumblings of Celtic doom. The Bargello David almost certainly missed with his first two shots. But the third, by fortunate chance, landed right between Goliath's eyes. Of course, the story had a happy ending. Nothing else is possible for a truly Italian statue.

Guardian, 21 August 1982

No Mean City

I am an Audrey Hepburn Roman. For it was neither Emperor nor Pope, red-shirted revolutionary nor black-mustachioed poet who first attracted me to the Eternal City. Thirty years ago, in a now demolished cinema, I saw Miss Hepburn looking like an elf from a Harrods window display and sitting at the foot of either the Spanish Steps or the Victor Emmanuel Monument. It was love at first sight with the scenery against which the film was set; absolute infatuation – not with the cathedrals and castles, the great monuments to the Risorgimento or the triumphal arches that only time can defeat. It was infatuation.

Miss Hepburn herself must take some credit. For Humphrey Bogart in a raincoat at Ava Gardner's funeral in the Verona cemetery and Montgomery Clift in tears on the platform of Termini Station as Jennifer Jones disappeared in a cloud of steam and dust did not call me to the Tiber's banks in the same clear imperative tone. It was a little romantic comedy called *Roman Holiday* which made me want a Roman holiday of my own. Perhaps by their nature such films encourage hopes which are never quite achieved. No doubt some of my contemporaries dreamed of Audrey Hepburn. I fantasised about the spiral of grey and terracotta clutter in which her celluloid ninety minutes were spent. For all of us it has been thirty years of frustration.

I, at least, have had my moments. But Rome – not having been built in a day – needs a whole lifetime, not a series of weekends, to understand. After three days, all that remains of the old passion is a feeling of unfairness, a resentment that so much antiquity has been crushed into so small a space. The Romans have more ancient monuments than they can decently handle or properly display. The whole city seems to be organised on the same principle as the Tate Gallery. For it stores underground and unseen marvels which other towns would put on exclusive and exalted show. Athens behaves almost as badly. But at least the Elgin Marbles are on permanent loan to a provincial gallery.

Part of Rome's problem is the passive reverence that it has for its antiquity. Any municipal sewerage undertaking which decorates its manhole covers with the initials which were once clutched in the claws of the Legion's eagles must be controlled by a corporation with a profound sense of history. Indeed, Rome sometimes takes its veneration of the past to absurd extremes. Babington's (English) Tea Rooms are an exact reproduction of station buffets which used to sustain (if not enliven) inter-war railway journeys. Timeless teacakes await their destiny within the protection of glass cases. As is the Roman way with relics, they are respected and passed by.

The Romans are not so much indifferent to the past as over-familiar with it. The Colosseum is in the middle of a traffic island and cat-lovers protest that their feline friends who inhabit the Forum are left to starve during the winter. The excavations provide a glimpse of the practical, indeed prosaic Empire. It was built by a race of heating and ventilation engineers on the most carefully laid bricks in the western hemisphere. The Caesars ruled a nation of soldiers, scholars, slaves, and plumbers of genius. Their lineal descendants see the drains and ducts increasingly exposed each day. The temptation to think of Rome's thousand baroque churches as an interesting example of modern craftsmanship must be almost irresistible.

On Easter Sunday afternoon there were fewer than twenty people awaiting the opening of the Basilica of San Clemente. I suspect that in the league table of Roman churches it occupies a place at the top of the second division. Yet it literally represents history piled on history, the past overlaid by the past time and time again. Three churches have been built on the same site. And the first of them used a Roman temple for its foundations. In an hour it is possible to glimpse (if not remotely to comprehend) how the Romans put together the passages which led to their Mithraic temple and the sort of ceilings which must have impressed Angelica Kauffmann when she lived across the road from the house where John Keats died. Yet it stands in a street which bears the name of another saint.

Being of modest disposition it is the second order of antiquity which I particularly admire. I do not possess sufficient spiritual grace to shudder in the Colosseum. It takes a more sensitive soul than mine to recoil at the memory of barbarities which were committed almost two thousand years ago. But I could not *enjoy* a visit there. For it is all spent force and decayed power, the black and broken teeth of a pugilist who was once a champion of the world. A thunderbolt may strike me before the sentence is completed. But, as the lightning flashes, I am prepared to admit that I find St Peter's similarly overpowering. I want my cathedrals to inspire awe, not induce agoraphobia.

And I want Rome to be full of small surprises, like those that time has scattered across the Forum – an almost overgrown boulder which, under its grass, turns out to be a Corinthian capital and a broken column which shows how the Roman masons dovetailed their marble together. The great monuments of the Forum are all temporarily hidden under the world's most comprehensive scaffolding and seem to be encased in giant and eccentrically shaped greenhouses in which the translucent sun-blinds have been all pulled down.

I do not mind. The Rome I want to see is the Rome of hidden gardens and unexpected courtyards, little chapels built under the shadows of great basilicas and bridges over narrow alleyways between episcopal palaces. Classical scholars will be shocked by my flippant romanticism and will fear that Roman culture never touched me until Audrey Hepburn came into my life. They will be wrong. The Empire's influence stretched as far as south Yorkshire. I saw *Roman Holiday* at the Capitol, Sheffield Lane Top.

Guardian, 1 April 1983

Alas, for the Algonquin

It was not until the last day of my recent visit to America that I realised how many wonders were hidden within the Pocono Mountains. By the time that I was allowed to look inside the official tourist brochure I was on my way back to England, home and the beauties of the Sparkbrook division of Birmingham. Until that final day my demanding hosts insisted that I ate, drank, slept, read and engaged in occasional conversation. As a result, no opportunity was afforded me to visit the Egg and Dutch Door Gift Shop with its examples of 'egg art from over 70 countries'. Nor did I see the Pocono Snake Farm, where trained and experienced personnel handle and discuss 'rattlers, tarantulas, alligators, 15-foot pythons and more'. I even missed the House of Basketts, 'which has often been compared to a museum', and Claws 'n' Paws wild animal park and its 'Zany Zoo Photo Critters'. However, my travels did in one respect broaden my mind. For I did experience the Pocono Candle Shop.

The Pocono are clearly the candle centre of the United States. If the Pope ever visited Business Route 209, East Stroudsburg (not to mention Route 611, Bartonsville, where American Candle is located), Catholicism would take on a new dimension and the incense industry would plunge into secular decline, like stained glass production, shipbuilding and the ability (in America at least) to recognise the absurd. For the speciality of the Pocono Candle Shop is 'the hand-dipped scented taper' which produces perfumed as well as flickering flame. 'There's husbandry in heaven,' said Banquo, sniffing the air, 'their candles no longer smell', and thereby acknowledged endless spiritual and commercial possibilities. A candle that exudes the odour of sanctity is more than a column of coloured wax with a wick inside. It is a triumph for Yankee ingenuity and it could become the symbol of the new 'moral majority' that is about to take over the US of A.

The odorous candle comes in a variety of odours. For the country lover there is lily of the valley, honeysuckle, lilac bouquet, bayberry and heather. The more sophisticated nostril can choose between Shalimar, Charlie, Estée Lauder and 'similar to White Shoulders'. The smell of pine is specially reduced. And if candle lovers journey to the Pocono in search of visual rather than nasal delight, they can buy candles that look like ice-cream cones, cupcakes, fruit sundaes, mice (or cheese-primed traps), lemon meringue pie (with plate as candlestick and fork as snuffer), bunches of roses, Whistler's mother or the White House. There are even animated candles encased in flameproof brandy glasses which, when ignited, make seagulls seem to fly, butterflies appear to flutter and crosses look as though they are shimmering in the sun on a distant hill. Imagine, therefore, my delight when, after my escape from the Pocono Candle Shop, I discovered in my room evidence that the America I had been brought up to believe in did once really exist. There by my bedside was *The Best American Wit and Humor*, copyright 1931 by Albert and Charles Boni, Inc.

Ogden Nash, Will Rogers, Alexander Woollcott, Dorothy Parker, Robert Benchley were all there. S. J. Perelman's absence I particularly regretted, not because I have ever laughed at anything

he wrote but because our paths briefly crossed and I used to gaze
on him in awe as the man who told the pretentious James Thurber
that the *New Yorker* was 'just another ten cents magazine'. Anyone
who says that cannot be wholly bad, despite responsibility for the
scripts of various Marx Brothers films – though I suspect that
some senior members of the Reform Club (where our passing
acquaintanceship occurred) would not agree. In those days Mr
Perelman was about to emulate Phileas Fogg and travel round the
world in just over eleven weeks, starting, as Jules Verne's hero had
started, from the Reform. To make that possible, Mr Perelman
almost joined the club, but even after his circumnavigation was
over he had still not completed the many important rituals which
novice clubmen must perform before initiation into full brother-
hood. His reluctance to fill in various forms was taken as a sign
of flippancy, and eventually patience was exhausted. 'We have,' a
Committee Member said to me one day, looking appropriately
grim, 'imposed the ultimate sanction on Perelman. His letters are
no longer being readdressed.'

If bathos really is a 'performance absurdly unequal to the
occasion', one of the few better examples than the Reform Club's
revenge is Robert Benchley's warning to Dorothy Parker, after a
suicide attempt: 'If you don't stop this sort of thing, you'll make
yourself sick.' Apart from Mrs Parker's explanation as to why she
always refused the public appointments offered her by the President
(wholly unsuitable for quotation here, but available upon request),
Mr Benchley's reproof is the only aphorism to come out of the
gloomy Algonquin dining room which I recall. Critical as I am of
the way in which that incestuous little group persuaded themselves
that they had a place in the world of American letters, I assumed
that I had only to read more of what they wrote to become convinced that they had the right to be spoken of in the same breath
as Theodore Dreiser, Eugene O'Neill, Ernest Hemingway, Ezra
Pound and Scott Fitzgerald. So I turned eagerly to *The Best American Wit and Humor.*

I turned first to George S. Chappell's 'Through the Alimentary
Canal with Gun and Camera', a title first brought to my attention
twenty-five years ago – but, then, actually misquoted in a way that
improved its impact. The discovery that the version in vogue at

the University of Hull twenty-five years ago – 'With Rod and Line Up the Alimentary Canal' – was superior to the only good joke in Mr Chappell's prize piece seemed as unnatural as finding a unicorn in the garden. I turned quickly to Robert Benchley and was rewarded at once with the splendid opening line: 'In America there are two classes of travel – first class and with children.' But instead of going on to discuss the two conditions which he so tantalisingly describes, Mr Benchley qualifies his definitions in a way that is more lugubrious than laconic: 'Travelling with children corresponds roughly to travelling in Bulgaria.' And just in case that explanation has not sufficiently diminished the force of the first sentence, he adds another: 'They tell me there is nothing lower in the world than third-class Bulgarian travel.'

Alexander Woollcott's contribution, 'Capsule Criticism', on the other hand, improved as it went along. But, then, it largely consisted of amusing quotations from other people's work. And that technique, *Listener* readers will agree, is sometimes the last refuge of the desperate essayist. Desperate or not, Mr Woollcott earns my eternal gratitude for one passage concerning Beerbohm Tree supervising a rehearsal of *Henry VIII* and looking 'in pained and prolonged dissatisfaction' at the 'collection of damsels that had been dragged into the theatre as ladies-in-waiting to the queen'. Mr Tree had one request: 'Just a little more virginity, if you don't mind.' The inclusion of that story confirms that Mr Woollcott recognised a good anecdote when he heard one. But that talent does not, in itself, qualify him for membership of the pantheon of American humorists.

To my mind *The Best American Wit and Humor* produced only a single candidate for the receipt of that illustrious accolade – 'Senator Glenn of Illinois, replying to an attack on President Hoover'. The Senator defended the Chief Executive and Commander-in-Chief by analysing both the character of the incumbent and the qualifications of his critics. Thus, 'no man who has reared no children of his own, no bachelor, can feel the same impulse of love and affection for childhood as does the President of the United States of America'. I suspect that such risible speeches are made from time to time in Westminster – indeed, I may well have made some myself. But there is a particularly American absurdity about a defence of the President that is based on his love of children. Suddenly I understood it all. With Senator Glenn up there on the Hill, Mr Benchley and Mrs Parker just found the competition too hard to take. The next time I fly to America and search in vain for amusing articles for the *New Yorker* I shall know whom to blame. The society that produced the Pocono Candle Shop and the House of Basketts needs no humorous fiction.

Listener, 14 May 1981

'Morningside becomes Electra'

This year I shall travel to Edinburgh by train. Indeed, my window seat, 'facing engine: right', is already booked. Uncertainty and improvidence usually combine to prevent such careful planning. But for a journey to Scotland, along the route pioneered by George Stephenson, exploited by George Hudson and neglected by the LNER, meticulous preparation is essential. The properly positioned passenger can, within barely an hour, see both of the North of England's great churches. First there is York Minster, its three white towers rising out of the see of medieval parishes over which the Archbishop presides. Then there is Durham, built in rich brown stone at the top of a rich brown stone cliff and towering so far above the River Wear that a traveller on the wrong side of the train notices only the gorge that God cut into the land and misses the monument to His glory that men erected at the escarpment's edge. And at the end of the line, the castle is just visible to travellers who squint upwards through the starboard side carriage window as they wrestle into their coats. Anyone who travels to Edinburgh on the wrong side of the train has no right to attend a festival of the arts.

Edinburgh being a city of multiple delights, the joys of approaching by road are hardly less than the pleasure of arriving by rail. The Great North Motorway cuts through Yorkshire's least spectacular landscape. But once in Durham and past Corbridge, there is the highway that General Wade built in a straight line. It may rise and fall 100 feet within 100 yards, but it does not deviate an inch to left or right. Once through the border hills, where the skyline seems 100 miles away, the land is more fertile and green than the storybooks about Scotland allow. Then, somewhere north of Lauder, there is the first sight of the capital, looking like Camelot must have looked when Guinevere first saw Arthur's distant kingdom. The whole city seems to have been crowded on a hill that is crowned with spires, steeples, towers and turrets. On closer inspection, some of them turn out to be blocks of flats, built as belated alternatives to the traditional tenement.

My first sight was over twenty years ago and the experiences of the last two decades have all merged into a single confused happy memory. Epstein in an underground market, the Berlin Philharmonic at the Usher Hall. Albert Finney in *Luther* at the Lyceum. *A Midsummer Night's Dream*, *Dr Faustus*, *King John*, *Richard III* and *The Recruiting Officer* witnessed from the hard seats of the Assembly Hall, chamber music in Leith on a Saturday morning; American students chewed up by *Pal Joey* and swallowed down by *Follies*; Degas in the Scottish National Gallery; incalculable Troiluses cuckolded by countless Cressidas in what now seems like every theatre in every year. I have stayed in every sort of Edinburgh lodging, from cheap digs in university hostels to a Coldstream-decorated bedroom in the official residence of the Secretary of State for Scotland. But I cannot recall which provided the best breakfast. I was always too anxious about getting to George Street or the Grassmarket to notice the porridge and kippers.

In the early years of our acquaintance I was infatuated with Edinburgh and exhibited all the flirtatious foolishness of that condition. An inferior production of one of Shakespeare's slighter comedies was transformed by Joan Sutherland's Titian presence in the next row of the stalls. Lunch at the George was rendered almost inedible by the heart-pounding arrival at the next table of von Karajan – described, I now recall, by Sir Thomas Beecham as 'a kind of musical Malcolm Sargent'. Supper, cheek by jowl with Marlene Dietrich's locally recruited accompanying musicians in a little coffee shop, was almost as exciting as seeing the star herself in the late-night show. Eavesdropping on their conversation, I discovered that the bandsmen were intrigued by her age, impressed by her professionalism and irritated by her musical director – a man by the name of Burt Bacharach, who, they confidently predicted, would sink back into obscurity after his departure from Scotland. I stepped out to Miss Dietrich's performance with all the confident insouciance of an insider.

I doubt if many of the performances were as good as I imagined them to be at the time. John Whiting's *The Devils* was the last play to keep me awake at night and a young lady (whose name has since been forgotten by the world and by me) playing Katherine in *Henry V* was the last actress to make me wish that I possessed a velvet cloak lined with white silk, a collapsible top hat, a silver-topped cane and a bunch of red roses. I know that I sat through the whole uncut film version of Eugene O'Neill's aptly named *Long Day's Journey into Night*; I was so impressed that I entitled the piece I was writing for the *Sheffield Telegraph* 'Morningside becomes Electra'.

It was Marlene Dietrich's performances (I saw the identical act twice in consecutive years) that I recall most clearly. She hung on to the curtain almost as much as Donald Wolfit in *King Lear*, but he communicated with the audience in a louder voice. The ends of familiar lines kept drifting at us across the footlights, '. . . back room will have' and '. . . moths around a flame'. But nobody minded missing the rest of the words. During the final encore, a man in a high box craning farther forward – partly because she was inaudible – almost overbalanced on to the stage. I know that he would have died happy, and the audience would have just screamed for another chorus, and that Miss Dietrich would have gone on looking like a lady at whose feet men died every day.

I do not expect to be lured on to the Rhenish rocks at Edinburgh this year. Nor do I imagine that I shall join the Festival Club in the hope of seeing a cello soloist drinking a bottle of lager or on the chance of catching a glimpse of a ballerina eating a ham sandwich. I shall go to Cramond and walk along the forbidden causeway into the Firth of Forth. I shall amble around the Old Town and look again at the El Grecos in Scotland's permanent picture collection. And I shall do it all with a calm deliberation that the atmosphere of the Festival made impossible in the late fifties. Of course, I shall see a couple of plays and be coerced into attending a concert. Performances in foreign languages (including broad Scots dialect) will not be on the itinerary. I shall never attend more than one event in a day.

And I shall enjoy it all immensely. I do not claim that the years have brought wisdom or even discretion. But there is no point in growing either up or old unless the passage of time produces a calm, unknown in youth. This year I shall not nibble at everything Edinburgh has to offer. I shall not even bite into a wide selection of Festival delights. I shall chew on a few carefully chosen items and return to London refreshed rather than exhausted, elated by the memory of selective pleasures, not bewildered by a jumble of overlapping joys. Of course, when it is all over, I shall travel south by train to see Durham and York again. Those sights in themselves justify a visit to Edinburgh.

Listener, 20 August 1981

Under the Quadruple Eagle

Assuming (as I certainly do) that you leap from your Thursday morning breakfast table the moment the letterbox rattles and (without thought of coagulated bacon fat, cold coffee or rigid toast) turn at once to the literary highlight of the week, you will be reading the column exactly seven days after my return to England from a visit to Austria. I now possess a grey felt feather-decorated hat of the sort worn by the male chorus in *The Sound of Music*, several tin shields and plastic medallions which I promised to nail on my walking stick, a glass jackboot with a litre mark to prove that it was designed neither for flowers nor feet but as a drinking vessel, and four boxes of lethal chocolates called Mozart Balls. What I remembered as I struggled through Heathrow – so loaded down with the treasures of the Hapsburg Empire that I dropped my bottle of Ballantine's whisky on the unyielding custom-house floor – was my day trip to Mayrhofen.

I visited the little Tyrolean holiday resort on one of the warmest days of the Austrian autumn. But, because of the state of what I laughingly call my wardrobe, I wore a heavyweight three-piece tweed suit and thick-soled brogues. As the temperature rose, I envied neither the elderly aboriginals (ventilated through the wizened knees and atrophied thighs that hung down beneath their lederhosen) nor the American tourists (cool in check golf trousers and Lacoste sports shirts) who outnumbered the local inhabitants by five to one. My only regret was that I lacked a striped flannel shirt, a white starched collar with rounded corners, a knitted silk tie, a gold watch-chain and cornelian fob, and a brown felt hat of the sort worn by the sophisticated metropolitan impresario in *The Sound of Music*. Complete with such accoutrements I would have looked like Englishmen did for 150 years as they strode through the Bavarian, Swiss and Austrian Alps.

The composite picture of those moustachioed hiking and reading heroes that I carry in my mind knows no national frontier. Robert Donat as Mr Chips finding Greer Garson in the foothills mist, Alfred Marshall inspired by the rocky terrain of the lower slopes to discover the *Principles of Economics*, Basil Radford and Naunton Wayne (ulstered up to their eyebrows) more worried about the Test Match than the snow warning, may have penetrated my memory from the Tyrol, the Bernese Oberland or the high southern tip of Germany. But whatever the exact location, the sharp light and the clear air were the same. I understand exactly why the gentlemen from nineteenth-century England were infatuated with the jagged horizons and the bright blue sky.

I once tried to express my generic affection for the Alps to a high official of the Swiss Foreign Ministry during a formal visit that I made to that peaceful and prosperous country. We were eating lunch at an inn that overlooked the Reichenbach Falls – not the cascade into which Conan Doyle cast Sherlock Holmes, but a Helvetic beauty spot of the same name. To my surprise my host was less than gratified. His annoyance at my inability to identify the nationality of various individual mountains was only one of the causes of his indigestion. His cosmopolitan poise was completely shattered by a troupe of local musicians who had been employed to entertain us with accordion, zither, harp and glockenspiel as we worked our way through baked ham and whatever William Tell called bubble and squeak. As if demented, he kept muttering 'cuckoo clock' under his breath.

The imprecation encapsulated his complaint about the civilised world's perception of his homeland, and its constant confusion with less worthy neighbours. He blamed it all on Graham Greene. In vain did I attempt to convince him that the line about 500 years of peace producing nothing more than an ornithological timepiece had been written into *The Third Man* script by Orson Welles. Ignoring my pedantry, 'The cuckoo clock,' he cried, 'comes from the Black Forest. Yet the Germans never get the blame. They get all the credit for intercontinental ballistic missiles, while the Swiss contribution to the flying bomb is always forgotten.' I found it impossible to console him.

Nor was I able, adequately, to respond to his next assault on the ignorance of Switzerland's so-called friends and countries that would have been allies had Swiss neutrality allowed such a relationship. Apparently, anybody of any consequence in world history had been born in, exiled to or inspired by his native land. Not being a cricketer, the Foreign Ministry official did not understand my metaphorical suggestion that Voltaire and Rousseau were only entitled to bat for Switzerland under the special overseas players' residence qualification. 'We are,' he insisted, 'thought to be of no consequence because we have never been led by a demagogue, bent on world conquest.' His properly derisive comment about Mussolini prompted a young friend who was with me to say that, no doubt, a Swiss dictator would make the watches run on time. If he followed her drift he treated the flippancy with well-merited contempt and began to cross-examine me about where I obtained my first mental picture of the Alps.

Embarrassed to admit that it was from a Hollywood musical called *The Emperor Waltz*, starring Bing Crosby as a gramophone salesman (complete with attentive spotted dog) and Joan Fontaine as a countess who preferred the high altitudes of the Tyrol to the high life of Vienna, I struggled to recall some more acceptable literary source. 'John Buchan's *Mr Standfast*,' I suggested. 'Which Alps were those?' he asked me. I could not answer. 'A *Farewell to Arms*,' I offered in desperation. 'The Ligurian Hills,' he said, in flat contradiction. I turned in panic from fiction to history. Hannibal's elephants, Barbarossa's bare feet, Napoleon's descent on Lodi, Rivoli and Castiglione. Each time he demanded that I identify the country in which the incident took place long before the countries were invented. At first I felt confident about Bonaparte's Italian campaign, which I was sure took place in Italy. Then, when I recalled the promiscuous behaviour of nineteenth-century Piedmont, I did not even feel certain of that. Anyway, are the Apennines Alps?

At any rate, I learned my lesson, and last week I made cautious progress through Zurich (Switzerland) to Innsbruck (Austria) and home via Munich (Bavaria, Germany or the FDR, according to taste). At each stop I worked hard at remembering not to offer schillings where only marks were legal tender. And I was more careful even than usual to make sure that the words 'cuckoo clock' did not escape my lips.

I was particularly anxious to be on my best behaviour in Mayrhofen. For there I was the guest of an hotelier, banker, shopkeeper and mayor of infinite amiability. And my dress proclaimed my Anglo-Saxon origins with such flagrant bravado that I felt like the Private of the Buffs – drunk last night but today standing in Elgin's place as the representative of all that is best in Britain. Faced with the prospect of an ascent in a chairlift, I put all thought of vertigo aside. 'Let cringing natives whine and kneel, a British boy will die' – or words to that effect. So, when I bought a Swiss Army penknife, I was both careful not to compare it unfavourably with the superior thwittle made in Sheffield since Chaucerian times and to observe that it cost less in Austria than in the quite distant country of its manufacture.

Had it not been for the tea, I would have kept it up right to the end of my trip. But the Holiday Inn at Innsbruck had an unhappy habit of providing essential afternoon refreshment in its separate constituent parts – hot water, teabags, little cartons of synthetic milk and slices of tired lemon. I left for the Hotel Arabella in Munich looking forward to a decent pot of tea. At first, room service brought me a pot of hot water and nothing else. When (driven back to the final compromise) I agreed to accept teabags, they expressed surprise that I was dissatisfied with the original water, which had, by then, sunk to the temperature of Bavaria's national beverage. Suddenly my nerve snapped and I forgot all the careful distinctions between the different Alpine regions. 'I know why the von Trapps really left,' I said, reaching for my grey felt hat. Bless my homeland forever.

Listener, 15 October 1981

Forever England

It is the memorial tablet which I remember best. I know little of learning's ancient seats, and all that I had to compare with that cold grey scroll was the roll of honour which I recalled from New England. In Harvard they proclaimed presidents – two Adams, two Roosevelts and a Kennedy. In Rome they celebrated saints. And the heavenly alumni of the English College outnumbered the presidential graduates of Harvard by more than two to one.

The marble tablet sanctified the wall of an archetypal Roman palace hall, cooled by a colourfully tiled floor and decorated with portraits of assorted grandees who stared at each other over the visitor's head. The grandees were cardinals. And the double doors which opened off the hall led to an austere refectory and a baroque chapel. It was Holy Saturday when I first visited the English College, and the choir was rehearsing its Easter Sunday offering.

The choristers looked like any other group of students. The occasional beard bristled. Denim and corduroys were *de rigueur*. If they even owned shovel hats and cassocks, their working clothes were kept locked away in cupboards like the track-suits and squash rackets of more secular scholars. It seemed impolite to ask if collars were turned around outside the college gates. So I have no idea if the walking-out dress of my father's day had been abandoned with the other manifestations of the old Catholicism.

In his time, they all looked like members of a students' union drama group playing Father Brown – serious, bespectacled boy priests who smoked obsessively and blinked in the sharp Roman sunlight. After more than fifty years in the college scrapbooks, the pictures had faded and turned brown. But my father, pince-nez on the bridge of his nose, was unmistakable. He wore them at the Catacombs for the St George's Day mass, in the villa outside the city where the college spent the hot summers and even when playing football in a courtyard sprinkled with vegetables and bundles of heavily bound books.

It was, the Rector assured me, a good life in the English College in the 1920s, with plenty of wine at meals and all the intellectual stimulation that the Gregorian University could offer. The lectures were given in Latin. My father remembered more about the Latin than the wine. Thirty years on he could still translate a gravestone inscription on sight. But when I returned from Yugoslavia bearing a no more than medium-dry bottle of Ljubljana plonk, he swallowed it down as if it were vinegar and announced that it tasted like Fennings' Fever Cure.

If the college cocktail – a powerful combination of gin, brandy and Punt e Mes – was invented in his day, he no doubt thought of it as an additional penance imposed upon him by a vengeful teetotal God. Perhaps he took comfort in its appearance. For it was the colour and consistency of milkless tea. I suspect that in spite of the pleasure that he found in the quiet, contemplative atmosphere, every image of home produced a painful combination of comfort and regret, and that he clung in desperation to the memories of England.

A year ago I found an old picture postcard which depicted the sylvan delights of Palazzola ora Collegio Inglese. It was addressed to home, but never posted. Where the message might have been written, an indelible pencil had engraved the county cricket scores: 'Notts 414–8 v Hants 118 + 136–2' and 'Leics 251 + 68–3 v Glam 151'. I can imagine his furtive guilt as he copied them down from an international edition of *The Times* which lay, like so many of the world's rewards, beyond his permanent possession.

His greatest pleasure – at least in later life – was doing nothing very much, but doing it in the company of his family. Indeed, I never knew a man who was so fond of hearth and home. In the summer he might spend the early evening cutting the grass or weeding the borders. But by eight o'clock he was back in the living room reading, listening to the radio and making gentle conversation. If our talk turned into serious discussion, he was always concerned lest it became an argument. He liked things to be ordinary.

Yet, at the age of seventeen he had set off for Rome indentured to salvation and bound apprentice to the Church for seven foreign years. In those distant days most seminarists did not return home until the final vows were taken. And since the roads that led to Rome were prohibitively expensive, the parents of the putative fathers did not see them between admission and ordination. In fact Frederick Hattersley, being a star student of some sort, returned briefly to Nottingham for one of the ceremonies that marked his progress to priesthood. I am astonished that he tore himself away from Nottingham a second time.

But he did. And in the college library, together with the deeds of its foundation and conversion from a crusaders' hospice into a house of prayer and learning, is the record of his admission into holy orders. He swore to return to England as a missionary and, if the Lord willed, a martyr. For the English College was the home of the English lost cause, although the young men thought that they would win the final victory.

In the chapel there was a little obelisk, moved for safe keeping from the battlefield on which an English student fell fighting for the Pope's right to remain a secular prince and stand in the irresistible path of the *Risorgimento*. Like the gilded cage from which the doves ascended on the day that Thomas More was canonised and the press cuttings of King George's visit to the Vatican, it was a sad symbol of an undying affection for the England from which the Reformation had exiled the Collegio Inglese. Or at least tried to exile it. For to my father, England, like Ernest Hemingway's Paris, was a movable feast.

Guardian, 18 June 1983

When Heaven is Found in Rome on a Hot August Afternoon

If it is hot in heaven, it must be just like Rome in August – at least Rome during the day, when all the city shines as gold as Siena and the streets are almost empty. In the evening when the buildings turn grey and menacing again, there are points of Rome which are more like purgatory. I could hear Trevi from half a mile away – not the sound of the water tinkling out of the fountain, but the buzz of the tourists standing shoulder to shoulder and staring at the coin-infested lake into which they have thrown their hundred-lira pieces.

After dark, young Italians sit in such crowded rows upon the Spanish Steps that it is impossible to climb from top to bottom without stepping on bed-rolls or negotiating guitars. But during the day, Rome is empty. It is as if Nicholas Breakspear's Interdict has worked at last.

It is not of course entirely empty. A few assiduous Americans, painted like Red Indians against the sun's rays, take careful photographs of the Colosseum. Businessmen – distinguishable from the rest of the world because they wear jackets and ties – sit in the air-conditioned foyers of the better hotels and look anxious.

In the parks and gardens a few near-naked young men concentrate hard on scorching themselves mahogany brown. Nuns run, in groups, from shade to shade, guidebooks in hand. But compared with May or September, Rome on an August afternoon is so deserted that it belongs to any visitor prepared to brave its blistering pavements.

Normally, Rome's most characteristic noise is the music of motor horns. I cannot distinguish between warning and greeting, threat and promise. Though I feel reasonably certain that I have never heard an apology. But in August, it is not only possible to drive in silence and safety past the Capitoline Hill and round the Victor Emmanuel Monument, the visitor in the hired car also has a reasonable chance of changing lane without having both nerve and eardrums tested by variations on a theme by Klaxon. At the end of my first day I had broken my personal record for accident-free motoring in the Eternal City. It now stands at the length of my whole visit.

The Colosseum is my least favourite ruin in all the world. In November, I applaud the ancient Christians for tearing off its thin veneer of civilised marble and using it to build St Peter's. But with the temperature above a hundred, it is possible to think more about Roman holidays than butchery. My theory is that feeding Christians to wild animals was a winter sport. Certainly it had one thing in common with British football.

The dictator of the time insisted on a membership scheme. The fans were issued with brass tokens, and woe betide any enthusiast classified as XXVII who tried to get in through gate XXV. Only in bright sunlight can you see the numbers carved in stone.

But it is the Forum that gains most from the city's desertion. Normally, the visitor looks up – up at the great temples turned basilicas, up at the columns which still stand, up at the almost complete triumphal arches and up at the ruined walls which mark its boundaries. With only a few mad Englishmen and dogs wandering along its badly maintained paths, it is possible to look down at the little bits of Forum and realise what their crumbling neglect demonstrates about Rome's history.

Rome has more history than it can manage. And another patch of first-century paving stone is therefore neither here nor there. There is no point in (or possibility of) sweeping it clear of earth and surrounding it with perfectly mown grass. So it sticks out of the ground as no more than a hazard – made all the more hazardous by the wild flowers with which it is camouflaged. But it is worth stubbing your toe, if it makes you remember that Mark Antony may have stumbled on the same spot. When surrounded, such embarrassments are ignored in the hope that no one else will notice. In summer it is possible to stop and stare.

The Pamphili Gardens offered almost complete solitude. A pair of lovers lay gently together in the shade of the shuttered, white villa. And a yoga enthusiast tied himself in knots under a palm tree. But apart from them, and a couple of young army officers who rode – very proper and very erect – across one corner of the great lawn, nothing moved. The fish in the ponds were dead or sleeping. The grasshoppers complained but did not hop when their grass was disturbed. Ornithologists will tell me that birds never migrate for the summer to cold climates. But whatever the reasons, no wing flapped.

There is a special romantic attraction in total desertion – Goldsmith's village, the submerged township that sometimes reappears from under the dam, the church without a congregation and the water wheel which no longer turns. 'Tell them I came and no one answered. That I kept my word,' he said.

Rome in August does not possess the appeal of benign desolation – just the charm of a city which, for once, can be seen in calm comfort. But even that is only possible for those who can stand the heat. I love it. What a pity that heaven – unlike the Pamphili Gardens on a summer's afternoon – is going to be temperate and crowded with people whom I do not want to meet.

Guardian, 13 August 1988

Death Throes of a Pathetic Empire

For years I have held the devout belief that nothing is so sad or so serious that we should not laugh about it. Had I written that sentence ten days ago, I would have followed it with examples of personal tragedy and public catastrophe which I have found funny. The jokes might not have been amusing. But at least they would have been distasteful. Sensitive toes would have been shattered by the sudden application of my crude boot. Decent people would have been offended. My mother would have been fearful to go shopping in case she met one of the unfortunates at whom I poked fun. But all is changed, suddenly changed. I have been to Romania and I have seen things about which I cannot raise even a smile.

I avoided the explicitly ghastly sights – the orphanages, the hospitals and the queues which quickly gather when a farmer sets up a stall to sell tomatoes or cucumbers. There are few more repulsive sights than a well-fed politician posing for a photograph with a starving child. The tragedy of Romania is the misery that hangs over the whole nation.

For me the tragedy is emphasised by a feeling of guilt. The criminal lunatic who ran the country for almost twenty years was kept in power, at least in part, by Western democracies. He was a thorn in the flesh of the Warsaw Pact. So we gave him a status and standing that prolonged his reign of terror. And his reign was not just terror alone. It was worse than that. A whole nation was pauperised and demoralised.

As I travelled around the ravaged country, there were sights and sounds which, in other circumstances, would certainly have raised a smile. A classics scholar from Jerusalem told me that the whole Romanian psyche was conditioned by the conviction that they were the true heirs to the Roman Empire – but Italians keep taking the credit for Plautus and Juvenal, not to mention Mark Antony, Augustus Caesar and St Paul. Normally that serious analysis of national psychosis would make me giggle fair to burst. But, at the time and in the place that the theory was advanced to me, I was nearer to tears than laughter.

We were in the huge marble, oak and gold palace that Ceauşescu was building – for no particular reason – on the outskirts of Bucharest. The gold was the real thing – none of your cheap gilt rubbish – and the marble was so monumental that Buckingham Palace could easily have been accommodated in one wing, the Hofburg in another, while the smaller palaces and chancelleries of Europe could have been tucked away in various extensions and annexes. The classical columns at the front of the building were bigger than the pillars at Baalbek. Before Christmas, shifts of 20,000 workmen laboured for twenty hours each day to complete the memorial to demented tyranny. I might well have laughed at the human folly had I not recalled what was happening in other parts of the capital city.

Barefoot beggars were running along beside anyone who was reasonably dressed, kissing their hands as they implored them to give a few coppers. Families were living in concrete barracks – without running water or integral sanitation – because their façades were thought to be more in keeping with the spirit of the revolution than the old but comfortable cottages which they replaced. Dimly lit corridors were still in gloom which had been created by the edict that only 40-watt bulbs were consistent with working-class solidarity. Men and women are now learning to type, because before Christmas the ownership of typewriters was prohibited by law.

But it was not these generalities of deprivation that wiped the grin off my face. One incident gave me an almost personal insight into what life is really like in so poor a country. I had developed a technique for running the gauntlet of men and women who loitered in the hotel lobby in order to offer all sorts of dubious delights to foreign visitors, and I prepared to repel a middle-aged man who approached with hand extended. More agile than some of the touts, he cornered me in the swing doors. He was a geography teacher, but in his school there were no geography books or atlases. He had come to town to see if any of the journalists who were covering the elections possessed suitable texts which they no longer wanted.

There are, I know, worse deprivations than a shortage of geography books. Indeed, there was a time when, confronted with stories of such underprivilege, I would have said that some people do not realise when they are well off. But it was the absurdity of his plea which made it especially moving.

I felt a similar pang of painful pity as I waited for the plane to take me home. The Americans with whom I had spent my Romanian days had searched the city for something to take back to the US and had found nothing in the shops except shapeless clothes and sweetish white wine. But at the airport there was a duty-free shop. The good family men pushed their way towards the counter, ready to demonstrate that no extravagance was too great as long as they could prove that out of sight was not the same as out of mind. Where the Swiss watches and Italian handbags should have been there were Mars bars in faded wrappers and small boxes of Lego.

The stories which I tell cannot compare with tales of famine in Ethiopia or descriptions of death on the streets of Calcutta. They are, like much of Romania, simply pathetic. I am sure that tonight there are men and women laughing in every part of that distressful country. But when I think of them I cannot even raise a smile.

Guardian, 26 May 1990

East of Suez

The church was Victorian, Gothic, dilapidated, and virtually identical to a thousand other churches scattered about the English suburbs. But a water buffalo suckled its calf in the shade of the spire, and the birds in the churchyard trees were royal blue and emerald green. A mile away, on the railway station wall, a faded notice confirmed the official price for hiring an 'authorised coolie'.

The marks of British India are still indelibly printed on Jhelum City, even though independence came in 1947 and Jhelum is in the Islamic Republic of Pakistan, a corner of the old Empire which does not always come to mind when we think of the two-hundred-year Raj.

Raj is a Hindi word. But in old India languages overlapped. British soldiers bound their legs with strips of cloth which, in their manly way, they preferred to call puttees rather than bandages, the English equivalent. And Pakistan has towns called Nuttall and Jacobabad.

Whatever it used to be called, most of the images and icons of the Raj are associated with what is now Pakistan. We stole the Koh-i-Noor from Lahore, the city in which Rudyard Kipling served his apprenticeship as a writer, and Zamazamah, the great brass cannon on which Kim once sat, is still on its plinth in the Mall. The marble columns of Lahore's palatial fort are engraved with graffiti of the Indian Army. 'The Wiltshires for ever'. 'God save the 51st'. 'Corporal Horace Cornish'.

And the history is not concentrated in a single city. The names of the provinces read like battle honours: Baluchistan, Punjab, Sind and the North West Frontier. Even the Bengal Lancers are now a Pakistani regiment.

On the lawn, high in the mountains outside the Khyber Rifles mess, a pipe band entertains visitors with the Tunes of Glory. In the anteroom, behind the long verandah, portraits of commanding officers mark the passage of the years with an almost imperceptible change from fiercely whiskered Englishmen to fiercely whiskered Pathans. The regiment guards a frontier which was marked out by a British officer, and has never been challenged since he drew the line. Lookouts watch for marauding tribesmen from pickets which flash their messages by heliograph, 'winking like fun', long before the radio or telephone were invented: 'Are you there? Are you there? Are you there?'

Of course, the riflemen identify with the achievements of their imperial predecessors. But they are not alone in looking back not with nostalgia, but with real admiration for the old order. A gnarled and toothless Baluch separatist, who had spent a dozen years in British jails, spoke with affection about the government which had kept him manacled to his cell wall. He almost convinced me that when Learoyd, Ortheris and Mulvaney marched north-west out of Peshawar, they did not sweat in vain. Given the slightest provocation, Pakistanis of almost every political persuasion will describe the contents of their bounteous inheritance. They begin with the English language, preserved in Parliament, on official documents, and as the sole means of communication in the better schools. It is said to open doors which remain closed to Urdu speakers.

The list continues with the practices of Parliament, if not quite yet complete democracy. The conviction is so clear that it seems rude even to be surprised, and it is quite impossible to say that even if British India was good for the Indians and Pakistanis, it has proved an historical disaster for Britain, encouraging neglect of industry, belief in class, and the myth of superpower status long after the glory faded. But if we cannot understand why they like us so much, it is easy enough to realise why we became addicted to them.

The fascination concerns the verb to teem. Urban Pakistanis hustle, bustle and jostle their way through life apparently without even questioning the justice of a destiny which crushes so many of them into towns and leaves the mountains of the north-west and the plains of Punjab almost empty. They are just as genial in the country. Nomads hang flags in the trees above their temporary shacks, just for the pleasure of seeing the colours flutter in the breeze. And the village shops combine work with pleasure by never closing, but containing beds on which their proprietors sleep when business is slow.

Kipling writes with particular affection about the Afghan caravans and rickshaw wallahs. Transport has changed, but the fascination persists. Nowadays, the rickshaws have three wheels; the front end of a moped is harnessed between the shafts. But they still zig-zag through the streets like angry horse-flies. The Afghans now drive lorries and buses, but they are decorated in the same old style. The coaches and the lorries' cabs are packed with as many human beings as can be squeezed inside them. Moving or still, Pakistan teems.

The sahibs from Sandhurst and Camberley also admired the warlike qualities of the Pathans and Punjabis, the Sindi tribesmen, and the warriors from Baluchistan. New recruits still arrive at the Khyber Rifles depot, already able to shoot and march as well as a regular soldier. The Pakistani was a worthy opponent, brave, proud and resourceful. The British admired his military bearing. Nevertheless, we shot him as and when duty required.

Now affection for the British is the essential ingredient of Pakistan's charm: that and the strange ability of the East to convince a visitor that he is a party to its virtues but wholly detached from its vices. As I left the depot, the Khyber Rifles' pipe band played 'Will Ye No Come Back Again?'. Indeed I shall.

Kipling said that after ten years' service a soldier was in thrall to old India. Despite all the doubts, it happened to me in as many days.

Guardian, 18 May 1991

Feeling Bushed
at the Passing-out Parade

Hail to the Chief and no more nonsense about his failing health. Ignore the reports of gastric flu. Last Wednesday, George Bush did what millions of minor politicians have dreamed of doing but never dared to do. Faced with yet another interminable official dinner, he behaved like Billy Bunter asked to translate a Latin unseen. When the going got tough, the Fat Owl of the Remove held a handkerchief to his face and, muttering 'nosebleed', ran from the classroom. The President's technique was, of course, more sophisticated and his performance was augmented by carefully rehearsed secret service agents. But the principle was the same.

I have applied it in a small way myself. Watching the television record of the sudden collapse and swift recovery, I was reminded of compulsory swimming in the first year of the Sheffield City Grammar School. Horrified by the idea of spending an hour in water into which sixty other little boys had sweated (and heaven knows what else), I always turned up at the baths with a bandage on my left hand. After two terms even Mr Smith (who had been excused war service because of the steel plate in his head) began to wonder why I trapped my fingers in the back door every Friday.

The problem was how to recover by Saturday and therefore be allowed to play football. Clearly, President Bush faced a similar dilemma last week in Japan. Thanks to the resources at the disposal of the world's most powerful person, he may be able to convince the American public that he is too ill to listen to after-dinner speeches on one day, and fit to stand for re-election the next. But if he tries to perform the trick too often, he will become a chronic invalid whose sudden seizures (although only likely to strike immediately before other people's speeches) disqualify him from high office.

Julius Caesar got away with it. But Julius Caesar did not have to stand for re-election or listen to doctors who diagnosed his disease on the evidence of television news reports. Remember, Mark Antony told Rome that on the Lupercal, 'we thrice did offer him a kingly crown which he did thrice refuse'. Bored out of his mind by the repetition of the same unacceptable proposal, he feigned what came to be known as the 'falling sickness'. History does not record the effects on his opinion-poll ratings.

President Lincoln never attempted the stratagem because he knew that, medically speaking, it is impossible to fool all of the people. In the case of George Bush, I am one of the undeceived. The mild nausea of which he complained before the dinner began was clearly the idea of the CIA's psychological warfare division and it prepared the ground brilliantly. Later elements of the plan were less convincing – due, I suspect, to a desire to protect the President's purpose and reputation. According to Marlin Fitzwater, Mr Bush collapsed in his chair and was 'lowered to the ground by the Secret Service'. For veracity, he should have hit the floor with a thud. He was said to have vomited 'into his own napkin'. Elderly men, on the point of unconsciousness, aim with less care. A real invalid would have sprayed the table. If Donald Wolfit had played the part, there would not have been a dry eye (or anything else) in the house.

Although I am critical of the President's performance, I have nothing but sympathy for his decision to pass out. It is easy enough to imagine how he felt. The small talk had gone on for more than an hour. All the aspects of Japanese life with which Mr Bush was familiar – dwarf trees, paper tearing, fat wrestlers and surprise attacks on American naval bases – were exhausted as topics of conversation.

The Prime Minister was about to give him a lecture on how to make motor cars, video machines and cameras. Then he would have to read the speech which the State Department had prepared for him. If, by mistake, he missed out the line about visiting Kyoto, a thousand journalists would speculate about the political significance of the altered text. Who can blame him for activating the plan code-named Convenient Colon?

Now that the example has been set at the very top, minor politicians will find the temptation to follow it irresistible. Guests will fall like flies at the Mansion House and Guildhall. All over England, preparations for the annual mayor's banquet will include the establishment of the casualty clearance stations in the council chambers. MPs will only be allowed to leave Foreign Office receptions on the production of a medical certificate. At regional dinners of the CBI, male nurses will be employed as bouncers with the task of keeping people in, not out.

A new word will pass into the language. In specially prepared recovery rooms in the Ritz and Savoy, men will re-fasten their shirt collars, wink and refuse further medical attention. 'Are you sure that you are fit to travel home?' anxious doctors will ask. 'I'm fine,' they will reply. 'Just Bushed.'

Guardian, 13 January 1992

Politics of Naked Fear

Lord Acton was wrong. It is failure, not power, that corrupts. Continuous power convinces politicians they have an invincible right to impose their beliefs on the misguided minorities which failed to support them. In politics, arrogance and integrity often go hand in hand. But repeated failure breeds the fear that only apostasy will bring success.

That is the spectre haunting the Democratic Party of the United States. Last week at the party's national convention, the phrase repeated most frequently was 'five out of six' – the ratio of defeats to victories in a quarter century of presidential elections. The dilemma, which delegates discussed with candour born of desperation, was how close to Republicans do Democrats have to move before they can change the record of failure to five out of seven? What is left of the old liberal wing of the party were openly expressing the fear that, by November, the presidential candidates would be divided by age rather than ideology.

Ideology has always been the most illusive ingredient in the Democrats' make-up. A coalition which combined the near-socialist intellectuals of the north-eastern seaboard with the Dixiecrats of the Deep South always had difficulty in defining its philosophical basis. And now that the strange alliance has broken down – and the blue collar vote which once sustained it in the cities has withered to a quarter of its post-war size – the party is struggling to find a new identity. The non-combatants in that contest are the liberals – i.e., the radicals (in the European rather than the American sense of the word), the heirs to Roosevelt's New Deal and (to their critics) the bleeding hearts and pinkos.

The liberal rhetoric was put on show for the convention's nomination day. Edward Kennedy demanded 'equality in life as well as in law', a view of society which when expressed in Great Britain is denounced as Bolshevism. Mario Cuomo advocated income redistribution and declared class war in a single paragraph: 'The neediest deserve most help from the rest of us ... Surrender that principle and we might as well tear the donkey from our lapels, pin elephants on instead and retreat to elegant estates behind ivy-covered walls where, when they detect a callus on their palms, they conclude that it is time to put down their polo mallets.'

It would be wrong to read Governor Cuomo's mind and assume that he was warning the candidates not to ape the Republicans. But he was warning somebody. Next day, in his acceptance speech, Governor Bill Clinton made his formal appeal for support from the deserted followers of Ross Perot, the man who won those voters' allegiance by declaring that the least government is best government and that ideology is the curse of democracy. There is no record of Mr Perot ever advocating equality or redistribution.

Even serious politicians attempt to attract the floating and homeless vote, often by disavowing their party's past. But usually the dispossessed minority fights back with more than a single day of coded messages. Last week, in New York, the liberal wing of the Democratic Party had almost given up the fight. Asked what had happened to Americans for Democratic Action (ADA), once the pace-maker of progressive policies, a distinguished alumnus of that now virtually defunct organisation replied, 'Remember how Labour treated the Militant Tendency?' The liberals in the Democratic Party have lost their influence because they have lost their nerve.

Part of the dilemma is intellectual. The shining hour of American domestic liberalism was Lyndon Johnson's presidency, the years of the Great Society Programme when the federal government took positive action to help the poor and reduce racial discrimination. But Operation Headstart, the Bootstraps initiative and reformation of 'the hundred year promise' of emancipation coincided with the war in Vietnam.

The progressive movement within the Democratic Party was shattered. Some of its members wondered how their colleagues could support Medicare at home and napalm abroad. Others thought that holding back communism was an essential part of the liberal agenda. After twenty years of disagreement, the liberal faction has still not regrouped. It is in no condition to meet the pincer movement which is closing in. On the left J. K. Galbraith, the doyen of ADA Democrats, concludes that a contented majority – including millions of families who have grown recently and precariously prosperous – will not vote for a more equal society.

On the other extreme, philosophers of the new right suggest holding down the illegitimate birth rate by 'ripping away every sort of government support that there is'. The old liberals lack the confidence to deal either with the despair in their ranks or the increasingly strident claims of their natural enemies.

The result is a Democratic platform which reflects at least some of the prejudices of the new right. 'We will ... require people who can work to go to work within two years in available jobs either in the private sector or in community service to meet current needs.' That is what the Republicans (and the Chicago economists) call 'workfare' – compulsory work instead of welfare payments. When asked on television if he felt comfortable with such a proposal, Senator Pat Moynihan, once the ADA man par excellence, said that it all depended on what was meant by 'require', 'can work' and 'community service'. If long-standing liberals are gambling on Governor Clinton's syntax, they will need to employ all their traditional linguistic agility in order to reconcile 'workfare' with Edward Kennedy's promise to 'Make war on poverty, not on the poor'.

Attempts to rehabilitate old liberal values have been seriously handicapped by the rise of a more modern sort of radicalism. That too is at least in part the product of the damage done by the Vietnam war. After Eugene McCarthy was forced to abandon his challenge to President Johnson, and Robert Kennedy (who took up the banner of withdrawal from Vietnam) was assassinated, the standard was carried into the presidential campaign by George McGovern. As well as contriving to be beaten by what was then the largest plurality in history, he changed the rules by which the Democratic Party was run. His changes institutionalised single-issue politics.

This year's Democrats are sincere, and virtually unanimous, in their determination to end discrimination against women. They are collectively revolted by the prejudice that blights the lives of homosexual men and women. The passion to right that wrong is only matched by the pride which some delegates take in proclaiming what the platform calls 'sexual orientation ... irrelevant to ability'. A keynote speaker from California introduced herself as a 'single-parent mother of two and a lesbian' in the manner of a Labour Party delegate announcing the constituency which she represents. At least two of the great liberal issues have found a home.

The 'right of every woman to choose' between birth and abortion is not only written into the platform, it was applauded with unrestrained enthusiasm whenever it was repeated in a speech. And it was reiterated and endorsed by virtually every speaker. Indeed, support for Rowe versus Wade (the court ruling which protected choice) combined with the red ribbon of solidarity with Aids victims to become the two abiding themes of the convention.

Nobody dismissed the demands of what are now called 'African Americans' or argued that the poor should be ignored. But, except during the escape of ideals on nomination day, they were not the issues that the leadership wanted to promote.

Women's place in society, like gay rights, is a reform which can be actively promoted without causing massive offence to middle-class America. When Governor Clinton asserted that 'it makes a difference whether the President believes in a woman's right to choose – and I do', the *New York Times* did not report the declaration as a reckless adherence to principle. It regarded his statement as an 'appeal to women, many of whom resent Mr Bush's opposition to abortion'.

Enthusiasm for Rowe versus Wade is almost certainly a net vote winner with the middle classes. Were it otherwise, few people believe that the support for choice would figure so prominently in the putative president's programme. In 1964, President Johnson signed the Civil Rights Bill and said, *sotto voce* to a young aide, 'I think we delivered the South to the Republicans for the rest of your lifetime.' This year's mood is better illustrated by determination to remedy the error which was identified by its official pollster: 'a profound disillusionment and less faith in the Democratic Party' by the whole lower-middle classes.

For this is the Democratic leadership which, despite its undoubted commitment to 'health care our families can afford', has tailor-made most of its manifesto to the financial prejudices of middle America. 'We cannot,' the platform says, 'tax and spend our way to prosperity.' That is, in itself, an unexceptional statement of the obvious. It is also a refutation of the allegation that Republicans make against Democrats – using the Republicans' own words.

Parties which accept their opponents' rhetoric, if only to refute it, are in deep ideological trouble. The Democrats' platform has made that concession in abundance.

'In the last decade, mounting payroll taxes have fallen disproportionately on the middle classes ... welfare was meant to be a promise of temporary help for people who have fallen on hard times ... measures to keep our schools safe, including alternative schools for disruptive children ... America is the "world's strongest military power" and we must remain so.' Each promise is, on its own merits, defensible. Each commitment is an acceptance of the Republican agenda.

It has taken the Democrats no more than four years to learn the cynical lesson which is most accurately described as the Willie Horton Syndrome. Michael Dukakis, fighting the 1988 election, fell into the liberals' trap. Horton was a convicted murderer who, when let out of prison for weekend rehabilitation leave, committed rape. Dukakis, as Governor of Massachusetts, had supported the prisoner's furlough scheme and, when challenged on television, did not pretend otherwise.

That, according to the Democrat realists, was the moment when the Republicans won the presidency. Clinton is not the man to repeat the mistake. The Democratic leadership will not even promise to resist the growing demands for capital punishment. The southern governor upholds a state's right to decide whether or not it executes its citizens.

Occasionally the smooth façade of middle-class acceptability cracks. Some of the voters who are being wooed with talk of family values were certainly alienated by Jesse Jackson's novel view that the Virgin Mary was a one-parent family who would have been punished by Pontius Pilate for terminating her pregnancy and reviled by the local Pharisees for producing an unwanted child. But that is the price a party pays for abandoning its idealism. The vacuum is filled by absurdity dressed up to look like moral outrage.

Such spectacles are also the price the Democrats pay for the vacuum in liberal leadership. Dukakis has become a proven vote loser. Jerry Brown is never credible and sometimes barely intelligible. Mario Cuomo is always about to step forward but never does. Edward Kennedy, with most of the right ideas and all of the energy, spent twenty years disqualifying himself from ever standing for president. It is said that he is at last contented. The epitaph for American liberalism is that it is happily married and settled down into cautious respectability.

Guardian, 22 July 1992

An Expedition to Oblivion

Until last Sunday I could only find comfort in the thought that as soon as I had finished *Daniel Deronda*, read *A Pilgrim's Progress* and flipped through *Buddenbrooks*, I would rush out and buy a copy of *A Year in Provence*. Now I realise that I was wrong to fret about the yawning gap in my recent education. My error is easily explained. Before I saw the first episode of the television adaptation, I had not understood that Peter Mayle's bestseller is a cookery book.

Back in the 1940s, my mother would get *Mrs Beeton* from the local library at Christmas and, in the intervals between her search for an exciting way to disguise the wartime rations, I gazed lasciviously at the full colour photographs of exotic puddings. They were all I could think of when, a year or two later, I arrived at the Sheffield City Grammar School and was given a copy of G. K. Chesterton's *Tremendous Trifles*. Now, apart from making a bad joke about Rosamond Lehmann's *The Salad and the Sauce*, I steadfastly refuse to regard recipes as a branch of literature.

I should have realised from the start that nothing good, as distinct from profitable, could possibly come from the word processor of Mr Mayle. For he has chosen – of his own free will and whilst neither pursued by police nor hounded by poverty – to abandon England. I understand why exile is sometimes unavoidable. The pursuit of work, the wish to find lost families, the search for a climate which reduces rheumatic pains or cures consumption – they are all explanations that can be offered in mitigation of the decision to leave home. But even then, the emigrants should set sail swathed in the gloom that Ford Madox Brown captured in *The Last of England*.

Shakespeare's characters knew how to deal with abroad. When his heroes were not beating France in battle, they were making flowery speeches about the country of their birth and affection and its superiority over all other nations. Bolingbroke only turned really nasty (and into *Henry IV, Parts I and II*) when he was exiled by Richard II. It is difficult to imagine John of Gaunt leaving his sceptr'd isle for a French farmhouse in close proximity to a restaurant that insisted on serving three desserts to all of its customers. The dying Falstaff 'babbled of green fields', not hexameters of yellow rape.

Rupert Brooke was particularly severe on gaudy melon flowers – especially as compared with unofficial English roses. And Robert Browning, who had a decent excuse for living in Italy, still longed for England in April. For patriots who want their love and loyalty to be expressed in more prosaic language, J. B. Priestley provides a simple description of his own feelings which ought to make every voluntary exile blush a deep red, white and blue: 'Never once have I arrived in a foreign land and cried, This is the place for me! I would rather spend a holiday in Tuscany than in the Black Country, but if I were compelled to choose between living in West Bromwich or Florence, I should make straight for West Bromwich.'

Mr Priestley was scathing about writers who needed the inspiration of exotic locations. No wonder. It is worth noting that Mr Mayle went to Provence to write a novel and produced what, if television has done him justice, turns out to be a gastronomic guide book.

I share Mr Priestley's view. Not for me the opinion so eloquently expressed by the Oscar Wilde dowager: 'We do not need to travel, we are already here.' Until last Sunday I assumed that most of my fellow countrymen believed with me that, although abroad is fine for a visit, in the long run, there is no place like home. But it was Jeremy Paxman who disturbed my complacent chauvinism. Introducing the *Did You See?* discussion on Mr Mayle's menu of the week, he announced that half of the English middle classes fantasised about spending a year, and more, in Provence. The gold-grey farmhouse, the Mistral and the butcher with didactic views on herbs were all part of their dream come true.

For a moment I toyed with the idea that Mr Paxman might be mistaken. Then – dismissing the notion as heresy – I began to consider the implications of what he had said. A nation in which even a part of the middle class longs to live in foreign idleness is a nation in decline – a country which has lost its faith in reality and takes refuge in a mirage. The Mayle idyll is an expedition to oblivion. It may be comforting to pretend that Thomas Cook sells one-way tickets to Arcady, but the need for such placebos is only felt by a nation which has lost an empire and failed to find a timeshare. It is impossible to imagine the self-confident Victorians or the real Elizabethans taking refuge in such escapism. They thought of making a hardworking heaven either in England or the English replicas which they built abroad.

My hope is that *A Year in Provence* will be a profound failure – not because of the quality of the adaptation or the performance of the actors, but because millions of viewers find the whole idea of the Mayle Drain too depressing for Sunday evening viewing. *Eldorado*, the down-market version of the same syndrome, is already doomed. If the middle classes demonstrate their continued fascination with Never-Never Land, I shall become so depressed that I may decide to emigrate.

Guardian, 8 March 1993